perspective

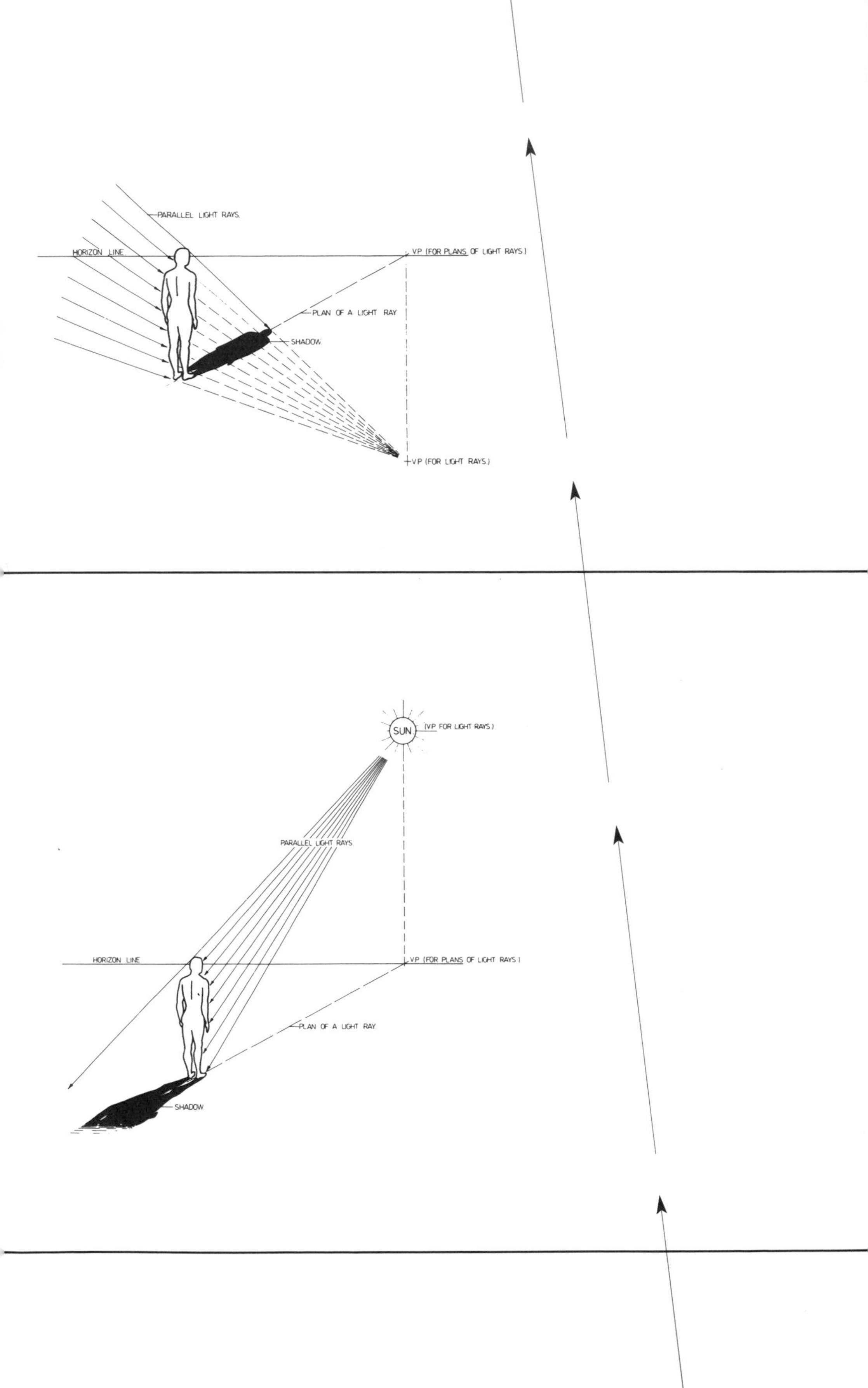
PARALLEL LIGHT RAYS.
HORIZON LINE.
V.P. (FOR PLANS OF LIGHT RAYS.)
PLAN OF A LIGHT RAY
SHADOW
V.P. (FOR LIGHT RAYS.)
SUN.
(V.P. FOR LIGHT RAYS.)
PARALLEL LIGHT RAYS
HORIZON LINE
V.P. (FOR PLANS OF LIGHT RAYS.)
PLAN OF A LIGHT RAY
SHADOW

robert w. gill

perspective

FROM BASIC TO CREATIVE

Originally published as two separate volumes, *Basic Perspective* and *Creative Perspective*.

This single-volume edition first published in 2006 in paperback in the United States of America by Thames & Hudson Inc., 500 Fifth Avenue, New York, New York 10110

thamesandhudsonusa.com

Library of Congress Catalog Card Number 2005907415

ISBN-13: 978-0-500-28607-4
ISBN-10: 0-500-28607-8

Printed and bound in Singapore

Contents

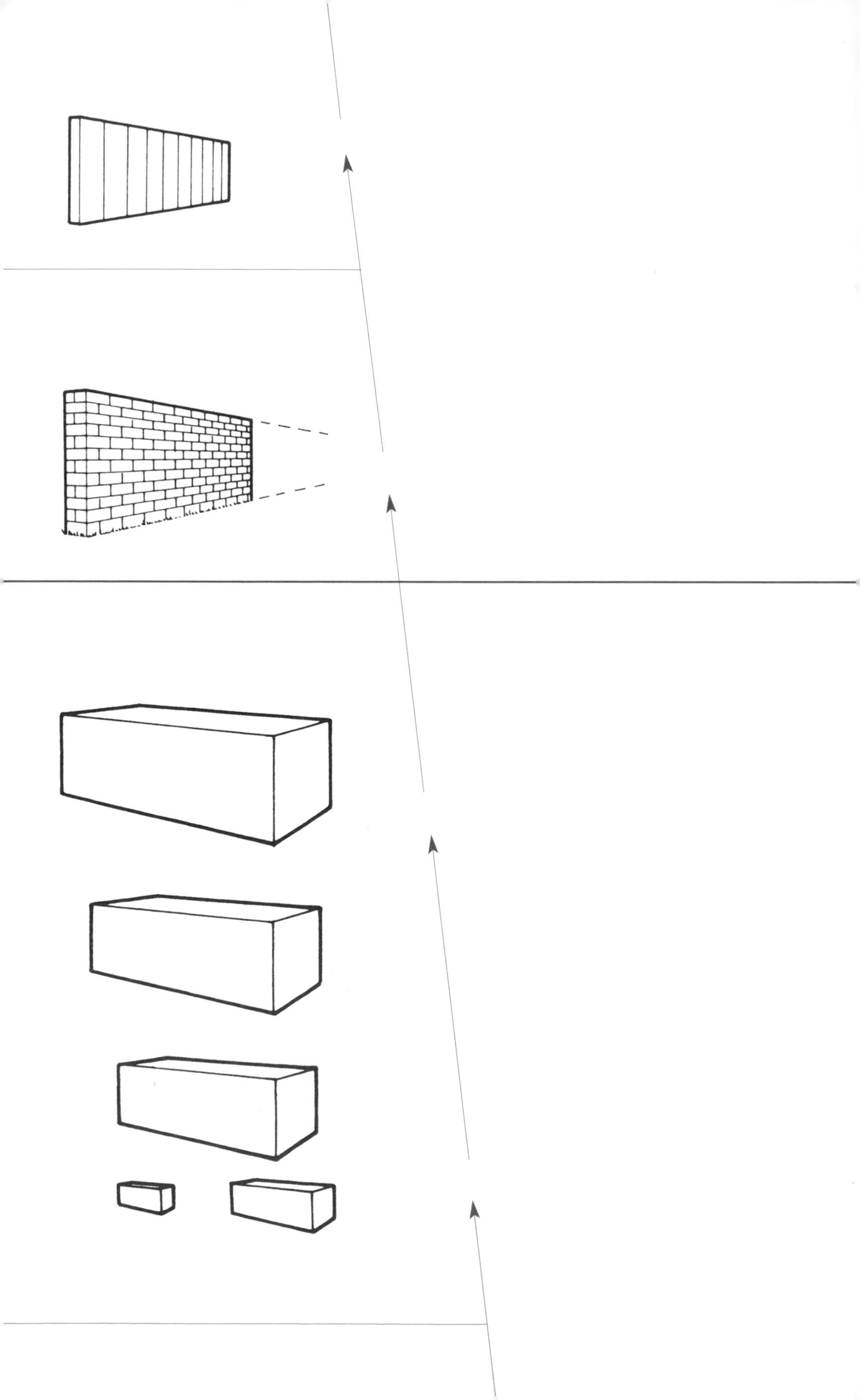

one

basic perspective

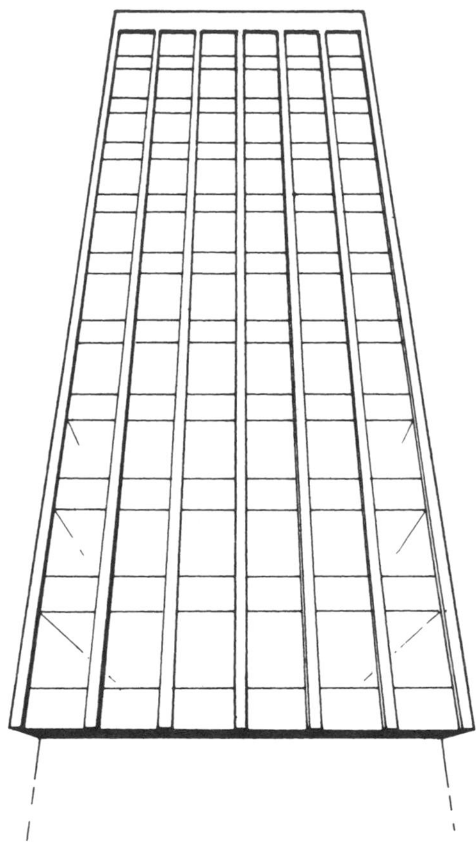

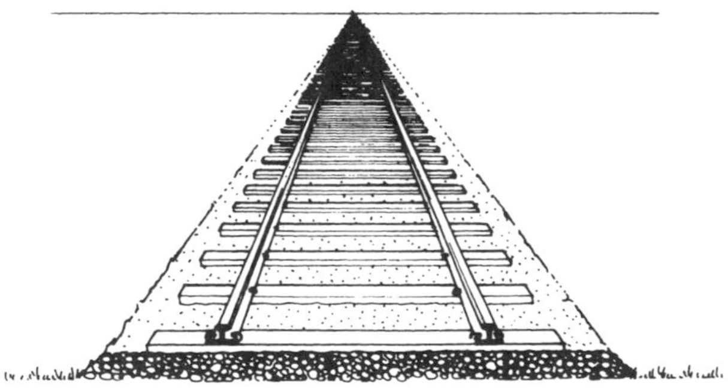

An Introduction to Basic Perspective

It is impossible to look at an object or view without being aware of the existence of perspective, the optical effect which gives a sense of distance and solidity to what is seen.

The examples shown in Fig. 1 are well known, and either these or similar ones are seen daily. Parallel railway lines appear to converge or come together as they recede into the distance. Tall buildings, when looked at from street level, appear to taper as they recede from the spectator. This is known as 'convergence'.

The spaces between the telegraph poles and between the fence posts (though we know that they are equally spaced) appear to get smaller as they recede from the spectator. This is known as 'foreshortening'.

The telegraph poles and the fence posts also appear to become smaller as they recede from the spectator. This is known as 'diminution'.

From these examples it can be seen that convergence, foreshortening and diminution occur simultaneously, but for convenience they are discussed separately. (See Figs. 2–4 for further examples of these factors occurring simultaneously.) By examining the examples shown, it is possible to observe and set down a number of visual rules. The most important of these is that parallel lines appear to converge as they recede from the spectator. The second of these rules is that equal distances appear to become foreshortened as they recede from the eye. The third visual rule is that objects of similar size appear to diminish in size as they recede.

Perspective drawing is a linear presentation, and therefore these three visual rules are the main ones that concern us here, but there are other factors which can also be observed when looking at an object or view. Shade and shadow play an

1 Some of the special effects of perspective –convergence, foreshortening and diminution.

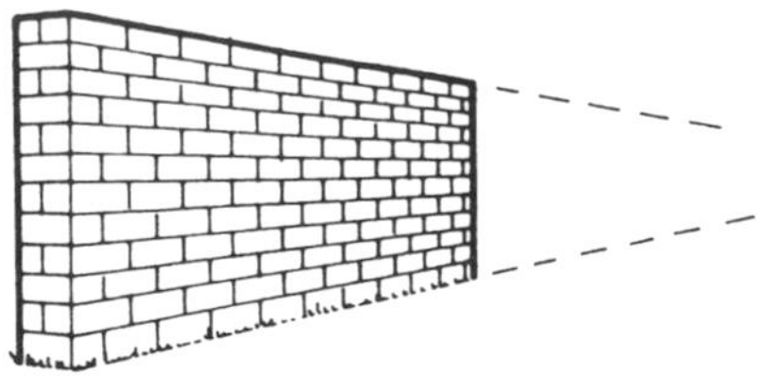

View of brick wall as seen by Spectator 2

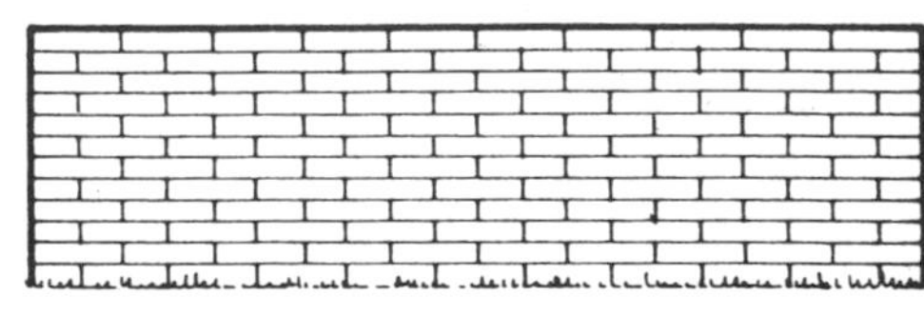

View of brick wall as seen by Spectator 1

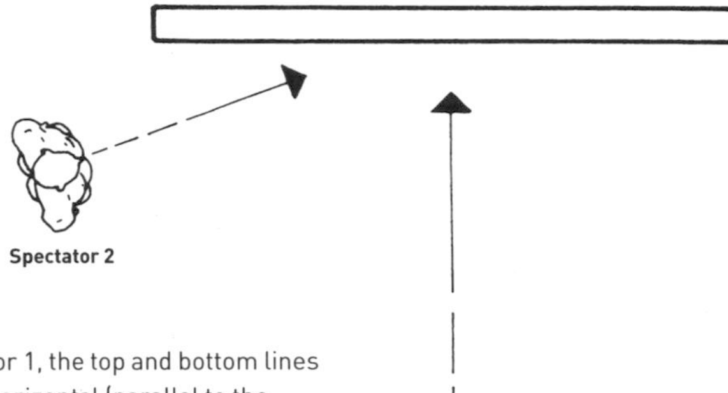

2 Convergence.

In the view of the brick wall seen by spectator 1, the top and bottom lines and all other lines parallel to these will be horizontal (parallel to the ground). In the view seen by spectator 2, these lines no longer appear parallel or horizontal but, instead, seem to come together as they recede. In this view of the brick wall, not only do the lines converge but the true length of the wall no longer appears.

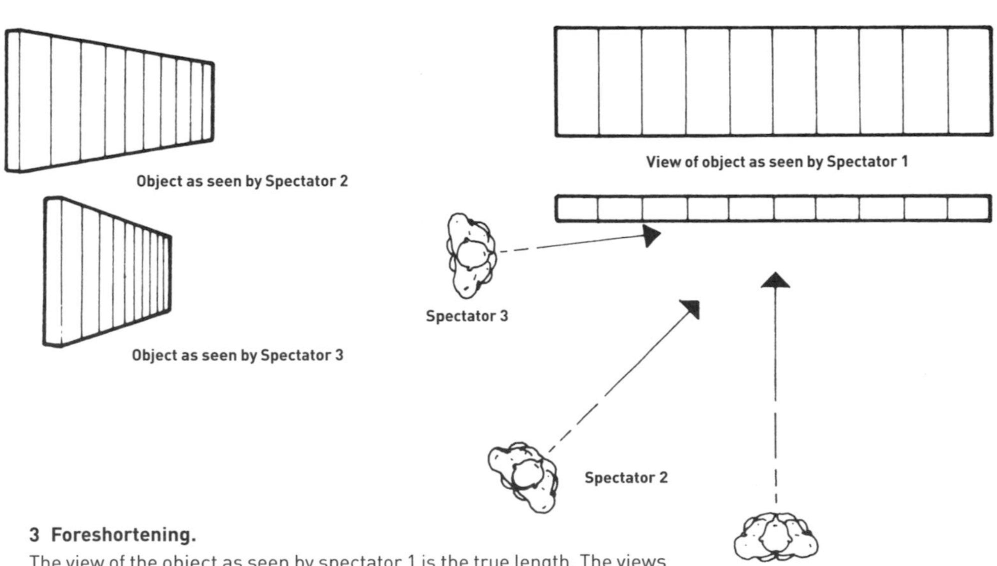

3 Foreshortening.

The view of the object as seen by spectator 1 is the true length. The views seen by spectators 2 and 3 appear shorter the further round the spectator moves from the 'straight-on' view. The vertical lines on the face of the object are equally spaced over its whole length, but as the object is rotated and the distance between the spectator and the lines increases, the spacing between the lines, and their length, seem to diminish.

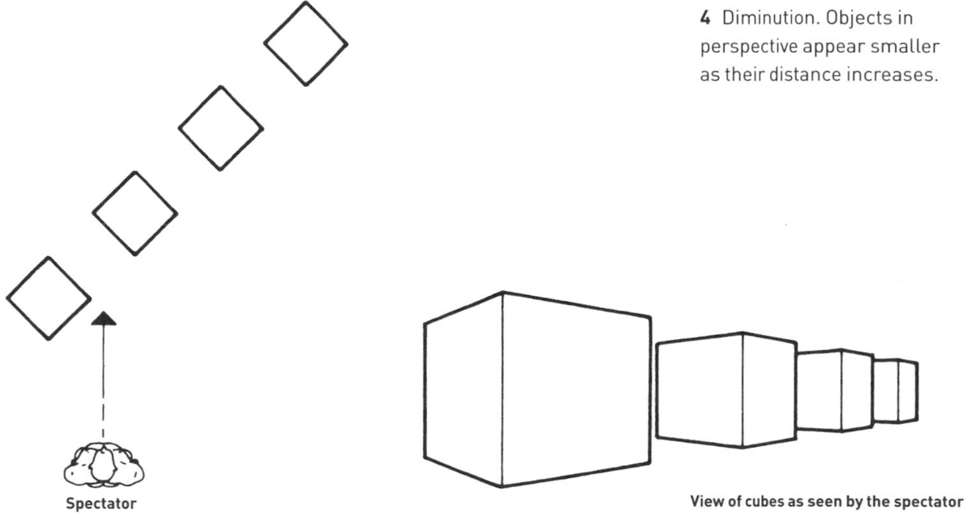

4 Diminution. Objects in perspective appear smaller as their distance increases.

important part in helping us to get a complete picture of a view or object. Shade exists when a surface is turned away from the light; shadow exists when a surface is facing the light but the light is prevented from reaching it by an intervening object.

We can also see more *detail* on an object viewed from a short distance than when it is seen from further away. In Fig. 6, detail diminishes as the distance between the spectator and the carriages increases, and is only suggested at the far end of the train; as the eye travels along the train it helps to 'fill in' the missing detail. Note that the reduction of detail is not only desirable to give a sense of perspective but is also necessary because of the greatly reduced size of the farthest carriage.

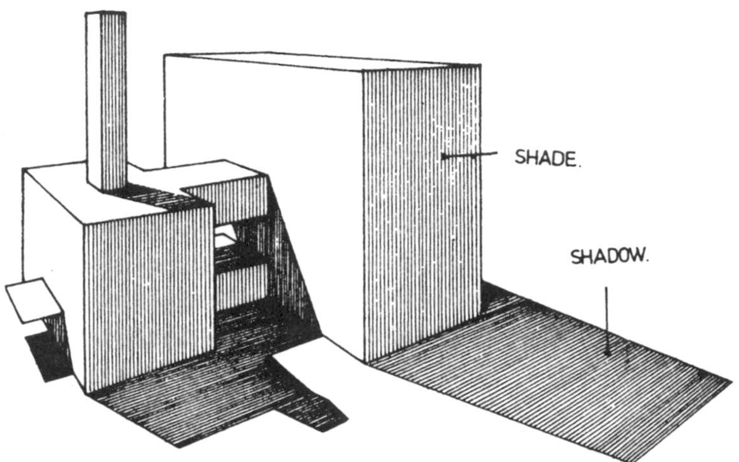

5 Shade and shadow. Light is needed to see an object, but in reality it is only the shades and shadows created by the light that are used in the rendering of an object

6 Diminution of detail as distance increases.

Tone and colour tend to become greyer or more neutral as the distance from the spectator increases. The five surfaces in Fig. 8, all assumed to have the same dark tone, appear to become greyer as they are seen from farther and farther away; similarly, light tones become greyer as the distance from the spectator increases. Colours are bright and clear when close to, but, like tones, they become greyer or more neutral as their distance increases.

Textures and patterns appear clearer and more detailed when close to the spectator than when viewed from a distance. Blades of grass, the bark and leaves of trees and the

7 Diminution of texture and pattern with distance.

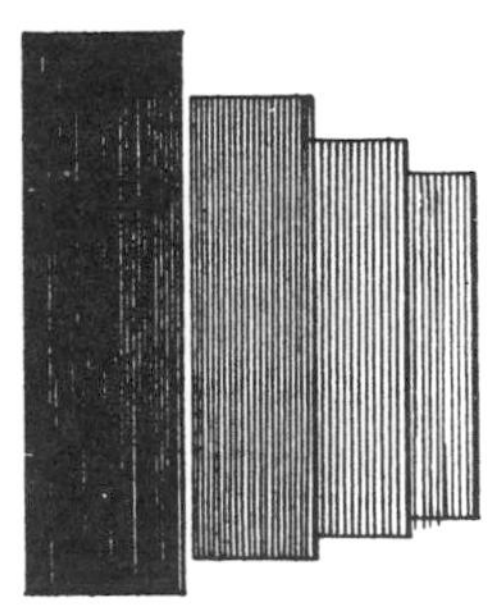

8 Diminution of tone and colour with distance – the 'atmospheric effect'.

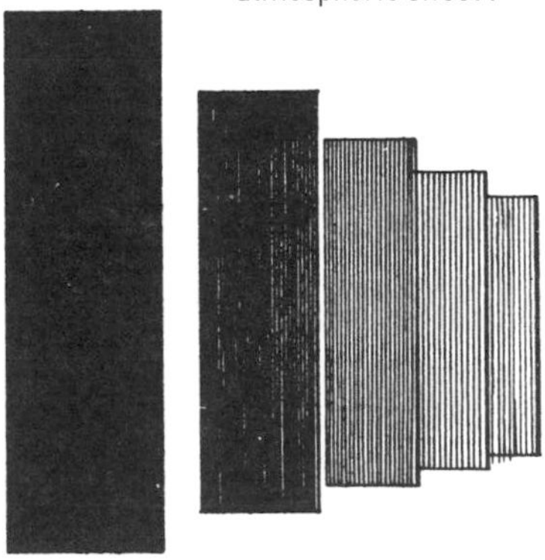

9 The difference between a fixed eye position and a moving eye when looking at an object.

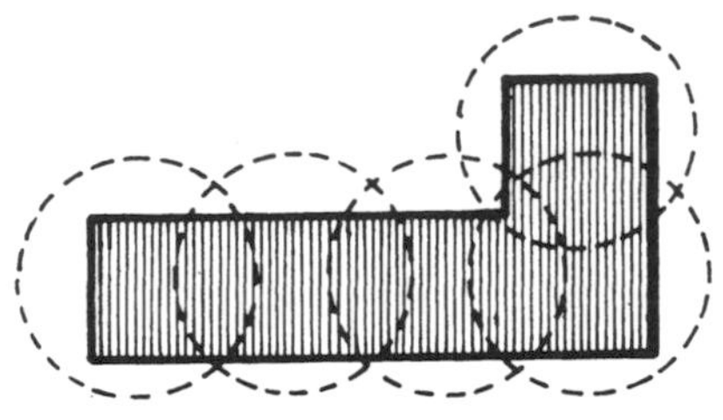

Moving eye position: The eye moves constantly over the object.

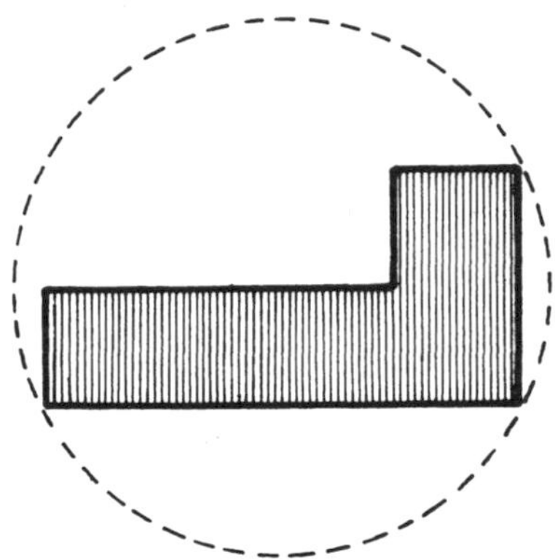

Fixed eye position: Drawing is limited to one view/one look.

features of people are seen clearly by a spectator close to them, but as the distance from the spectator increases he sees less and less detail until only a lawn or a tree or a person can be distinguished.

Although convergence, foreshortening and diminution are basic to a sense of depth and space in a drawing of a three-dimensional object, shade and shadow, detail, tone and colour together with texture and pattern are important when the perspective drawing is to be rendered.

A thorough understanding of these seven basic principles of perspective is necessary to all draughtsmen engaged in representational drawing. These principles are applied to different purposes and with varying degrees of thoroughness by artists, architects, engineers, industrial designers, interior designers, illustrators and others.

Once the basic principles are understood it will be found that their application to actual problems will help to produce greatly improved drawings based on visual facts instead of vague guesswork.

First, it is necessary to understand how we look at things. When looking at an object or view our eyes constantly move and change focus to take in the overall appearance together with its detail, colour and size. From this we form a mental picture of the object or view together with its relationship to other objects around it. However, a drawing of this object or view is limited to one 'look' or a fixed eye position (like that of the camera), and from this one 'look' it is possible to produce a drawing, just as it is possible to take a photograph of it with a camera. There are other factors which affect this also (see *Cone of Vision*, p.20), but at this point it is necessary only to understand the 'one-look' principle as applied to drawing.

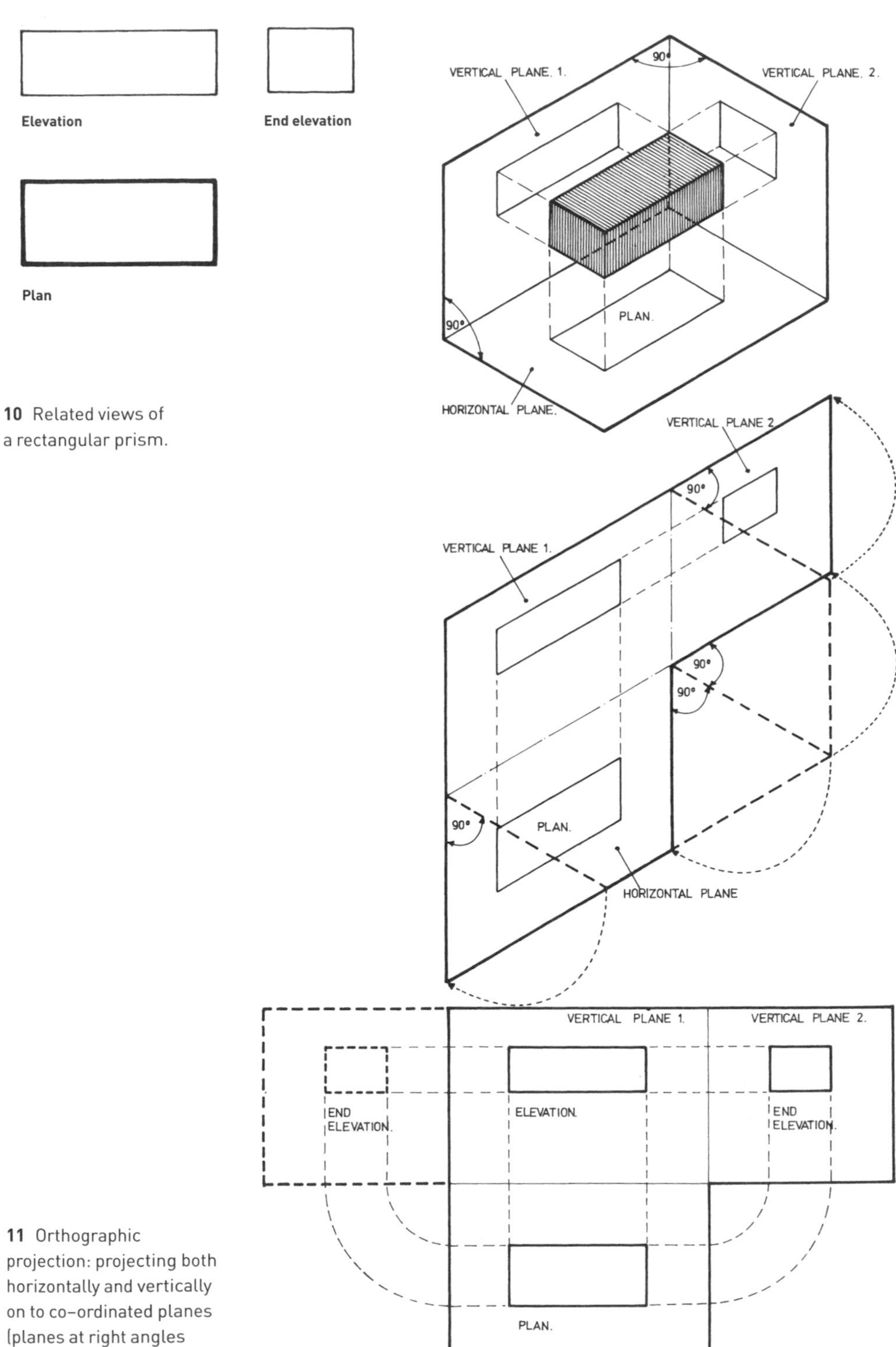

10 Related views of a rectangular prism.

11 Orthographic projection: projecting both horizontally and vertically on to co-ordinated planes (planes at right angles to one another).

1.1 Terms Used in Perspective Projection

The most important thing to understand from the beginning is that a perspective drawing can show only that which can be seen from a specific viewpoint. A perspective drawing is a technical drawing, unlike the artist's drawing, which is his own interpretation of what he sees. It is because a perspective drawing is a technical drawing that an accurate system of setting up is necessary. The system shown here is considered the most accurate yet evolved, and produces as nearly as possible a drawing of a three-dimensional object which coincides with the actual view of the object seen from the chosen viewpoint.

The first requirement when setting up a perspective view of an object is to obtain accurate information. This information is usually in the form of plans, elevations and sections. It is from the plan, usually, that the perspective view is projected (a plan of suitable size should be obtained), and heights, etc. are measured from the elevations and sections. For the purpose of explanation the plan and elevations of a simple rectangular prism are shown in Fig. 10, using orthographic projection.

Orthographic projection is simply the method of drawing three-dimensional objects in two dimensions by means of related views called plans, elevations and sections. This means a parallel or perpendicular projection. Most buildings, furniture and fitting designs are prepared in this way.

If the object is placed so that its sides are parallel to the co-ordinated planes, as shown in Fig. 11, the faces of the object (in this case a rectangular prism) can be projected back onto the planes parallel with the faces and the plans and elevations can be drawn.

To explain the next step fully it is necessary to imagine that the co-ordinated planes are 'hinged'. The horizontal plane is swung downwards through 90°, and the vertical plane 2 is swung round through 90° so that the three planes, i.e. the projections, will lie in the same plane, which allows the draughtsman to work in two dimensions when portraying three-dimensional objects. In actual practice the projection is made by first drawing the plan, then the front face (elevation) immediately above and the end elevation beside the front elevation. This is known as 'first-angle' projection, and it means that each view is so placed that it represents the face of the object remote from it in the adjacent view.

The first-angle projection is used in the British Isles and in Europe generally, the Netherlands being the exception. The Dutch, like the Americans, use what is known as 'third-angle' projection, in which the plan is immediately above the elevation of the front face of the object. The end elevation, which is placed next to the front elevation, is of the adjacent end. In practice, architects often combine both first- and third-angle projections, so that the plan is located as in first-angle projection and end elevations are placed as in third-angle projection. This arrangement is recommended for general use.

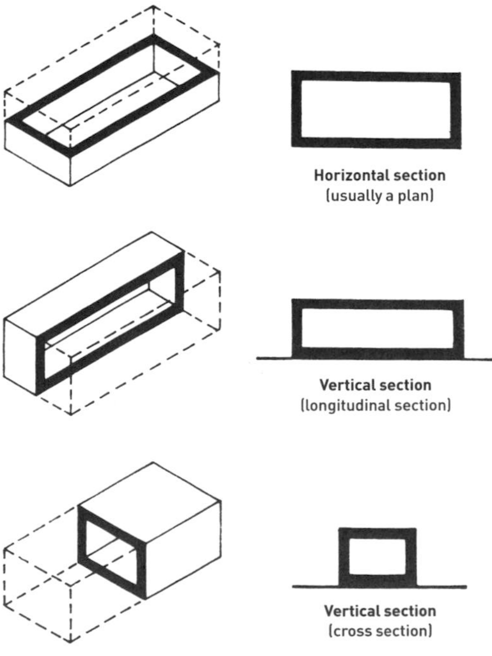

12 The sections used in orthographic projection, and their relationship to the actual object.

Sections

A section is a view of an object when it has been cut straight through in (usually) either a vertical or horizontal direction. The most-used sections are illustrated in Fig. 12 but they by no means cover all the possibilities.
The horizontal section is the plan (sectional plan), and usually there is a plan or horizontal section at each floor level in a building, including the foundations and the roof. If the object is cut longitudinally and vertically the view is called a longitudinal section, or long section. If the object is cut across and vertically, the view is known as a cross section.

Sections are used in orthographic projection to show interior details and/or details of construction.

Therefore sections should be taken through important parts of objects and buildings.

Station point

This is the chosen point from which the object is to be viewed. It is also known by other names, such as the 'observer', 'viewing point' or 'eye position', but 'station point' is preferred by most authorities.

The station point should always be chosen in relation to the nature of the object. A station point chosen too close to an object will give a dramatic appearance to the perspective drawing which is seldom acceptable. It is usually advisable to avoid this effect by moving a little further back from the object.

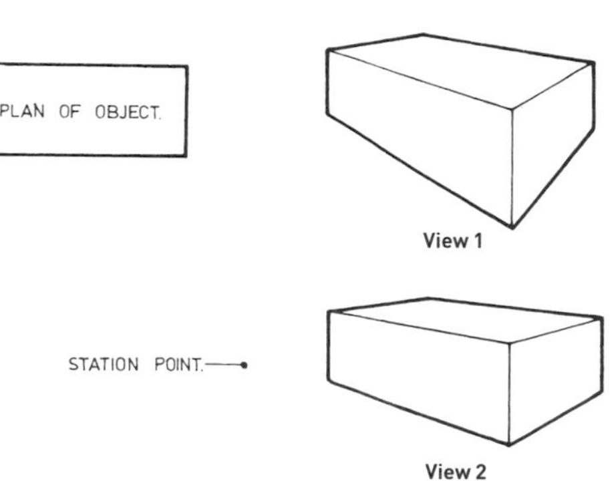

13 Selection of station point in relation to an object.

Selecting a suitable station point is a matter of judgment and experience, and it should never be finally chosen until its position has been checked with the 'cone of vision' and also the size of the final drawing considered. (See *Cone of Vision*, p. 20, and *Picture Plane*, p. 23.) It is often advisable, when selecting the position of a station point, to look at a similarly shaped object: if you are drawing a rectangular prism, look at a cigarette packet or a matchbox, as a check.

Unless otherwise stated, the height of the eye above the ground at the station point is taken as 5 ft (1.5 m).

In Fig. 13, view 1 shows a perspective drawing of a rectangular prism resulting from a badly chosen station point. Distortion is clearly evident, which makes this view unacceptable. The remedy in this case is simply to move the station point further back from the object. View 2 shows another perspective drawing of the same rectangular prism resulting from a much better position for the station point. The lack of distortion makes this view acceptable.

Centre line of vision

The centre line of vision, or, as it is sometimes known, the 'direct line of vision' or the 'direct line of sight' in perspective drawing is a line from the station point to the centre of interest

14 *Right* Station point and centre line of vision (plan).

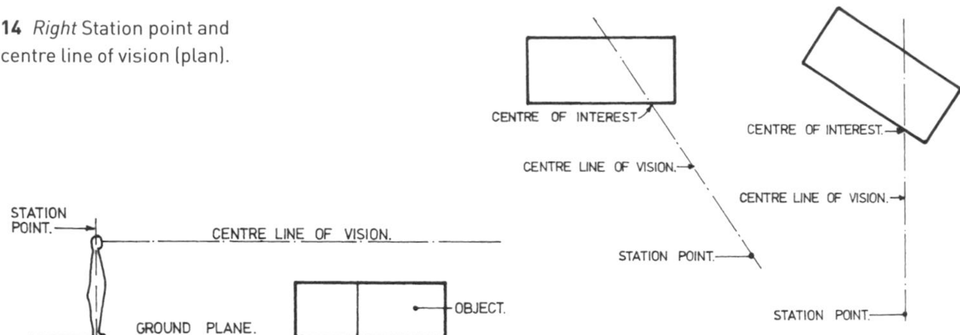

15 *Above* Station point and centre line of vision (elevation).

of the object – in other words, the point on which the eye is fixed. This line is always represented as a vertical line in perspective drawing. When the station point is located and the direction of the view (centre line of vision) is decided upon, the plan should be turned round until the centre line of vision is vertical, and usually with the station point at the bottom. This is done for convenience, to make it easier to produce a perspective drawing using a T-square and a set square. The centre line of vision is always taken to be parallel to the ground plane, which is shown as a horizontal plane for the purpose of perspective drawing (see *Ground Line*, p. 34).

Cone of vision

The field of vision is known to be more than 180° but it is not possible to see clearly over this whole range. The normal maximum range within which it is possible to see clearly and easily is accepted as being a cone of less than 90° and is seldom if ever shown as more than 60°. For the purpose of perspective drawing it is usually limited to 60° or less. Where possible, the student is advised to use a cone of vision of much less than 60°, say 45° or even 30°, as these will normally be adequate for his purposes and will give a much more satisfactory result than a wider cone of vision.

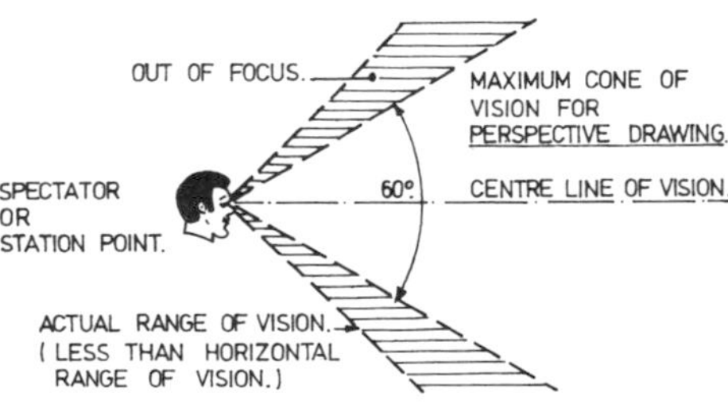

16 Cone of vision in plan (*top*) and elevation.

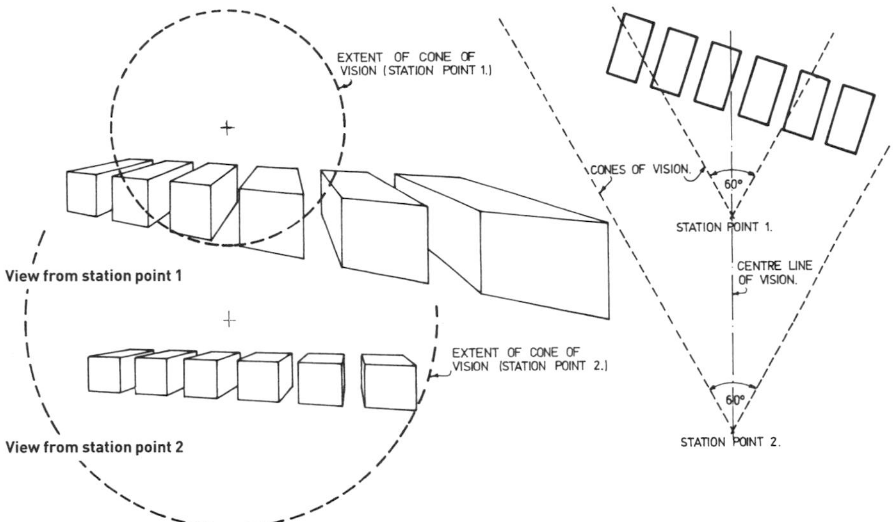

17 Two alternative station points, and what is seen from them.

As can be seen from the diagrams, any object or part of an object which would not normally be seen clearly because of its lying outside this cone of vision will be distorted if we try to draw it. To obtain a wider coverage with the cone of vision it is necessary to move back from the object; it is not enough simply to widen the cone of vision. When deciding on the position from which to view the object it is necessary to fit the whole – or the part which is to be included in the drawing – inside the cone of vision. This fact governs the distance from which one should view the object. When a station point is being considered and its position checked with the cone of vision, it should be checked on the plan and also on the elevation. The reasons for this will be obvious when the object is, for example, a tall building.

The centre line of this cone is the centre line of vision. This line is represented in plan by a vertical line and in elevation by a horizontal line. The apex of this cone is the station point.

From examination of Fig. 18 a number of points can be learned. The first of these is that the smaller the angle for the cone of vision, the greater the distance required between the object and the station point to obtain the same coverage. The second is that even though the plan of the cone of vision appears to confirm the location of the station point, when this

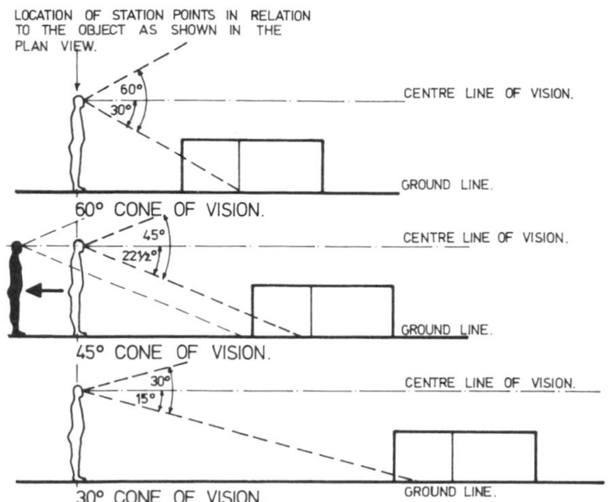

Elevations showing locations of the three possible station points located on the plan.

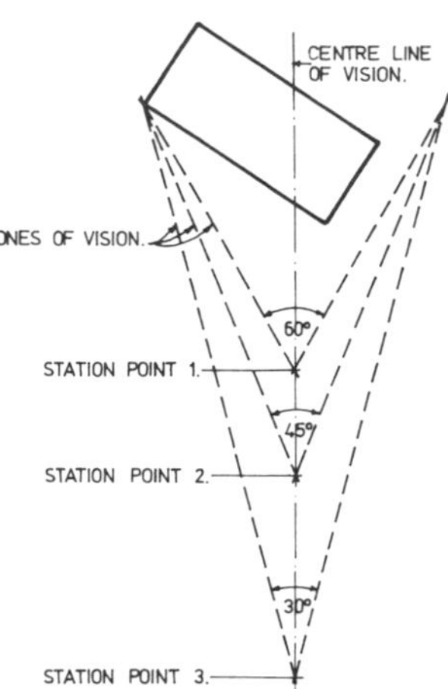

Plan of object with three possible station points based on 60°, 45° and 30° cones of vision.

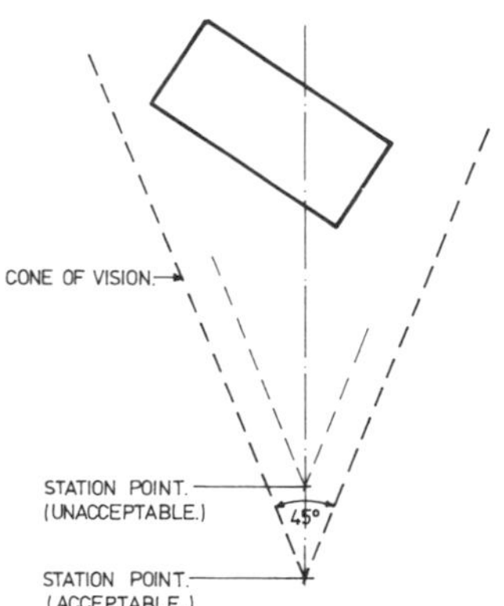

Plan of object with confirmed station point using a 45° cone of vision.

18 Cone of vision: examples of its use to locate the limits of a drawing.

is checked in the elevation it can be seen that in each case the station point must be moved further back from the object. (For the purposes of illustration it is intended to use a 45° cone of vision for the examples in this book.)

The elevation of the 45° cone of vision shows the station point repositioned so that the whole of the object falls within the cone of vision. (The repositioned figure is shown in black.) This means that a perspective drawing made using the new confirmed station point will not contain distortions.

It can be seen that it is the cone of vision that governs the distance of the station point from the object. Ignorance of this fact is responsible for many of the badly distorted perspective drawings that are produced.

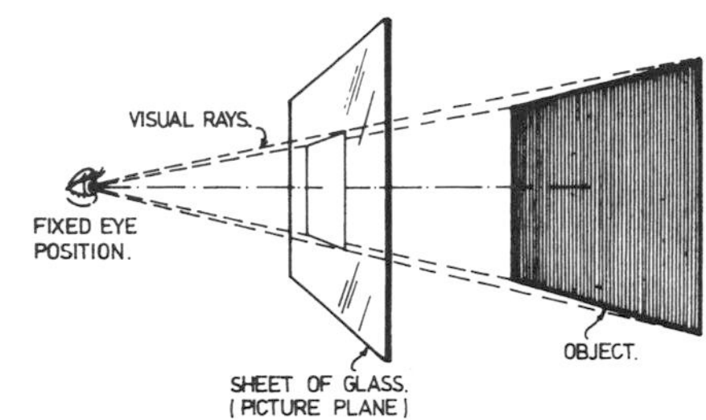

Picture plane

This is an imaginary vertical plane on which the perspective drawing is supposed to be done. The perspective drawing is in fact the plotting of the positions where the visual rays from the eye (station point) through the points of the object intersect the picture plane. Imagine a fixed eye position looking through a sheet of glass (e.g. a window). It would be possible to trace the shape of the object on the glass exactly as it is seen. As shown in Fig. 19, this principle remains true whether the picture plane is placed in front of or behind the object.

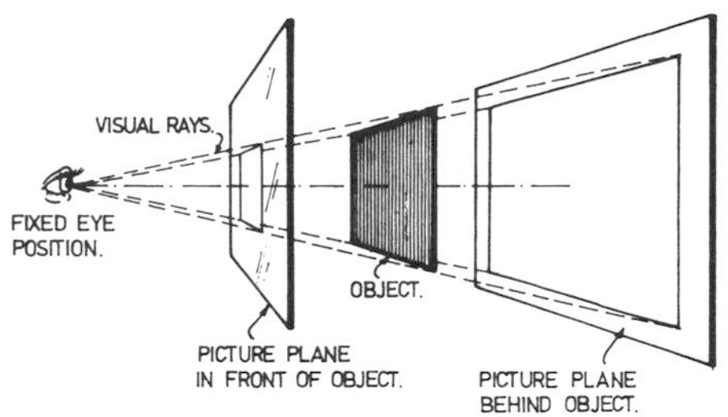

19 The principle of the picture plane in relation to the object and the eye.

In perspective drawing the picture plane is an imaginary plane, normally at 90° to the ground plane, on which the perspective drawing is supposed to be made. The picture plane can be inclined to the ground plane for special views, which are dealt with later (see aerial views, p. 89), but in what are known as 'one-point' and 'two-point' perspectives the picture plane is always taken to be perpendicular.

From Fig. 19 it can be seen that the picture plane may be placed in front of, behind or, if necessary, even through the object. In other words, the location of the picture plane is a matter of personal choice and convenience, so long as it is perpendicular and at 90° to the centre line of vision.

The exact situation shown in the diagram can be drawn in plan where the plan of the object, the station point (spectator) and the centre line of vision are prepared for perspective drawing as previously described. The plan view of the perpendicular picture plane will be represented by a straight line drawn in a selected position at 90° to the centre line of vision.

It will be obvious that the picture plane cannot remain perpendicular, as shown in Fig. 20, when a perspective drawing is being done on a flat sheet of paper. As explained on p. 17, a plane can be 'hinged' so that a vertical plane can be brought into the same plane as the horizontal plane for drawing purposes. This can be done without altering the image of an object drawn on the plane.

By using vertical projection, distances marked on the plan of the picture plane can be projected either above or below the plan of the picture plane to a selected position where the perspective drawing is to be made. This is explained more fully in Fig. 21.

The upper diagram in Fig. 21 shows the visual rays from the spectator (station point) passing through the points of the object and meeting the picture plane. From Fig. 19 it can be seen that by joining these points where the visual rays meet the picture plane the perspective view can be drawn. Also shown are the plans of the visual rays from the station point through the points of the plan of the object and meeting the picture plane. From this it can be seen that lines projected up from the points where the plans of the visual rays meet the picture plane coincide with the points of the perspective of the object. This simply means that by working with a plan of the object together with a plan of the picture plane it is possible to locate the vertical lines on which the points of the object will be located on the elevation of the picture plane.

When the picture plane is swung down so that it falls in the same plane as the plan, as shown in the lower diagram of

Diagram showing a spectator looking at an object with a picture plane placed behind it.

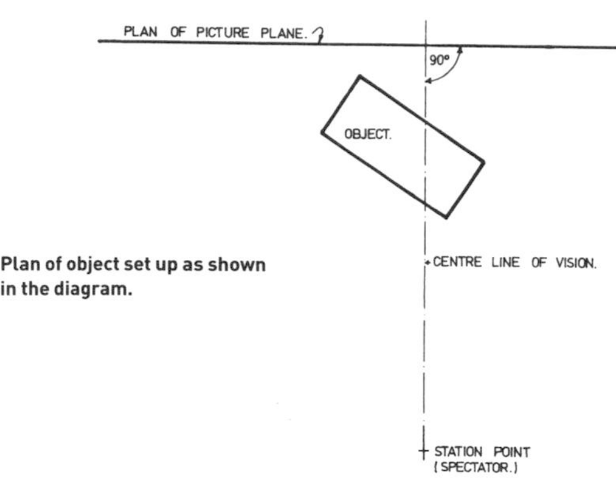

Plan of object set up as shown in the diagram.

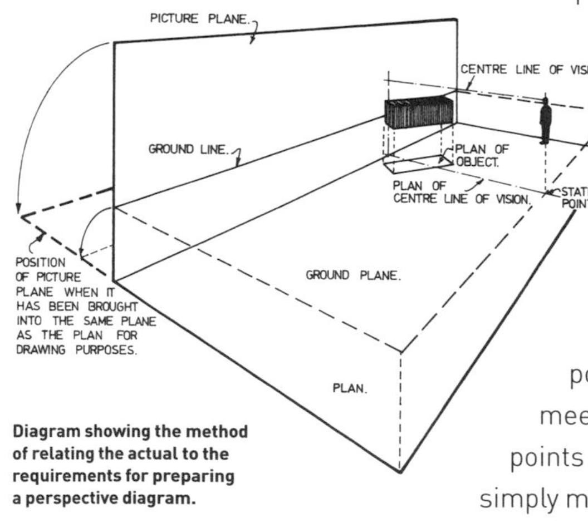

Diagram showing the method of relating the actual to the requirements for preparing a perspective diagram.

20 The spectator and the object in their relation to a selected picture plane.

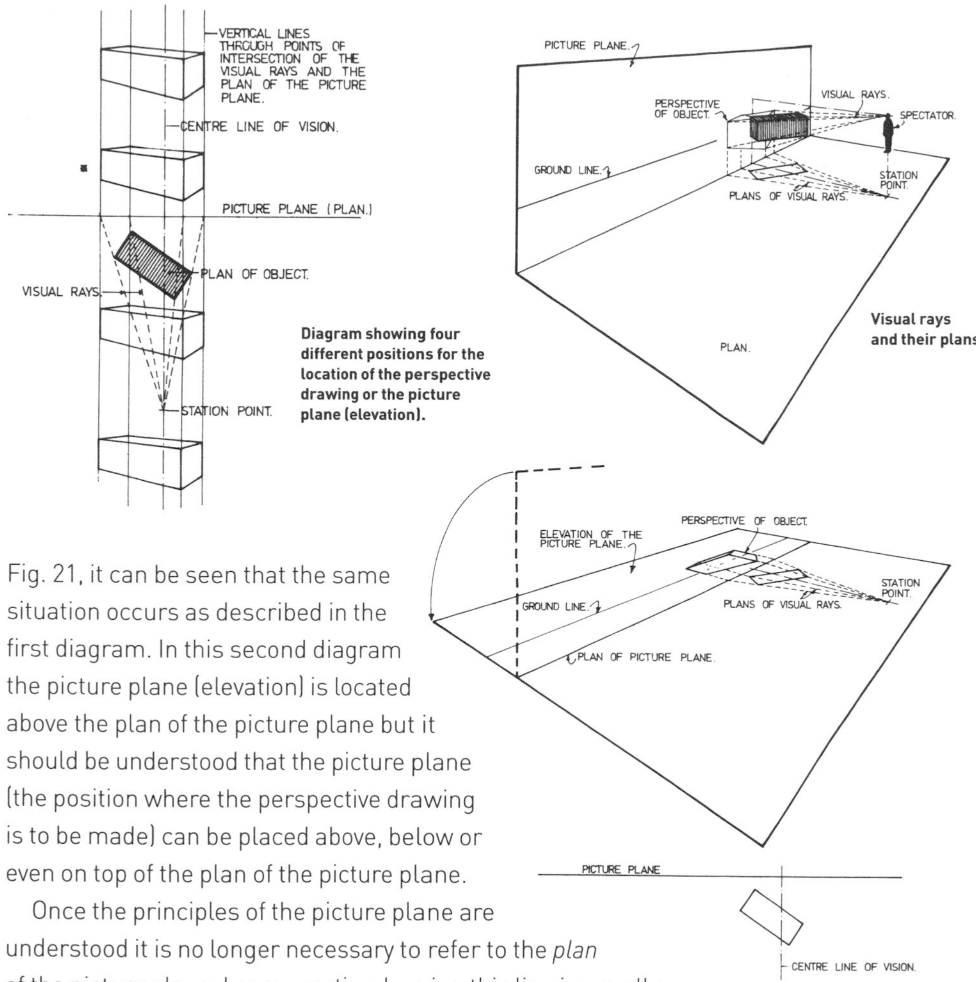

Diagram showing four different positions for the location of the perspective drawing or the picture plane (elevation).

Visual rays and their plans

Identification of plan of picture plane.

Fig. 21, it can be seen that the same situation occurs as described in the first diagram. In this second diagram the picture plane (elevation) is located above the plan of the picture plane but it should be understood that the picture plane (the position where the perspective drawing is to be made) can be placed above, below or even on top of the plan of the picture plane.

Once the principles of the picture plane are understood it is no longer necessary to refer to the *plan* of the picture plane. In perspective drawing this line is usually referred to simply as 'the picture plane', and this is the name which will be used in diagrams and text from this point on.

The location of the picture plane is a matter of choice, convenience or control of the size of the perspective drawing required. The closer to the spectator the picture plane is located the smaller the drawing, and, naturally, the further away the larger the drawing. However, it is only the *size* of the drawing which is affected; the view of the object remains the same. Fig. 22*a* explains this.

By drawing the visual rays from the station point through the points of the object to the selected picture plane the overall size of the perspective drawing can be measured.

21 The picture plane brought into the same plane as the plan, to allow for a perspective drawing to be made.

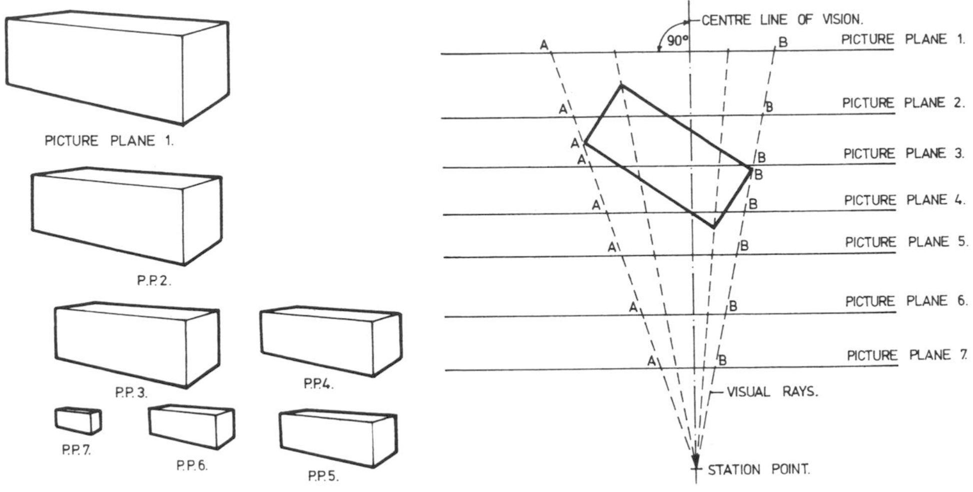

22a The effect of moving the picture plane: only the size of the drawing is changed.

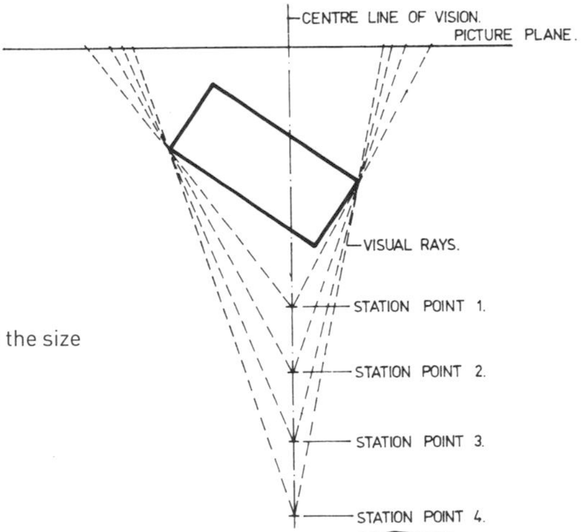

CENTRE LINE OF VISION.
PICTURE PLANE.
VISUAL RAYS.
STATION POINT 1.
STATION POINT 2.
STATION POINT 3.
STATION POINT 4.

22b The effect of moving the station point: both the size and the view of the object are changed.

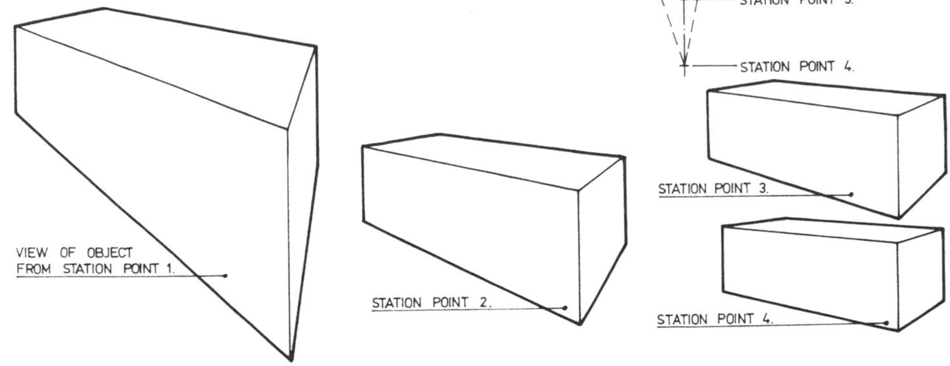

VIEW OF OBJECT FROM STATION POINT 1.
STATION POINT 2.
STATION POINT 3.
STATION POINT 4.

A check on the finished size of the perspective drawing to be made at this point can save a great deal of effort and time. The complete control of the size of the finished perspective drawing from the beginning is a valuable aid to anyone preparing any type of perspective drawing.

Fig. 22*a* shows seven different locations for the picture plane, chosen at random. Points *A* and *B* are the extreme ends of the object seen from the station point shown. These two points can be located as shown on each picture plane, and measurement of the distance between them will give the overall length of a perspective drawn using each location for the picture plane.

By contrast, using a fixed picture plane and different station points changes not only the size of the drawing but also the view of the object. The diagram in Fig. 22*b* has four station points located at different distances from the object along a common centre line of vision. (For the purpose of illustrating this point the cone of vision has been ignored in the views from station points 1, 2 and 3.) By comparing the views of the object seen from the different station points it can be seen that they differ considerably from one another even when allowance is made for the obvious distortions in the view from station point 1.

A thorough understanding of these facts will enable the student, from the beginning of a project, to control the drawing size and fit a perspective drawing into any given size without difficulty.

The position where it is intended to draw the perspective on the paper is the picture plane in elevation. This can be clearly understood by referring to Fig. 21, where the actual construction of the perspective drawing can be seen on the picture plane behind the object.

Vanishing points

Any two or more parallel lines will, if extended indefinitely, appear to converge and meet at a point. This point is known as

23 Why the vanishing point is at the observer's eye level.

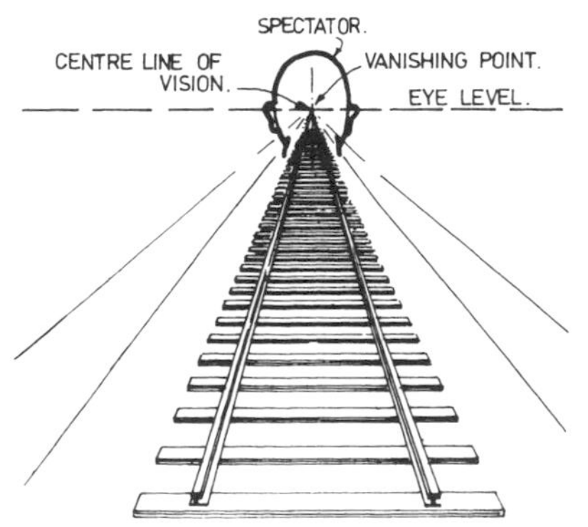

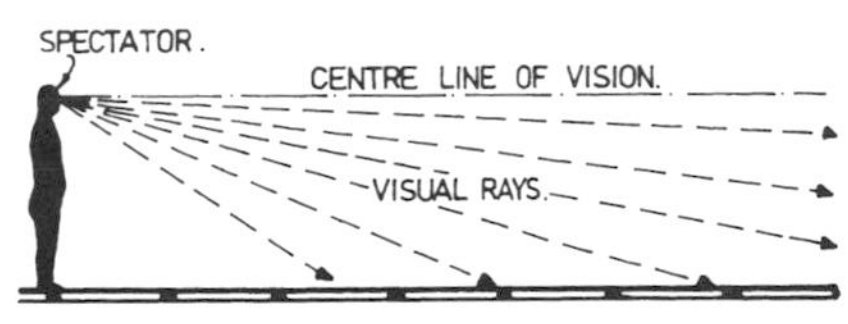

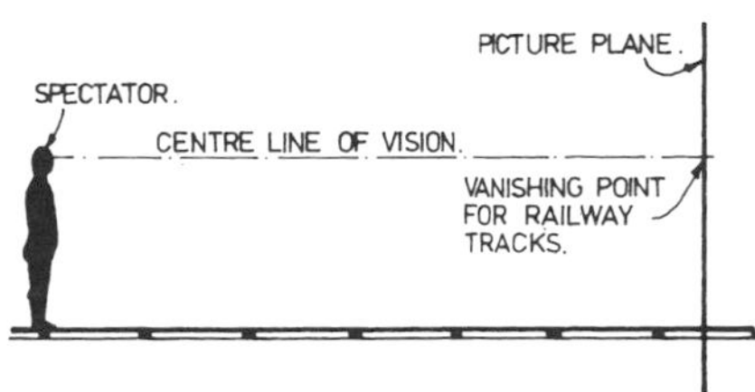

the vanishing point. Regardless of direction, each set of parallel lines will converge towards its own vanishing point.

In perspective drawing it is necessary to locate exactly the vanishing points for parallel lines. To do this, the relationship between parallel lines and sight lines must be understood. When a spectator looks along railway lines, the centre line of vision is in fact parallel to the tracks. (The centre line of vision is parallel to the ground plane.) Because these lines are parallel they will converge until they meet at a common vanishing point. The second diagram in Fig. 23 shows how the angle between the centre line of vision and the visual rays decreases as the distance between the spectator and the point observed increases. From this it can be seen that the visual rays will finally coincide with the centre line of vision, which means that the vanishing point will be on the eye level.

Therefore the vanishing point for the railway lines is at the point at which the sight line (the centre line of vision in this case) parallel to them intersects the picture plane. Because the sight line, which is parallel to the railway lines, vanishes to the same vanishing point as the railway lines it can be assumed that all lines parallel to the railway lines will converge to the same vanishing point. From this it can be assumed that in all cases where a sight line parallel to a line or side of an object meets the picture plane (in plan), that point will be the vanishing point for the line or side of the object and all lines parallel to it.

Once the principle of locating vanishing points has been understood it can be applied to perspective drawing. It has been established in Fig. 23 that a sight line (the centre line of vision in the case of the spectator looking along the railway lines) parallel to a side of an object vanishes to the same vanishing point as all lines which are parallel to that side. This means that the method of finding the vanishing point for a side of an object is a simple matter of drawing a sight line parallel to the side. The point of intersection between the picture plane and the sight line is the vanishing point in plan.

By reference back to the explanation of the picture plane (p. 23) it can be seen that the actual location of the vanishing points will be above or below their plan position (depending on the location of the elevation of the picture plane). Also from the

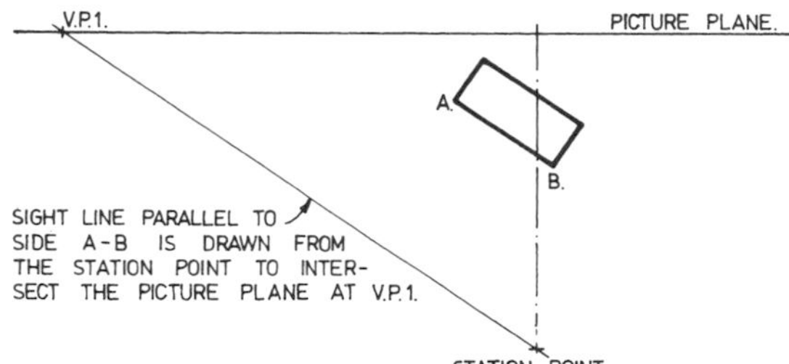

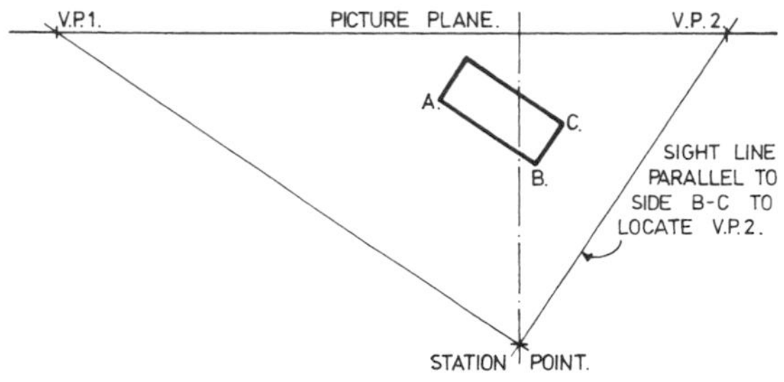

24 The method of obtaining the vanishing points for a simple rectangular prism, and the actual vanishing points in relation to their plan positions.

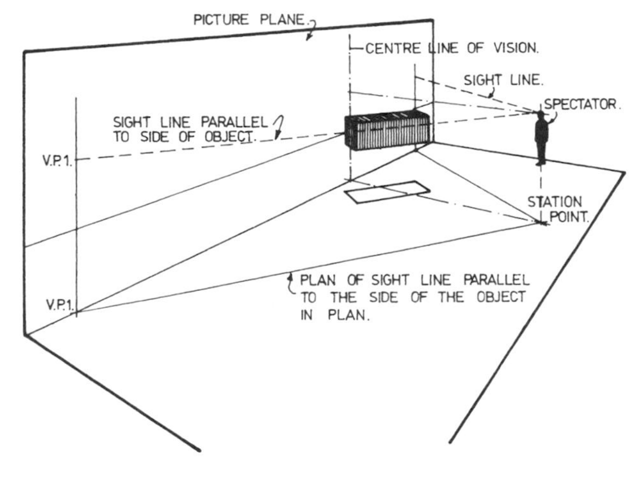

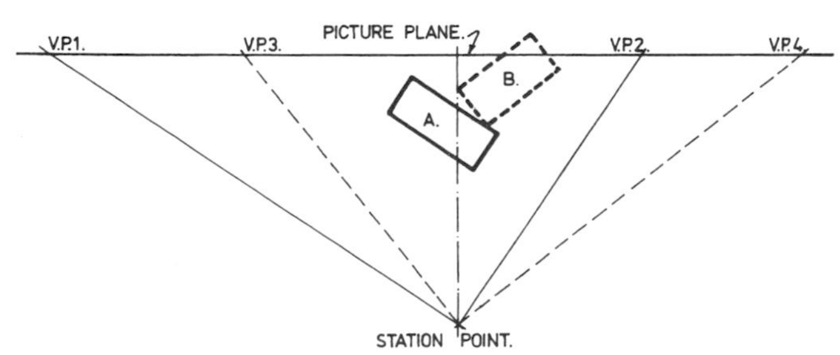

25 The method of obtaining vanishing points for two objects at different angles to the picture plane.

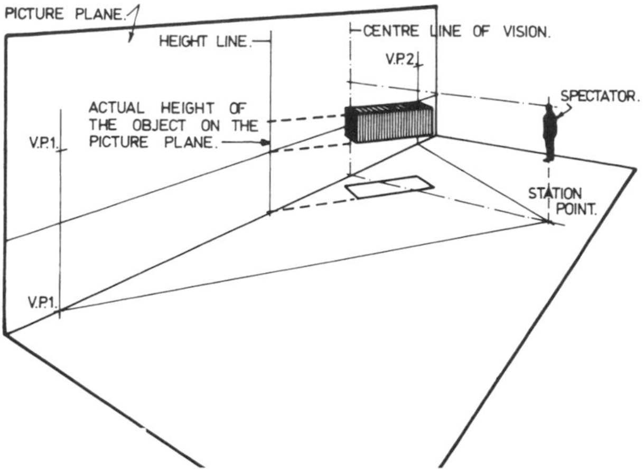

26 Locating the height line: a side of the object is projected to meet the picture plane.

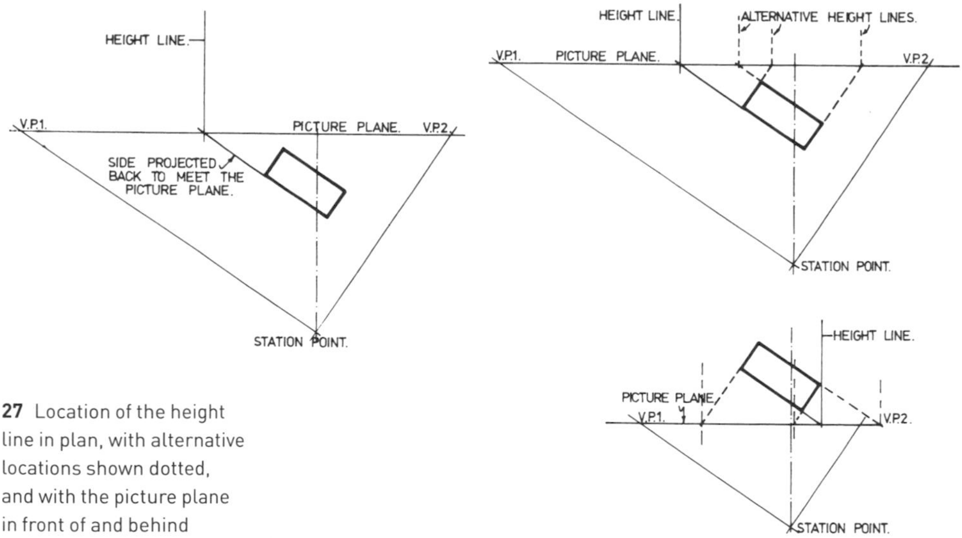

27 Location of the height line in plan, with alternative locations shown dotted, and with the picture plane in front of and behind the object.

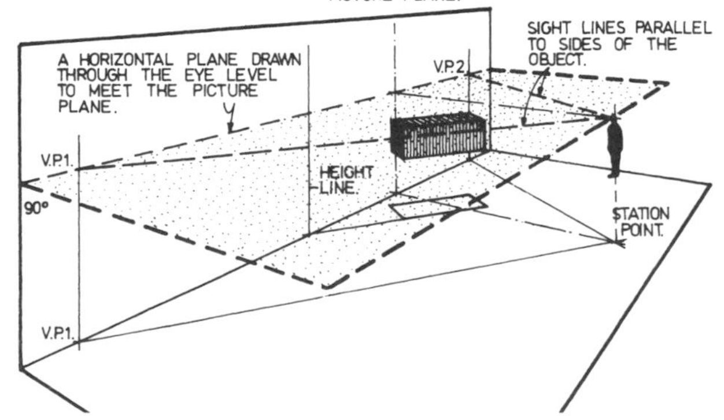

28 A horizontal plane through the spectator's eye level intersecting the picture plane at the horizon line.

explanation, and from Fig. 23, it is known that the vanishing points for lines parallel to the ground plane will be on the eye level. (This is further explained in Fig. 29, p. 32.)

For objects at an angle to each other, since it has been established that each set of parallel lines will converge to a single vanishing point, by treating each object separately the vanishing points for each side can be found and each object drawn in perspective. This is also true for objects with more than four sides or irregularly shaped objects. The important thing to remember is that each set of parallel lines will have its own vanishing point, so it does not matter how many different directions are included in any one object or group of objects. Provided the vanishing points are found for each set of parallel lines in each direction, any shape can be drawn in perspective.

Height lines

The height line in perspective drawing is the line used for measuring all vertical heights. These heights are measured using the same scale as that used for the plan and elevations. The location of this line is found by projecting a line as the continuation of a side of the object in plan either backwards or forwards, as necessary, to meet the plan of the picture plane. From this point a vertical line can be drawn on the elevation of the picture plane and it is on this line that vertical heights can be measured. Fig. 26 shows graphically the relationship between the plan and the actual side of the object projected back to meet the picture plane and the plan. From this it can be seen that the top and bottom of the extended side meet the picture plane on the line projected up from the plan location of the height line and, because the top and bottom lines are parallel, the distance between them is the same as the height of the object. Therefore actual heights can be measured on the height line because the height line is in actual fact a continuation of the side being measured. This remains true for all the sides of the object, therefore the most convenient side should be chosen to be projected either backwards or (if the picture plane is in front of the object) forwards to the picture plane to locate the height line.

Fig. 27 shows the alternative locations for the height line when other sides are extended. It can be seen that any side can

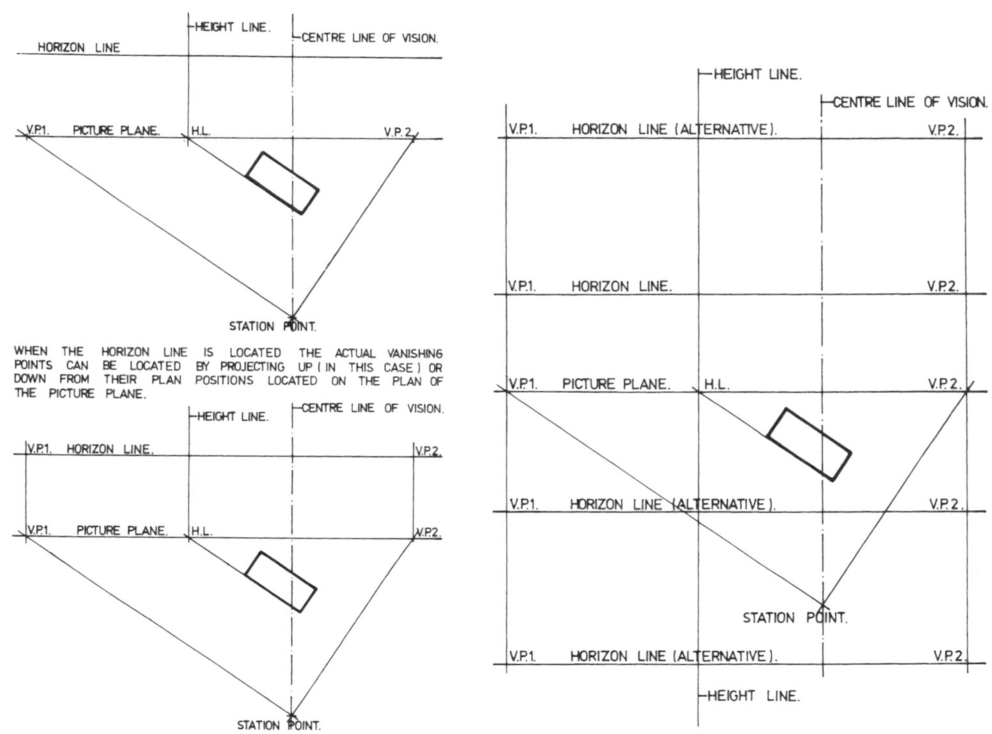

29 Locating the vanishing points on the horizon line. Note that the various alternative locations for the horizon lines do not alter the relationship between the vanishing points, the centre line of vision and the height line. Any of the alternative locations would be satisfactory for drawing the perspective view of the object.

be extended but it should also be obvious that a convenient side should be used to locate the height line, otherwise inaccuracies can be expected. This is explained more fully later on in this book, but generally the side chosen should be one prominent in the view of the object from the selected station point, and for preference it should be on the side which has the greater distance between the centre line of vision and the vanishing point.

Eye level or horizon line

When the spectator's centre line of vision is parallel to the ground, the eye level coincides with the horizon line. This means that if a horizontal plane is drawn through the spectator's eye level it will meet the picture plane, producing a straight horizontal line parallel to the ground plane and the same distance above it as the spectator's eye. The line produced on the picture plane by the intersection of the horizontal plane through the eye level of the spectator is known as the eye level or the horizon line. (In perspective drawing, the term 'horizon line' is preferred, and will be used from here on.)

The important fundamental in perspective drawing is the height of the eye level above the ground plane. As previously described, the elevation of the picture plane can be located as convenient (within certain limits), so wherever the horizon line is drawn can be assumed to be the elevation of the picture plane – in other words, the position where it is intended to draw the perspective view. This is usually directly above or sometimes below the plan of the picture plane, whichever is more convenient. It is necessary in perspective drawing to project up (or down) from the plan of the picture plane to locate the vanishing points and the height line on the horizon line.

The positioning of the horizon line on the elevation of the picture plane is a matter of convenience. The position is limited only by the equipment and space available (i.e. the size of the drawing board and the length of the set square to be used for the vertical projections).

A few important points regarding the horizon line and its use are worth remembering. The horizon line in a perspective drawing shows the position of the spectator's eye level. It is advisable to draw objects using an eye level normally used for viewing that object in reality unless some special viewing position is required for some specific reason. Generally a horizon line placed towards the top of the picture or above it means a high eye level, sometimes called a 'bird's-eye view'. This is often used in perspective drawing when the top of the object is important. The horizon line placed about the centre of the picture usually means a normal eye level (i.e. 5 ft above the ground). A low horizon line (near the bottom of the picture) usually means a low eye level or 'worm's-eye view'.

When locating the horizon line on the picture plane it should be decided at what height the eye level is to be, so that space

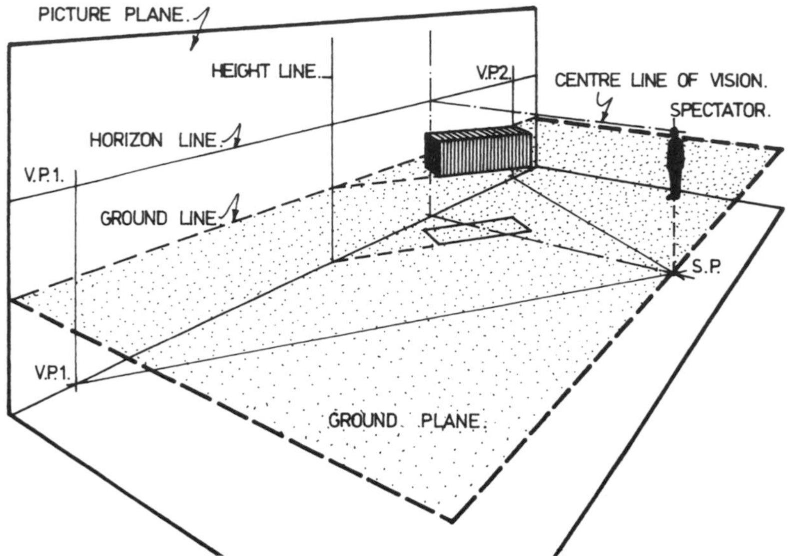

30 The relationship between the ground line and the horizon line.

can be provided either above or below the horizon line as may be necessary for the perspective drawing to be done.

Ground line

The ground plane is a horizontal plane representing the ground on which the spectator and the object are supposed to stand or to which they are supposed to be related. The eye level of a spectator is measured as some distance above (or below) the ground, depending on the spectator's position relative to the ground, e.g. a spectator standing on the top step of a ladder will have a higher eye level than a spectator standing on the ground.

The ground line is the intersection of the ground plane and the picture plane. This is explained graphically in Fig. 30, where the object and the spectator are shown in relation to the ground plane and the picture plane. The spectator is standing on the ground in what is known as the 'normal' position, that is to say the eye level is assumed to be 5 ft (1.5 m) above the ground. Unless something different is specified, this assumption is always made.

The ground line is seen to be a horizontal line parallel to the horizon line. In perspective drawing, the ground line is

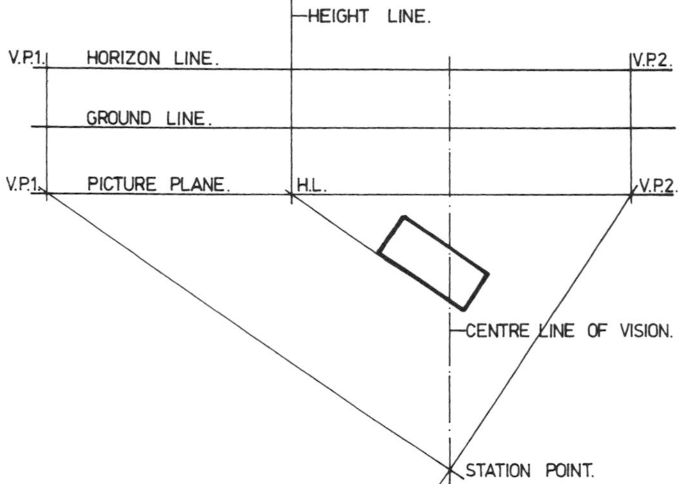

31 The distance between the horizon line and the ground line, as it would be measured on the height line in setting up a perspective drawing.

located (Fig. 31) by measuring down from the horizon line the distance of the selected eye level (using the same scale as that used for the plan and elevations) and at this point a horizontal line is drawn, representing the ground line. This places the ground line at the required distance below the horizon line or the spectator's eye level. In other words, the horizon line and the ground line are related to each other so as to produce a perspective drawing of an object when looked at from this specific eye level.

The location of the horizon line is a matter of convenience but the ground line is always located in relation to the horizon line, therefore they should be thought of as inseparable, and when the horizon line is located the ground line should be located with it.

In practice the ground line need be located only where it intersects the height line, which means that the height line should be used to measure the distance between the horizon line and the ground line. The reason for this will become obvious as the method of drawing the perspective view is described.

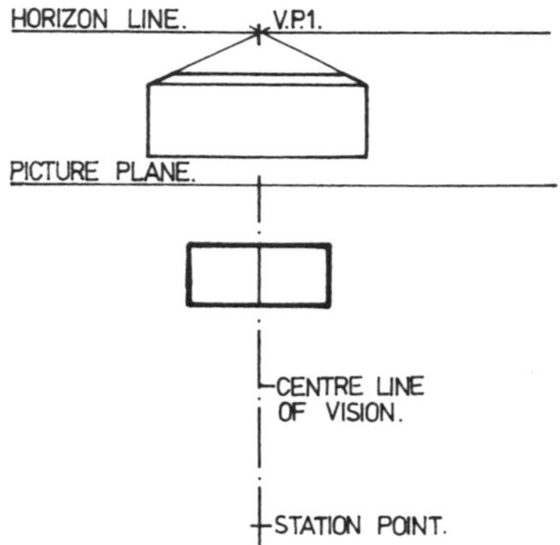

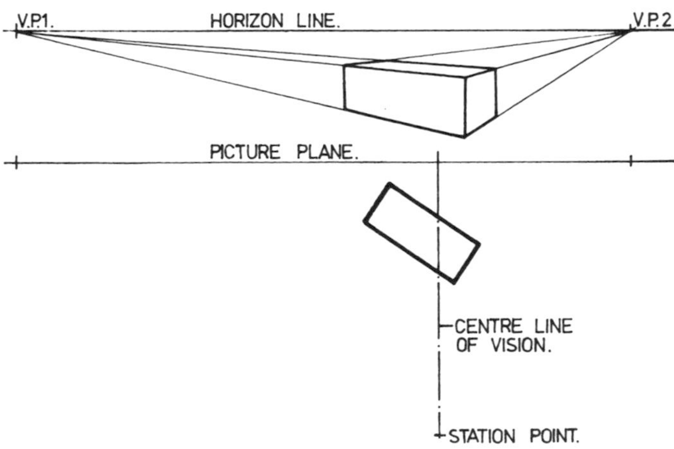

32 *Top* One-point perspective. *Bottom* Two-point perspective.

1.2 Drawing the Perspective: One-Point and Two-Point

With the location of the ground line the preparations for drawing the perspective view are complete. All that remains is for the actual perspective view to be drawn, but before proceeding to this it is necessary to understand the various types of perspective drawing in general use.

There are three types of perspective drawing. Each type has a different relationship between the lines of the object and the picture plane. In perspective drawing, any set of parallel lines may be parallel to, at right angles to, or oblique to the picture plane. Lines which are parallel to the picture plane remain parallel in the perspective. A set of lines which are at right angles to or oblique to the picture plane vanish to a vanishing point in perspective. The three types of perspective drawing are distinguished by the number of vanishing points required by each type.

One-point perspective has two sets of lines parallel to the picture plane and a third set at right angles to it. Since a set of parallel lines not parallel to the picture plane converges to a vanishing point, this set-up will require only one vanishing point and is called 'one-point' perspective.

Two-point perspective has one set of lines parallel to the picture plane (the vertical lines only) and two sets oblique to it. Parallel lines oblique to the picture plane converge to a vanishing point, which means that this set-up will require two vanishing points.

Three-point perspective has three sets of lines oblique to the picture plane, thus requiring three vanishing points. Three-point perspective is more difficult to construct than the other two types and is not used as frequently as the others. It is not illustrated at this stage, but is dealt with later (p. 73).

The most-used type of perspective drawing is probably two-point perspective; because of this, the explanations used so far have been illustrated with two-point principles, but as will be seen, these principles remain true for each of the three types of perspective drawing.

Two-point perspective drawing

Figs. 33–35 show the steps for the preparation of a plan and the setting up of conditions for the drawing of a perspective view of an object. If these steps are followed in the sequence shown here, it will be found that perspective drawings can be prepared quickly and accurately.

Step 1. Either obtain or prepare information regarding the object, i.e. plan, elevations and, if necessary, sections. For the purposes of illustration the same rectangular prism is used as for the preceding explanations, and it is shown in orthographic projection.

Step 2. Select the direction of the view and the station point, i.e. the centre line of vision and the position from which it is proposed to view the object.

Step 3. In perspective drawing, the plan of the centre line of vision is always drawn as a vertical line, so it is necessary to rotate the plan and the station point until the centre line of vision is vertical.

33 Two-point perspective drawing: steps 1–5.

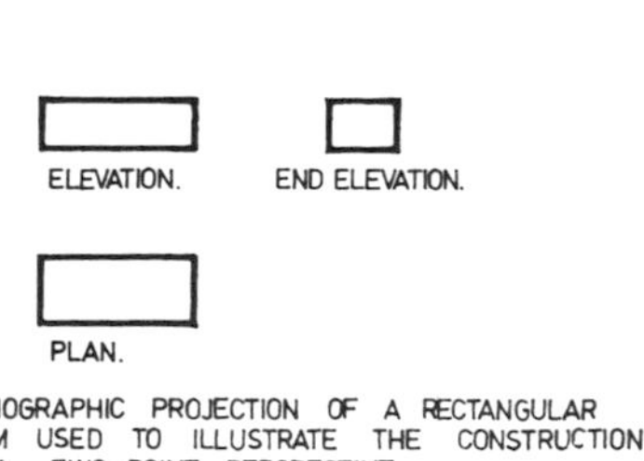

Step 1. Obtain information.

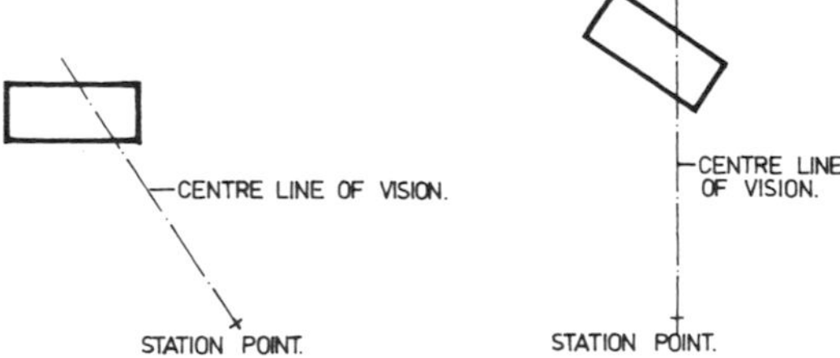

Step 2. Locate station point and the direction of view.

Step 3. Centre line of vision to be vertical.

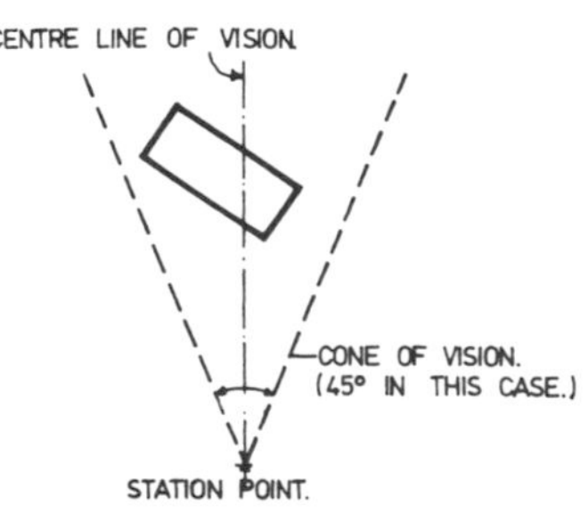

Step 4. Check the location of the station point with the cone of vision.

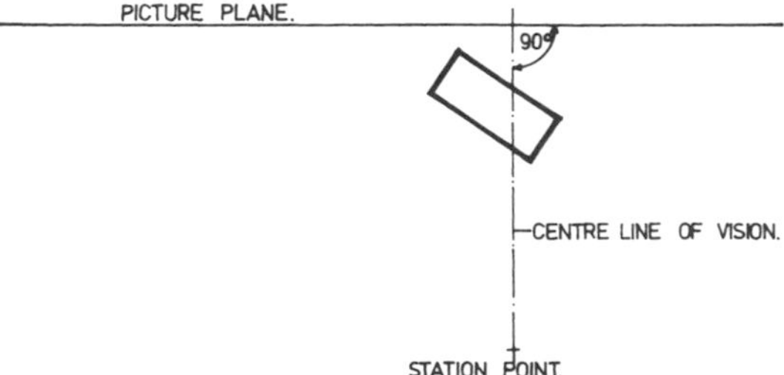

Step 5. Locate the picture plane at 90° to the centre line of vision.

Step 4. The location of the station point should be checked at this stage with the cone of vision. (The cone of vision suggested in the earlier explanations was 45°.) If the whole of the object intended to be included in the drawing falls within this cone of vision, the position of the station point can be taken as confirmed. If not, it will be necessary to move the station point back from the object. (It is not sufficient to simply widen the cone of vision: see Figs. 16–18, *Cone of Vision*.)

Step 5. Locate the picture plane in the desired position. The picture plane is always drawn at 90° to the centre line of vision. (See Figs. 19–22 for an explanation of the picture plane.)

Step 6. Locate the two vanishing points required for the perspective drawing of this object from this station point. From the station point draw lines parallel to the sides of the object to meet the picture plane. Where these lines and the picture plane intersect are the required vanishing points. (See Figs. 24 and 25 for an explanation of the vanishing points.)

Step 7. Locate the height line by projecting a convenient side of the plan of the object to meet the picture plane. (See Fig. 27 for an explanation of the height line.)

Step 8. Locate the horizon line in a convenient position either above or below the plan. In this example it is intended to draw the perspective view above the plan, so the horizon line is drawn at a convenient height above the picture plane. Project up from the plan the positions of the vanishing points and the height line in the picture plane (plan) to locate them on the horizon line. (See Figs. 28 and 29 for an explanation of the horizon line.)

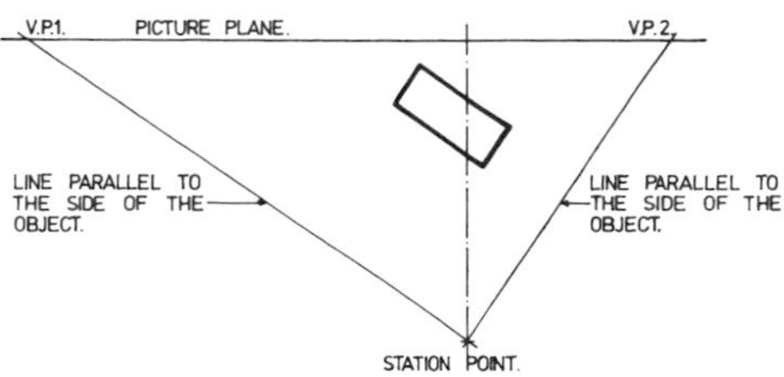

Step 6. Locate vanishing points.

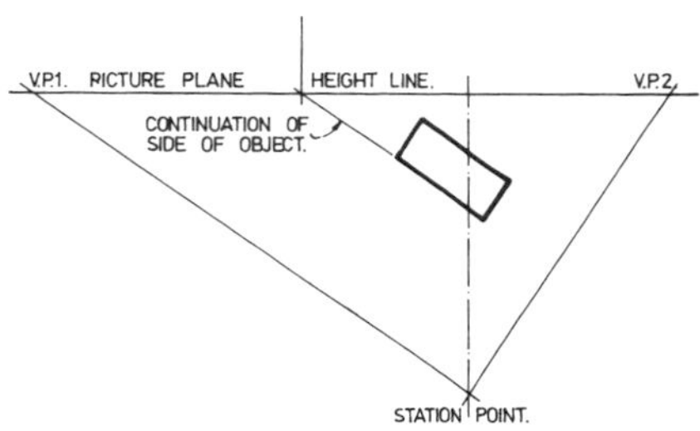

Step 7. Locate the height line.

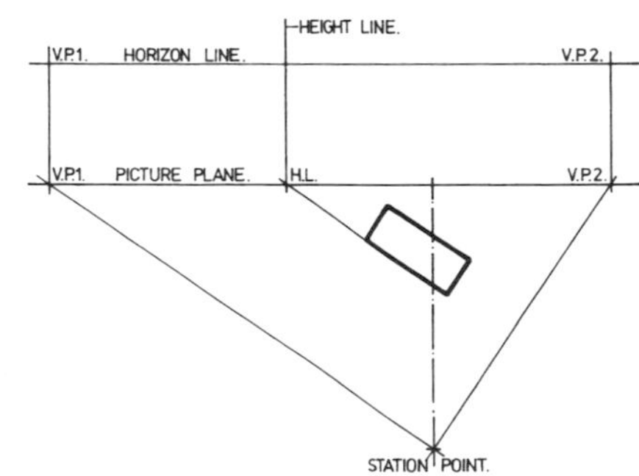

Step 8. Locate the horizon line and project up to locate vanishing points on the horizon line.

34a Two-point perspective drawing: steps 6–8.

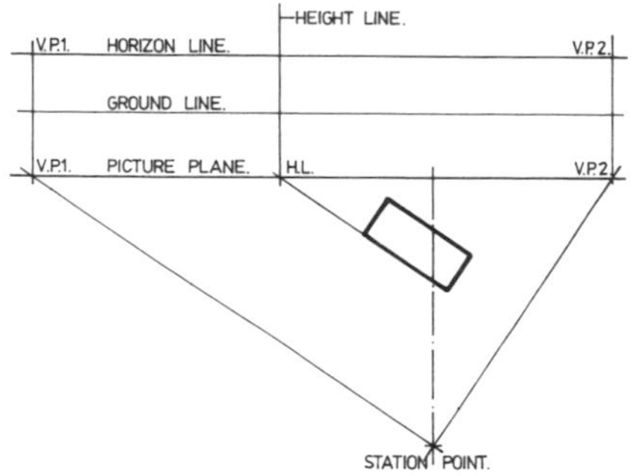

Step 9. Locate the ground line.

34b Two-point perspective drawing: step 9.

Step 9. Locate the ground line at the required distance below the horizon line. (See Figs. 30 and 31 for an explanation of the ground line.)

The next step is to draw the perspective view of the object. Once the set-up has been completed (steps 1 to 9), the actual drawing is done using visual rays, vertical projections and perspective lines, i.e. lines to the vanishing points, in the sequence shown in Fig. 35.

Opinions may vary as to the sequence used in the drawing of the perspective view. Any sequence can be used; for instance, some people prefer to locate the base of the object in the perspective view first. But whichever sequence is adopted the student is advised to follow it and only deviate from it when absolutely necessary, otherwise he can easily become confused in the early stages of his studies in perspective drawing. Many needless, time-consuming mistakes in perspective drawing are made because the wrong line or point is used. The student is advised to name each line clearly as soon as it is located. Similarly, as each point is located it should be identified so that it can easily be followed through the construction, and any mistakes quickly found and rectified.

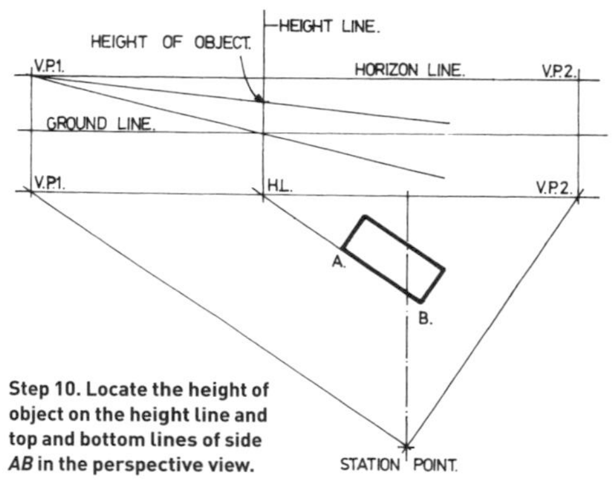

Step 10. Locate the height of object on the height line and top and bottom lines of side *AB* in the perspective view.

35a Two-point perspective drawing: step 10.

Step 10. It is usually advisable to draw first the perspective view of the side of the object which is used to obtain the height line. To do this it is necessary to locate the height of the object on the height line. From the elevations the height of the object can be measured. Measuring from the ground up, the height of the object is located on the height line. From vanishing point 1, a line is drawn through the intersection of the height line and the ground line. The bottom line of the side of the object which was projected back to find the height line will be located on this line. (See Fig. 27.) From vanishing point 1, a second line is drawn through the measurement of the height of the object on the height line. The top line of the side of the object which was used to locate the height line will be located on this line.

Step 11. From the station point, visual rays are drawn through the points of the object, i.e. the ends of the side used to find the height line, to meet the picture plane. From the points where these visual rays meet the picture plane, vertical lines are projected up to the lines representing the top and bottom lines of the side in perspective. With the location of the vertical lines at each end of the side of the object in perspective the side can be drawn as it will appear to a spectator looking at the object from the selected station point.

Step 12. By drawing the visual rays from the station point through the remaining points of the object and projecting up vertical lines from the points where they meet the picture plane, the drawing of the object in perspective can be completed. From the diagram it can be seen that vanishing point 2 is used for the sides at right angles to the side drawn first. Vanishing point 1 is used for the side parallel to the side drawn first. It will be seen from the diagram that the point at the back of the object need not be sighted (that is to say, the visual ray need not be drawn) as this point can be located by drawing lines back to the vanishing points from the established sides of the object. However, it is often advisable to sight this point when accuracy is required.

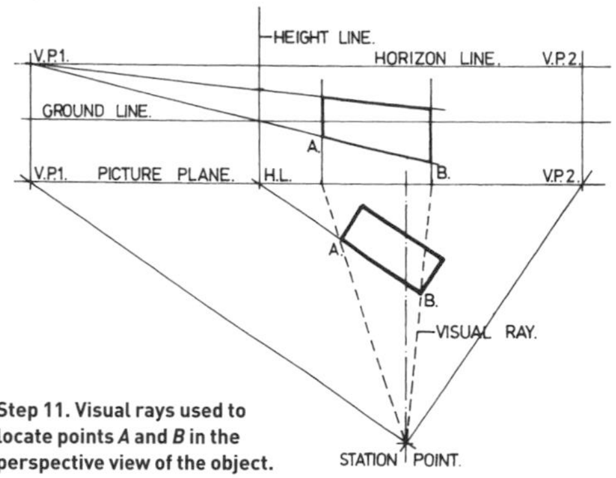

Step 11. Visual rays used to locate points *A* and *B* in the perspective view of the object.

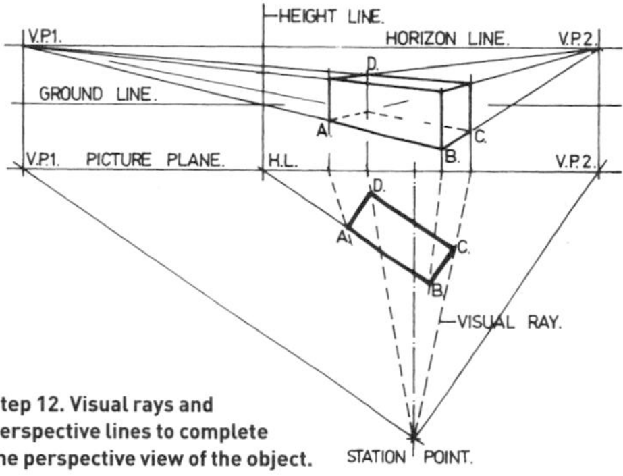

Step 12. Visual rays and perspective lines to complete the perspective view of the object.

35*b* Two-point perspective drawing: steps 11 and 12.

The method shown here (Figs. 34 and 35) is considered the easiest and most convenient but in some cases, e.g. objects with a very complex elevation, it is preferable to place the plan

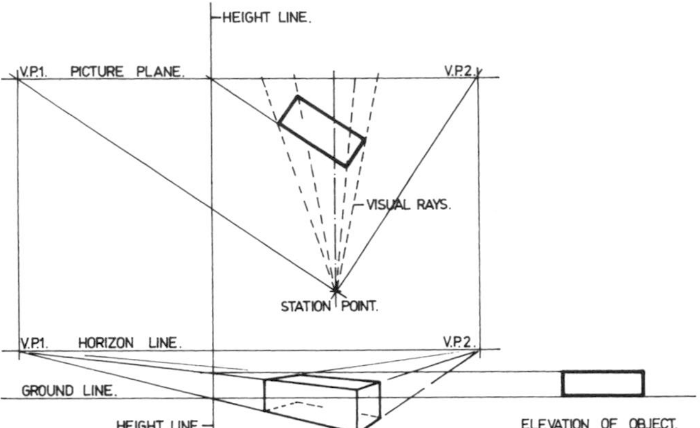

36 An alternative method of setting up a perspective construction and drawing.

as shown in Fig. 36 and to project directly across to the height line. As can be seen, the result is exactly the same as for the previous method.

The horizon is placed below the plan (as in the preceding method, any location can be used so long as it is directly above or below the plan of the picture plane). The construction is identical to that shown in Fig. 34. When the ground line has been located an elevation is then set up (on whichever side is the more convenient) so that its ground line coincides with the ground line in the perspective construction.

The height of the object is located on the height line simply by projecting a horizontal line across from the top line of the elevation of the object to intersect the height line. The perspective view of the object can now be drawn as shown in Fig. 35*b*.

One-point perspective

The second of the more commonly used types of perspective drawing is the one-point perspective. In a number of ways one-point perspective is easier and quicker than the two-point but the principles are very much the same. The principles explained in Figs. 13 to 21 apply to one-point perspective even though the more common two-point perspective has been used to illustrate them. The main differences between the two types of perspective are in the selection of the station point and, because of this difference, in the number of vanishing points required by each.

In two-point perspective the station point is positioned so that the centre line of vision is at an angle to a side of the object, so that all four sides of a rectangular prism are at an angle to the spectator. This means that two vanishing points will be required to draw the object in perspective from this station point.

In one-point perspective, on the other hand, the station point is located so that the centre line of vision is at right angles to a side of the object. This means that this side and all lines parallel to it will be parallel to the picture plane, therefore they will remain parallel in the perspective drawing, and not converge to a vanishing point. In the rectangular prism used to explain the method of drawing an object in one-point perspective, the sides parallel to the picture plane are at right angles to the centre line of vision. In this case the centre line of vision is a sight line parallel to a side of the object, therefore the vanishing point for these sides parallel to the sight line will be located at the intersection of this sight line and the picture plane (plan). (See Figs. 23 and 24, *Vanishing Points*.)

A height line as such is not required in one-point perspective. The method used for locating the height line in two-point perspective (Fig. 27) can be applied in one-point perspective but when the sides of the rectangular prism used here are projected (back, in this case) to meet the picture plane it is possible to link up the points projected back and produce a true elevation of the object.

Once this particular aspect of one-point perspective is fully understood it can be used to save a considerable amount of time and effort. This is discussed further in the section dealing with interior perspective, where it is shown to be a distinct advantage to locate a side of the object in the picture plane so that one wall of the interior can be drawn in the perspective as a true elevation.

The method used for setting up a one-point perspective is shown in Fig. 37, and again it is emphasized that if the set-up is done in sequence it will be found easy to follow.

Step 1. Either obtain or prepare information regarding the object, i.e. plan, elevations and, if necessary, sections. For the purposes of illustration the same rectangular

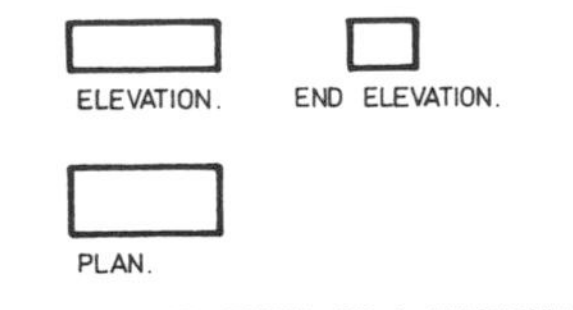

Step 1. Obtain information.

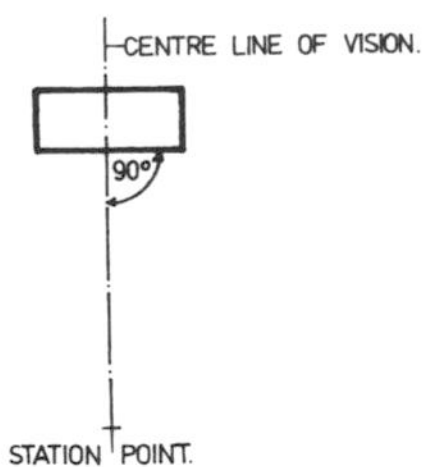

Step 2. Locate station point and the centre line of vision at 90° to a side of the object.

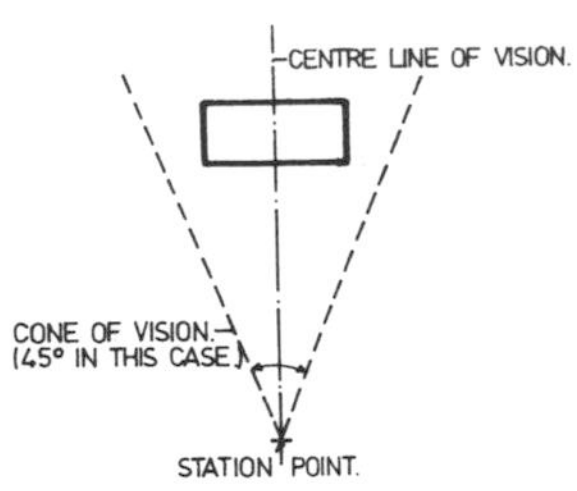

Step 3. Check the S.P. with the cone of vision.

37a One-point perspective drawing: steps 1–3.

prism is used as for the preceding explanations and the two-point perspective.

Step 2. Select the direction of the view and the station point, i.e. the centre line of vision and the position from which it is proposed to view the object. In one-point perspective the centre line of vision will be at right angles to one of the sides of the object. As with two-point perspective, the centre line of vision is always drawn as a vertical line, so it is necessary to rotate the plan and the station point until the centre line of vision is vertical.

Step 3. The location of the station point should be checked at this stage with the cone of vision. (The cone of vision suggested in the earlier explanations was 45°.) If the whole of the object intended to be included in the drawing falls within this cone of vision, the position of the station point can be taken as confirmed. If not, it will be necessary to move the station point further back from the object. (It is not sufficient to simply widen the cone of vision; see Figs. 16–18, *Cone of Vision*.)

Step 4. Locate the picture plane in the desired position. The picture plane is always drawn at 90° to the centre line of vision. (See Figs. 19–22 for an explanation of the picture plane.)

Step 5. Locate the vanishing point required for the perspective drawing of this object from this station point. As previously described, the centre line of vision is used as the sight line parallel to the sides of the plan of the object. Where this sight line and the picture plane intersect is the vanishing point for all lines parallel to the centre line of

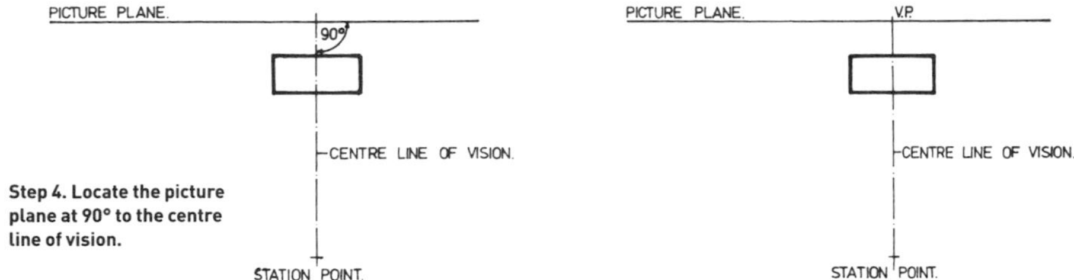

Step 4. Locate the picture plane at 90° to the centre line of vision.

Step 5. Locate the vanishing point for the sides of the object parallel to the centre line of vision (sight line).

37*b* One-point perspective drawing: steps 4 and 5.

vision, i.e. all lines at right angles to the picture plane (See Figs. 24 and 25 for an explanation of the vanishing point.)

Step 6. Locate the horizon line in a convenient position either above or below the plan. In this example it is intended to draw the perspective view above the plan, so the horizon line is drawn at a convenient height above the picture plane. Project up from the plan the position of the vanishing point in the picture plane (plan) to locate it on the horizon line. (See Figs. 28 and 29 for an explanation of the horizon line.)

Step 7. Locate the ground line at the required distance below the horizon line. (See Figs. 30 and 31 for an explanation of the ground line.)

Step 8. No height line as such is required in one-point perspective but it is necessary to locate the elevation of the object on the elevation of the picture plane. The simplest method of doing this is to project up from the plan, as shown in the diagram. The height of the object can be

37*c* One-point perspective drawing: steps 6 and 7.

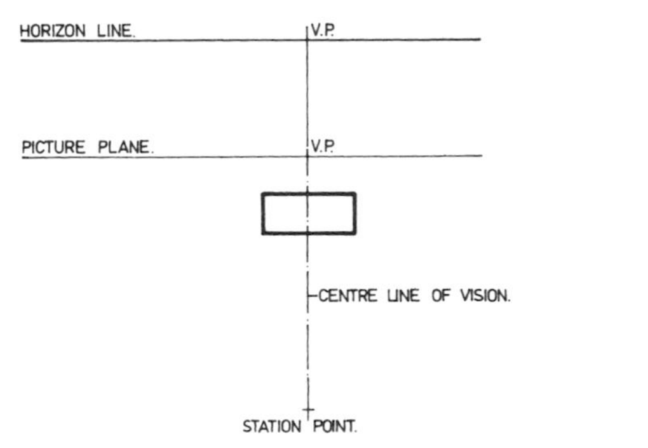

Step 6. Locate the horizon line and project up to the vanishing point on the horizon line.

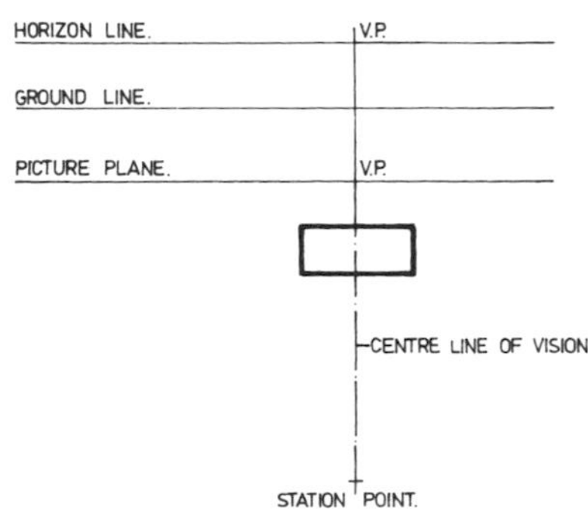

Step 7. Locate the ground line.

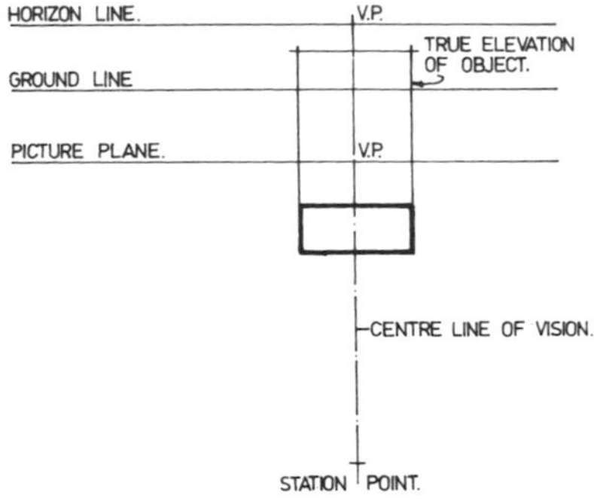

Step 8. Locate true elevation of object on elevation of picture plane.

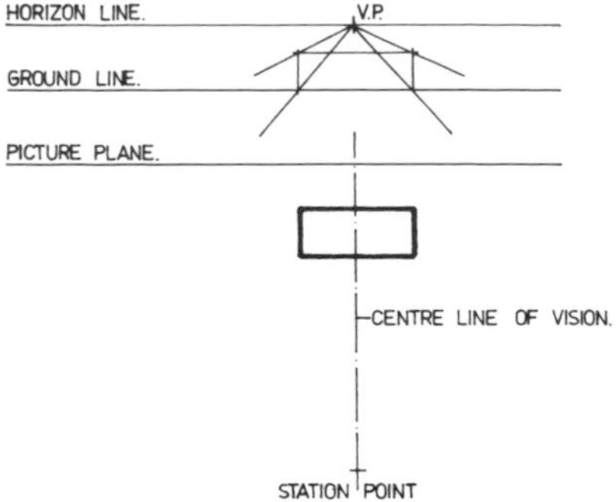

Step 9. From the vanishing point, draw perspective lines through the points of the elevation.

38*a* One-point perspective drawing: step 8 and 9.

measured on the elevation and located on the elevation of the picture plane (measurement is set out from the ground line up). From this measurement the top line of the object can be drawn, thus completing the elevation of the object.

The next step is to draw the perspective view of the object. Once the set-up has been completed (steps 1 to 8), the actual drawing is done using visual rays, vertical projections and perspective lines, i.e. lines to the vanishing point.

Fig. 38 shows the sequence used for drawing the perspective view of the object, and if this or any other logical sequence is followed, time and wasted effort can be minimized. In one-point perspective, as in the two-point method, lines and points should be identified and named as soon as they are located. Acquiring this habit from the beginning will eliminate many of the time-consuming mistakes which, more often than not, are the result of using the wrong line or point.

Step 9. It is usually advisable to draw first the perspective lines of the object, i.e. lines from the vanishing point through the points of the elevation of the object on the picture plane. It will be on these lines that the lines of the object which are at right angles to the picture plane will be located.

Step 10. From the station point visual rays are drawn through the points of the front face of the object, i.e. the ends of the front face, to meet the picture plane. From the points where the visual rays meet the picture plane, vertical lines are projected up to the lines representing the top and bottom lines of the ends of the object in perspective (the perspective lines located in step 9). Horizontal lines are drawn from the points of intersection and result in the outline of the front face of the object in the perspective drawing.

Step 11. By drawing visual rays from the station point through the two remaining points of the plan of the object (rear face) and projecting up vertical lines from the points where they meet the picture plane, the drawing of the object in perspective can be completed.

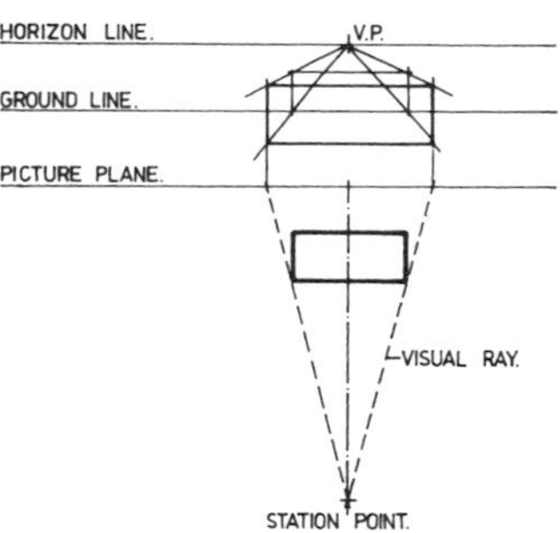

Step 10. Visual rays used to locate the front face of the object in the perspective view.

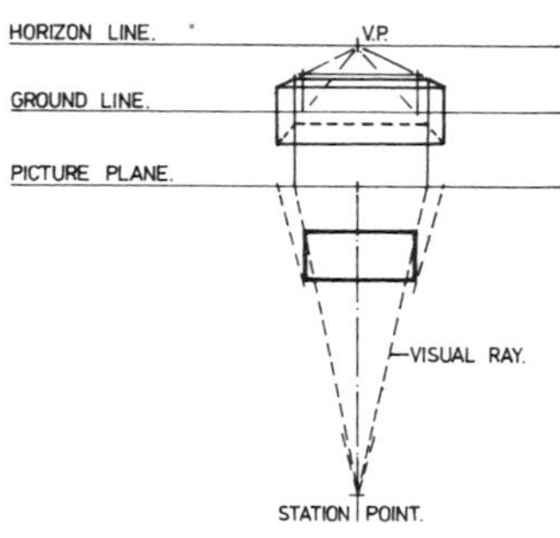

Step 11. Visual rays used to locate the rear face of the object in the perspective view.

38b One-point perspective drawing: steps 10 and 11.

The method shown in Figs. 37 and 38 is considered the easiest and most convenient, but in some cases, e.g. objects having a very complex elevation, it is preferable to place the plan as shown in Fig. 39 and project directly across to the elevation of the object on the picture plane. In this method, the horizon line is placed below the plan (as in the previous method any location can be used so long as it is directly above or below the picture plane). The construction is identical to that shown in Fig. 37. When the ground line has been located an elevation is then set up (on whichever side is more convenient) so that its ground line coincides with the ground line in the perspective construction. The height of the object is located in the perspective view by projecting a horizontal line across from the top line of the elevation of the object. The perspective view of the object can now be drawn as described in Fig. 38. As can be seen, the result is exactly the same as for the previous method.

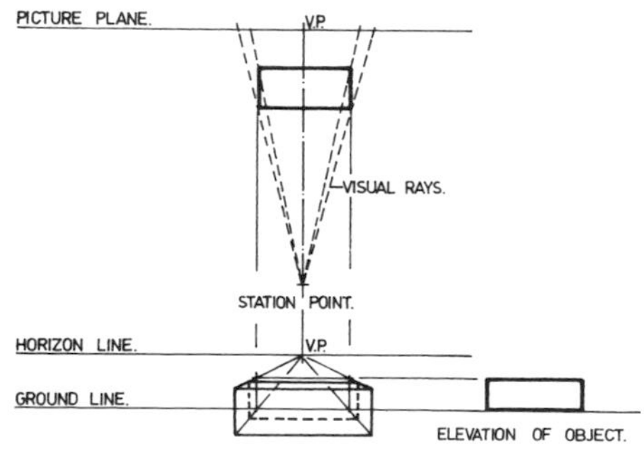

39 One-point perspective drawing: an alternative method of setting up.

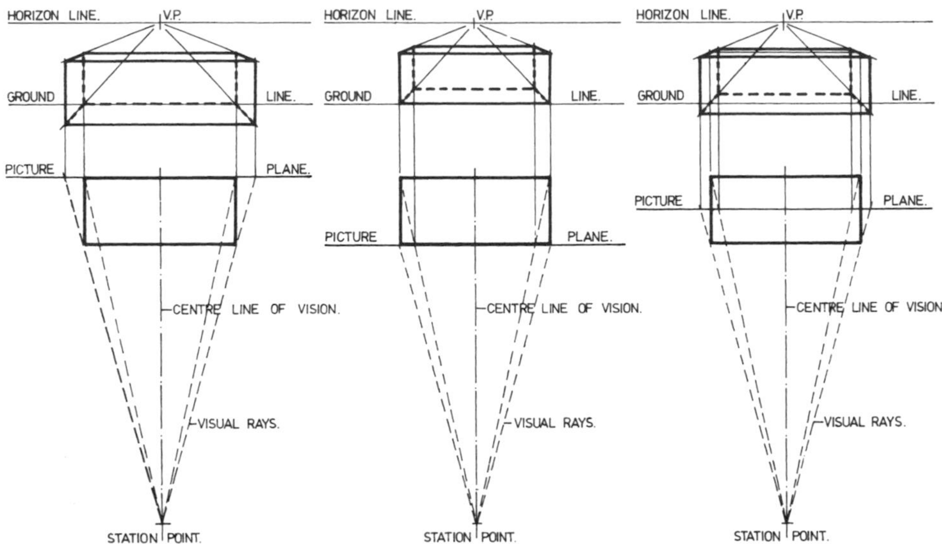

40 Three different locations for the picture plane, with fixed positions for the object and the station point.

Fig. 40 shows three examples of one-point perspective drawings resulting from three different locations for the picture plane. As with two-point perspective, only the size of the perspective is affected by moving the picture plane; the view of the object remains the same. (The greater the distance between the station point and the picture plane the larger the resulting perspective drawing and, naturally, the smaller the distance the smaller the perspective drawing.)

The location of the picture plane is a matter of choice, convenience or regulation of the size of the perspective drawing. The three positions for the location of the picture plane shown in the diagram either coincide with a face of the object or pass through it. It will be seen that the relationship of the plan of the object to the picture plane is maintained in the relationship of the perspective view and the ground line: that is to say, if the plan of the object is in front of the picture plane the perspective drawing of the object will be in front of the ground line, and vice versa. An understanding of this will help in setting up a perspective drawing because it will enable the student to locate the horizon line and the ground line in such a position as to allow enough room for the perspective drawing to be done without overlapping work already completed.

One-point and two-point perspective constructions combined

One-point and two-point perspectives are each treated as a separate type of perspective drawing but, as can be seen from the examples and explanations so far, they are based on exactly the same principles and are in fact interchangeable in a sense. The only difference between the two types is the angle of the centre line of vision to the side of the object at which the spectator is looking. Fig. 41 shows a spectator looking at two objects, one of which is parallel to the picture plane and will be drawn in one-point perspective. The other object is at an angle to the picture plane, so it will be drawn in two-point perspective. The station point, the centre line of vision and the picture plane are common to both objects, so that if each object is treated separately – the object parallel to the picture plane being drawn first as a one-point perspective and then the object at an angle to the picture plane as a two-point perspective – the resulting combination will show each object as the spectator would see it and each object will be in its correct relation to the other.

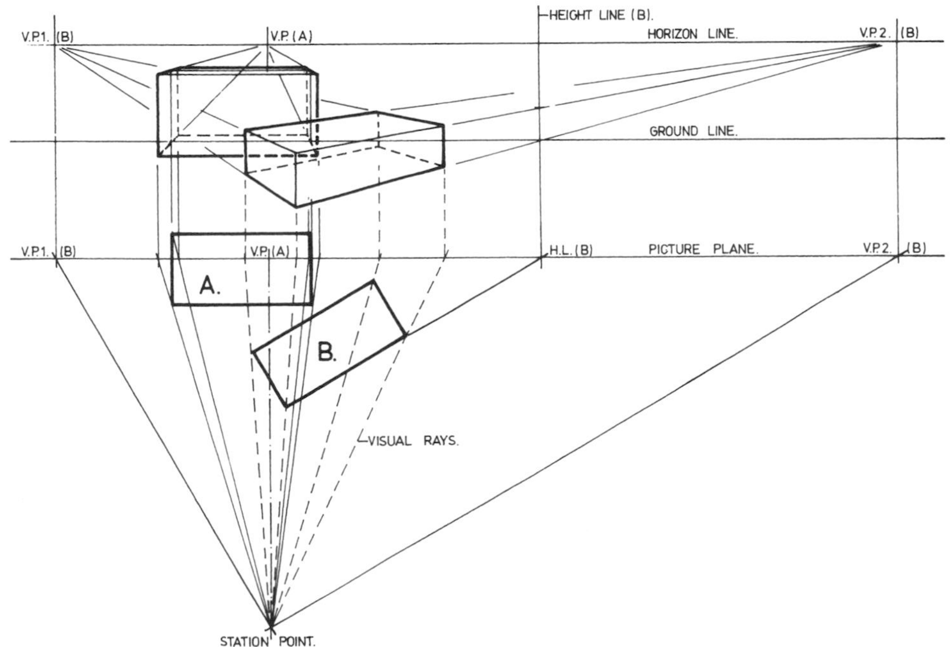

41 Set-up combining one-point and two-point perspective construction.

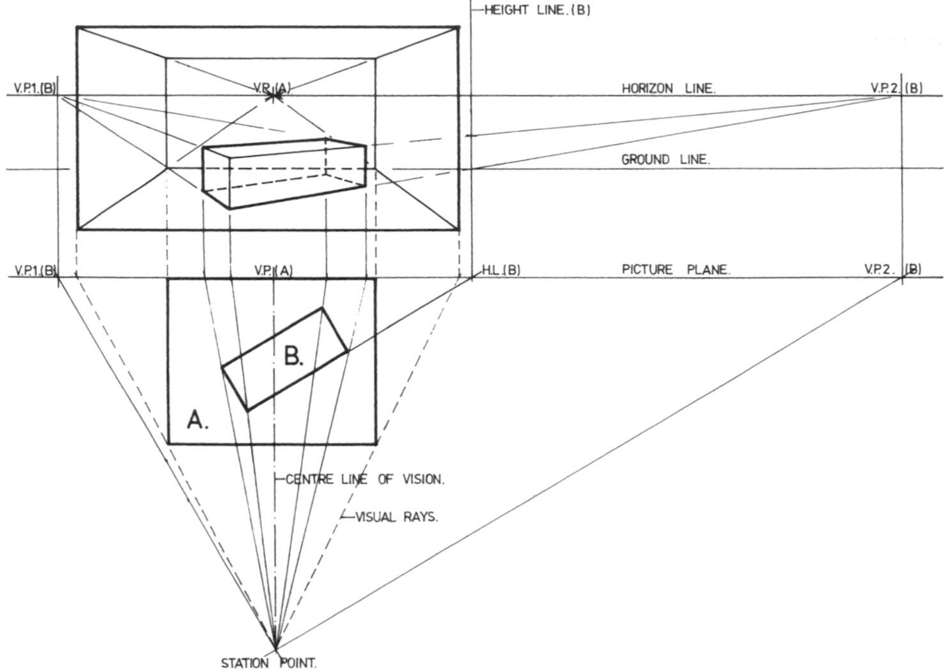

42 Another combination: two-point perspective inside a one-point perspective.

When producing a drawing containing more than one object or one set of vanishing points it is advisable to work on one object or one set of vanishing points at a time, to avoid confusion.

That one-point and two-point perspectives can be combined in one drawing is important because it allows for a wide variety of drawings which can be simply and quickly set up without the long and laborious sets of projections that are sometimes necessary to obtain the same results if only one type of perspective construction is used.

Fig. 42 shows another perspective view containing both one-point and two-point perspective constructions. In this example one object is located inside the other. The larger object is placed parallel to the picture plane and is therefore drawn as a one-point perspective. The smaller object, which is positioned inside the larger one, is located at an angle to the picture plane, therefore it will be drawn as a two-point perspective. From this example it can be seen that this combination is very useful when working on interior perspectives of rooms, etc.

Interior perspectives using one-point construction

Interior perspectives can be either one-point or two-point perspectives and in many cases both are used in one drawing, but it is usually the one used to set up the room which is the main construction that identifies the type of perspective used. The selection of a one-point or a two-point perspective for a specific drawing is often a matter of personal choice but it should be understood that while both types are accurate, one-point interiors are usually quicker and easier to set up and draw. This aspect can be only partly appreciated at this stage but it should become clearer as the student becomes more proficient at drawing perspective views of objects.

Another reason for the popularity of the one-point perspective for interior views is that it is easier to 'control', which means that there is less likelihood of unfortunate angles 'appearing' and other mistakes or accidents occurring which may not become evident in a two-point perspective construction until the drawing is well advanced. As with most things, experience is important in perspective drawing when it comes to controlling what is likely to happen; time spent in the beginning of a project 'controlling' as much as possible is seldom wasted.

Fig. 43 shows the set-up and perspective view of a simple room. To avoid confusion, it is shown without furniture or any details such a skirtings, architraves or light fittings. The method used for setting up the perspective view of the room is exactly the same as for any other one-point perspective but in this case the station point is located within the object to be drawn, which means that the wall behind the spectator will not be visible to him and therefore it will not appear in the perspective view.

It will be found that the use of the maximum angle for the cone of vision (60°) is advisable in interior perspectives, particularly of small rooms, because the

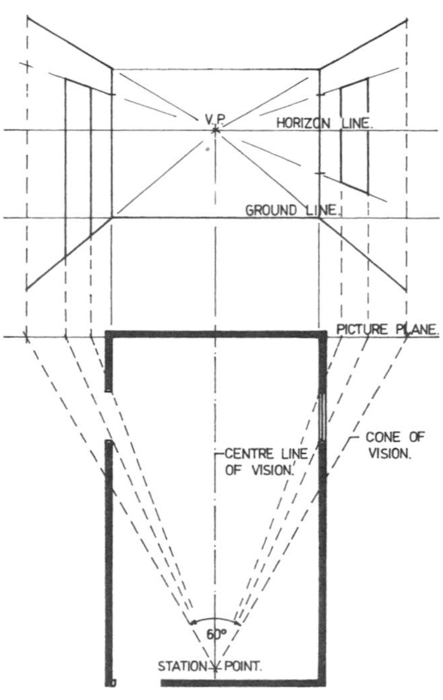

43 A simple one-point interior perspective set-up and drawing.

recommended small angles (30°–45°) will be found much too restricting.

Once the main room is set up in the perspective view it is necessary to locate the positions of the door and the window. Because the end wall of the room coincides with the picture plane it is drawn in the perspective view as a true elevation, which means that measurements can be made on it using the same scale as that used for the plan. As the height of the door in the left-hand wall and the height of the top and bottom lines of the window in the right-hand wall are known (obtained from the plan, elevations and sections of the room, not shown here) they can be measured on the end wall. Because the door is in the left-hand wall (at right angles to the picture plane) it will be necessary to locate the measurement on the left-hand end of the end wall to allow this height to be projected back along the left-hand wall. The top line of the door will be located on this line. To locate the door it is necessary to sight its position in the plan in the usual fashion. (From the station point draw a visual ray through the sides of the door and from the points of intersection of these visual rays and the picture plane project vertical lines up to the wall in the perspective view. Using these vertical lines and the perspective line at the height of the top of the door, the actual door can be drawn in the perspective view.)

The window in the right-hand wall is located and drawn in the same way as the door. In this case, the height of the top and bottom lines of the window are set out on the right-hand end of the wall to allow for these heights to be projected back along the right-hand wall. The actual position of the window in the perspective view of the wall is located using visual rays as before.

This example is kept simple to avoid confusion, but to include more detail would only mean repeating the procedures a greater number of times. The measurements of heights on the walls, irrespective of the reasons for them, are located in the same way as described and the locations of any features shown on the plan are sighted in the normal way, so that regardless of the complexity of the interior the method remains the same.

The location of a point in perspective

There are a number of different methods which can be used to locate a single point in perspective. Whichever method is used it should be understood that the principles are basically the same for each of them, and the variations are mainly in the way in which the point is related to its surroundings, e.g. picture plane, walls, etc.

Three different methods are shown in Figs. 44–47 and it can be seen in each diagram that two lines are used to relate the point either to the picture plane or, as in Fig. 47, to two walls of the room in which the point is situated. Two lines are required to locate a point in perspective with the point situated at the intersection. These lines are located in plan, which means that they can be drawn in perspective thus locating the point at their intersection in the perspective view.

Figs. 44–47 show methods of locating points in perspective related to a one-point interior perspective, because it is in this type of perspective that it is usually required, e.g. for locating light fittings on ceilings. However, it will be seen on examining the diagrams that with the exception of Fig. 47 the points are related only to the picture plane, so they use the same picture plane as the main perspective but are in no other way related to the main perspective construction. In other words, the method of locating a point in perspective requires the point (or points) to be located in plan in relation to the station point, the centre line of vision and the picture plane, and regardless of what is going on around this plan the set-up of the position of the point can be plotted in perspective. Therefore these methods can be used for locating points in either one-point or two-point perspective constructions.

In Fig. 44, to locate point *A*, which is on the floor plane (ground plane):

44 The most usual method of locating a point in perspective (located on the floor plane).

Step 1. From point *A* in the plan draw a line to meet the picture plane at 45° or any convenient angle.

Step 2. From the point of intersection of this line and the picture plane project up a vertical line to meet the ground line. (This point is sometimes known as the starting point.)

Step 3. Locate vanishing point 2 by drawing a sight line from the station point parallel to the line from point *A* to the picture plane. Where this sight line meets the picture plane is the plan position of vanishing point 2.

Step 4. Project up vertically from the plan position of vanishing point 2 to locate it on the horizon line.

Step 5. From point *A* in plan draw a line parallel to the centre line of vision to meet the picture plane (the end wall of the room in this case), and continue this line up to meet the ground line.

Point *A* in plan can be seen in the diagram to be located at the intersection of the two lines – one at 45° to the picture plane and the second parallel to the centre line of vision (at 90° to the picture plane).

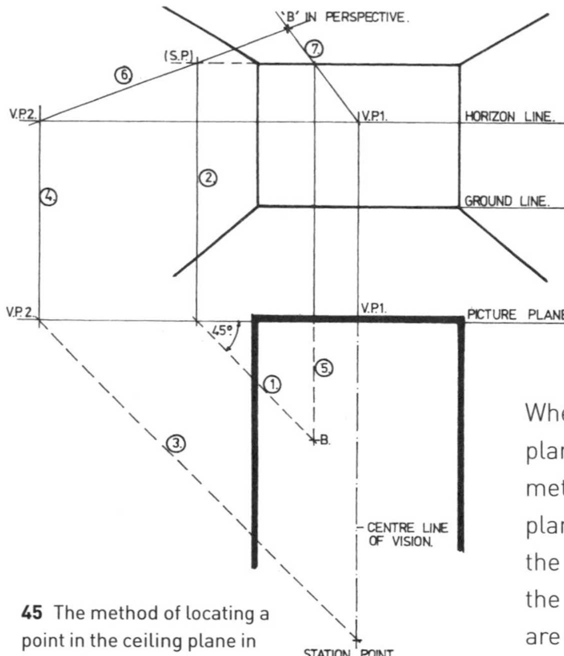

45 The method of locating a point in the ceiling plane in one-point perspective.

Step 6. From vanishing point 2 through the starting point, draw a line representing the perspective view of the line from point *A* to the picture plane, meeting it at 45° (in plan).

Step 7. Finally the perspective view of the line parallel to the centre line of vision (in plan) can be drawn using vanishing point 1.

When the point is located in the ceiling plane, as shown in Fig. 45, the same method is used as for a point in the floor plane (ground plane) except that instead of the ground line being used in steps 2 and 5 the ceiling line is used. In Fig. 45 the steps are numbered to tie in with the description of the method for point *A* in the floor plane.

The alternative method of locating a point in perspective shown in Fig. 46 is based on the preceding method but uses a visual ray instead of a line parallel to the centre line of vision. The seven steps for locating point *C* in perspective are:

Step 1. From point *C* draw a line to meet the picture plane at 45° (any convenient angle can be used). Where this line meets the picture plane is the point known as the starting point (S.P.).

Step 2. Locate the starting point on the ground line by projecting up vertically from the plan position of the starting point in the picture plane.

Step 3. From the station point draw a sight line parallel to the line from point *C* which meets the picture plane at 45°. The intersection of the sight line and the picture plane is the location of vanishing point 2 in plan.

Step 4. Locate vanishing point 2 in the horizon line by projecting a line up vertically from its position in plan.

Step 5. From vanishing point 2 draw a line through the starting point and continue it as far as necessary.

Step 6. From the station point draw a visual ray through point *C* (in the plan) to meet the picture plane.

Step 7. From the point in the picture plane where the visual ray through point *C* meets it, project up a line to intersect the line from vanishing point 2 through the starting point. The point where these two lines intersect is the location of point *C* in perspective.

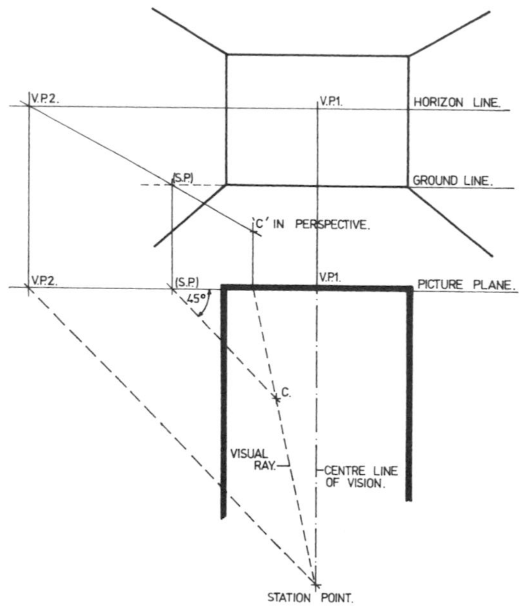

46 An alternative method of locating a point in perspective.

The third method of locating a point in perspective, shown in Fig. 47, is the quickest and simplest one when the point is within a shape or can be related to an object.

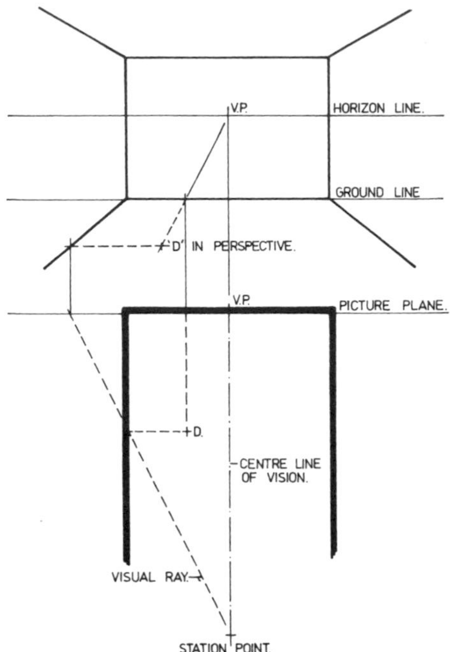

47 Another alternative method of locating a point in perspective.

Step 1. From point *D* (in plan) draw a line parallel to the side wall of the room to meet the end wall (picture plane). From this point on the end wall project up a vertical line to meet the ground line (point *D* is in the floor plane).

Step 2. From point *D* (in plan) draw another line, in this case parallel to the end wall (picture plane) to meet the side wall of the room.

Step 3. From the station point draw a visual ray through the point on the side wall where the line from point *D* meets it, to meet the picture plane. From the point on the picture plane where the visual ray meets it project up a vertical line to meet the floor line of the side wall in the perspective view of the room.

Step 4. The line drawn parallel to the side wall in the plan can be located in the perspective view by drawing a line from the vanishing point through the point in the ground line located in step 1.

Step 5. The line drawn parallel to the end wall in the plan can be located in the perspective view by drawing a line from the point in the floor line of the side wall (located in step 3) parallel to the end wall in the perspective view. Point *D* in perspective is located at the intersection of the two lines located in steps 4 and 5.

The location of a number of points in perspective

Fig. 48 shows the method used for locating more than one point (two points in this example) in perspective when the position of the station point, the centre line of vision, the picture plane and the height of the eye level are given.
The method is similar to the one used in Fig. 44 with one exception. Instead of using a line from the point in the plan to meet the picture plane at any convenient angle, a line is drawn through both points and continued on to meet the

picture plane. A line parallel to this line is then used to locate the vanishing point. The rest of the construction to locate the two points is exactly the same as the one described in Fig. 44.

The location of a single line in perspective

The location of a single line in perspective is exactly the same procedure as that used to locate two points in perspective. Fig. 49 shows a short line *GH* in plan, with *G* corresponding to *E* in Fig. 48 and *H* corresponding to *F*. The ends of the line *GH* have been made to correspond with points *E* and *F* in Fig. 48. The same station point, picture plane and centre line of vision have been used, to show that the methods employed for locating two points in perspective and for locating a line in perspective are identical.

This method can be used to locate any line in perspective and is, in fact, the simple basis of all perspective drawing. By comparing the diagram with previous diagrams (Figs. 34–42) it will be seen that location of a line in perspective is the same whether the line is the object or only a part of an object.

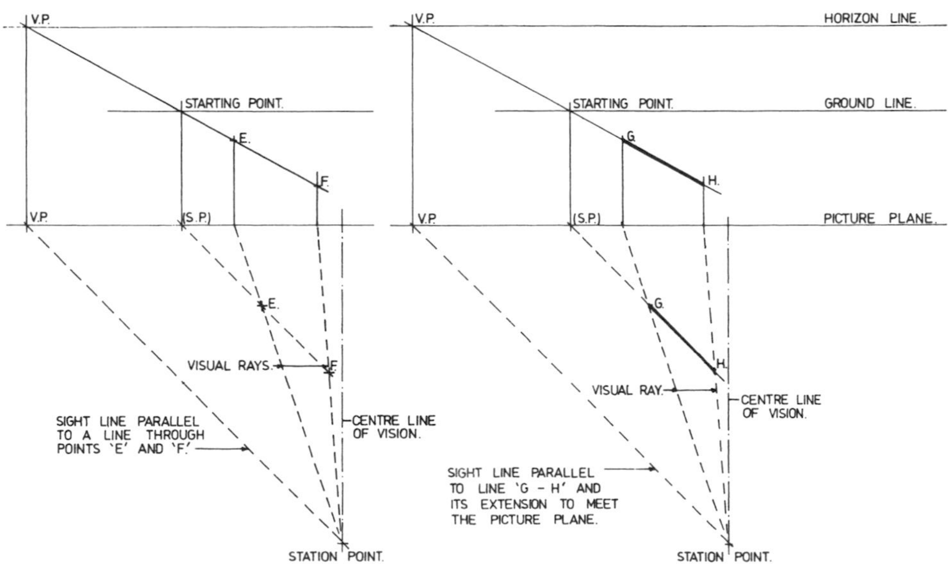

48 The method used to locate two points in perspective.

49 The method used to locate a single line in perspective.

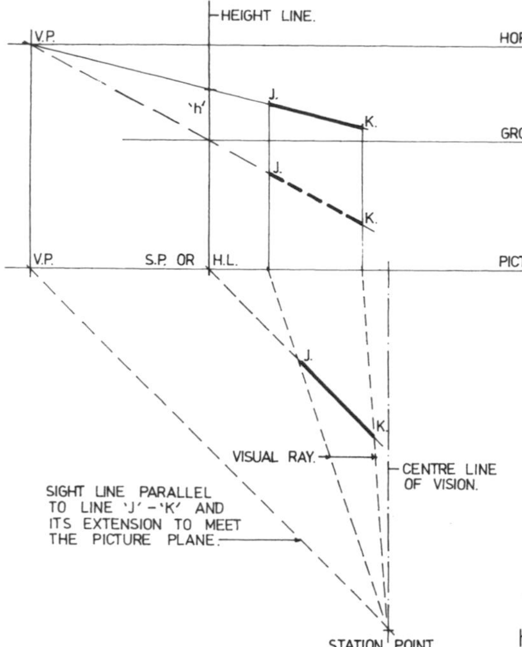

50 The method used to locate a single line above the ground plane in perspective.

Fig. 50 shows a method of locating and drawing a line in perspective when the line is situated above the ground plane. From this diagram it can be seen that the same plan is used whether the line is on the ground plane or above it. (The position of the line in perspective if it had been situated on the ground plane is shown dotted.) The location of a height line is essential for this exercise. By reference to Figs. 26 and 27 it will be seen that the starting point is in fact the point on the picture plane where the height line and the ground line intersect. This means that the height line is located in this exercise simply by projecting a line up vertically from the starting point in the picture plane (plan). Once the height line has been located, the required height *h* of the line above the ground can be measured and a line drawn through it from the vanishing point. (The line *JK* will be located on this line.) When this line is drawn, the vertical lines from the points of intersection of the visual rays from the station point through the ends of the line in plan are projected up to meet this line, thus locating the length of the line in perspective.

The methods shown in Figs. 49 and 50 are used in Fig. 51 to locate and draw four lines in perspective. This diagram looks very complicated but in reality it is only the one method repeated four times with all the construction lines shown. Each separate line can be followed through from its position in the plan to its required position in the perspective. If each line is located and drawn before the next is considered, what looks like a complicated drawing is greatly simplified.

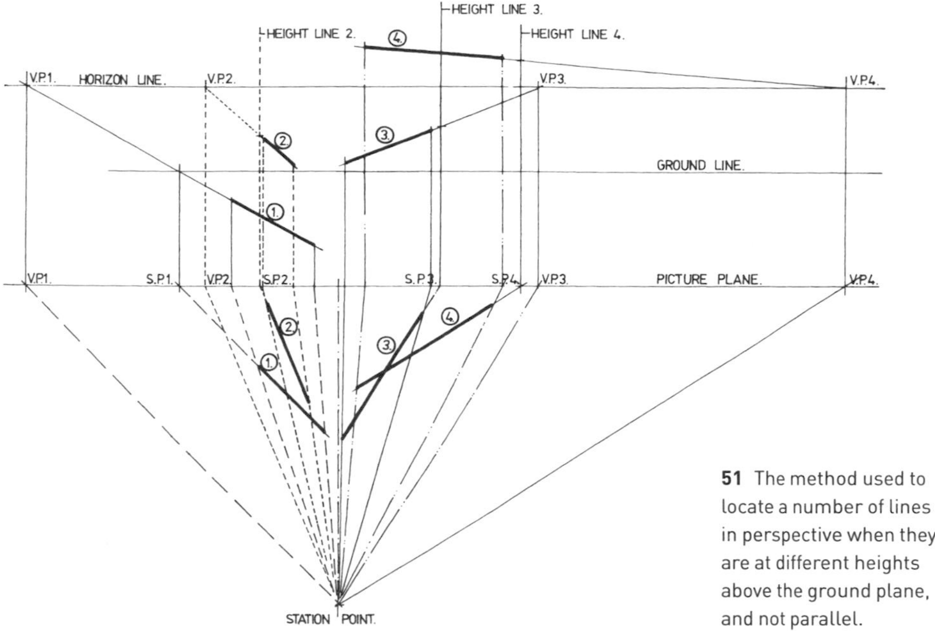

51 The method used to locate a number of lines in perspective when they are at different heights above the ground plane, and not parallel.

Inclined lines and planes in perspective

Up to this stage, only lines parallel to the ground plane have been considered. Many objects contain not only lines parallel to the ground plane (horizontal lines) and vertical lines but also lines inclined to the ground plane, so that it is necessary to locate vanishing points for these inclined lines.

Parallel lines which are inclined to both the picture plane and the ground plane will appear to converge to a vanishing point. The most important rule to remember when working with inclined lines and planes is that the vanishing point for inclined lines or an inclined plane is always directly above or below what its position would be if the lines or plane were in the horizontal plane. This can best be explained when applied to a book (see Fig. 52).

The book, when closed and placed on a horizontal plane, can be drawn as a simple rectangular prism. The locations of vanishing points 1 and 2 are found as previously described. These vanishing points are the vanishing points for the sides of the book and all lines parallel to them. This means that while the book remains closed these vanishing

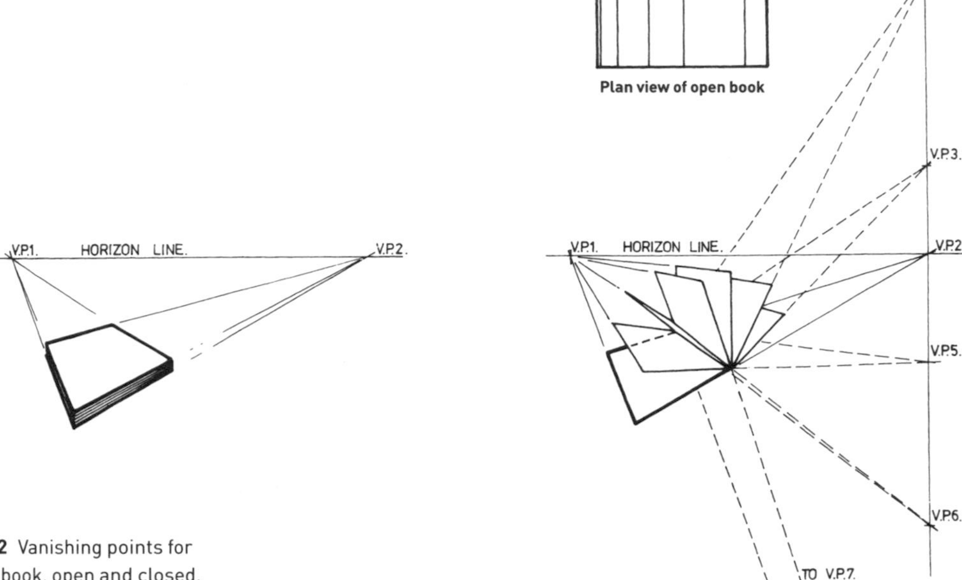

52 Vanishing points for a book, open and closed.

53 A spectator looking at an object which has inclined lines, and a view of the object as seen by him.

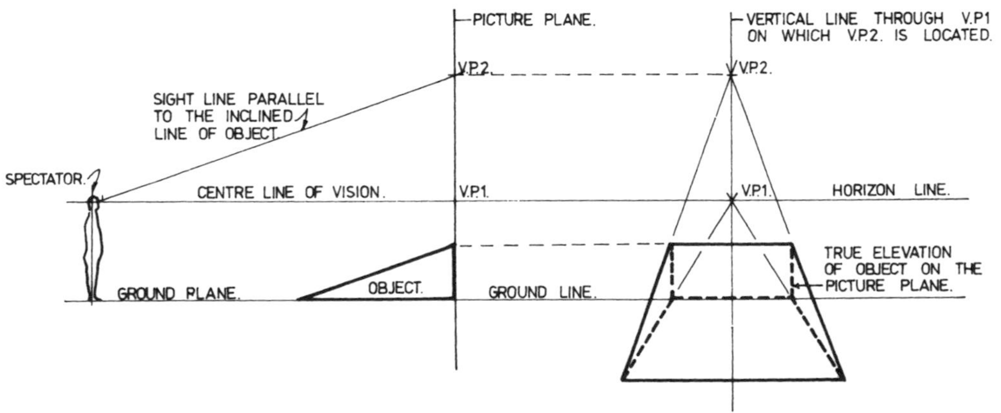

points will be the vanishing points for the individual pages of the book as well. When the book is opened and looked at in plan, the edges of the individual pages will remain parallel to the sides of the book because only the inclination of the pages is affected. This means that the vanishing points for the individual pages are located in plan in the usual way. (Draw a sight line from the station point parallel to a side of the object; the intersection of this line and the picture plane is the plan position of the vanishing point.) The vanishing point for the closed book and the individual open pages of the book in the plan construction having been established, it can be seen that the actual positions of the vanishing points for the open pages will fall in a vertical line through the vanishing point for the closed book, which will be in the horizon line.

It has been established previously that in all cases where a sight line parallel to a side or line of an object meets the picture plane, that point will be the vanishing point for that side or line of the object and all lines parallel to it. Therefore when drawing a perspective view of an object containing an inclined line or lines it is necessary to use a sight line parallel to the inclined line to locate its vanishing point on the picture plane. Fig. 53 shows a spectator looking at an object which includes inclined parallel lines. As previously described, the centre line of vision is a sight line and, because in this case the object is parallel to the picture plane (one-point perspective), the vanishing point for the lines of the object parallel to the ground plane will be located at the point where the sight line parallel to them meets the picture plane. Because the inclined lines of the object are directly above the lines in the ground plane, the vanishing point for the inclined lines will be directly above the vanishing point for the lines in the horizontal plane (ground plane).

In the view of the object as seen by the spectator in Fig. 53, it can be seen that V.P.1 and V.P.2 are located in a vertical line, and the height of V.P.2 above V.P.1 is found by projecting across from the elevation where the sight line parallel to the inclined lines of the object meets the picture plane.

The location of the vanishing point for the inclined lines of the object can be checked simply by setting up the horizontal and vertical planes of the object (in this case, in one-point perspective). This means that the base of the object is drawn in the ground plane and the vertical plane of the object, which coincides with the picture plane, is drawn in true elevation. A line joining a front corner of the base of the object to the appropriate top corner of the vertical plane in the picture plane is continued until it meets a vertical line drawn through V.P.1 at V.P.2 (the vanishing point for the inclined lines of the object). This exercise can be repeated for the second inclined line of the object, and if the draughting is accurate it too will pass through V.P.2.

Fig. 55 shows an alternative method for locating vanishing points for inclined lines based on the method used here to check the position of the vanishing point located by using an elevation.

One-point perspective has been used to explain the principles of locating vanishing points for inclined lines, but, as can be seen from the diagram in Fig. 52, inclined lines occurring in objects drawn in two-point perspective also have their vanishing points located by using the same principles.

Location of vanishing points for inclined lines in two-point perspective

The method of locating the vanishing points for inclined lines in two-point perspective (Fig. 54) is based on the two-point perspective construction previously described in Figs. 34 and 35, and all the horizontal and vertical lines of the object are located and drawn in the perspective view in the normal way. The method of locating the vanishing points for the inclined lines of the object is as follows:

Step 1. It is first necessary to produce an elevation of the object in relation to the picture plane and the station point. The most convenient position for this elevation is as shown in the diagram (beside the plan construction). A ground plane is drawn parallel to the centre line of vision at a convenient distance from it, to meet the picture plane

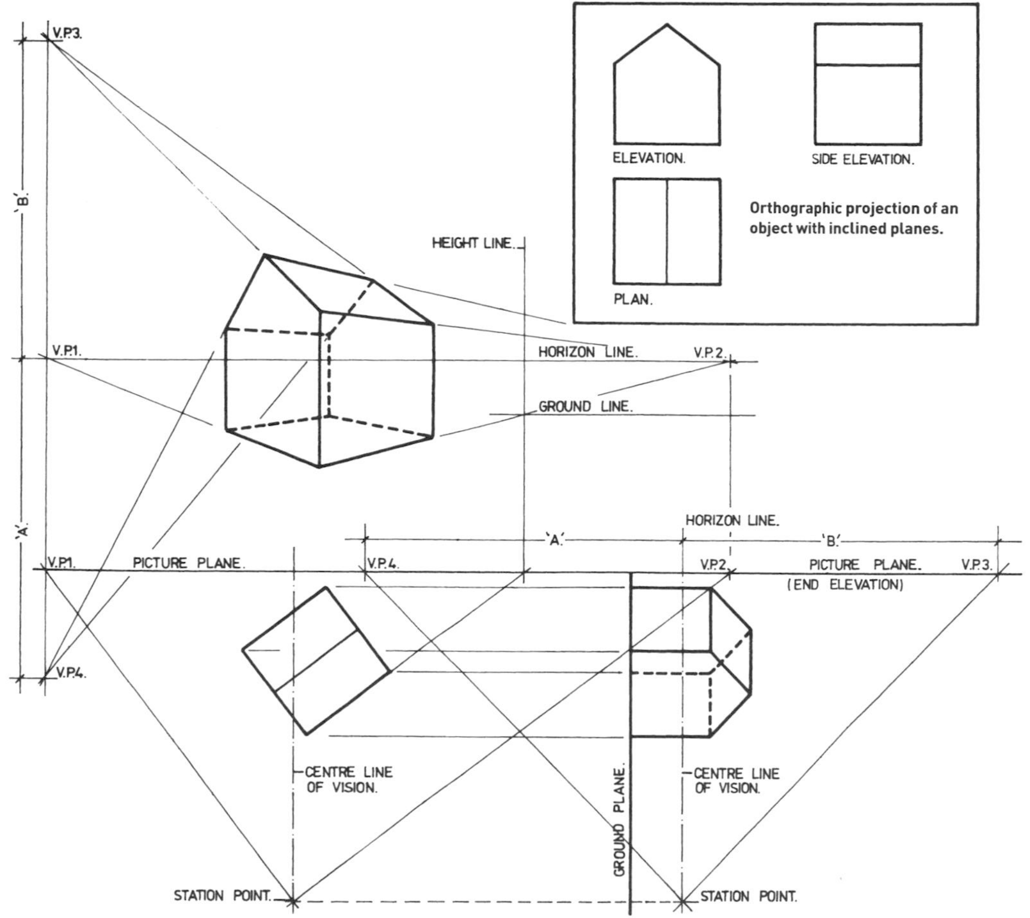

at an angle of 90°. The station point can be located in the elevation by projecting across from the station point in the plan position. The height of the eye level is known and can therefore be measured to locate the centre line of vision, which is drawn parallel to the ground plane. The elevation of the object is drawn by projecting across from the plan and using measurements obtained from the orthographic projection of the object (heights). The elevation of the object produced shows the true inclination of the inclined lines to the picture plane when the object is placed in the position shown in plan.

54 The method of locating the vanishing points for inclined lines in two-point perspective.

Step 2. As previously described, a sight line from the station point (in elevation) parallel to a line of the object will intersect the picture plane at the vanishing point for that line in perspective. Therefore, using the elevation produced in the preceding step, the location of the vanishing points V.P.3 and V.P.4 for the inclined lines of the object is a simple matter of drawing sight lines from the station point parallel to the inclined lines of the object to meet the picture plane. Where these sight lines meet the picture plane at V.P.3 and V.P.4 their height above or below the horizon line can be measured. In this case V.P.3 is a distance *B* above the horizon line and V.P.4 is a distance *A* below it.

Step 3. It has been established in Figs. 52 and 53 that the vanishing point for inclined lines will be directly above or below the vanishing point for the lines if they were in the horizontal plane. The inclined lines of the object shown here are in the plane used to locate V.P.1, so V.P.3 and V.P.4 will be located in a vertical line drawn through V.P.1. V.P.3 will be located at a height *B* above V.P.1, which is in the horizon line, and V.P.4 will be located at a height *A* below V.P.1. V.P.3 and V.P.4 can now be used to draw the inclined lines of the object in perspective as shown in the diagram.

This method is considered the most accurate, but because it requires the setting up of a special elevation the simpler and quicker alternative method is favoured by many. The alternative method is adequate for most projects but its accuracy is often suspect because it relies on the accuracy of the draughtsman to a much greater degree than the method shown in Fig. 54.

Alternative method

Fig. 55 shows the same orthographic projection as used in Fig. 54, but in this case a centre line has been drawn on the elevation with the inclined lines, and a horizontal line has also been drawn forming a triangle (this line is used here only for the purpose of explanation and is not normally necessary when preparing a drawing). The height of the object is measured in two parts as shown. The height *H* from the

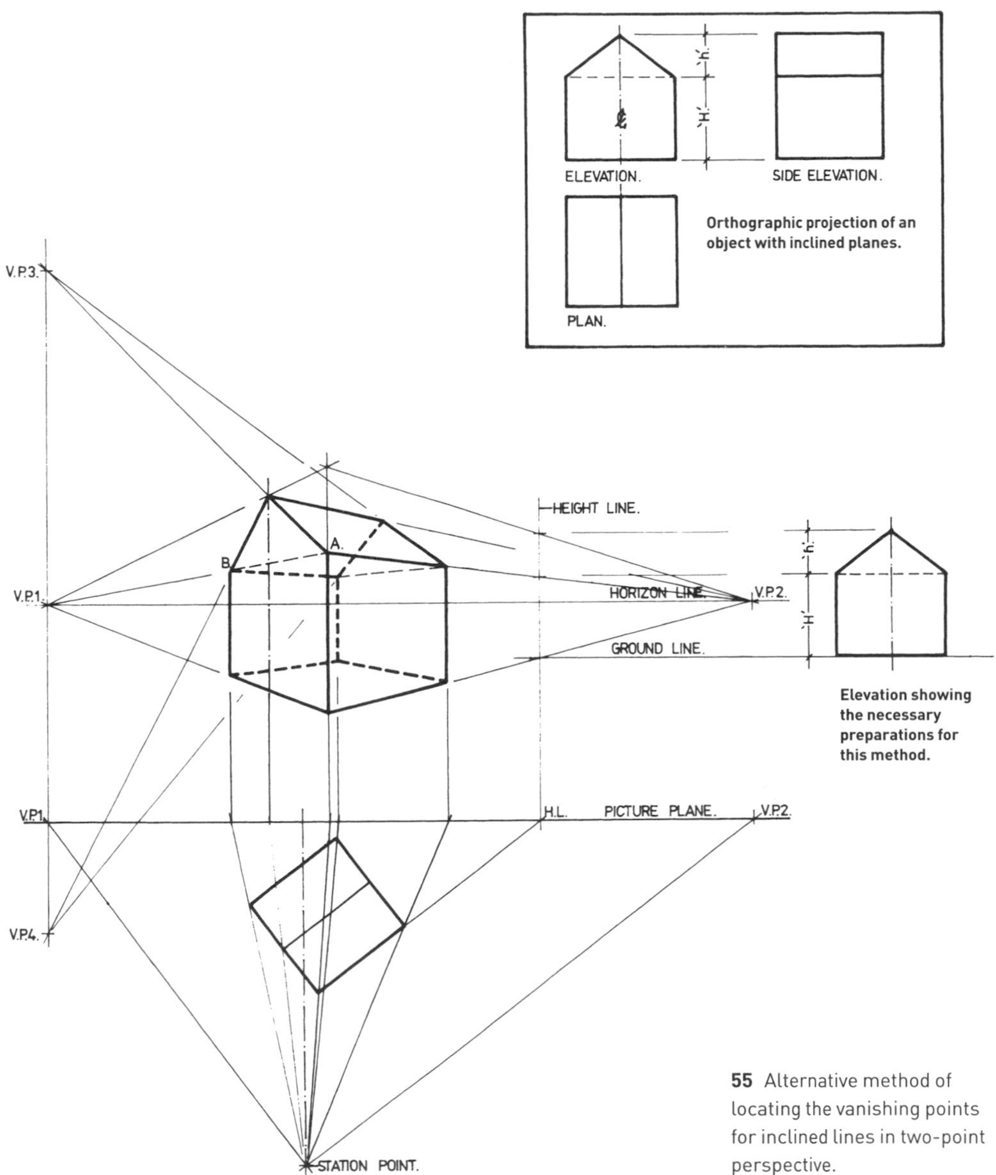

Orthographic projection of an object with inclined planes.

Elevation showing the necessary preparations for this method.

55 Alternative method of locating the vanishing points for inclined lines in two-point perspective.

ground to the lower end of the inclined line is measured and the vertical difference *h* between the lower end and the higher end of the inclined lines is also measured. These two dimensions and the centre line are all the preparations needed to locate the vanishing points for the inclined lines using this alternative method.

The method is based on the two-point construction previously described in Figs. 34 and 35, and all the horizontal and vertical lines of the object are located and drawn in the perspective view in the normal way. The method of locating the vanishing points for the inclined lines of the object is as follows:

Step 1. It is first necessary to locate the line in perspective on which the apex of the triangle formed by the inclined lines on the elevation of the object and the horizontal line shown in Fig. 55 will be located. Because, in this case, the apex of

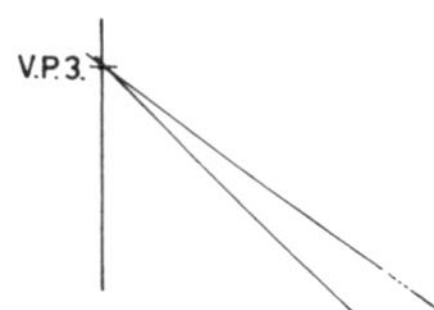

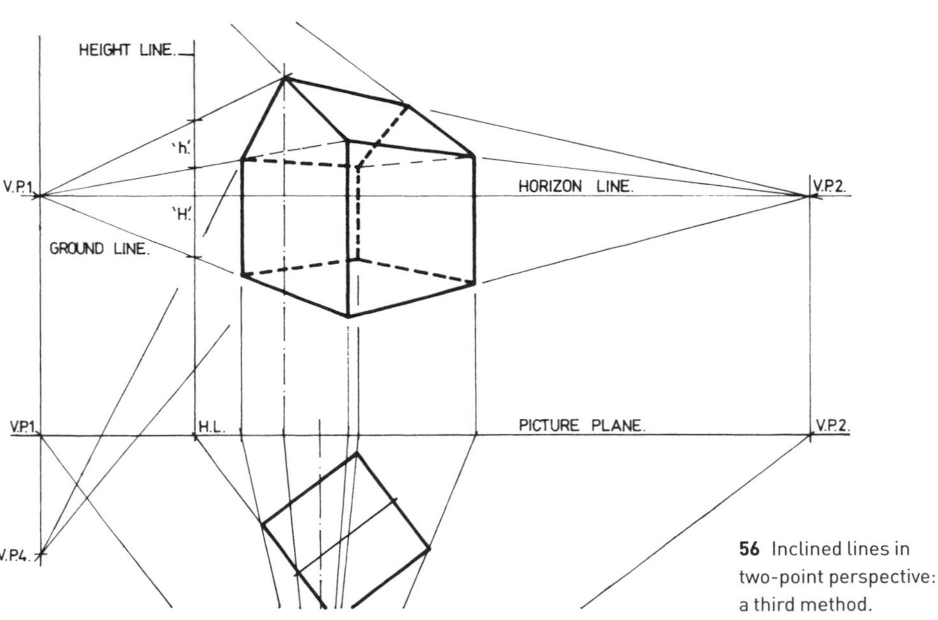

56 Inclined lines in two-point perspective: a third method.

the triangle also falls on the centre line of the building, this line is located in the plan and projected up and located in the perspective view in the normal way. Thus the apex of the triangle in perspective is located at the intersection of these two lines.

Step 2. From the point marked *A* in the perspective a line is drawn through the apex of the triangle (on the centre line) and continued to meet a vertical line drawn through V.P.1. Where these two lines intersect (V.P.3) is the location of the vanishing point for the inclined line used to locate it and all lines parallel to it. (The vanishing point for an inclined line is located directly above or below its position if the line were located in the horizontal plane.)

Step 3. V.P.4 is found in a similar way to V.P.3; a line is drawn from the apex of the triangle (on the centre line) through point *B* and continued to meet the vertical line drawn through V.P.1 at V.P.4.

Using V.P.3 and V.P.4 it is possible to complete the drawing of the object in perspective. From Fig. 55 it should be obvious to the student that if a height line was located by projecting the side containing the inclined lines, one set of projections could be eliminated, thus reducing the possibility of further compounding any errors which may have been caused by inaccurate draughting. Fig. 56 shows the same alternative method as used in Fig. 55, with the height line located by projecting the side containing the inclined lines back to the picture plane. (Any convenient side may be projected backwards or forwards to meet the picture plane to locate a height line – see Fig. 26.) Apart from the different position of the height line, the drawing of the object in perspective is completed in the same way as in Fig. 55.

Location of vanishing points for inclined lines in one-point perspective

Inclined lines in one-point perspective are treated in much the same way as they are in two-point perspective. The diagram in Fig. 53 shows the basic principles of locating the vanishing points for inclined lines. Figs. 57 and 58 show the

57 Inclined lines parallel to the picture plane in one-point perspective.

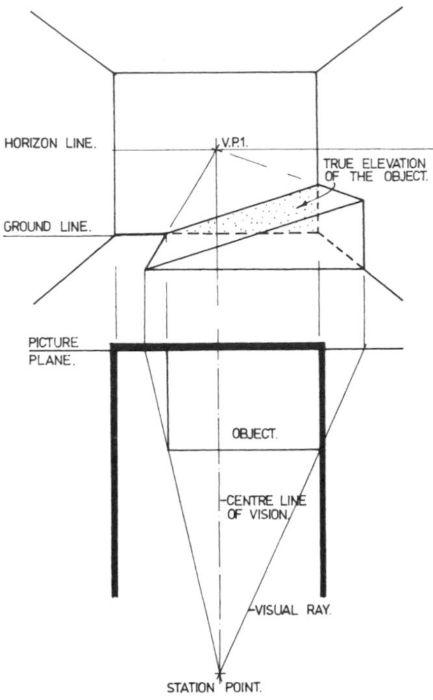

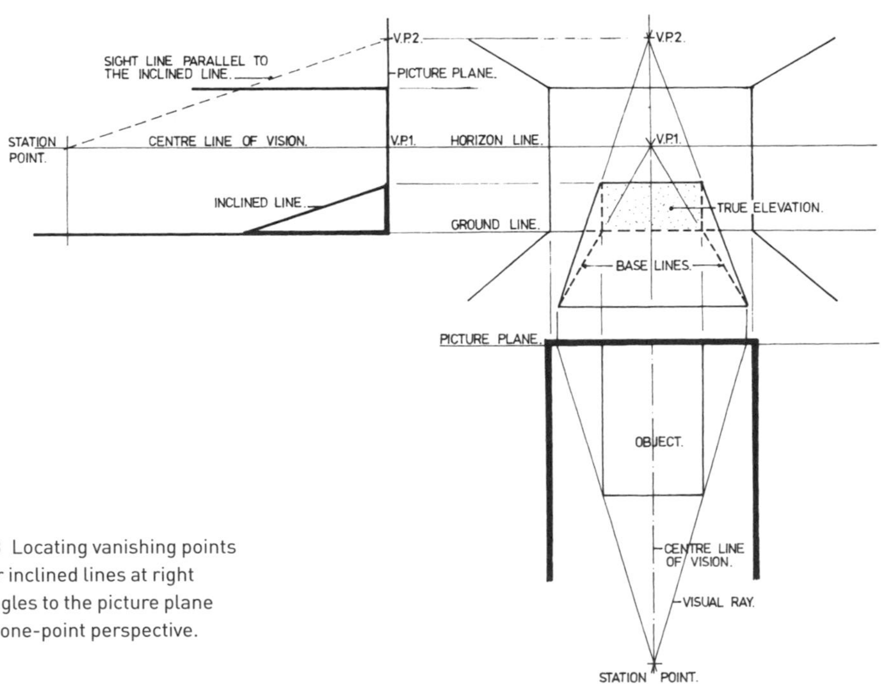

58 Locating vanishing points for inclined lines at right angles to the picture plane in one-point perspective.

methods used for setting up a one-point perspective of an object including inclined lines.

When dealing with inclined lines in one-point perspective the first thing to remember is that parallel inclined lines which are located parallel to the picture plane remain parallel, i.e. they do not converge to a vanishing point. The usual method for drawing inclined lines which are parallel to the picture plane is shown in Fig. 57. The object (a simple ramp in this example) is located in a room which is drawn in one-point perspective, using the method described in Fig. 43; this means that the end wall of the room coincides with the picture plane and is drawn in true elevation in the perspective view. One side of the ramp coincides with the wall (itself coinciding with the picture plane), therefore a true elevation of the ramp can also be drawn in the perspective view.

The drawing of the ramp is completed by using the vanishing point to locate the bottom line of the ramp on the floor and its top line on the right-hand wall. The width of the ramp is located by drawing visual rays from the station point through the points of the plan of the object. From the intersections of the visual rays and the picture plane vertical lines are drawn up to the top and bottom lines of the ramp. From these intersections the side of the ramp nearest to the station point can be drawn.

From this example it can be seen that the sides of the object, whether horizontal, vertical or inclined, if located parallel to the picture plane in plan, remain parallel to each other in the perspective view. It can also be seen that any inclined line parallel to the picture plane can be located in the perspective view by drawing a true elevation of the inclined line on the picture plane and locating it by using simple projection.

When the same object is placed in the same room but turned round so that the sides containing the inclined lines are at right angles to the picture plane, as shown in Fig. 58, the inclined lines will recede from the spectator, and so a vanishing point will be required for them.

First, the room is set up as described in Fig. 43. When the drawing of the room in the perspective view is completed, the object can be located and drawn.

Step 1. Locate and draw the elevation of the side of the object, which coincides with the end wall of the room. (The end wall of the room coincides with the picture plane.) This is done by projecting up from the plan and measuring the height on the elevation of the object.

Step 2. The lines of the base of the object are located and drawn on the floor plane by projecting up from the intersections of visual rays and the picture plane together with lines from vanishing point 1.

Step 3. Draw an elevation showing the object in its position in relation to the picture plane, station point, ground line and eye level (horizon line). From the station point (eye) a sight line is drawn parallel to the inclined line of the object to meet the picture plane at vanishing point 2 (the vanishing point for the inclined lines and all lines parallel to them).

Step 4. From V.P.2 in the elevation, project across to meet a vertical line drawn through V.P.1. This point will be the vanishing point for the inclined lines in the perspective view. Using V.P.2, the inclined lines can be drawn in the perspective view as shown in Fig. 58.

An alternative method can be used to find the vanishing point for the inclined lines, but, like the alternative method for locating vanishing points for inclined lines in two-point perspective (Fig. 55), it is less accurate than the method shown in Fig. 58. When this alternative method is used, the room is set up exactly as in the previous method. Steps 1 and 2 are the same as those described in the previous method; it is only steps 3 and 4 which differ.

Step 3. Select one corner of the base of the object in the floor plane and from it draw a line through the appropriate top corner of the elevation of the object in the picture plane, and continue the line until it intersects a vertical line drawn through V.P.1. The point of intersection of these two lines is the vanishing point (V.P.2) for the inclined lines.

Step 4. From the other corner of the base of the object in the floor plane a line is drawn through the appropriate top corner of the elevation of the object (in the picture plane) and continued to meet the vertical line through V.P.1 at V.P.2.

This method relies on the accuracy of the draughtsman, and if care is taken it is considered sufficiently accurate for most requirements. But if extreme accuracy is needed, the student is recommended to use the first method described here.

59 Comparison between the plan used for one-point and two-point constructions (i.e. vertical lines parallel to the picture plane) and the 'special' plan required for three-point perspective.

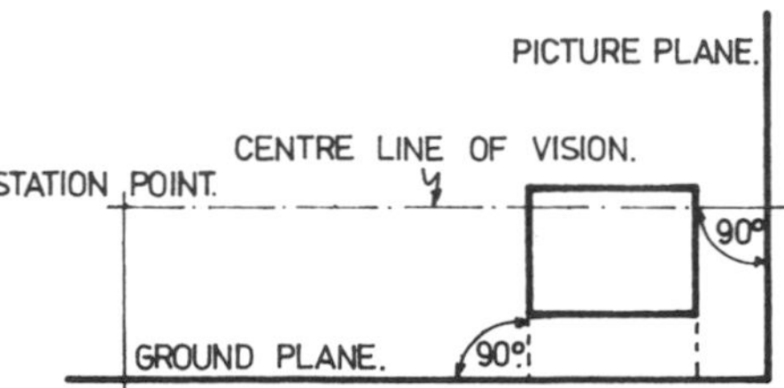

Elevation showing the object parallel to the ground and picture planes.

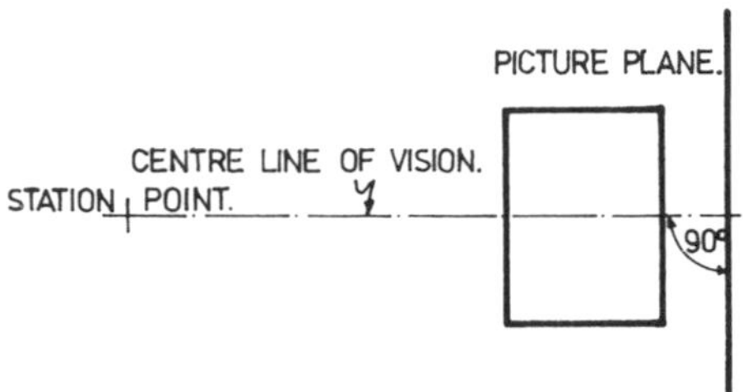

Plan showing the object parallel to the ground and picture planes.

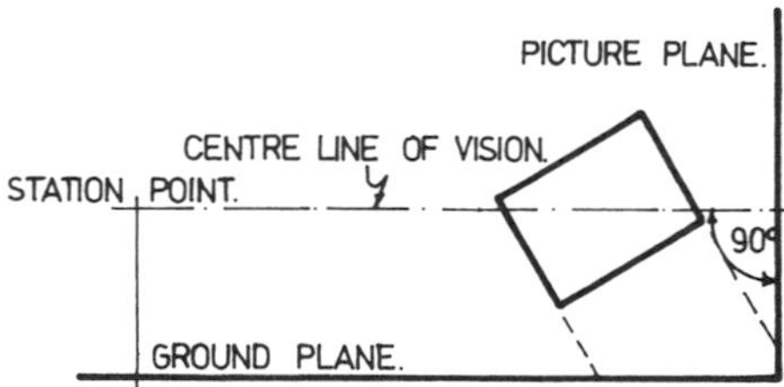

Elevation showing the object inclined to the ground and picture planes.

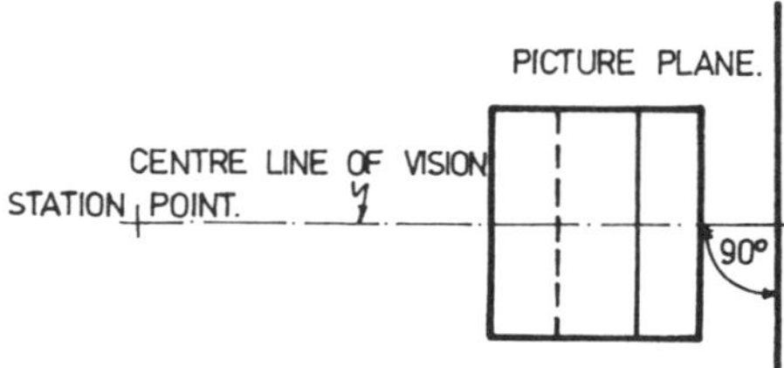

Plan showing the object inclined to the ground and picture planes.

1.3 Three-Point Perspective: Objects Inclined to the Ground Plane

In the previous examples of perspective, only those requiring one or two vanishing points have been used. Some aspects of these constructions have required extra vanishing points to help in the execution of the drawing, but the constructions have been based on either one-point or two-point constructions.

In these constructions it will be seen that the vertical lines of a rectangular prism, when parallel to the picture plane, i.e. at 90° to the ground plane, will be vertical in the perspective drawing. When the rectangular prism is inclined to the ground plane, however, these lines will no longer remain vertical in the perspective drawing, therefore they will have to be treated as inclined lines. This means that a vanishing point will be required for these lines which, in one-point and two-point constructions, were vertical. The addition of this vanishing point, which is known as the vertical vanishing point (V.P.3), is the reason for the name 'three-point perspective'.

The vertical vanishing point is located either directly above or directly below the intersection of the centre line of vision and the picture plane (on the horizon line). As previously described, the vanishing points for inclined lines will be directly above or below what would be the vanishing points for these lines if they were in the horizontal plane. The lines of the object which were vertical when the object was parallel to the ground plane will be visible when the object is inclined, and will appear as lines parallel to the centre line of vision (at right angles to the picture plane). Therefore, because the centre line of vision is considered as a sight line parallel to the sides of the object (in plan), the vanishing point for these inclined lines of the object will be located either directly above or directly below the intersection of the centre line of vision and the picture plane.

Fig. 59 shows the object in its normal position, i.e. located with its vertical lines parallel to the picture plane, so that it can be drawn in one-point perspective. Also shown in Fig. 59 is the object inclined to the ground plane, i.e. located with its vertical lines inclined to the picture plane, which means that a vertical vanishing point will be required before it can be drawn in perspective.

From the diagram in Fig. 59 it will be seen that, because the object is inclined, the lines which were vertical in one-point and two-point constructions will now be visible in the plan view of the object. This means that a 'special' plan must be prepared for three-point perspective. Using, as before, a simple rectangular prism for our example (see Fig. 60), the first step is the selection of the station point, the eye level and the picture plane in relation to the object. These are drawn in elevation, as shown in the diagram. The end elevation of the object is located and drawn at the required angle to the ground and picture planes.

From the elevation, horizontal lines are projected across to a convenient location where the plan view of the inclined object can be drawn together with the plan views of the picture plane, the station point and the centre line of vision. (The length of the object is measured on the orthographic projection.)

Only the vertical lines have been considered so far, but it should be remembered that not only the 'vertical' lines become inclined lines when the object is inclined to the ground plane. In the example shown in Figs. 59 and 60 the lines which were parallel to the centre line of vision (horizontal lines at right angles to the picture plane) will become inclined lines when the object is inclined to the ground plane.

From this information and the diagram it can be seen that three-point perspective is an exercise in the setting up of inclined lines. There are two methods of setting up three-point perspectives, one based on the one-point and the other on the two-point construction. If the lines of the

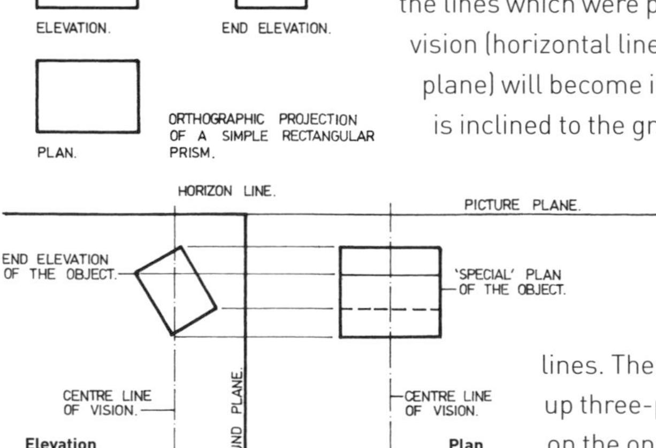

60 The method used for preparing a 'special' plan for a three-point perspective construction (when the object is inclined to the ground plane) based on a one-point construction. For the method based on a two-point construction, see Fig. 65.

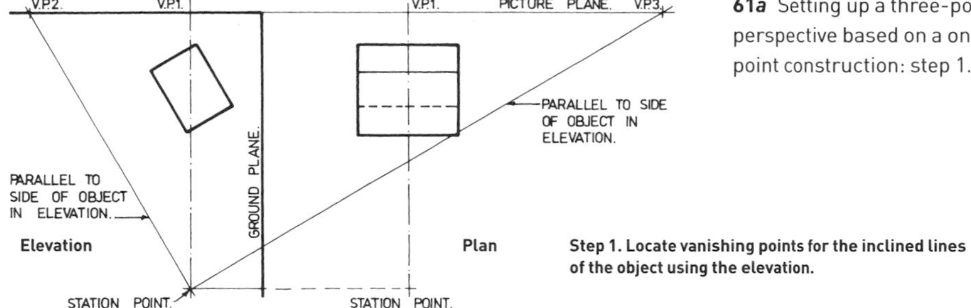

61*a* Setting up a three-point perspective based on a one-point construction: step 1.

Step 1. Locate vanishing points for the inclined lines of the object using the elevation.

object are parallel to the picture plane *or* the centre line of vision in the plan view, a basic one-point construction is used; if these lines are at an angle to the picture plane *and* the centre line of vision in the plan view, a basic two-point construction is used.

The first method explained here is the one based on the one-point construction, and it continues from Figs. 59 and 60. Having prepared a 'special' plan as described in Fig. 60, the location of the station point should be checked with the cone of vision and adjusted if necessary.

The method of setting up a three-point perspective based on a one-point construction is as follows:

Step 1. Locate the vanishing points for the inclined lines.
As previously described, the vanishing point V.P.1 for lines parallel to the centre line of vision is located at the point where the centre line of vision meets the picture plane. This means that the vanishing points for inclined lines parallel to the centre line of vision in the plan view will be in a vertical line through V.P.1. The heights of these vanishing points above or below the horizon line (V.P.1) are located by drawing sight lines parallel to the inclined lines of the object in the elevation. The points where these sight lines intersect the picture plane are the locations of the heights of the vanishing points for the inclined lines. These heights are located on the elevation, and even though they may overlap the plan construction (as they do in the example shown here), it should be remembered that all dimensions are measured from the horizon line in the elevation. The

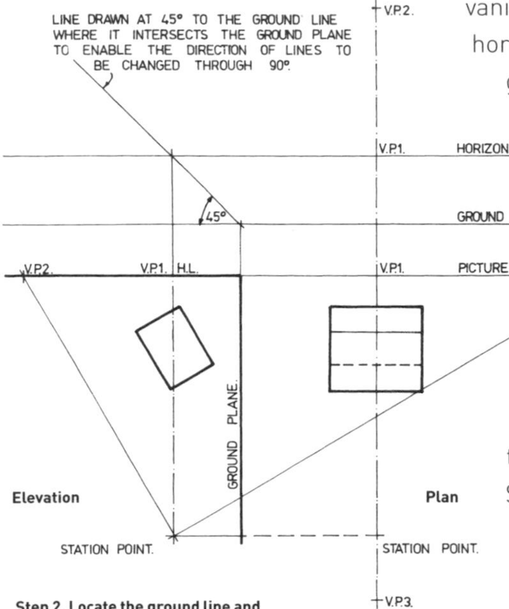

Step 2. Locate the ground line and the horizon line together with a line at 45° to the ground line to enable the direction of lines to be changed through 90°. (V.P.2 and V.P.3 are located on a vertical line drawn through V.P.1.)

61b Setting up a three-point perspective based on a one-point construction: step 2.

vanishing point V.P.2 for the lines which were horizontal when the object was placed on the ground plane (see Fig. 59) is located above the horizon line when the object is inclined to the ground plane and looked at from above. The vanishing point V.P.3 for the lines which were vertical when the object was placed on the ground plane is located below the horizon line when the object is inclined to the ground plane and looked at from above.

Step 2. The horizon line is located in a convenient position, as previously described, and the ground line is located below it in the usual way (the distance between the horizon line and the ground line being the height of the eye level, as required). The elevation of the ground plane is extended to meet the ground line (on the elevation of the picture plane where the perspective view is to be drawn) as shown in Fig. 61*b*. From the intersection of the ground plane (in the elevation) and the ground line a line is drawn at 45° to the ground line. This line is used to change the direction of lines through 90°. This construction makes use of the fact that if the centre line of vision in the elevation is extended it will meet the horizon line at the point where it intersects the line drawn at 45° to the ground line (where the centre line of vision meets the end elevation of the picture plane is the horizon line, as already explained). From this it will be seen that the ground line and the horizon line, though they change direction through 90°, remain parallel and therefore the same distance apart.

V.P.2 is located on a vertical line drawn through V.P.1 and its height above V.P.1 can be measured on the elevation. V.P.3 is located on a vertical line drawn through V.P.1 and its height below V.P.1 can also be measured on the elevation.

Step 3. Visual rays are used to locate the points of the object on the picture plane in the usual way. These visual rays are required not only on the plan but also in the elevation, as shown in Fig. *62a*. The best way to understand the construction required to locate a point of the object is to 'follow' one selected point. From the station point in the plan a visual ray is drawn through a selected point *A* of the object to meet the picture plane, and from this point on the picture plane a vertical line is projected up in the normal way. Point *A* is located in the end elevation of the object and a visual ray from the station point is drawn through point *A* to meet the end elevation of the picture plane. From this point on the end elevation of the picture plane a vertical line is projected up to meet the line drawn at 45° to the ground line. From this point a horizontal line is projected across to meet the vertical line located in the plan by projecting up from the point on the picture plane where the visual ray drawn through point *A* meets it. Point *A* in the perspective view is located at the intersection of the vertical line from the plan and the horizontal line from the elevation. The other seven points of the object are located in the perspective view in the same way.

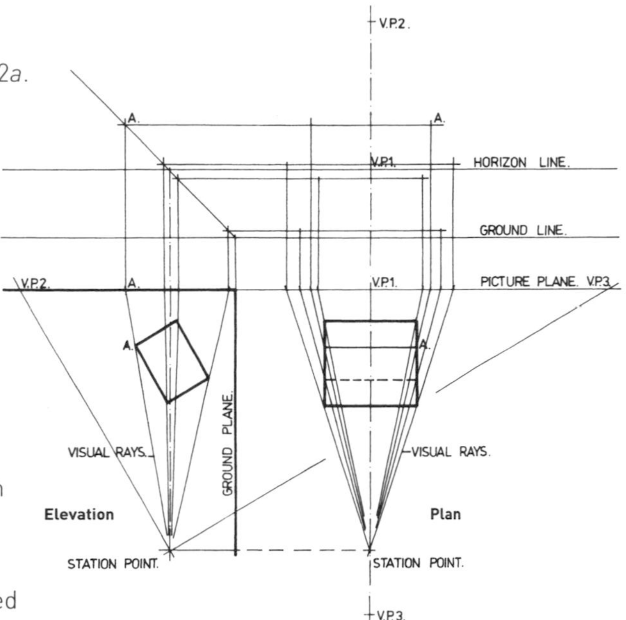

Step 3. Visual rays and projections used to locate the points of the object in the perspective view.

62a Setting up a three-point perspective based on a one-point construction: step 3.

Step 4. The object is drawn in the perspective view by identifying the points of the object and drawing the outline with the help of V.P.2 and V.P.3. Care should be exercised when identifying the points of the object; it is often advisable to follow the practice shown here of identifying each point where it occurs in each step. In this way points do not 'get lost', causing delays and frustration as well as unnecessary work in repeating steps to try and find mistakes.

62b Setting up a three-point perspective based on a one-point construction: step 4.

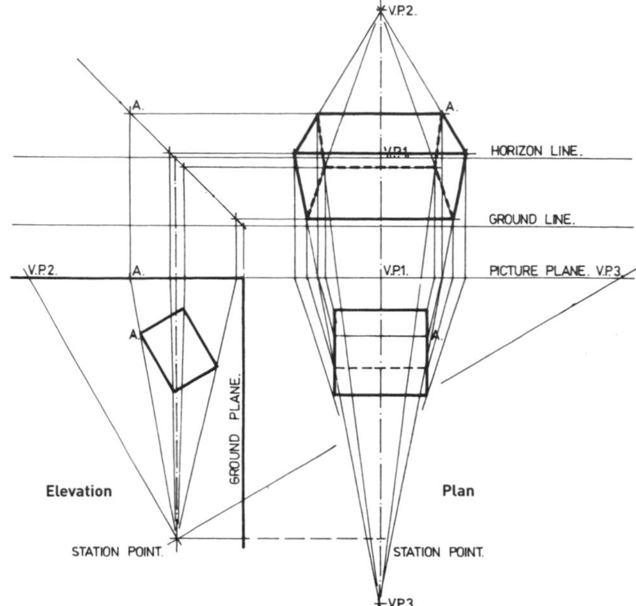

Step 4. Vanishing points (V.P.2 and V.P.3) are used to draw the perspective view of the object.

The example shown in Figs. 59–62 is based on an object inclined so that its top is visible to the spectator, and it is therefore referred to as an object viewed from above. Fig. 63 shows the same object inclined so that the bottom is visible to the spectator, and it is thus referred to as an object viewed from below.

The method used to draw an object inclined to the ground plane so that it is viewed from below, based on a one-point perspective construction, is the same as that used for the preceding example when the object is viewed from above. Only the locations of the vanishing points are changed, i.e. V.P.2 is below the horizon line and V.P.3 is above it.

The second, and probably the commonest, type of three-point perspective is the one based on a two-point construction. The principles remain the same whether a three-point perspective is based on a one-point or a two-point construction, so it is not necessary to repeat those principles here.

Like three-point perspectives based on one-point constructions, one based on a two-point construction requires a 'special' plan showing the object inclined to

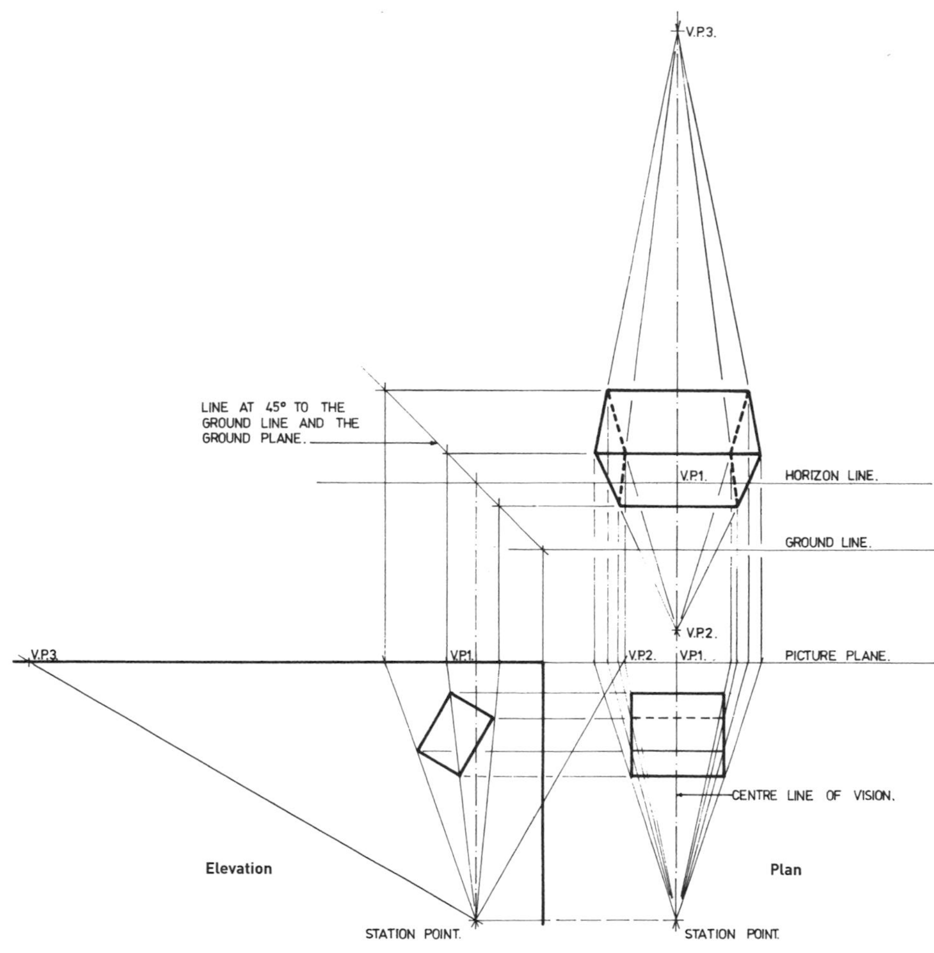

63 The construction used for a drawing of an object inclined to the ground plane and viewed from below, based on a one-point perspective construction.

the ground plane. Fig. 64 shows the orthographic projection of an object (a rectangular prism) used to illustrate the method of setting up a perspective view of the object inclined to the ground plane when a three-point perspective based on a two-point construction is needed.

As with other methods, it is necessary first to locate the station point and the centre line of vision. When the direction of the view of the object is decided it is necessary to rotate the plan until the centre line of vision is *horizontal* (Fig. 64, [directional]). The elevation of the object at right angles to the centre line of vision can then be drawn using projections from the elevation in the orthographic projection (to obtain the height) and from the plan.

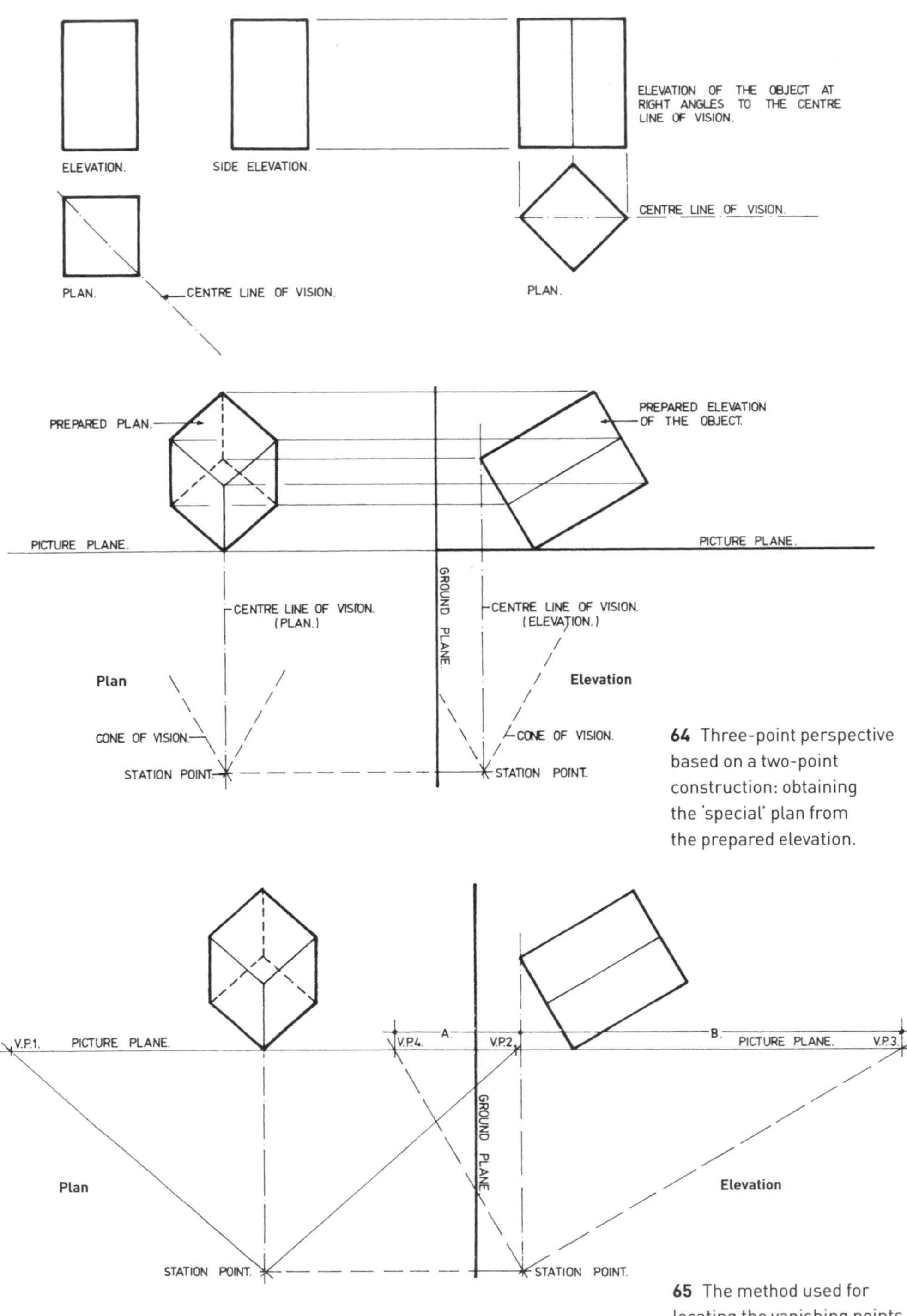

64 Three-point perspective based on a two-point construction: obtaining the 'special' plan from the prepared elevation.

65 The method used for locating the vanishing points.

The prepared elevation is set up (Fig. 64, [directional]) so that the picture plane is horizontal and a ground plane is drawn at right angles to it. The prepared elevation is drawn at the required angle to the ground plane and the picture plane. The station point is then located in the elevation and the height of the eye above the ground is chosen. At this stage the position of the station point should be checked with the cone of vision and adjusted if necessary.

The next step in the preparation of the 'special' plan is to locate the plan of the centre line of vision at right angles to the picture plane at a convenient distance from the ground plane (end elevation). By projecting across from the prepared elevation the 'special' plan can be drawn. Any dimensions (width) not obtained by projection can be obtained by measurement from the plan used to obtain the prepared elevation. All that remains is to locate the plan position of the station point by projection from the elevation. The construction is then ready for the preparation of a three-point perspective drawing of the object. (The plan position of the station point should be checked at this stage with the cone of vision and any necessary adjustments made before proceeding.)

The method for setting up a three-point perspective based on a two-point construction is as follows:

Step 1. Once the 'special' plan and the elevation have been prepared and set out as shown in Fig. 64 it is necessary to locate the vanishing points, including V.P.4 which in reality is not a vanishing point but the height above (or below) the horizon line at which V.P.1 and V.P.2 will be located.

V.P.1 and V.P.2 are located in the usual way by sight lines from the station point parallel to the sides of the object in the plan. V.P.3 and V.P.4 are located on the end elevation of the picture plane by drawing sight lines from the station point parallel to the sides of the elevation of the object (see Fig. 65).

Step 2. The horizon line for the perspective drawing is located at a convenient distance down on a continuation of the centre line of vision in the plan. The ground line is located

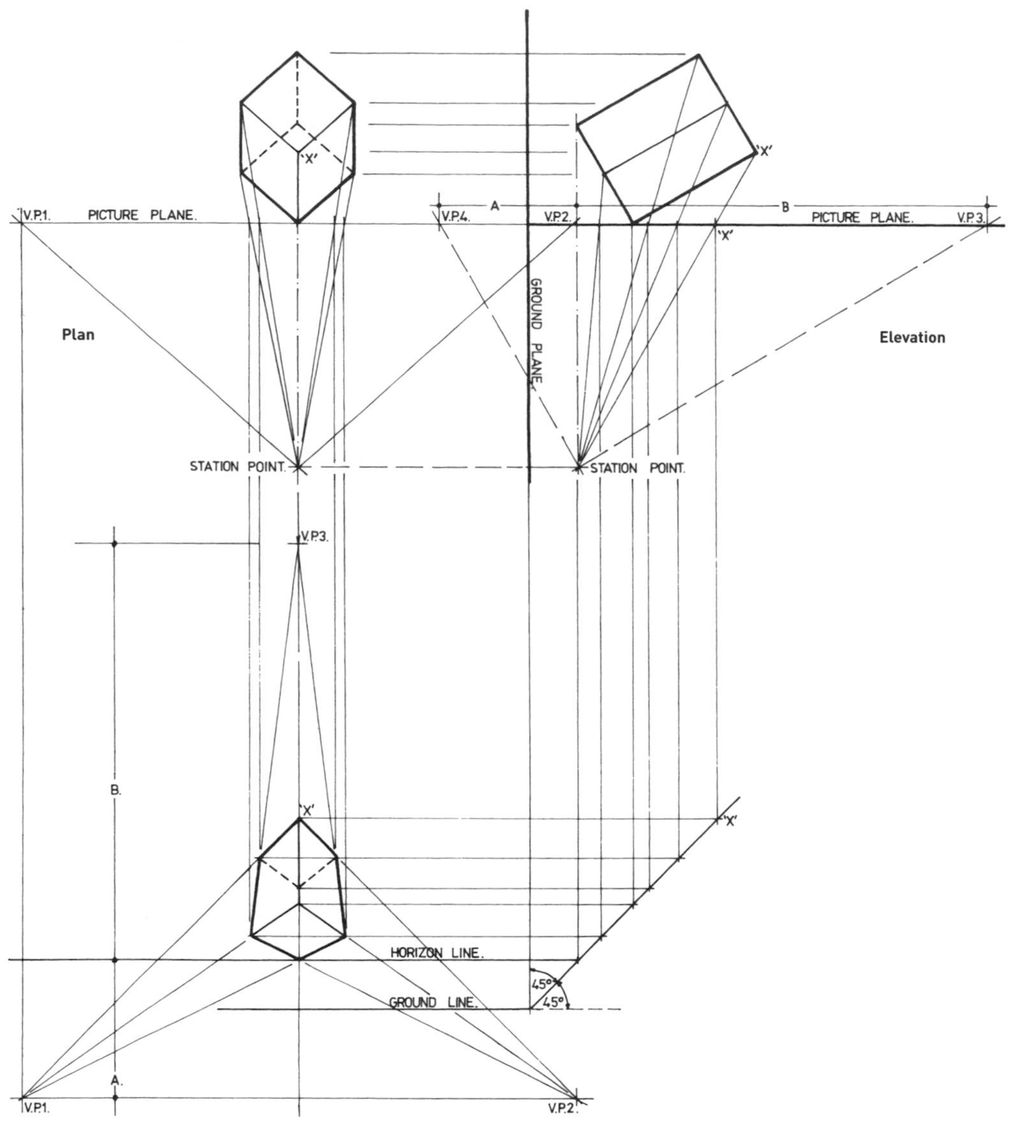

66 The construction of a three-point perspective (based on a two-point construction) when the object is inclined to the ground plane and viewed from below.

below the horizon line at the distance shown in the elevation and is extended across to meet the extension of the ground plane in the elevation. At the intersection of the ground line and the ground plane a line is drawn at 45° to both (see Fig. 66) so that the direction of lines can be changed through 90° as described in Fig. 61.

Step 3. From the elevation it can be seen that V.P.4 is a distance *A* below the point where the centre line of vision meets the end elevation of the picture plane (horizon line), which means that V.P.1 and V.P.2 will be located at height *A* below the horizon line. To locate V.P.1 and V.P.2 a line is drawn at height *A* below the horizon line in the perspective view and V.P.1 and V.P.2 are located on it by projecting their positions down from the plan view of the picture plane.

Step 4. V.P.3 (known as the 'vertical vanishing point') is located on the extension of the centre line of vision (in the plan) by measuring up from the horizon line the distance *B* which was established in the elevation: the distance from the intersection of the centre line of vision and the end elevation of the picture plane to V.P.3.

Step 5. The view of the object is drawn in perspective by using projections from both the plan and the elevation as previously described. All the points of the object are found in exactly the same way, so that it is necessary to describe the location of only one point here; the rest can be found by repeating the procedure for each point.

Point *X* is located in both the plan and the elevation. From point *X* in the elevation a visual ray is drawn back to the station point. At the point where this visual ray meets the picture plane a vertical line is drawn to meet the line drawn at 45° to the ground line. Here it changes direction through 90° and is projected across to meet a line drawn from the point on the picture plane where a visual ray through the plan of point *X* meets it. In this case point *X* in the plan falls on the centre line of vision and will be located in the perspective view at the intersection of the visual ray through point *X* in the elevation projected down and across and the extension of the centre line of vision from the plan. The remaining points of the object

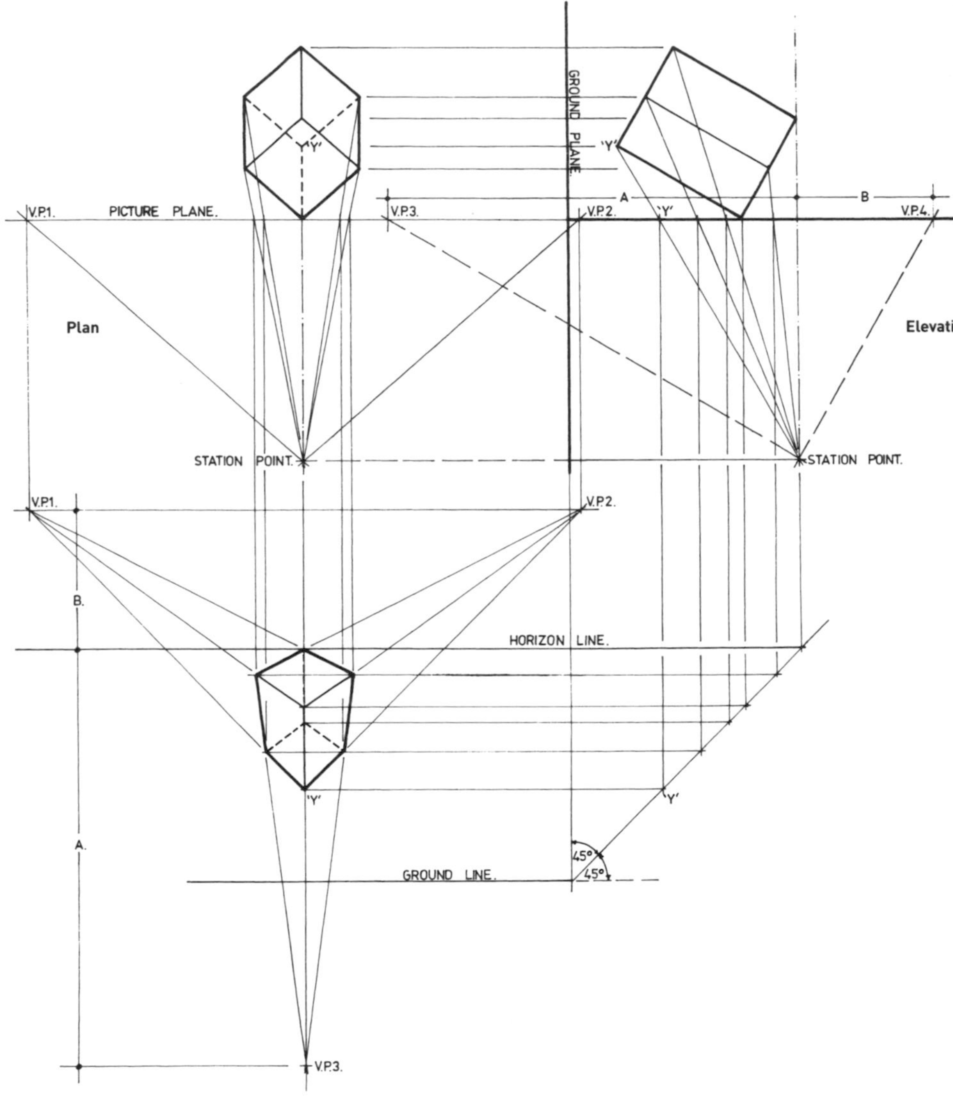

67 The construction of a three-point perspective (based on two-point construction) when the object is inclined to the ground plane and viewed from above.

are found in the perspective view in exactly the same way. When all the points have been found all that remains is to join them up, using V.P.1, V.P.2 and V.P.3 to produce the drawing of the object in three-point perspective.

When the object is inclined to the ground plane so that the spectator sees the top of the object instead of the bottom of it, the method is exactly the same as that described for the example shown in Figs. 64–66. In Fig. 67 the vertical vanishing point (V.P.3) is located *below* the horizon line and V.P.4 or the level of V.P.1 and V.P.2 is located *above* the horizon line – which is opposite to their positions when the object is inclined to the ground plane so that the bottom of it is visible to the spectator.

It can be seen from the examples of objects inclined to the ground plane, whether based on one-point or two-point constructions, that the principles are simply an extension of those discussed under the heading of 'inclined lines and planes in perspective' and, provided the main principles of perspective are thoroughly understood, three-point perspective is far less complicated than it may look at first.

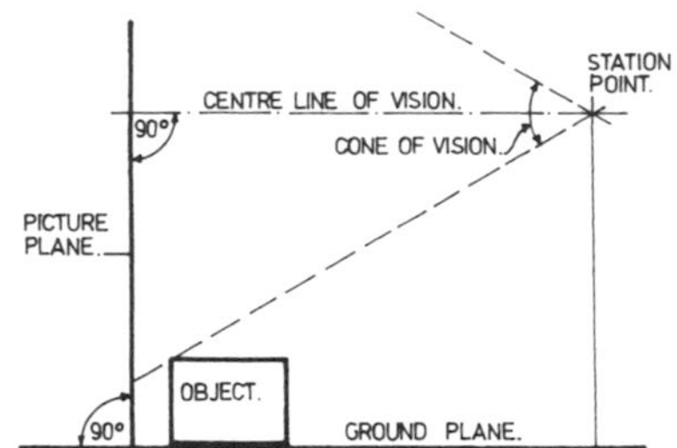

68 Station point too high: object becomes invisible.

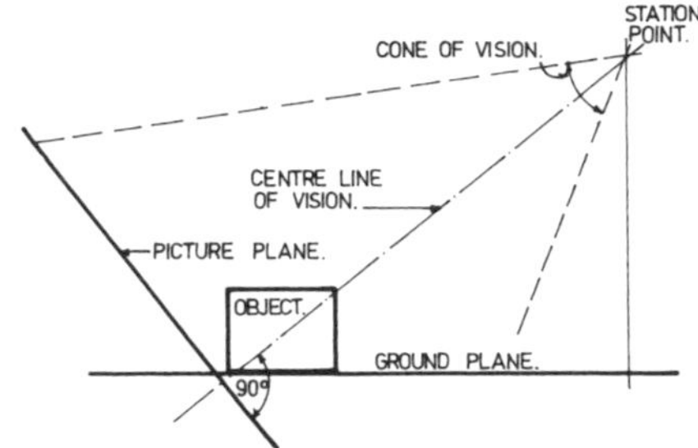

69 Centre line of vision and picture plane tilted: bird's-eye or aerial view.

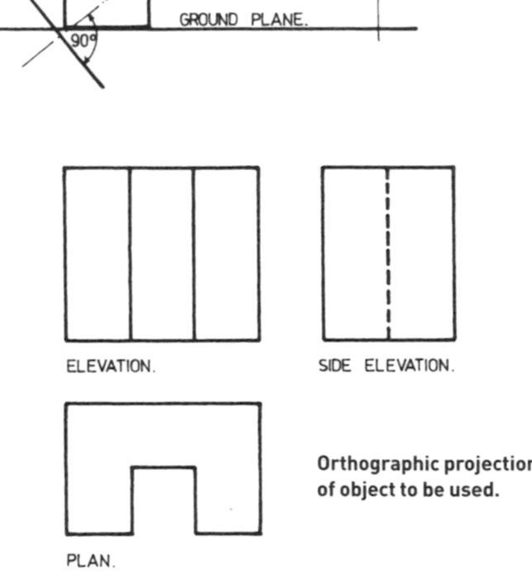

Orthographic projection of object to be used.

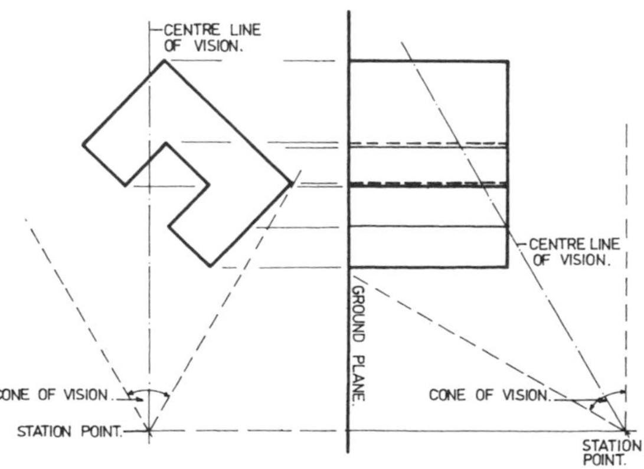

70 Setting up the plan and elevation for an aerial perspective: step 1.

1.4 Perspectives with an Inclined Picture Plane

For the best view of an object the eye should be focused on or near the centre of it. Similarly, when producing a perspective drawing of an object the best results are generally obtained when the centre line of vision passes through or near the centre of the object to be drawn. The picture plane is always at right angles to the centre line of vision, so when the station point is in a horizontal plane through the object a vertical picture plane is used, i.e. one at 90° to the ground plane. The higher or lower the station point is located in relation to the object, the more necessary it becomes to use an inclined picture plane in order to achieve the best results.

Fig. 68 shows an object in relation to a high station point and it can be seen that these conditions make it impossible to produce a satisfactory perspective drawing using a normal, that is to say vertical, picture plane. (The object falls outside the cone of vision, which means that the drawing of the object will be distorted if attempted under these conditions.)

Fig. 69 also shows the same object and the same station point, with the centre line of vision depressed until it passes through the object and is thus no longer parallel to the ground plane. Because the picture plane is always at right angles to the centre line of vision it too will now be inclined to the ground plane. If the picture plane is inclined to the ground plane it will be seen that the conditions are similar to those shown in Fig. 59, where the object itself was inclined to the ground plane. Because of this the construction will also be similar: both require a third vanishing point ('vertical vanishing point'). However, this construction has one advantage over the other three-point constructions in that it does not require a 'special' plan but can be carried out using a normal plan. This is why this method is specially favoured for aerial, bird's-eye or worm's-eye perspectives.

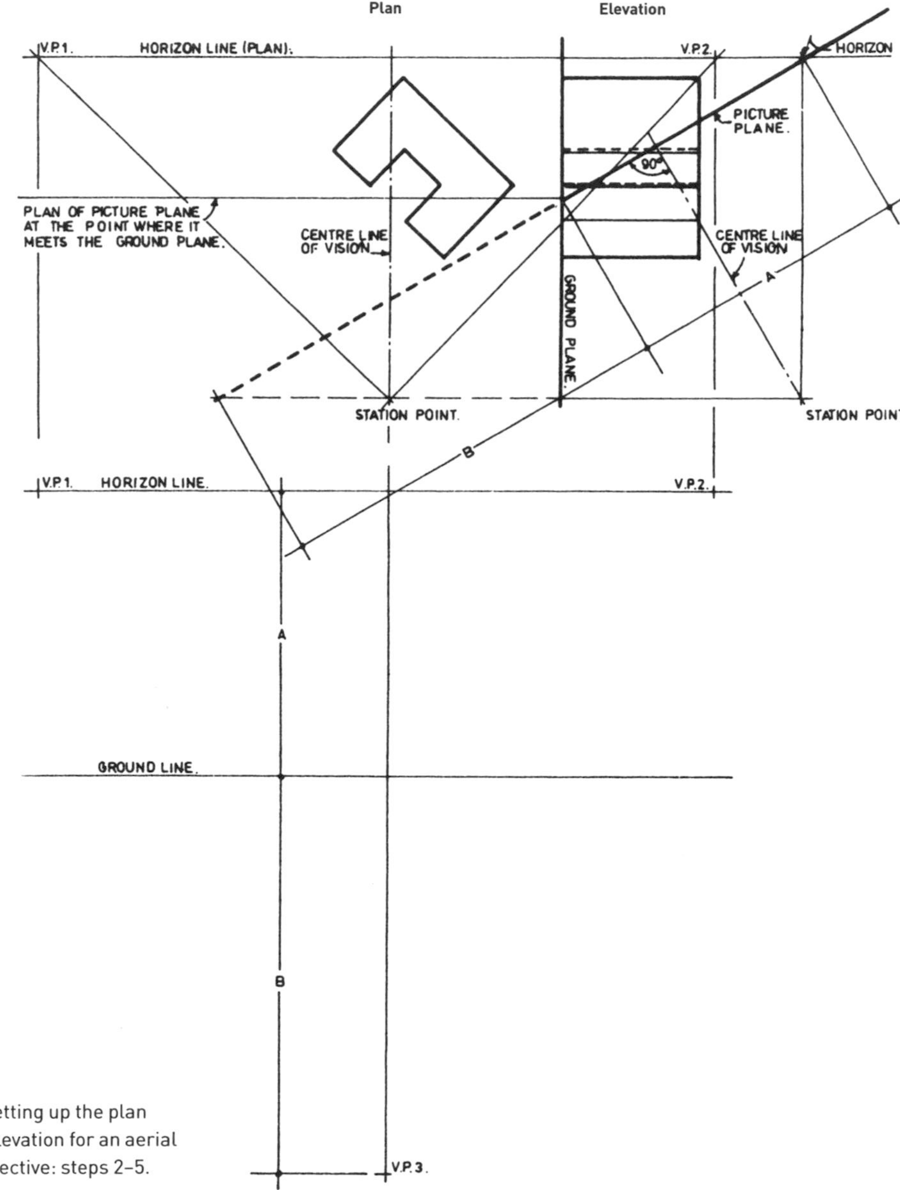

71 Setting up the plan and elevation for an aerial perspective: steps 2–5.

To draw an aerial or bird's-eye view of the object shown in orthographic projection in Fig. 70 it is necessary first to locate the station point in the plan and the elevation. When this is done the method of setting up an aerial view of the object, i.e. a perspective drawing of the object using an inclined picture plane, is as follows:

Step 1. The selection of the station point is a matter of choice within the limits of the cone of vision. When it is chosen, the plan is rotated so that the centre line of vision is vertical, as shown in Fig. 70. A prepared elevation is necessary, and is obtained by drawing at some convenient distance from the centre line of vision a ground plane (elevation) parallel to the centre line of vision. The elevation of the object can then be prepared in the normal way (by projection and measurement) and a suitable height above the ground selected for the station point. The centre line of vision is drawn in the elevation at the required angle to the object and the ground plane, remembering that usually the best results are achieved when the centre line of vision passes through the object to be drawn. The station point should be checked in both the plan and the elevation with the cone of vision and any necessary adjustments made.

Step 2. As previously explained, the location of the picture plane is a matter of choice and it is drawn on the elevation in the chosen position *at right angles to the centre line of vision*. (Fig. 71 shows the preparations necessary for an aerial perspective.)

Step 3. Because the picture plane is inclined to the ground plane it is necessary to locate the plan positions of the horizon line and the ground line (the plan of the picture plane where it meets the ground plane). As previously explained, the horizon line is always located on the picture plane at the point where a sight line parallel to the ground plane meets it. A sight line is drawn parallel to the ground plane in the elevation, and from the point where it intersects the inclined picture plane a horizontal line is drawn representing the horizon line on the plan view of the picture plane. From the point of intersection of the inclined

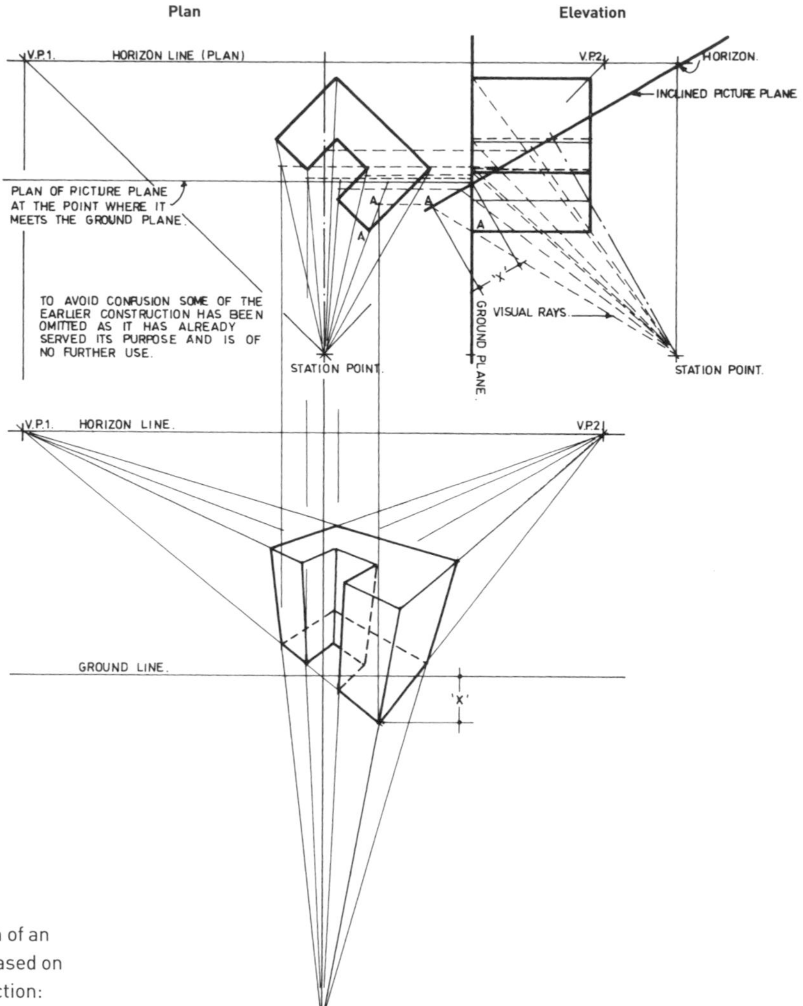

72 The construction of an aerial perspective based on a two-point construction: steps 6–8.

picture plane and the ground plane in the elevation a horizontal line is drawn representing the intersection of these two planes in the plan view, i.e. the ground line.

Step 4. The location of the vanishing points for the lines parallel to the ground plane will be located in the horizon line and are located in the normal way except that because the picture plane is inclined the horizon line is visible in the plan, which means that the sight lines parallel to the sides of the plan of the object are drawn to the horizon line instead of the picture plane (plan) as in previous examples.

V.P.1 and V.P.2 are located in this way and are the vanishing points for the horizontal lines of the object.

The vertical vanishing point (V.P.3) which will be the vanishing point for the vertical lines of the object is located on an extension of the elevation of the inclined picture plane by drawing a sight line parallel to the vertical lines of the object. In this example, because the spectator is above the object, V.P.3 will be located at a distance *A* below the ground plane in the elevation. The station point is at a distance *B* above the ground plane. Using these two measurements it is possible to locate the horizon line, the ground plane and the vanishing points for the perspective drawing.

Step 5. From the plan view of the centre line of vision a vertical line is drawn as a continuation of the centre line of vision, as shown in Fig. 71. At a convenient distance down this line a horizontal line is drawn representing the horizon line in the perspective view. The positions of V.P.1 and V.P.2 are located on this horizon line by projecting down vertically from their positions in the plan view. At a distance *B* below the horizon line another horizontal line is drawn to represent the ground line in the perspective view. At a distance *A* below the ground line V.P.3 is located on the extension of the centre line of vision.

The construction is now completed and all that remains is for the perspective drawing of the object to be done.

Step 6. From the station point in the elevation visual rays are drawn through the points of the object to meet the picture plane (Fig. 72). The points where these visual rays meet the picture plane are transferred by measurement to the perspective view. (Point *A* on the object is followed through the construction to help the student understand the procedure.)

Step 7. From the station point in the plan visual rays are drawn through the points of the object. To locate the points where these visual rays meet the picture plane it is necessary to project lines across from the positions where the elevations of visual rays intersect the elevation of the picture plane. Where these lines projected across from the elevation meet the appropriate visual rays in the plan are the positions where the visual rays in the plan meet the

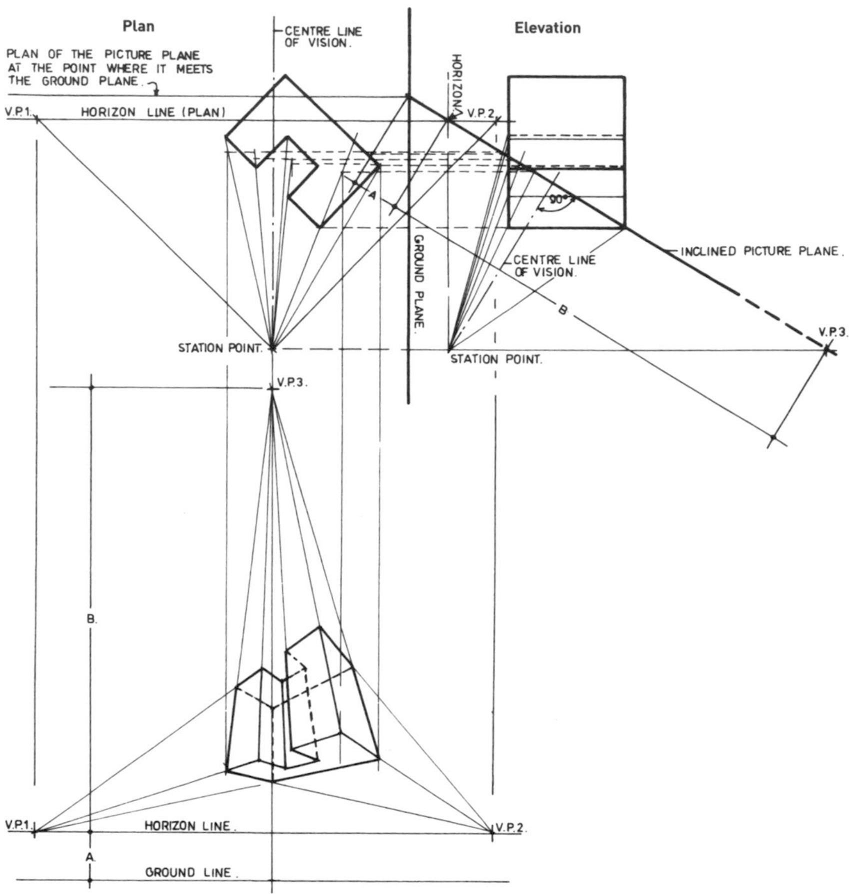

73 The construction of a worm's-eye view based on a two-point perspective construction.

picture plane. From these points where the visual rays in the plan meet the picture plane, projections are made down to the perspective view, and from these the points of the object can be located in the perspective view. (The heights above or below the ground line are located by measurement – see step 6.)

Step 8. By using V.P.1, V.P.2 and V.P.3 the points of the object are joined up to produce the drawing of the object in perspective using an inclined picture plane.

Fig. 73 shows the construction used for a worm's-eye view (seen from below). The method used for this example is identical to that used in the preceding one (Figs. 70–72). Because the station point is located at a lower level than

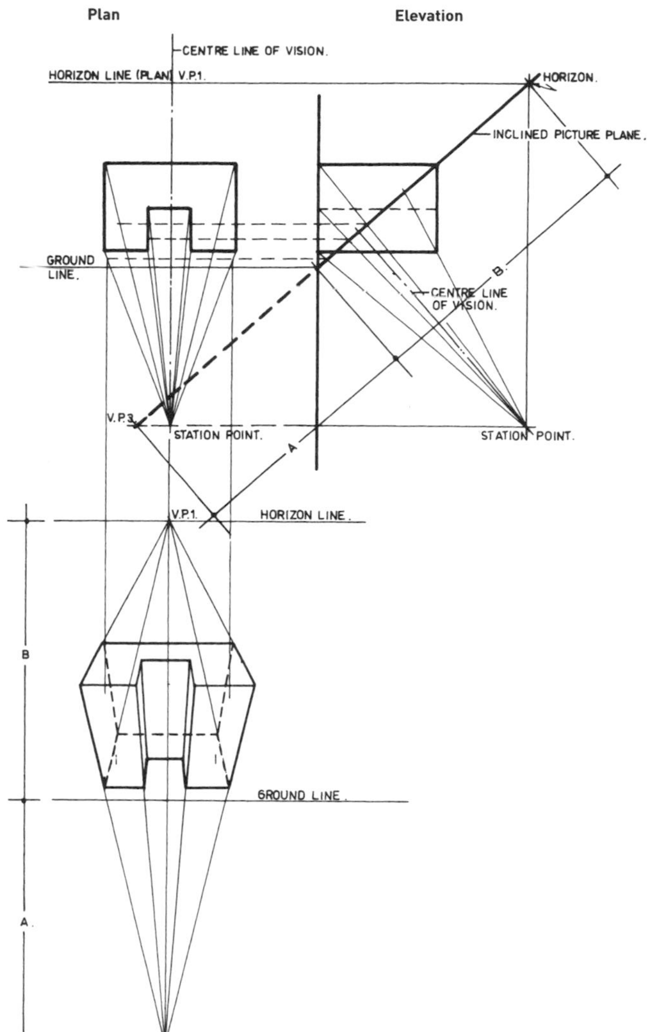

74 The construction of an aerial perspective based on a one-point construction.

it was in the previous construction the spectator will be looking up instead of down, so the vertical vanishing point will be located above the ground plane instead of below it. The method of construction is the same, and if Fig. 73 is compared with Fig. 72, the method for drawing a worm's-eye view will be easily understood.

Points located on the inclined picture plane in the elevation are located in the perspective view by measurement. These measurements are made along the picture plane, starting

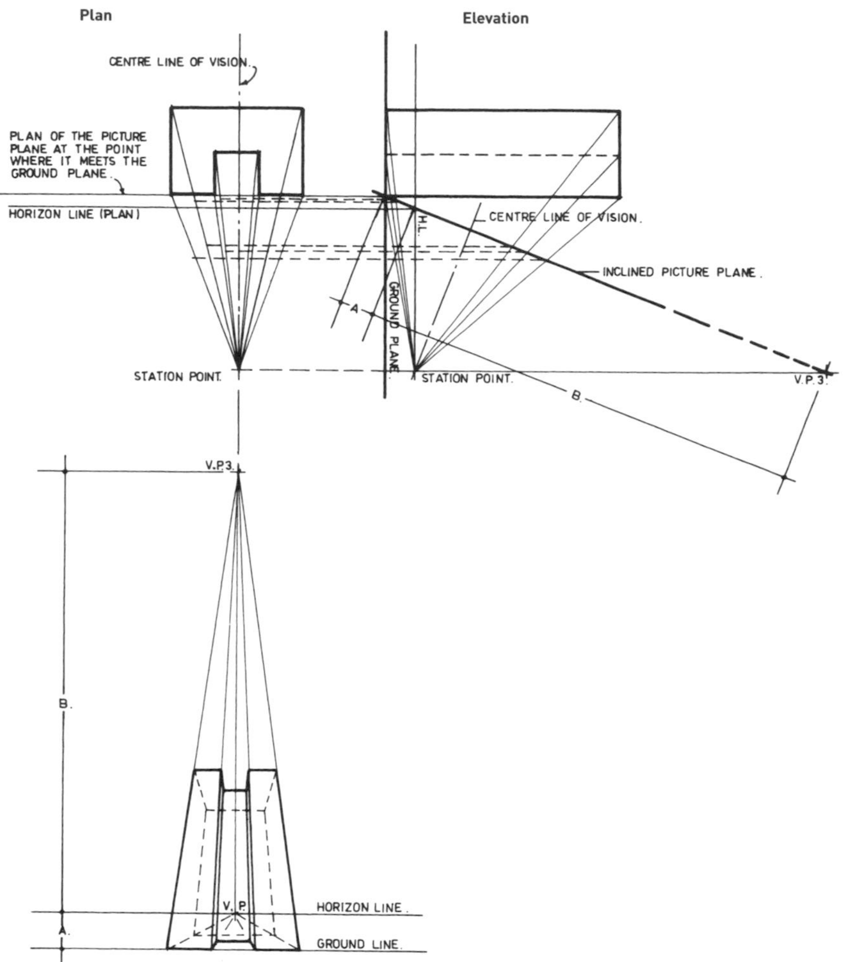

75 The construction of a view from a low station point (worm's-eye view) based on a one-point perspective construction.

from the ground plane (in the elevation). The ground line is the base line in perspective constructions, and all measurements are made from it.

Fig. 74 shows the method used for drawing an aerial view of an object based on a one-point construction. Again the method is similar to the one used for an aerial view based on a two-point construction, the only difference being in the placing of the object: in one-point perspective the object is located so that its sides are parallel either to the picture plane or to the centre line of vision, whereas in two-point perspective the object is located with its sides at an angle to the picture and the centre line of vision. The steps are carried out in the same order as for the two-point construction described in Figs. 70–72. (Note that the vertical vanishing point continues to be identified as V.P.3, to avoid any confusion.)

Fig. 75 shows the method used for the construction of a worm's-eye view of an object based on a one-point construction. For this example the object shown in orthographic projection in Fig. 70 has been increased to twice the height to show to better effect the results obtained with a worm's-eye view. Again the method is similar to the previous examples of perspectives with inclined picture planes, and this can be verified by comparison of Fig. 75 with Figs. 72–74.

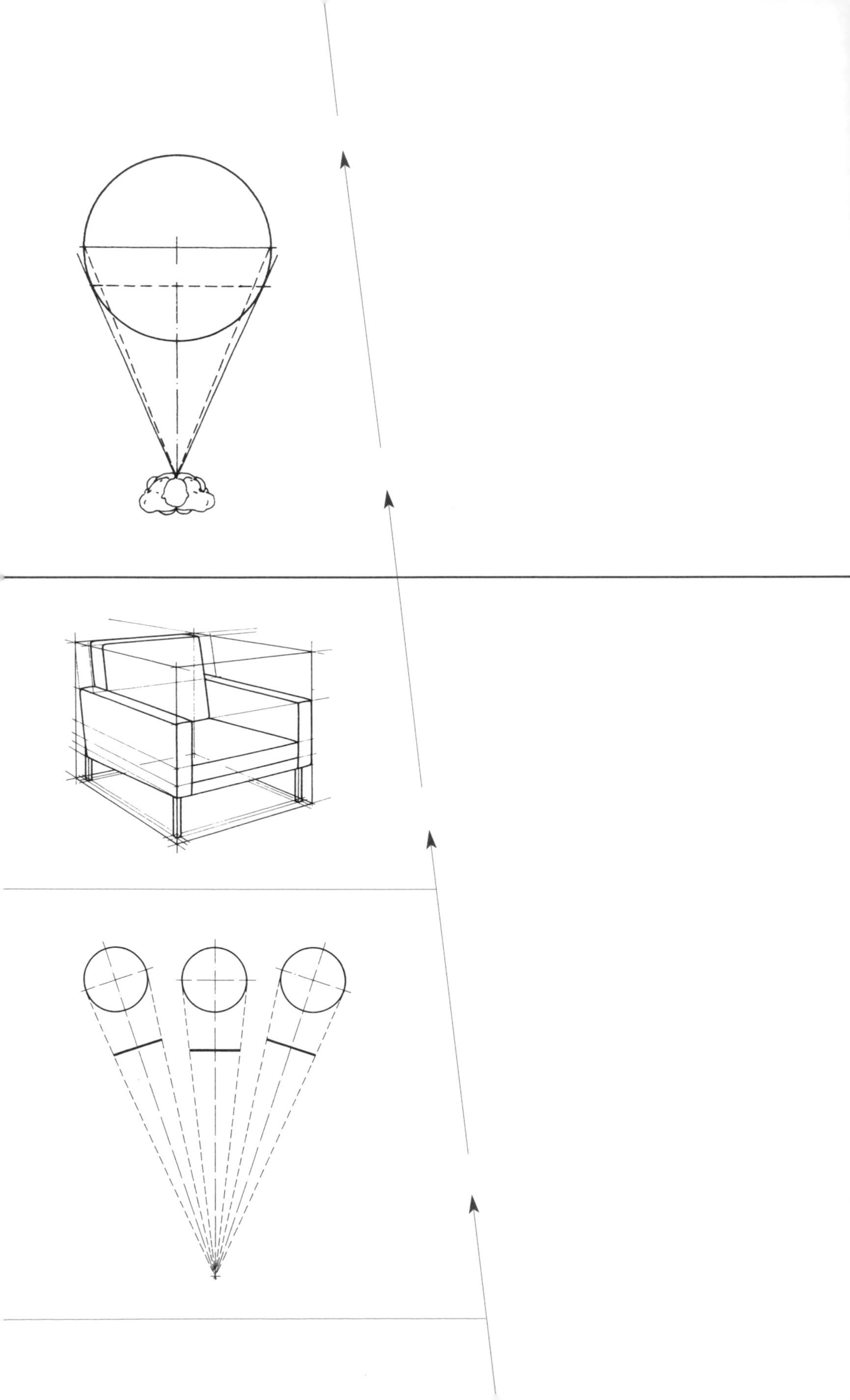

two

creative perspective

An Introduction to Creative Perspective

Before the basic principles of perspective projection can be developed and applied they must be understood. It is not intended here to become involved with the theory of perspective which has been fully explained in the first section of this book. However, the methods for constructing a one-point, a two-point, and a three-point perspective are recapped here to establish a starting point. The same basic principles are used in each of the three methods and it is only the relationship between the observer and the object which differs.

One-point perspective constructions (Fig. 76) are probably the simplest and quickest of the methods of setting up a perspective and are therefore popular with students. The eleven steps required to set up a one-point perspective view of an object are shown graphically and should need no further explanation. If the sequence shown is followed, little difficulty should be experienced in setting up any perspective view of this type.

In the case of a two-point perspective view of the same rectangular prism as used in Fig. 76, twelve steps are required; these are shown in sequence in Fig. 77. Again, it is recommended that, to avoid unnecessary confusion, this sequence be followed when setting up a two-point perspective view of any object.

Fig. 78 shows the basic method for setting up a three-point perspective view of the rectangular prism used in the two preceding examples. Because the prism is tilted, i.e. its top and bottom are no longer parallel to the ground plane, a special plan is required before the perspective construction can be carried out. The method for preparing this special plan is shown in Fig. 78 together with the steps required, in sequence. The three-point perspective constructions are the most complicated of all the perspective constructions but when it is realized that they are only developments or extensions of inclined lines in perspective they should be more easily understood.

There are a number of variations of the basic method of setting up a three-point perspective view of an object. The third point, which is the one which gives this method its name, is known as the vertical vanishing point, i.e. the vanishing point for those lines which were vertical in both the one-point and the two-point constructions. The example in Fig. 78 shows a three-point perspective based on a two-point construction. Three-point perspectives can also be based on one-point constructions and, though they are slightly simpler to construct, there is little difference in the underlying principles between them and the ones based on the two-point constructions. Another method which can be used to construct a three-point perspective view of an object is the one which uses an inclined picture plane. This method has an advantage over the one shown in Fig. 78 in that it does not require a special plan: this makes it eminently suitable for such large-scale aerial perspectives as city developments, airports, etc. If an inclined picture plane is used for this type of subject a normal orthographic plan, such as the ones used in one-point and two-point constructions, can be used.

If the methods shown and discussed here are examined, it will be seen that the basic principles are the same in each case, which means that they can be combined in the same drawing if required. Fig. 79 shows a composite drawing in which a one-point, a two-point and a three-point construction are used to portray the three different objects as they would be seen by an observer located at the station point. Once it is clearly understood that the basic principles of perspective projection do not change because the position of an object being viewed changes in its relationship to the observer, it is possible to go on to the next step. This step is the development, expansion and application of these basic principles so that they can be used to produce accurate perspective drawings with a minimum amount of wasted time and effort.

76a Setting up a one-point perspective view. Steps 1–7.

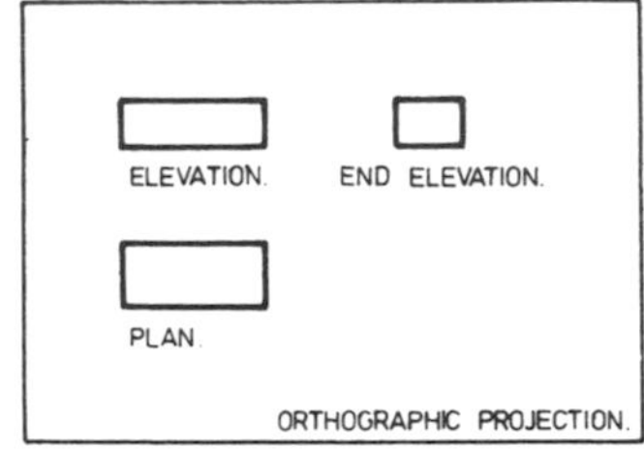

Step 1
Obtain information.

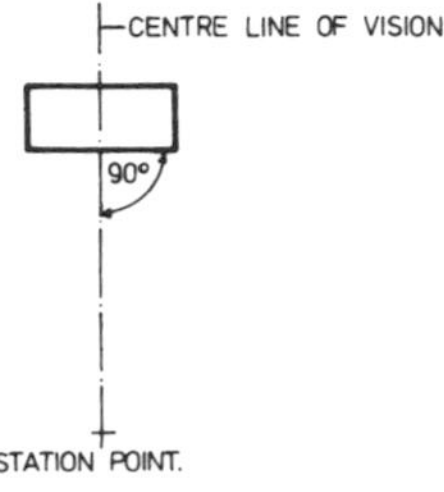

Step 2
Locate station point and the centre line of vision.

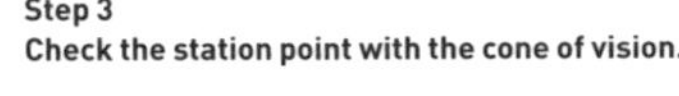

Step 3
Check the station point with the cone of vision.

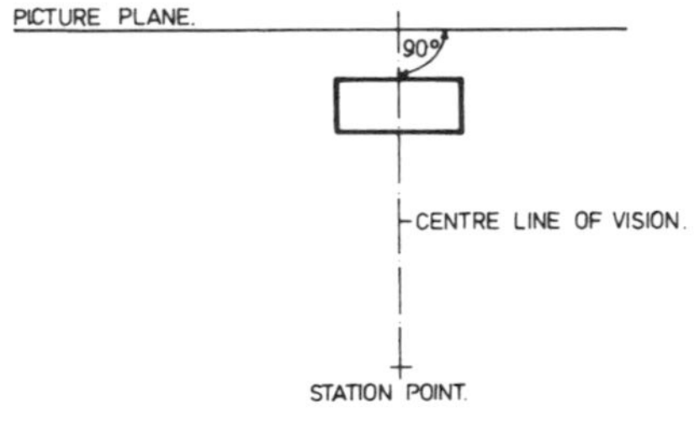

Step 4
Locate the picture plane at 90° to the centre line of vision.

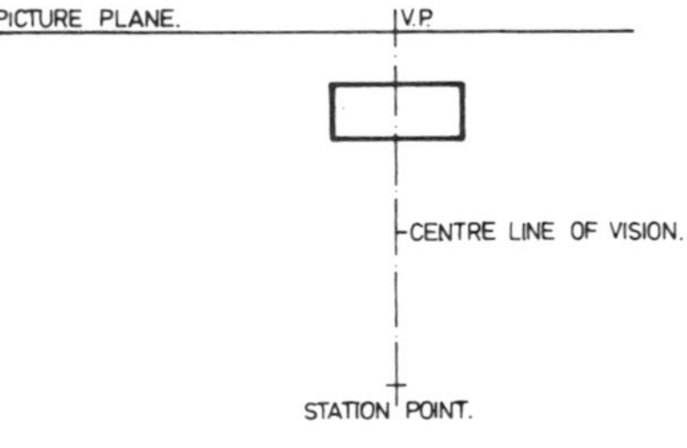

Step 5
Locate the vanishing point for the sides of the object parallel to the centre line of vision (sight line).

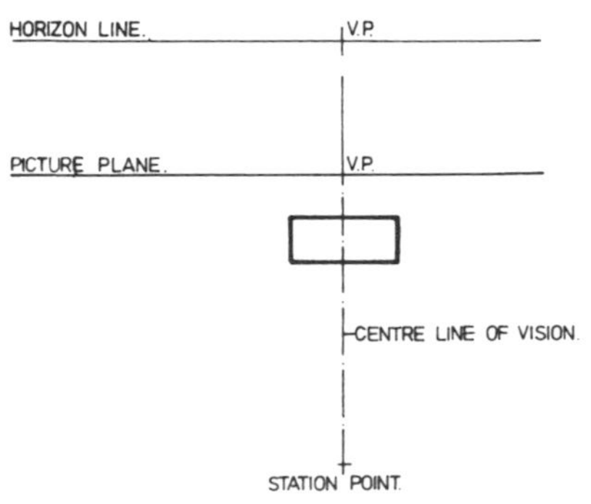

Step 6
Locate the horizon line and project up to the vanishing point on the horizon line.

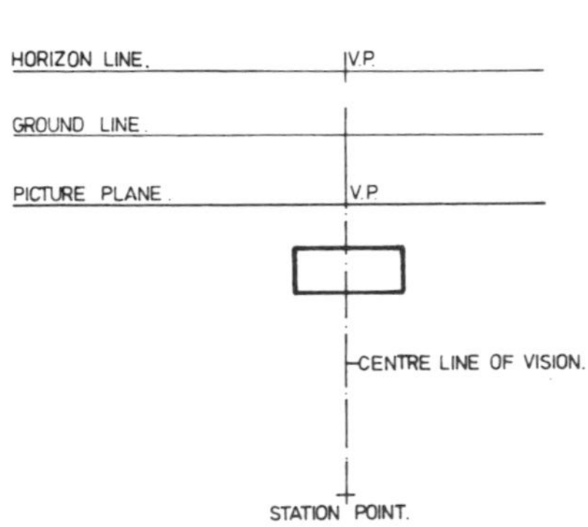

Step 7
Locate the ground line.

76*b* Setting up a one-point perspective view. Steps 8–11.

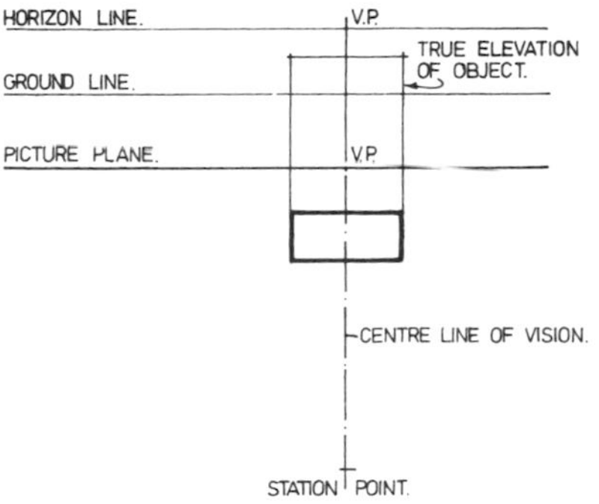

Step 8
Locate true elevation of object on elevation of picture plane.

HORIZON LINE.
V.P.
GROUND LINE.
PICTURE PLANE.
V.P.
CENTRE LINE OF VISION.
STATION POINT.

Step 9
From the vanishing point draw perspective lines through the points of the elevation.

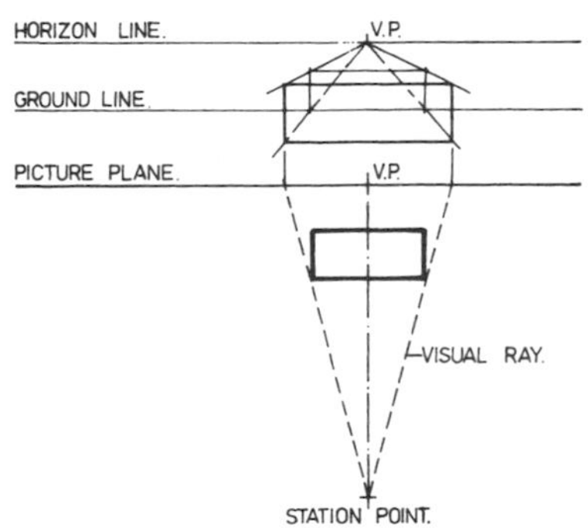

Step 10
Visual rays used to locate the front face of the object in the perspective viewpoints of the elevation.

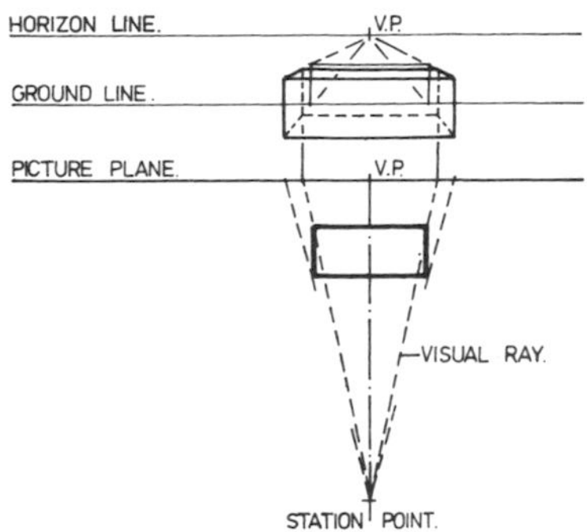

Step 11
Visual rays used to locate the rear face of the object in the perspective view.

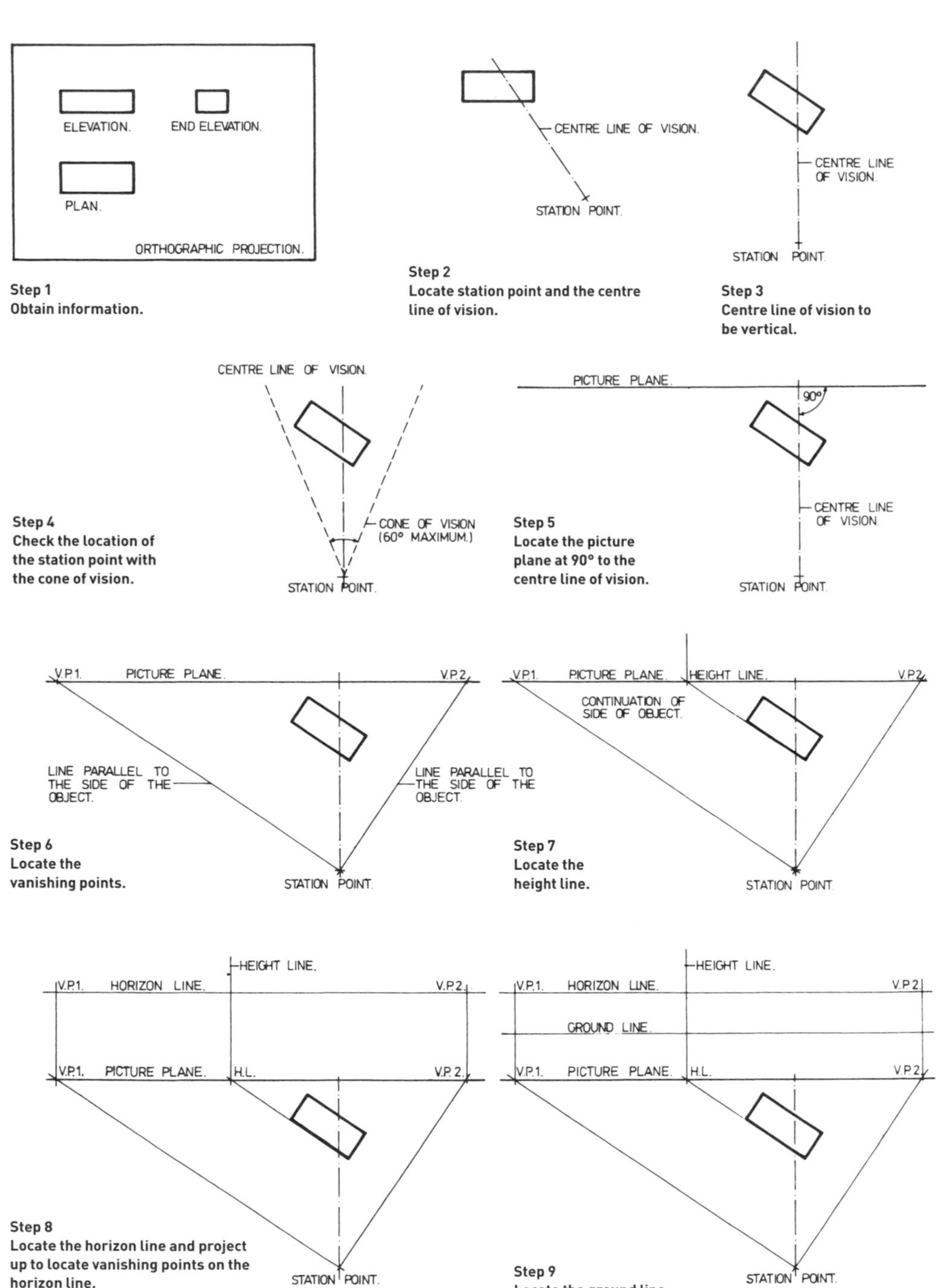

Step 1
Obtain information.

Step 2
Locate station point and the centre line of vision.

Step 3
Centre line of vision to be vertical.

Step 4
Check the location of the station point with the cone of vision.

Step 5
Locate the picture plane at 90° to the centre line of vision.

Step 6
Locate the vanishing points.

Step 7
Locate the height line.

Step 8
Locate the horizon line and project up to locate vanishing points on the horizon line.

Step 9
Locate the ground line.

77a Setting up a two-point perspective view. Steps 1–9

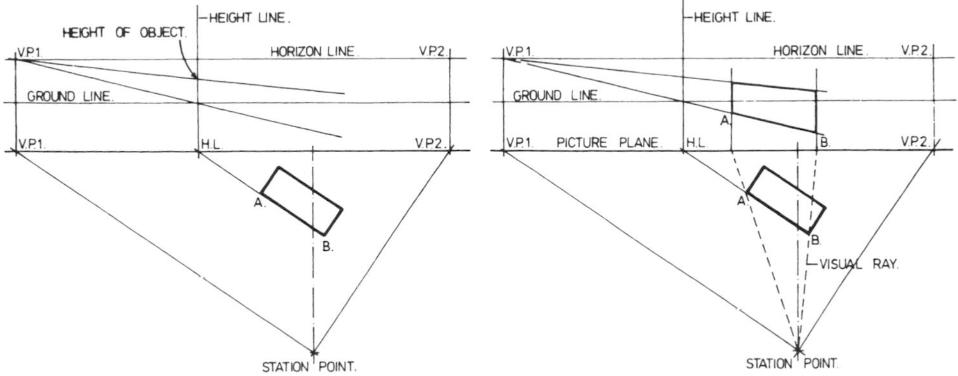

Step 10
Locate height of object on the height line and the top and bottom lines of side *AB* in the perspective view.

Step 11
Visual rays used to locate points 'A' and 'B' in the perspective view of the object.

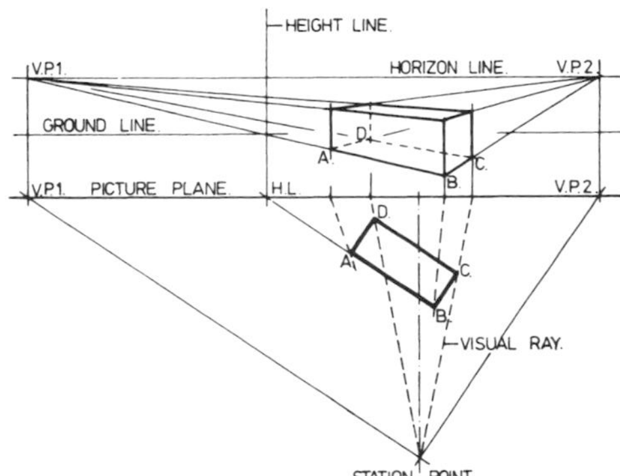

Step 12
Visual rays and perspective lines to complete the perspective view of the object.

77*b* Setting up a two-point perspective view.
Steps 10–12.

78 Setting up a three-point perspective view.
Steps 1–11.

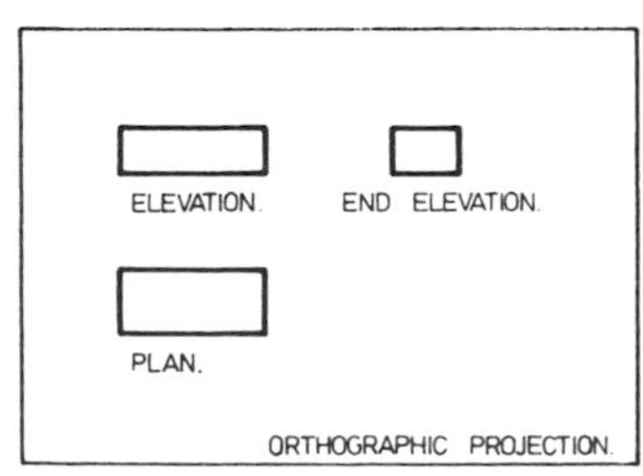

Step 1
Obtain information.

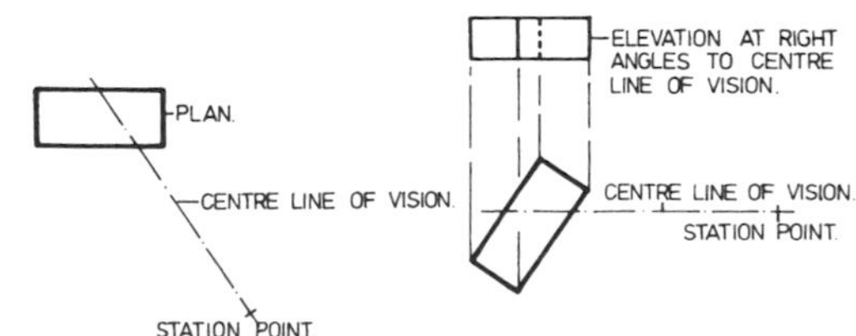

Step 2
Locate station point and centre line of vision.

Step 3
Prepare an elevation at right angles to the centre line of vision.

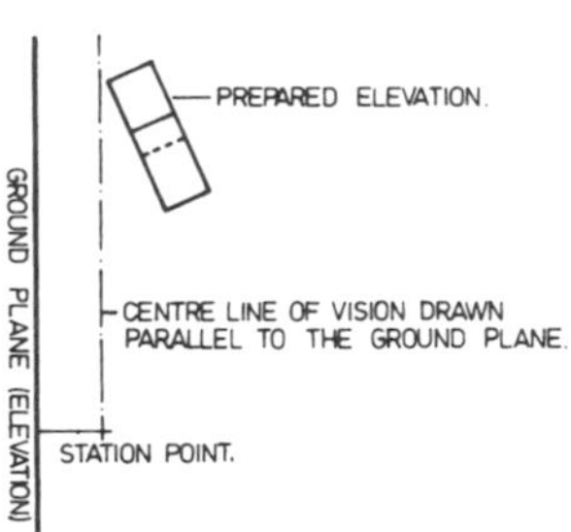

LOCATION OF SPECIAL PLAN AND PLAN CONSTRUCTION.

Step 4
Locate an end elevation of the ground plane at right angles to a normal picture plane. Locate station point, eye level, centre line of vision and the prepared elevation in its required position.

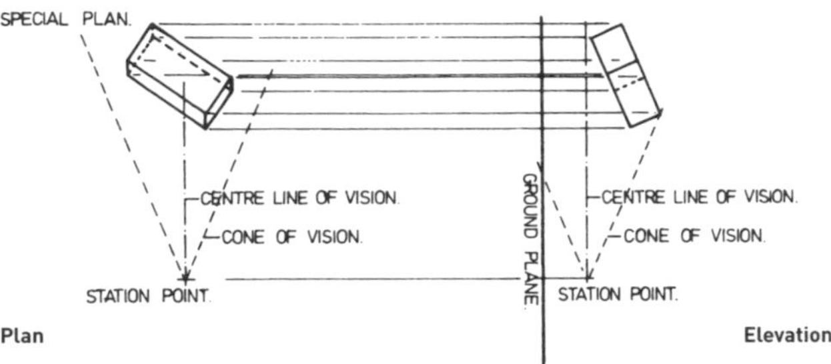

Step 5
Locate plan of the centre line of vision in a convenient position – by horizontal projection and measurement, the special plan is produced. (Check location of station point with the cone of vision.)

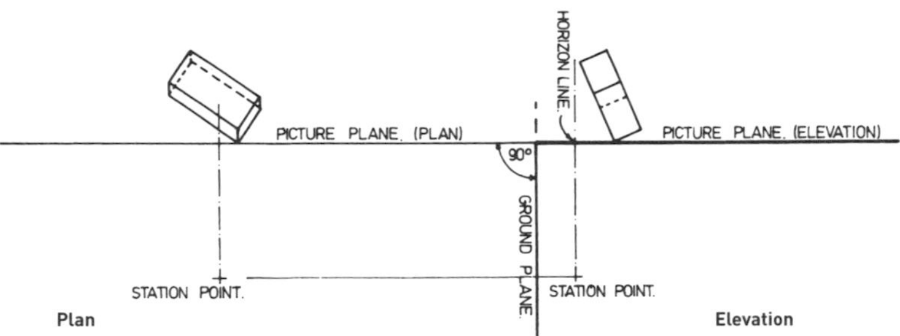

Step 6
Locate the picture plane (in both the plan and the elevation) in a convenient position.

Step 7
Locate vanishing points in both the plan and the elevation.

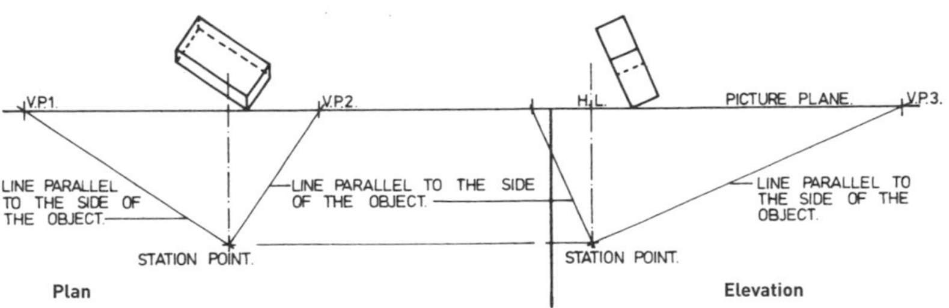

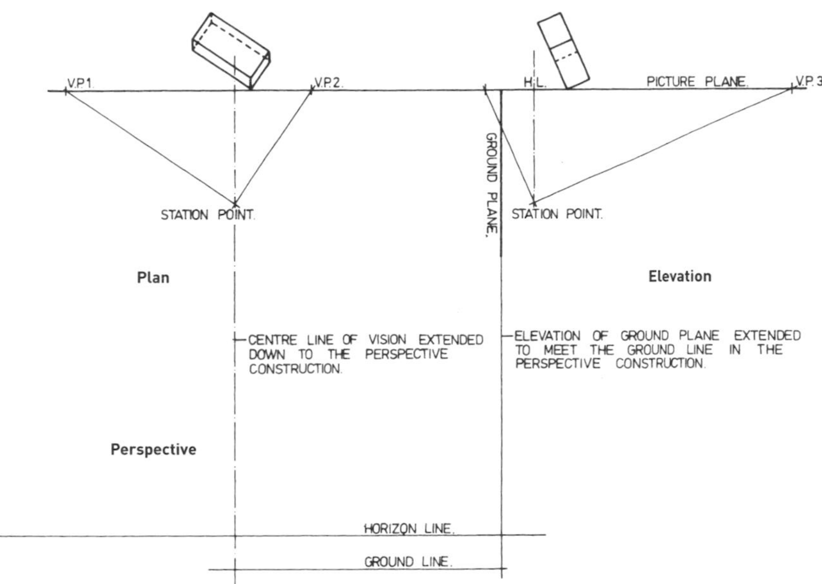

Step 8
Locate the horizon line and the ground line in a convenient position either above or below the plan. Extend the ground plane to meet the ground line in the perspective construction and also extend the plan of the centre line of vision down.

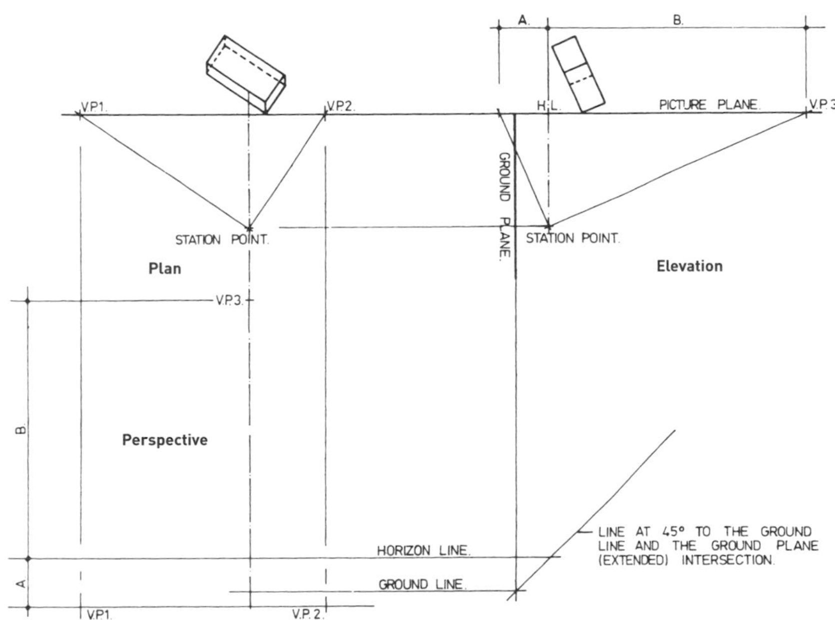

Step 9
Measure heights of V.P.3 (*B*) and V.P.4 (*A*) above and below the horizon line in the elevation. Locate V.P.3 at height *B* above horizon line and V.P.1 and V.P.2 at height *A* below it. Draw a line at 45° to the intersection of the ground line and the ground plane.

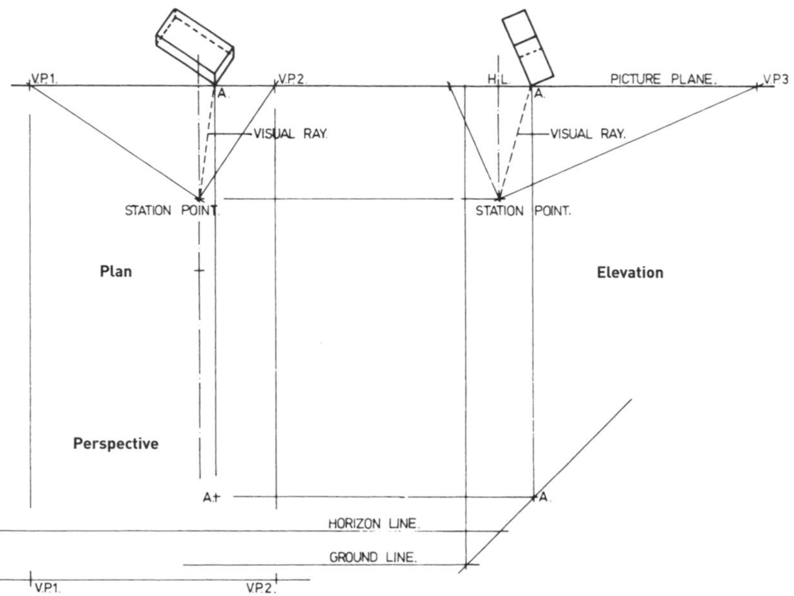

Step 10
Locate a point *A* in perspective by using a visual ray to locate the point on the picture plane and then using projections.

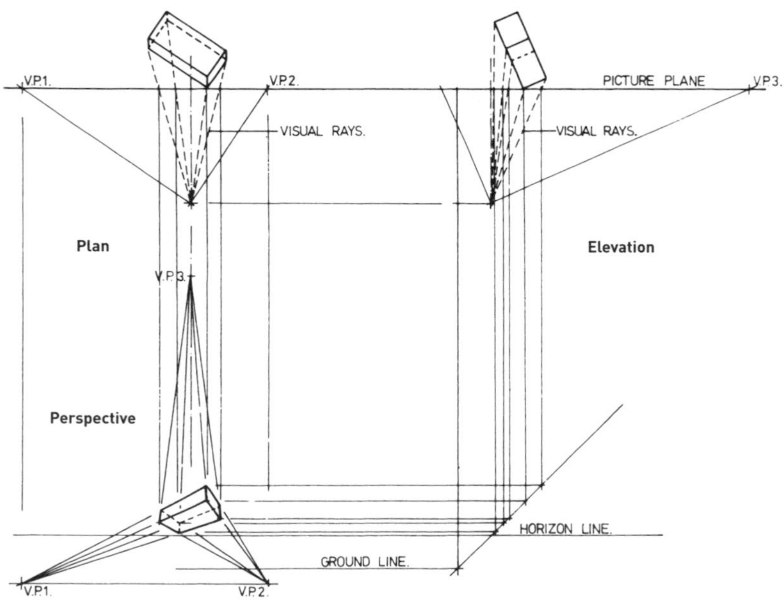

Step 11
Using visual rays, vertical and horizontal projections and perspective lines, the perspective view of the object is completed.

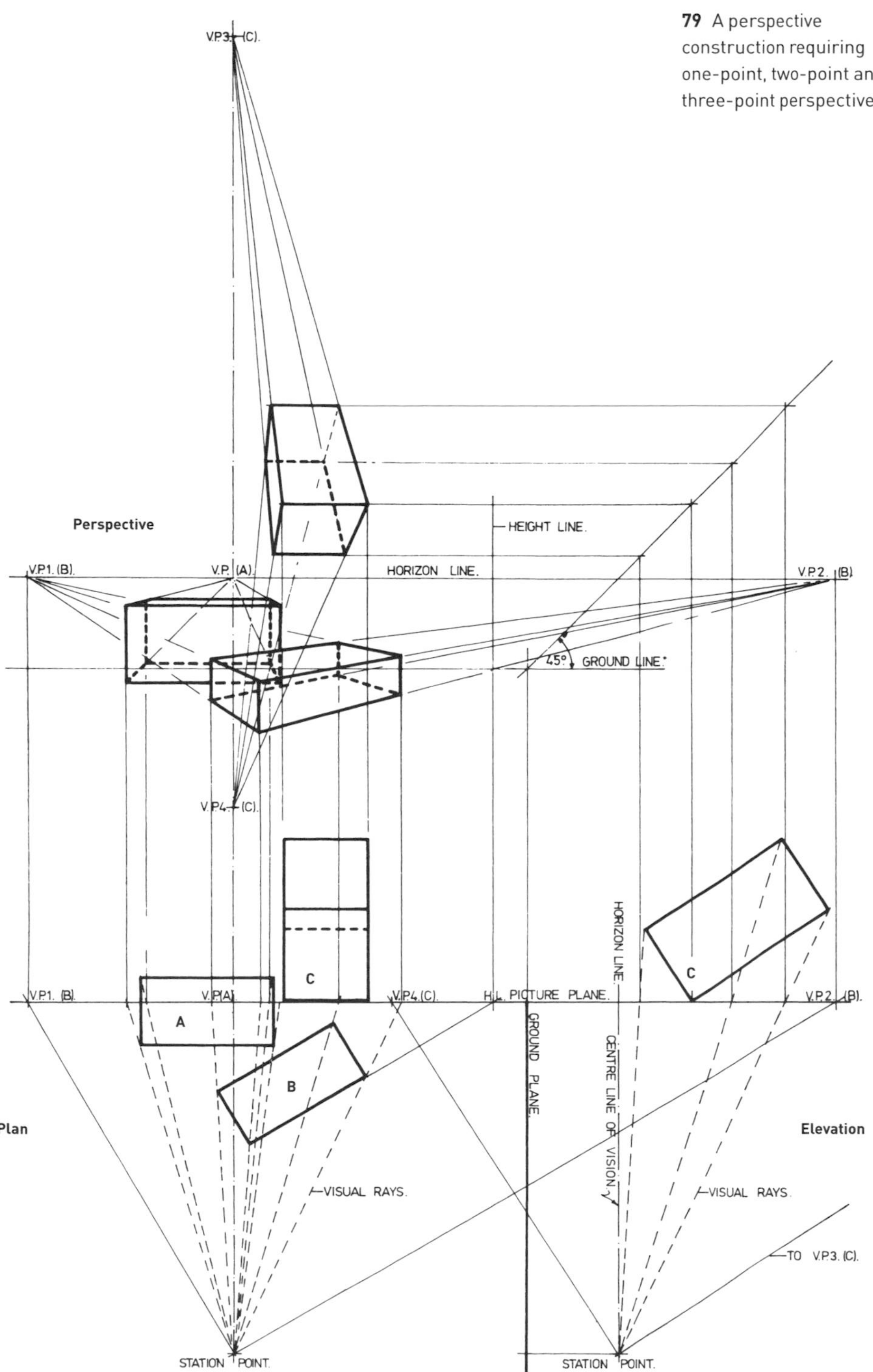

79 A perspective construction requiring one-point, two-point and three-point perspective.

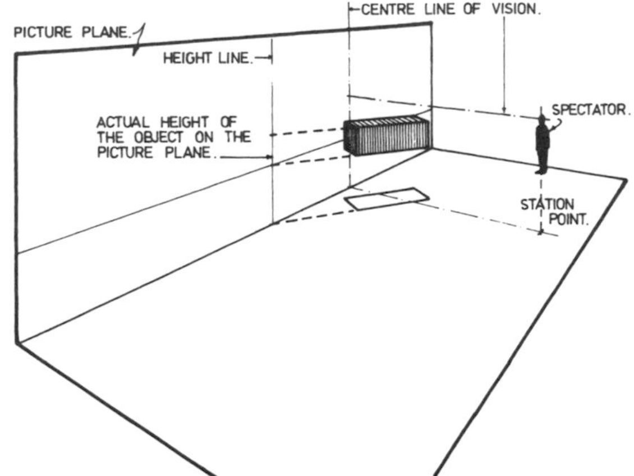

80 A side of the object projected back to meet the picture plane.

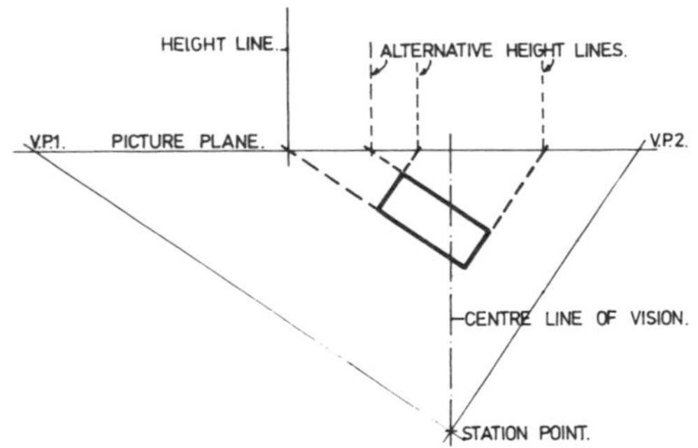

81 Alternative locations of height lines (shown dotted).

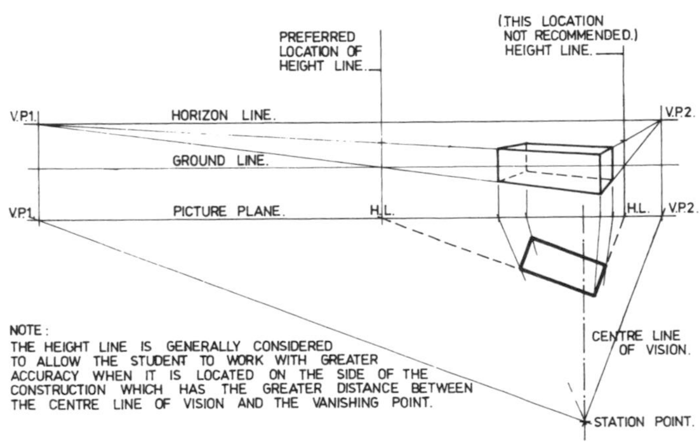

82 Preferred location for the height line.

.1 The Use of Alternative Height Lines for More Complicated Shapes

The height line in perspective drawing is the line used for measuring all vertical heights relating to the object being drawn. These heights are measured using the same scale as that used for the preparation of the plan and elevations of the object being used in the perspective projection. The location of this line is found by projecting a convenient side of the object (in plan) either backwards or forwards as necessary to meet the plan of the picture plane. From this point a vertical line is drawn on the elevation of the picture plane and it is on this line that vertical heights can be measured. Fig. 80 shows graphically the relationship between the plan and the actual side of the object projected back to meet the picture plane. From this it can be seen that the top and bottom of the extended side meet the picture plane on the line projected up from the plan location of the height line and because the top and bottom lines of the object are parallel the distance between them remains the same when they are projected to meet the height line. Therefore heights can be measured on the height line because it is in fact a continuation of the side being measured.

Any side of the object can be projected either forwards or backwards as necessary to locate a height line. Fig. 81 shows each of the four sides of the object projected to meet the picture plane, resulting in four alternative locations for the height line. Each location will be accurate because each height line is located by projecting a side of the object back to meet the picture plane. However, the most convenient height line is the one usually accepted. In this case it is the one which was located by projecting the side of the object used to locate the vanishing point which is the further from the centre line of vision (V.P.1. in this case). The use of this height line rather than one of the alternative ones is considered to result

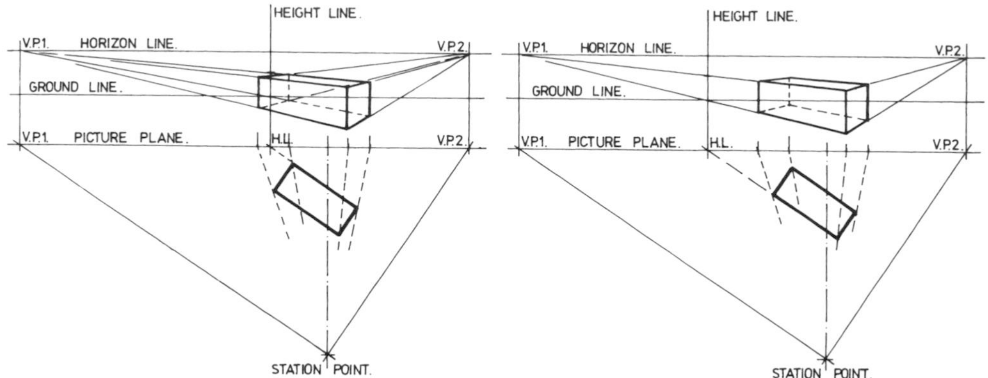

The selection of one of the two sides forming the back of the object for the location of the height line can not only increase the number of projections required in setting up a perspective drawing, thus increasing the possibility of error, but as can be seen in the diagram here it can also contribute to confusion.

The use of the recommended side for locating the height line can save extra work and reduce the possibility of error.

83 Locating the height line – the right and the wrong way.

in more accurate work because when the angle between two intersecting lines is small it is more difficult to locate the point of intersection than when the angle between the lines is nearer to a right angle. This can be understood by reference to Fig. 82 which shows a perspective line passing through a point measured on a height line at a small angle, i.e. from a vanishing point close to the centre line of vision, and one passing through a point on a height line at a much greater angle, i.e. from a vanishing point at a much greater distance from the centre line of vision.

The reason one of the two unseen sides of a simple rectangular object is not normally used to obtain the height line, though either could be used, is simply a matter of convenience. If one of these two sides were chosen it would require at least one extra set of projections which could consume extra time and increase the chance of error. Fig. 83 shows the extra set of projections required when one of the unseen sides is chosen for locating the height line and, for comparison, the use of the recommended side to obtain the height line which eliminates the extra set of projections.

Once the use of the height line is understood in its simplest form it can be used to save a great deal of time in the setting up of perspective drawings of more complex objects, and objects consisting of a number of components. Figures 84*a*,

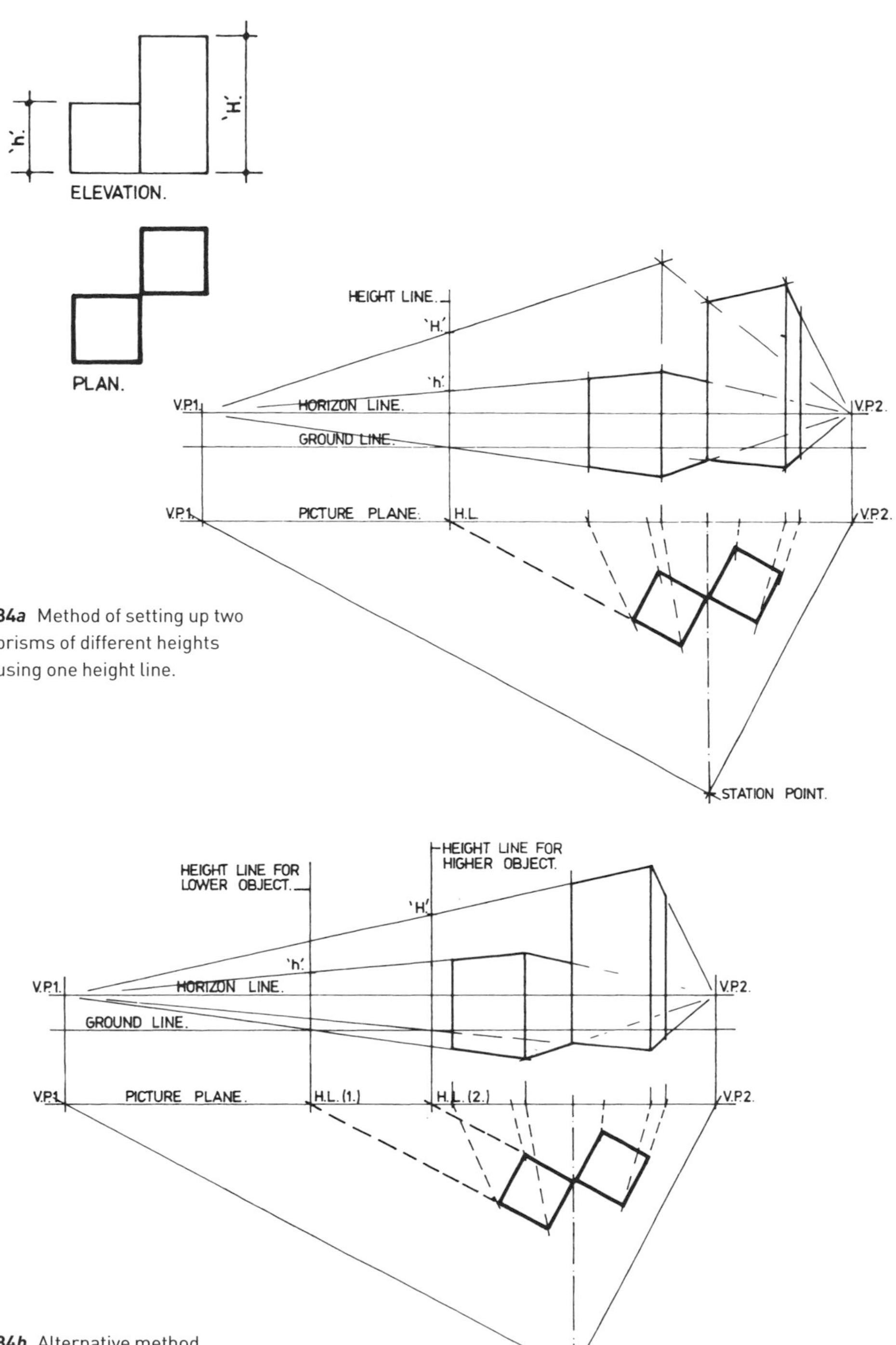

84*a* Method of setting up two prisms of different heights using one height line.

84*b* Alternative method, with two height lines.

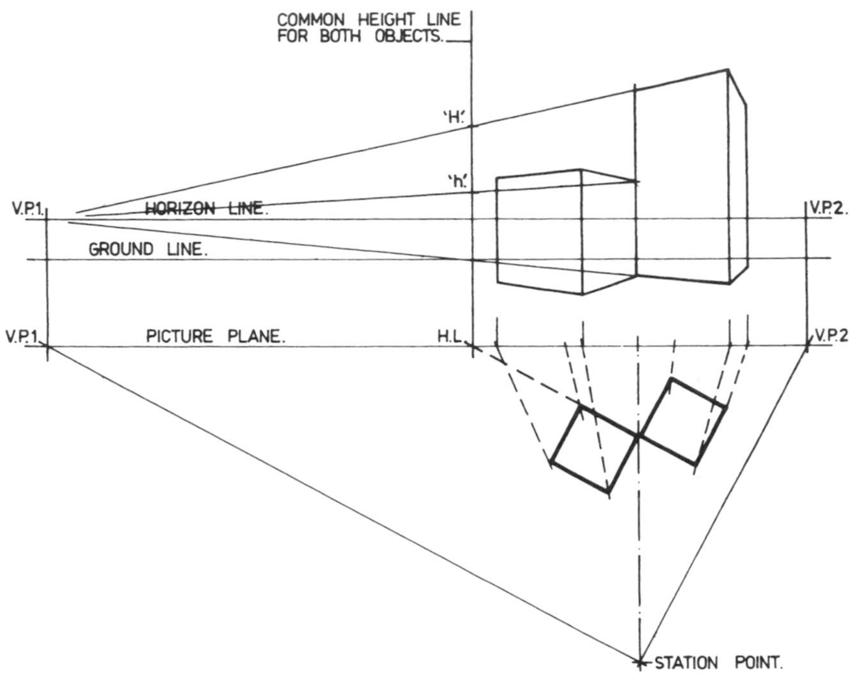

84*c* Alternative method, with one height line.

84*b* and 84*c* show three methods used to set up two simple rectangular prisms of different heights. It could be done using one height line but this would involve a large number of projections, as shown in Fig. 84*a*, which illustrates the method using a side of the lower prism to locate the height line. The projections required to draw the higher prism are unnecessarily complicated if this side is chosen. In this example there are two other alternatives open to the student. A separate height line can be used for each of the objects as shown in Fig. 84*b*. However, if the objects are examined it will be seen that only one height line is needed because if a side of the taller prism is projected back as shown in Fig. 84*c*, it coincides with a side of the shorter prism. In this case the use of this common height line will simplify the work required in setting up these two objects in perspective and not reduce the degree of accuracy, which is very important.

When confronted with a more complex shape in perspective drawing, such as the one shown in Fig. 85, it is often impossible to locate a common height line and therefore each part of the object must be treated as a separate object and a

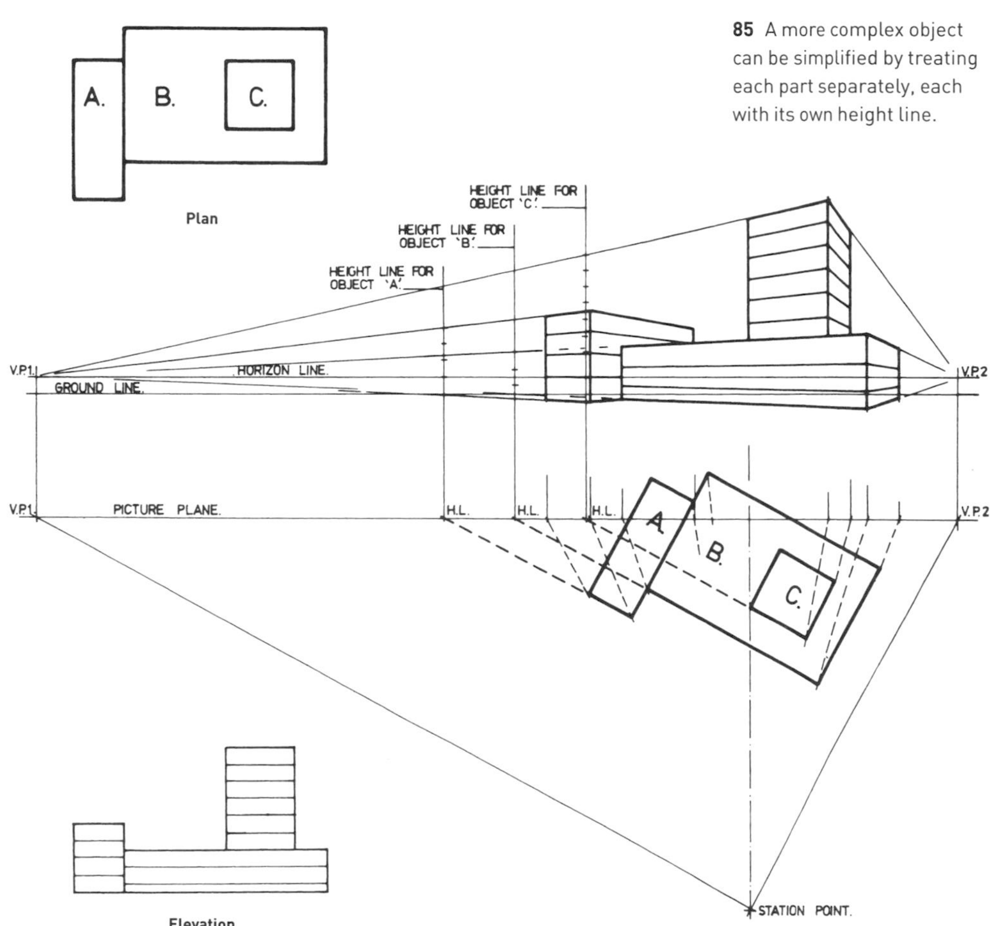

85 A more complex object can be simplified by treating each part separately, each with its own height line.

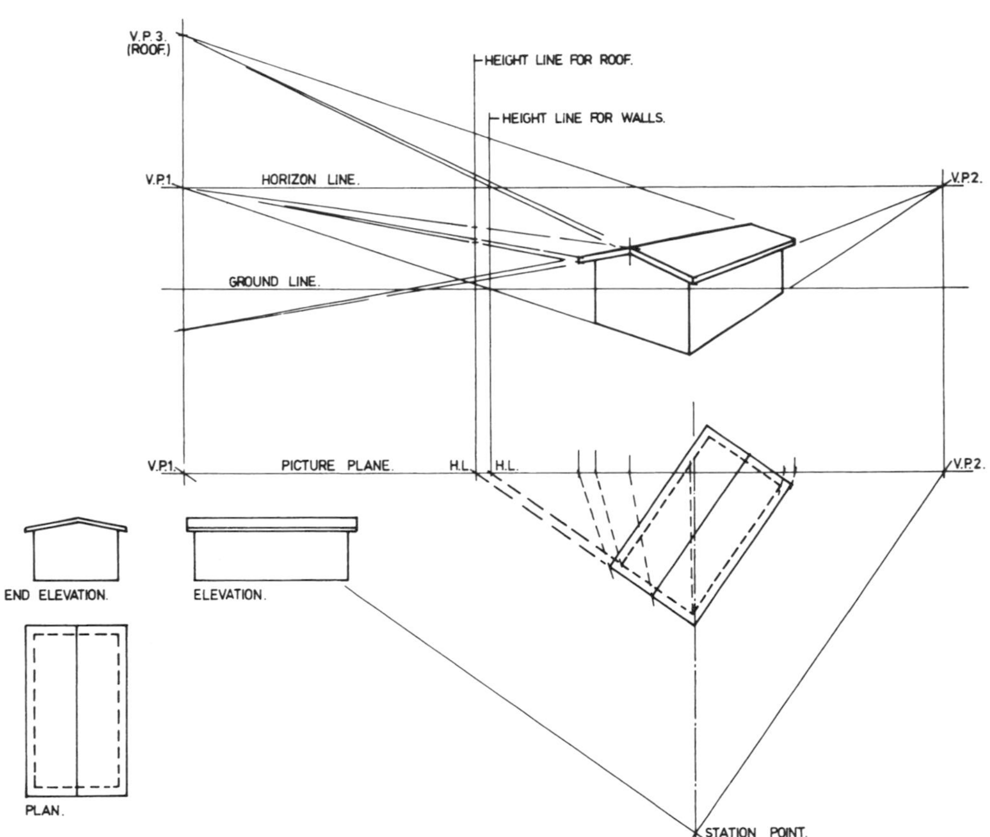

86 A case for using two separate height lines.

separate height line must be located for each part. In this case the first part to be drawn is the lowest section; this simplifies the drawing of the part located on it and the medium-height part can be left until last.

When preparing a perspective drawing of an object it is important to examine all of the possibilities so that unnecessary work is either eliminated or kept to a minimum, because unnecessary work often leads to the possibility of errors as well as wasted time. Fig. 86 shows a commonly encountered problem which can be greatly simplified if a second height line is used. In this case the pitched roof should be considered first and a height line for the roof located. The pitched roof should be treated as if it were a simple object containing inclined lines. When the roof is completed the walls of the building can be considered as a separate object, for which a separate height line will be required. This approach minimizes the amount of work necessary to produce a perspective drawing of an object of this type.

Once the delineator realizes that he is not limited to one or in fact any given number of height lines when drawing a perspective view of an object he will find that the use of alternative height lines is a great time-saver; if he exploits each one fully, he will avoid many inaccuracies which may otherwise occur in his work.

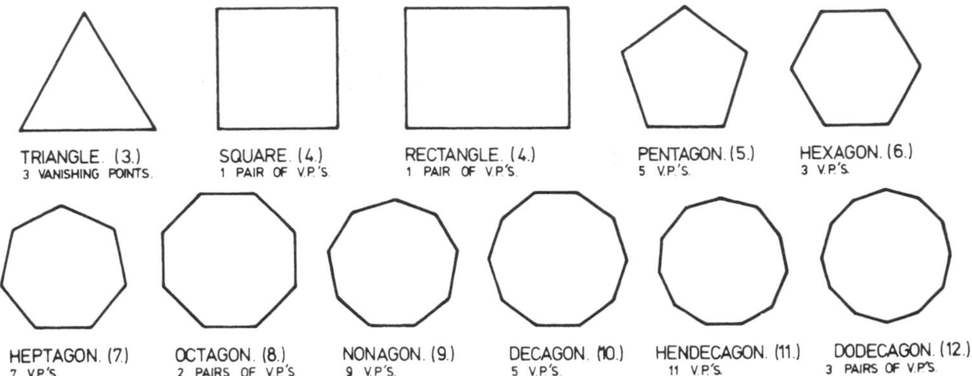

87 Eleven regular shapes, and the number of vanishing points required in each case, for setting up the shape in perspective.

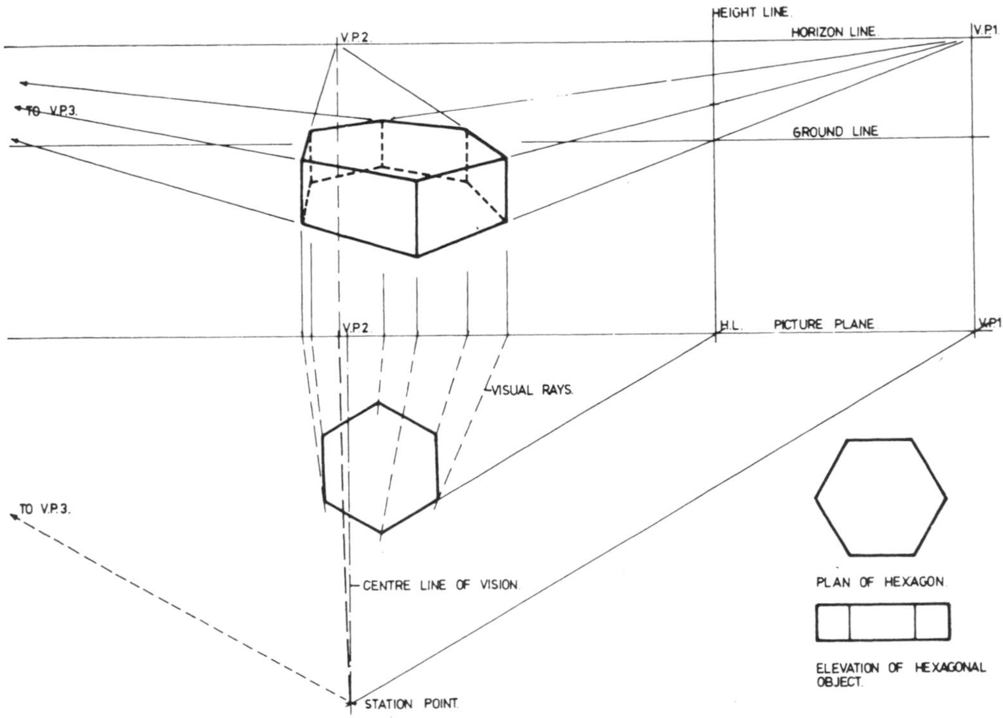

HEIGHT LINE.
V.P.2.
HORIZON LINE.
V.P.1.
TO V.P.3.
GROUND LINE.
V.P.2.
H.L.
PICTURE PLANE.
V.P.1.
VISUAL RAYS.
TO V.P.3.
CENTRE LINE OF VISION.
PLAN OF HEXAGON.
ELEVATION OF HEXAGONAL OBJECT.
STATION POINT.

88 The basic method of drawing a hexagonal object, using three vanishing points.

.2 Regular and Irregular Shapes

Regular shapes, which include squares, rectangles, triangles, and regular polygons, create no special problems. Drawing squares and rectangles in perspective has been covered thoroughly in the first section of this book so it is not intended to consider them further here. However, such shapes as triangles, pentagons, hexagons, heptagons, octagons, etc. are sometimes encountered in perspective drawing and the student should learn to examine the shape to ascertain firstly whether any of its sides are at right angles to another side and secondly whether any of its opposite sides are parallel to each other. These two factors dictate the number of vanishing points required to draw any of these shapes in perspective. For example, a hexagon is a six-sided figure in which no side is at right angles to any other side but which consists of three pairs of parallel sides: therefore only three vanishing points are required to draw a hexagon in perspective. If a triangle and a pentagon are examined in the same way it will be seen that the triangle will also require three vanishing points, and the pentagon will require five (Fig. 87). Pairs of vanishing points are required when a shape has sides at right angles to other sides, e.g. a square, a rectangle, an octagon, etc. The reason for this should be readily understood by referring to the basic principles of perspective projection. Fig. 88 shows the method used for setting up a perspective view of a simple hexagonal object. The selection of a station point, the centre line of vision and the location of the picture plane are the same as for any other shape. The location of the horizon line and the ground line is exactly the same as for any other perspective drawing of an object situated on the ground plane. The height line is located by projecting any convenient side back to the picture plane in the usual way and, similarly, each of the vanishing points is located by drawing

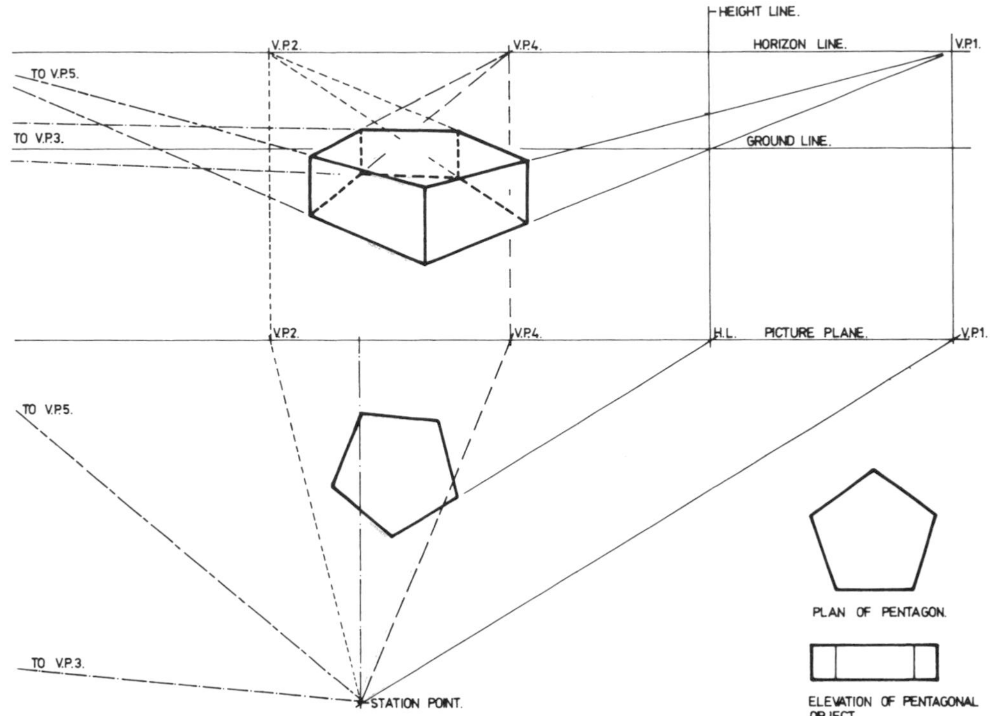

89 The basic method of drawing a pentagonal object, using five vanishing points.

a sight line from the station point parallel to the side to be drawn to meet the picture plane. If this is done in sequence, so that each side is drawn in the perspective view before the next is considered, drawing a hexagonal shape is no more difficult than drawing a simple rectangle.

A pentagon, unlike the hexagon, does not have any of its sides parallel which means that each side requires its own vanishing point (Fig. 89). Therefore five vanishing points will be required to draw it in perspective. None of its sides is at right angles to any other side, therefore pairs of vanishing points will not be required. The method is the same as for the hexagonal object except that five vanishing points are required instead of three. Some shapes, such as a triangle, pentagon or hexagon, can sometimes be drawn in perspective by simpler methods. The most popular of these is to construct a square around the shape, as shown in Figs. 90 and 91, because when the shape is contained in a square it can be drawn in simple two-point perspective by

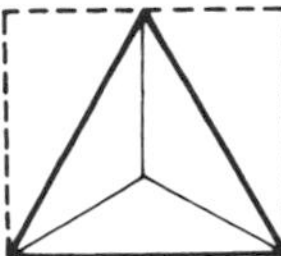

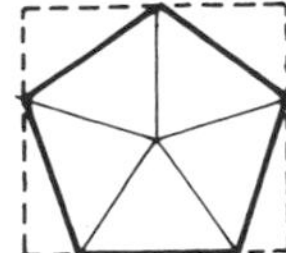

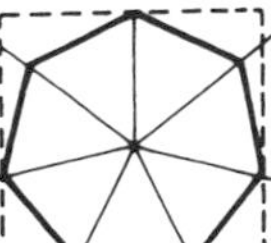

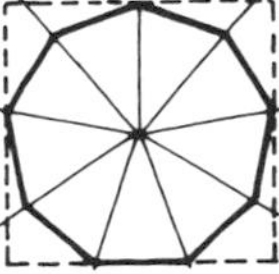

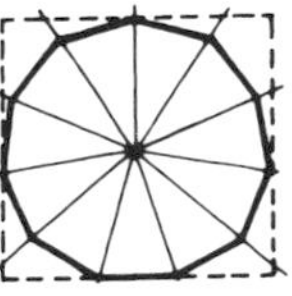

90 Five regular shapes 'in the box' (with squares constructed around them to allow perspective drawings to be made using a one-point or two-point construction). Where some of the points of the object do not touch the sides of the square, as in the heptagon, the nonagon and the hendecagon, lines are drawn from the centre of the object through these points to intersect the sides of the square. These points of intersection on the sides of the square can be used in the perspective construction in much the same way as the actual points of the object which do touch the sides of the square.

91 An alternative method of setting up a perspective view of a pentagonal object, using a square constructed round the plan of the object and simple two-point projection.

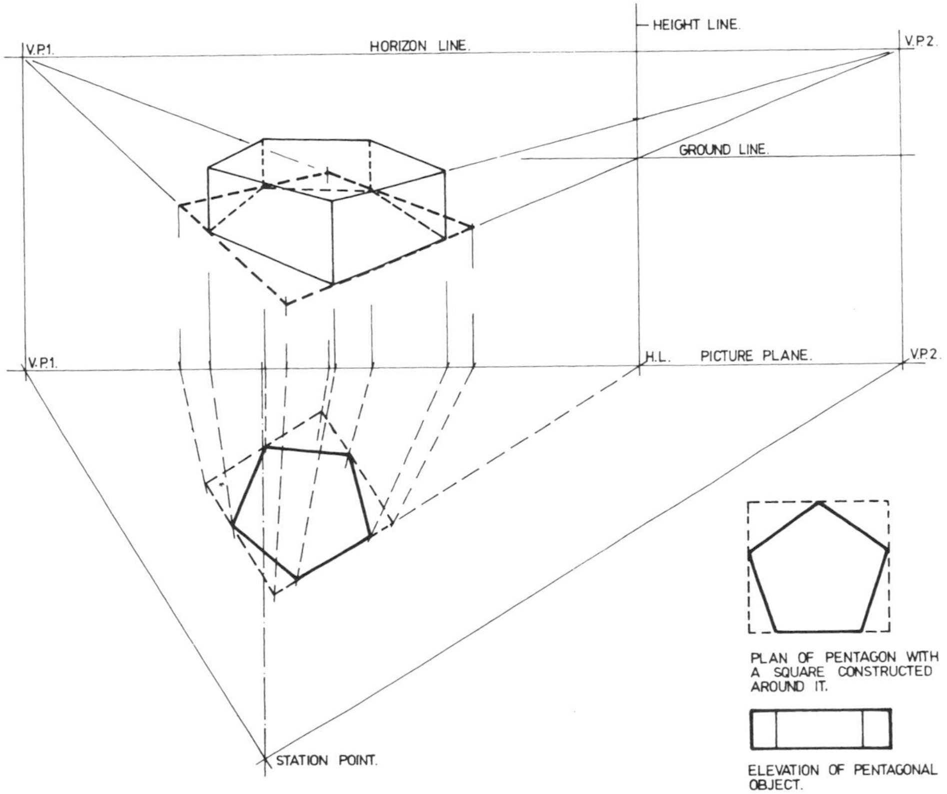

HEIGHT LINE.
V.P.1.
HORIZON LINE.
V.P.2.
GROUND LINE.
V.P.1.
H.L.
PICTURE PLANE.
V.P.2.
PLAN OF PENTAGON WITH A SQUARE CONSTRUCTED AROUND IT.
ELEVATION OF PENTAGONAL OBJECT.
STATION POINT.

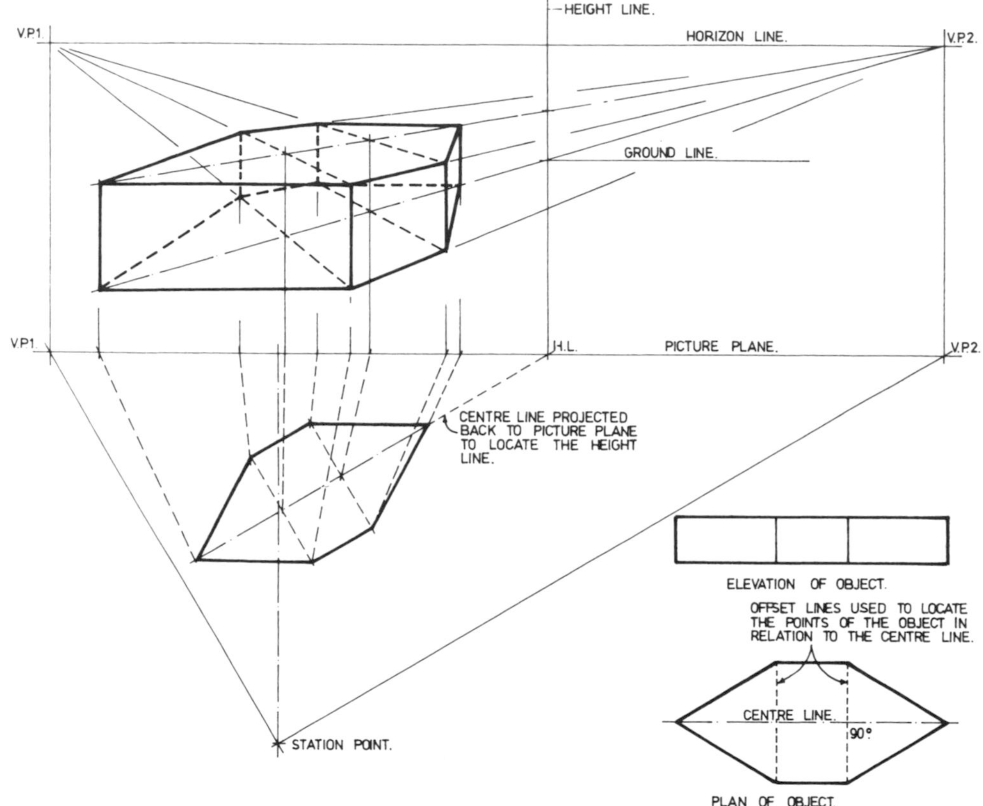

92 The use of a base line (which in this example is also the centre line) and offsets to set up a perspective drawing.

locating on the square the points where the shape contained in it touches the sides of the square. This method of setting up an object in perspective is known as 'placing the object in a box', and by this method even the most complex shapes can be drawn in simple one-point or two-point perspective. This 'box' method of drawing objects is dealt with more fully in Chapter 2.4 (pp. 127–28).

Another method which can be used in special cases for drawing regular shapes in perspective involves the use of a centre line at right angles to one of the sides. This side and the centre line can be set up as a simple one-point or two-point perspective and the other points of the shape can be located by using offsets from the centre line. This is the usual method for irregular shapes but it can be applied in some cases to regular-shaped objects with considerable success.

When dealing with irregular shapes such as irregular quadrilaterals, irregular polygons or irregular curves the use of a base line which can be established to suit the shape, together with offsets to locate the changes of direction, makes even the most complex shapes comparatively easy to draw in perspective. A simple shape such as the one shown in Fig. 92 can be set up in two-point perspective by drawing a centre line of the object on the plan together with two offsets on each side of the centre line (which is used as the base line in this example). The offsets are always drawn at right angles to the base line, which means that the base line and the offsets, instead of the sides of the object, are used to locate the height line and the vanishing points. Once these are established, the rest of the set-up is exactly the same as for any other two-point perspective.

The construction shown in Fig. 92 is for an object which is symmetrical about a centre line but from this example it should be clear to the student that this method will work equally well for an object which is not symmetrical about

93 For an asymmetrical object, a base line is arbitrarily drawn as convenient, with offsets to the outside angles of the object.

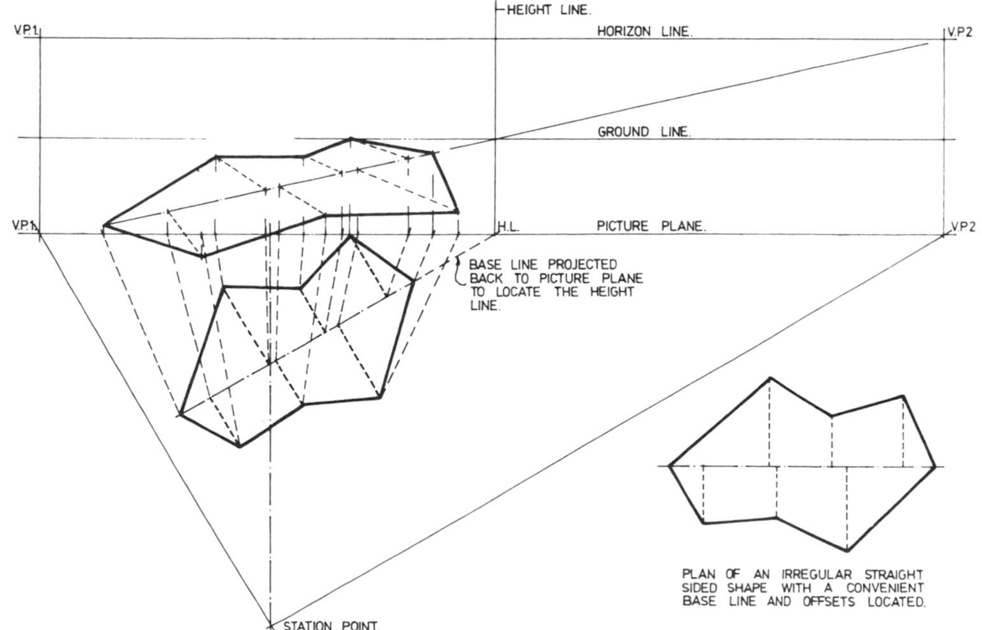

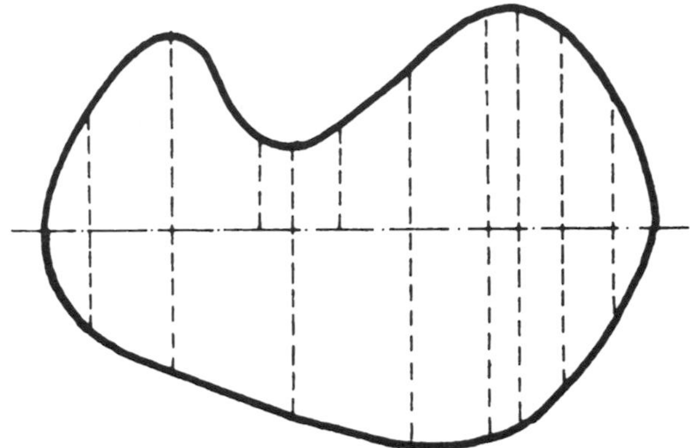

94 An irregular curved shape with a convenient base line and offsets located. The more offsets used, the greater the accuracy of the resulting perspective drawing.

a centre line. The irregular multisided object shown in Fig. 93 does not have a centre line about which it is symmetrical so a convenient base line must be established, together with sufficient offsets to locate all of the points where the sides of the object change direction. (It should always be remembered that the offsets must be at right angles to the base line.) Once the base line and the offsets are established, this object can be drawn in simple one-point or, as here, two-point perspective. This method is not limited to shapes with straight sides but can be used with considerable accuracy for irregularly shaped objects whose sides are made up of constantly changing curves, such as the example shown in Fig. 94. In this case the greater the number of offsets used the greater will be the accuracy of the perspective drawing of the object.

There are no hard-and-fast rules for locating the base line for an irregularly shaped object; the student should use his judgment and locate the base line in the position which eliminates as much unnecessary work as possible.

2.3 Perspective Drawings with a Grid Over the Plan

When none of the above methods seems to give the complete answer to a problem involving complex shapes an alternative which can be used is the grid method. Fig. 95 shows part of a map, somewhat simplified for the purpose of illustrating the method of setting up a perspective drawing of an object of this type. With particularly complex shapes such as this the use of a base line and offsets is not always advisable. Instead a simple grid can be constructed over the whole of the part of the map or object forming the subject of the perspective drawing thus producing a series of simple squares which can be drawn quickly and easily in either one-point or two-point perspective.

A grid of suitable size should be adopted with regard to the character and scale of the object to be drawn in perspective (Fig.96). Fig. 97 shows the method of setting up the grid in two-point perspective and locating the outline of the map by using visual rays through the points in the plan where the outline of the map intersects the lines of the grid superimposed on it. In this way an accurate perspective drawing of this part of the map can be obtained. If, in addition, the contour heights are available, it is possible to obtain not only the correct outline in perspective but also the accurate rise and fall of the land. The result is a complete and accurate picture of this part of the map in perspective. From the example in Fig. 98 it should be obvious that the height of the land above each intersection of the grid can be found. These heights (calculated from some base level, such as sea level in the example here) can be measured on the height line and projected in the normal way to their appropriate intersection, thus locating the level of the land at that point. This may be a tedious and time-consuming task but it has a number of applications, particularly where large building projects

95 Part of a simplified map, to be drawn in perspective.

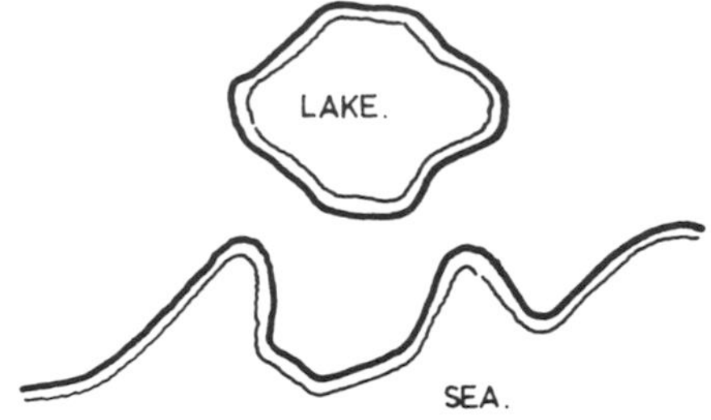

96 Grid superimposed on Fig. 95 to simplify the drawing of the map in perspective. Any convenient size of grid can be chosen, depending on the accuracy and the amount of detail required.

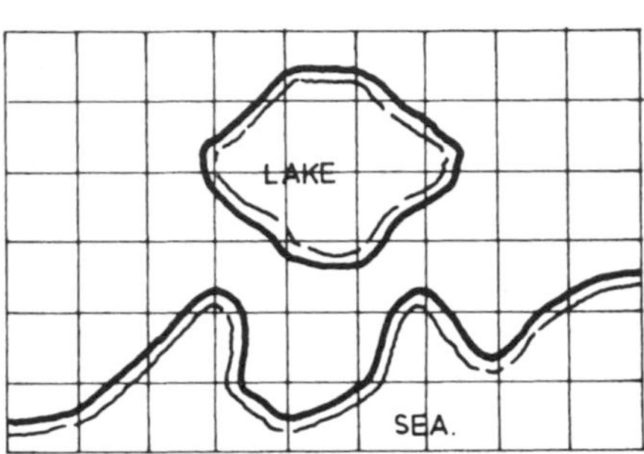

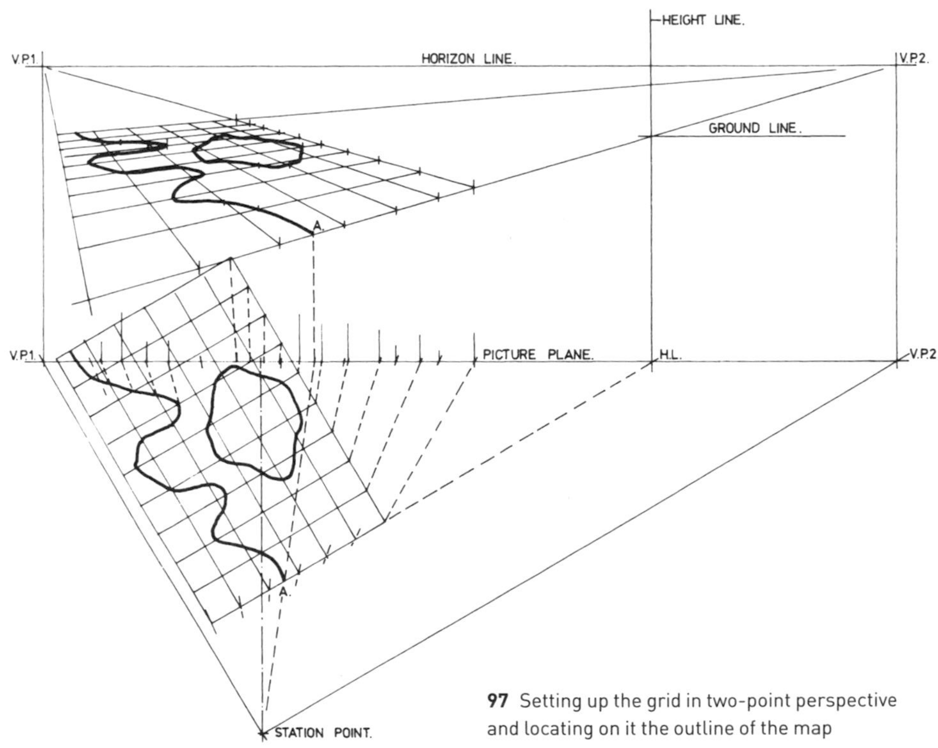

97 Setting up the grid in two-point perspective and locating on it the outline of the map

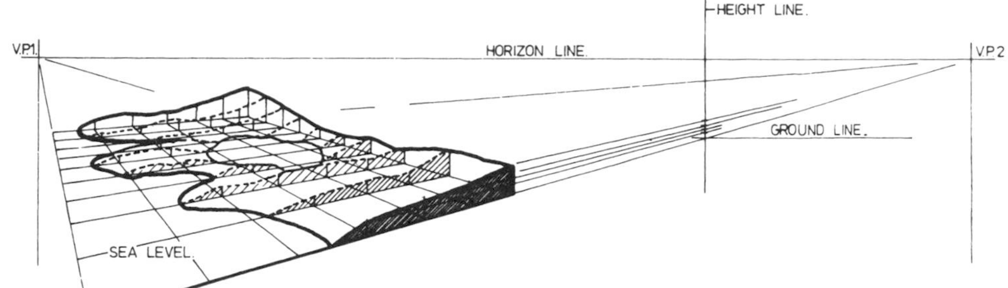

covering large areas of land are involved, or other developments such as bridges or large landscaping projects where accuracy is demanded in a basic perspective drawing.

The use of a grid over a complex shape has many other uses in perspective drawing besides the one shown here. By using a grid a complicated mural or a free-form pool, together with many other objects of complex shapes, can be shown accurately in a perspective drawing.

To obtain the most from any of the methods described in this book it is necessary for the student to use his powers of observation and his imagination when approaching any subject with a view to producing a perspective drawing of it. This will usually reward him handsomely in economy of time and in the high degree of accuracy obtained in the final drawing.

98 Using the perspective map of Fig. 97, heights (taken from contour lines) can be located at each intersection of the grid lines. This will allow sections to be set up along the grid lines, as shown, from which an accurate three-dimensional view can be drawn.

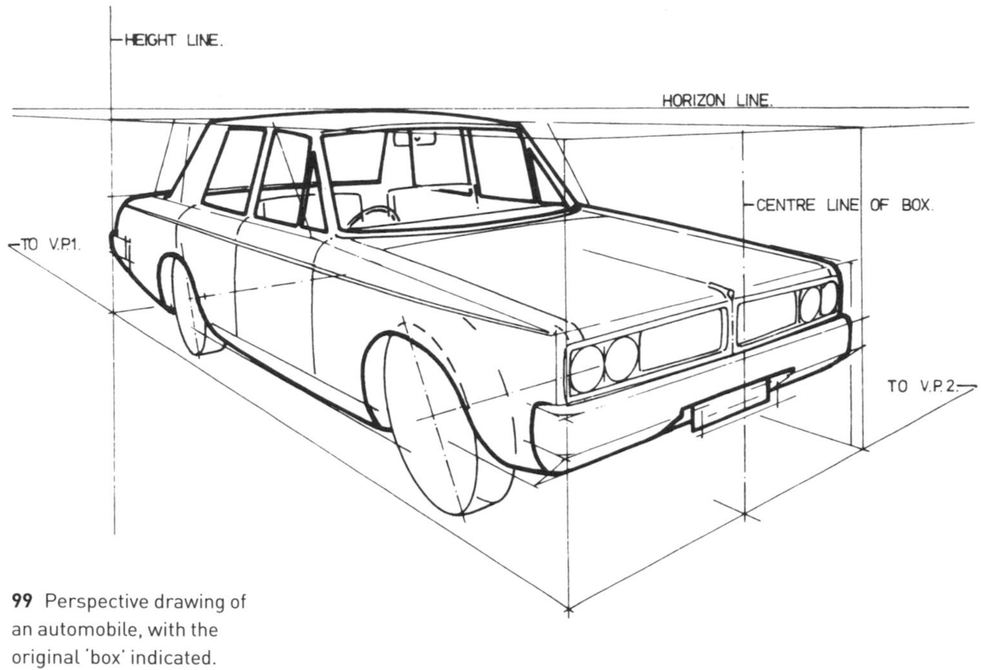

99 Perspective drawing of an automobile, with the original 'box' indicated.

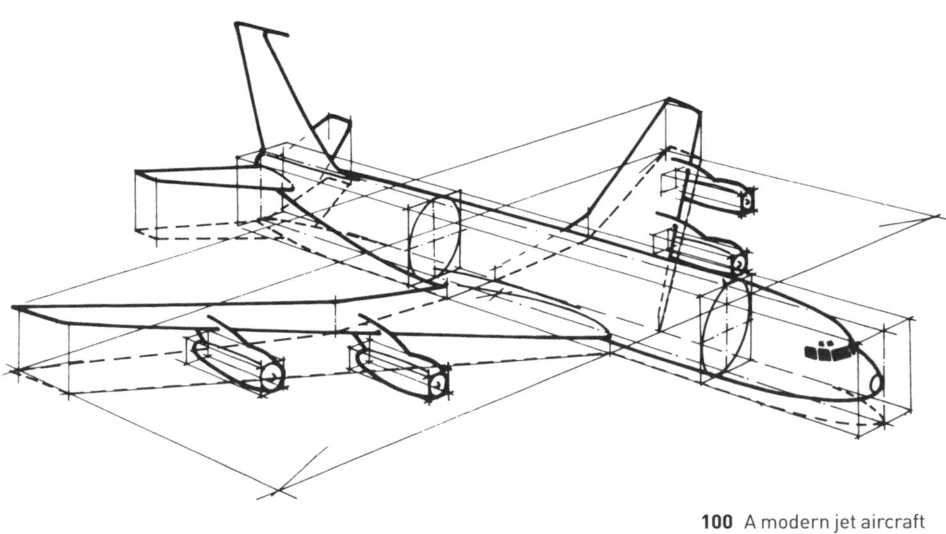

100 A modern jet aircraft drawn in perspective, with the 'box' outlines indicated. Details have been omitted, to show the method of construction more clearly.

.4 The Box Method

It is said, 'If you can draw a rectangular prism in perspective you can draw anything man can make.' This sounds at first like a gross exaggeration or the boast of a self-opinionated delineator trying to impress a prospective client. However, if the statement is examined a little more closely, and in conjunction with various problems, its basic truth becomes apparent.

By referring to the section on drawing regular and irregular shapes in perspective (Fig. 91) it will be found that if a pentagon is enclosed in a square, or 'put in a box', it can be drawn in one-point or two-point perspective in the normal way. In other words, the problem becomes a simple matter of a square box on which certain points are located; the required object is then drawn by joining up these points and removing the box.

The automobile is one object which has always caused the student a great deal of trouble in a perspective construction. However, if the automobile is placed in a box the only problem is to draw a rectangular prism. Once this rectangular prism has been drawn in perspective it remains only to remove parts of the box to obtain the general shape of the automobile (Fig. 99). From this point the degree of refinement is a matter of personal choice but the method for obtaining an accurate shape is based on the assumption that if you can draw a basic rectangular prism (box), you can draw any type of automobile. This still holds true even as the design of the automobile becomes more and more sleek in accordance with the current theories of aerodynamics.

This 'basic box' idea remains true even when drawing such complex shapes as modern jet aircraft. Again, if the aircraft is contained in a box and parts of the box removed according to the dimensions of the aircraft, what is left is an accurate perspective drawing of the aircraft (Fig. 100).

The types of objects with more or less complex shapes that can be fitted into a simple rectangular prism for the purpose

101 The 'box' method applied to two chairs.

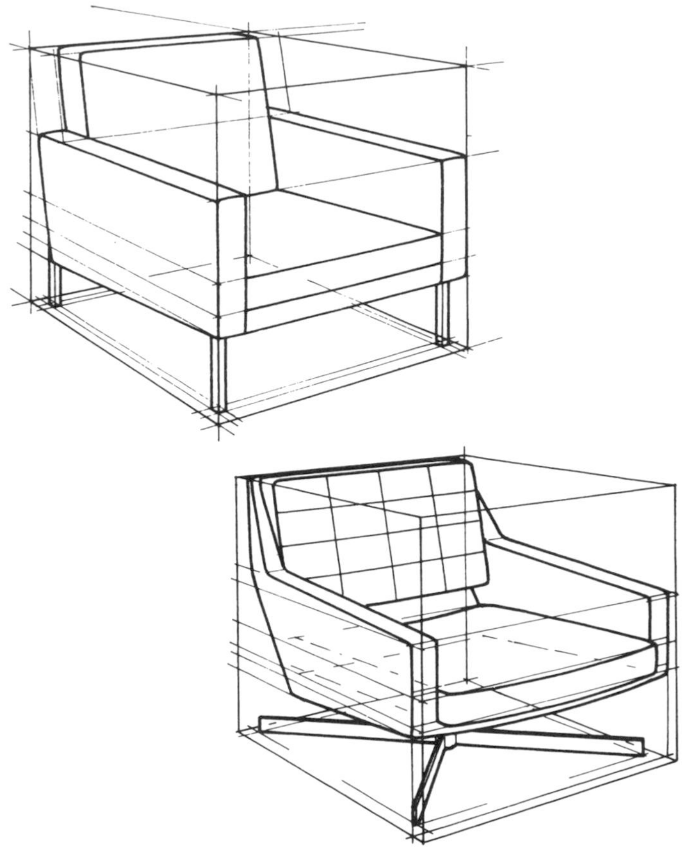

of drawing them in perspective are almost endless and include such objects as boats, ships, railway rolling stock, buses, road transport, machinery of all types, sculpture, equipment, furniture and fittings. Of these, the most common items with which the student has difficulty is the chair. In perspective drawing the chair is greatly simplified if it is first placed in a box from which pieces are cut out until the required shape of the chair remains. Fig. 101 shows the method of using the box for both a simple chair and a slightly more complex one. Without the box even the simple chair is difficult to draw in perspective but once the problem becomes a basic rectangular prism it is greatly simplified, and removing parts of the box to leave the required chair shape is a comparatively easy exercise. In other words, 'if you can draw a rectangular prism in perspective you can draw anything man can make.'

.5 Circles, Cylinders and Spheres

Perhaps the most difficult of all shapes to handle accurately in perspective drawing is the circle. The only time a true circle is seen in perspective drawing is when it is located parallel to the picture plane, i.e. at right angles to the centre line of vision, and as this very seldom occurs it can almost be discounted. Except for this rare occurrence, it is seen in a perspective drawing as an ellipse or a straight line. When a circle which is located at right angles to the picture plane and parallel to the centre line of vision coincides with the centre line of vision it is seen by the spectator as a straight line (Fig. 102), either horizontal or vertical depending on whether the circle is parallel to the ground plane or at right angles to it. As the circle is moved further away from the centre line of vision, in any direction, without changing its angle to either the ground or the picture plane, the spectator sees more of the face of the circle. That is to say the circle appears to him as an ellipse which increases in width as it is placed further from the centre line of vision.

At this point the student needs to understand something about the ellipse as a geometric figure in order to understand how it is handled in perspective drawing. An ellipse is an oval figure constructed on two unequal axes, a major axis and a minor axis, which always bisect each other at right angles. The ellipse consists of four identical quadrants, as shown in Fig. 103. The only other fact which need be known at this stage is that an ellipse can always be contained in a rectangle. An ellipse is among the more difficult figures for the student to attempt and the few instruments that are available for drawing ellipses are somewhat expensive. This makes it necessary for the student to look at the various other methods which can be used for drawing ellipses.

When using a freehand line to draw an ellipse it is necessary first to set up the major and the minor axes and

102 The appearance of a disk viewed at different distances from the centre line of vision.

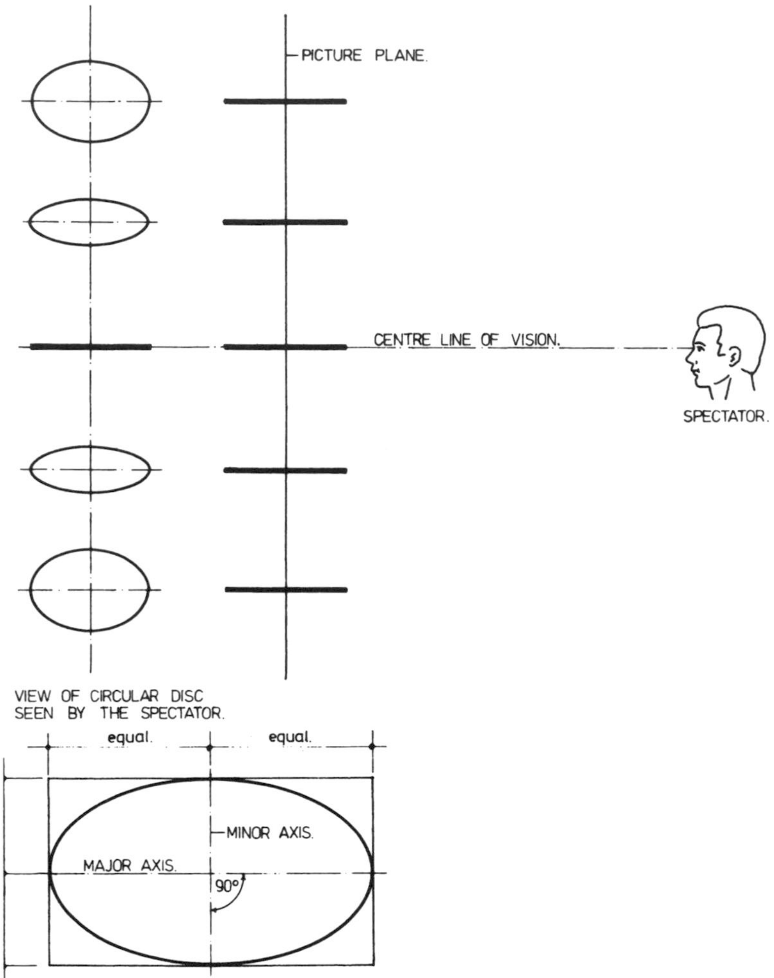

103 The geometry of the ellipse.

also the rectangle which will contain the final ellipse. Fig. 104 shows the steps required for drawing a freehand ellipse and also the finished ellipse. A great deal of practice is needed before acceptable ellipses can be produced in this way and a modification of this method will probably achieve better results for the student. This modification, shown in Fig. 105, consists of the same basic set-up of the major and minor axes together with the rectangle surrounding the ellipse. The next step consists of the accurate drawing of one quadrant only of the ellipse. A tracing is then taken of the quadrant, the major and the minor axes and the quarter of the rectangle to be

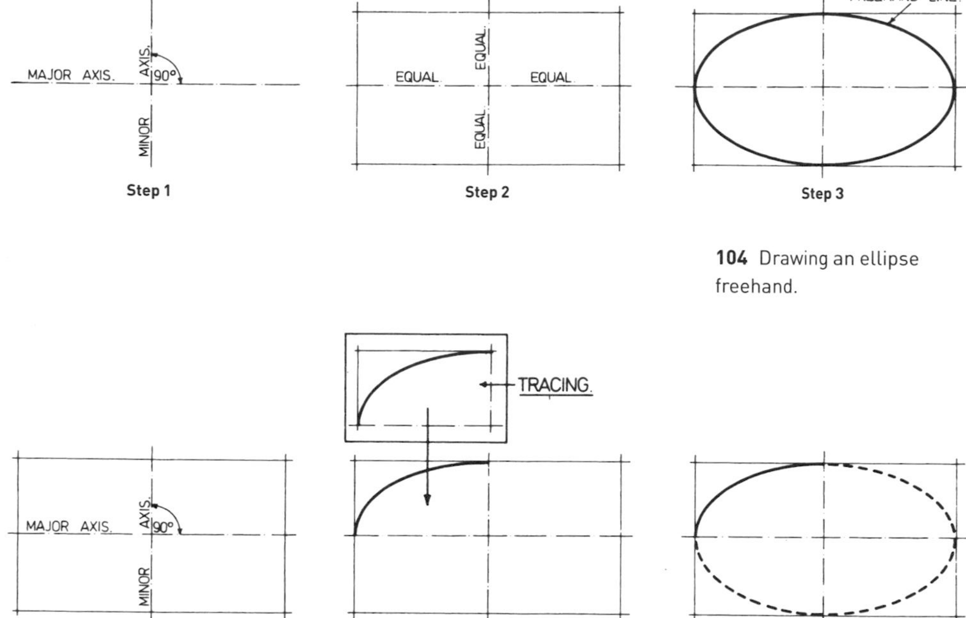

104 Drawing an ellipse freehand.

105 Alternative method for freehand drawing of an ellipse.

used as reference. Using the tracing the other three quadrants of the ellipse can be drawn to complete the ellipse. Again, practice is necessary before good ellipses are produced.

There are a number of other methods which can be used to produce an ellipse. Though some of these methods still rely on a freehand line finally to draw the ellipse they are considered more accurate than the freehand methods shown in Figs. 104 and 105 because more points on the curve of the ellipse are located. The method shown in Fig. 106 is one where the points on the curve are located by the intersection of lines. Half of the major axis is divided into a number of equal parts (four in this case). Half one end of the rectangle containing the ellipse is also divided into the same number of equal parts. From point *A* lines are drawn through the divisions of the major axis and from point *B* through the divisions of the end of the rectangle. The curve of the ellipse is then drawn using a freehand line through the intersections of these lines. The other three quadrants can be constructed in

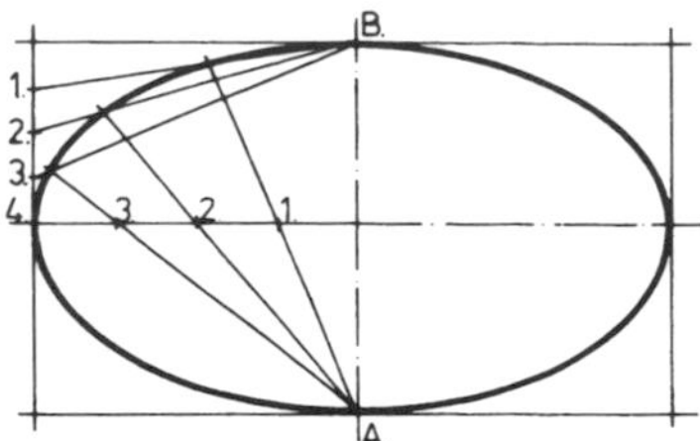

106 Drawing an ellipse by intersection of lines.

MAJOR AXIS
MINOR AXIS
Trammel
TRAMMEL

107 Drawing an ellipse: the trammel method.

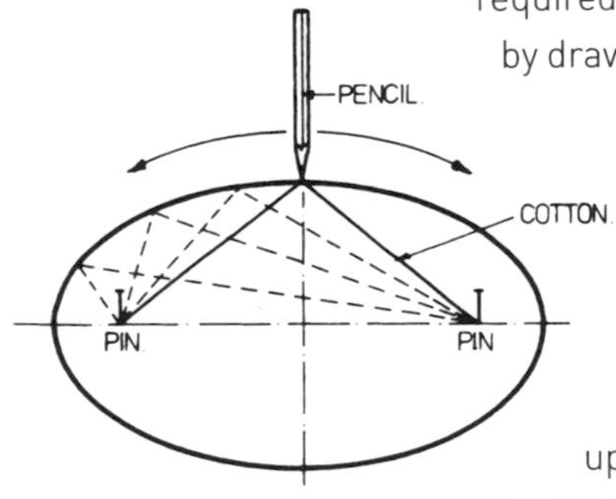

108 Drawing an ellipse with pins and cotton.

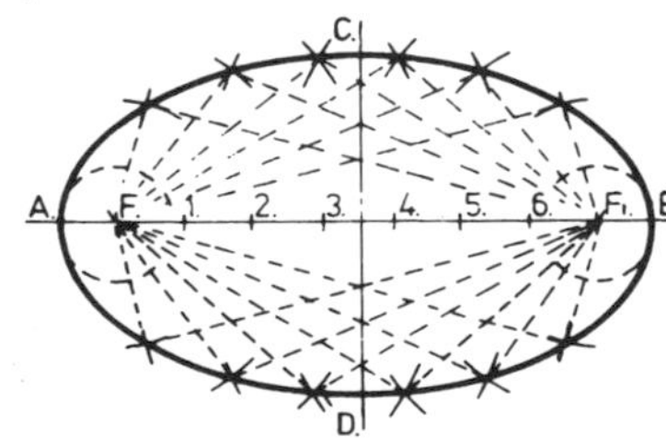

109 Drawing an ellipse: freehand method by arcs from the foci.

the same way or the completed quadrant can be traced as previously described and the ellipse can be completed with the aid of the tracing.

The method shown in Fig. 107 is known as the trammel method and is one of the most favoured because it avoids a mass of construction lines which are required by some of the other methods. This method requires the setting up of the minor and major axes. A straight strip of card or stout paper (a trammel) is placed along the major axis and half the length of the major axis is marked along the trammel. From the same end of the trammel half the length of the minor axis is also marked. The trammel is placed on the drawing so that the two marks separated by the difference between the two halves of the axes fall on the major and minor axes as shown. The trammel is moved so that the two marks on it always coincide with the two axes of the ellipse while the third mark on the trammel is used to locate points on the curve of the ellipse. As many points as required can be located in this way. The ellipse is completed by drawing a freehand line through the points located with the aid of the trammel.

Another simple method for drawing ellipses is shown in Fig. 108. This method consists of using two pins and a length of cotton. The two pins are located on the major axis at equal distances from each end. (This method also requires the setting up of the major and the minor axes as the first step.) The piece of cotton is then either tied or looped around the two pins with sufficient slack to allow a pencil point to coincide with one end of the minor axis when the cotton is held taut. The ellipse is drawn by moving the pencil around with the cotton held taut against it.

The method shown in Fig. 109 is based on a similar principle to the previous one but arcs of a circle are used to locate the points on the curve of the ellipse. The ellipse is a continuous line following a curve in such a way that the sum of the distances from any point in the curved line to two fixed points (foci) on the major axis remains

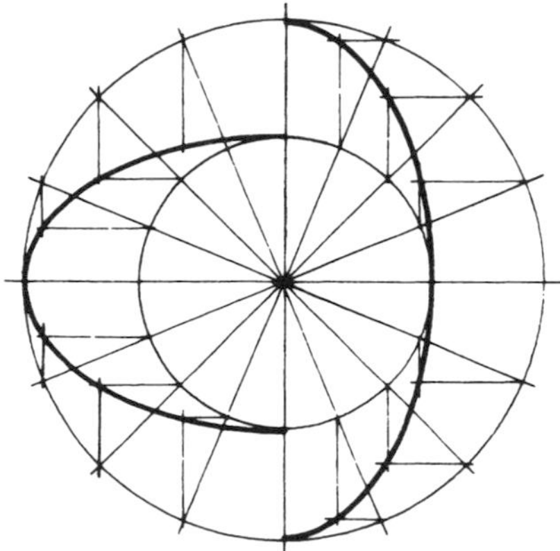

110 Drawing an ellipse: the concentric circle method.

constant. Reference to Fig. 108, in which the piece of cotton remained the same length throughout the exercise, will help the student to understand this principle. In this method as with each of the others the major and the minor axes are located first. The fixed points (foci) are located by swinging an arc from point *C* with a radius equal to half the length of the major axis to meet the major axis at *F* and F_1. The distance between these two fixed points is then divided into an odd number of equal parts (7 in this example). Using fixed point *F* as the centre an arc is drawn with a diameter equal to the distance from *A* to point 1. Arcs can then be drawn through each of the divisions using point *F* as the centre. Using fixed point F_1, arcs are again drawn through each of the divisions. By drawing a freehand line through the intersections of the arcs drawn from points *F* and F_1 the ellipse can be completed.

Fig. 110, the final method to be dealt with here, uses two circles with a common centre. The diameter of the larger circle is equal to the length of the major axis and the diameter of the smaller one is equal to the length of the minor axis. A convenient number of radials are drawn cutting the circumferences of both circles and from these points lines are drawn parallel to the axes. The intersections of these lines locate points on the curve of the ellipse which is drawn by using a freehand line to join the points.

Although the previous examples illustrate a number of methods which can be used for setting up ellipses, it should be noted that the methods used here are by no means all that

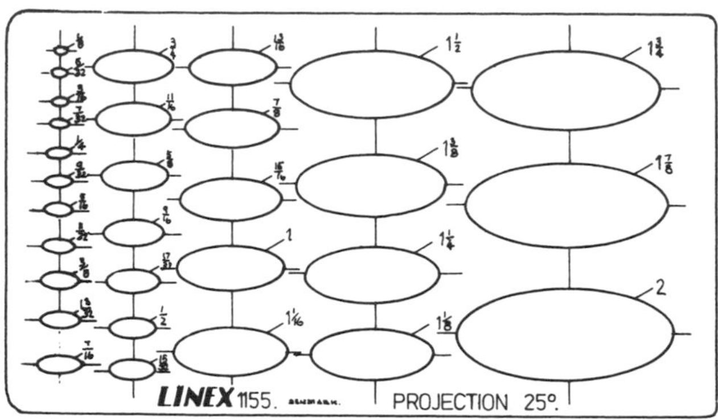

(Half full size)

111 Ellipse template.

are available to the student. However, the ones shown should be sufficient for the purpose of studying circles, cylinders and spheres in perspective.

One of the most valuable aids in drawing ellipses is the ellipse template. However, ellipse templates have one serious limitation: each template has only a limited number of sizes and projections, which means that a student needs access to a large number of templates, but because of the expense involved this is seldom possible. Therefore it is necessary for him to develop his ability to draw ellipses using less expensive methods.

Once the drawing of the ellipse has been mastered it is possible to proceed to the circle in perspective drawing. A true circle can always be surrounded by a true square. If the diagonals of the square are drawn they will pass through the centre of the circle. A true square can also be constructed within a true circle and, similarly, its diagonals will pass through the centre of the circle. Fig. 112 shows a true circle with a true square surrounding it and another constructed within its circumference. This knowledge is very important when circles are to be drawn in perspective because it is necessary first to enclose a circle in a framework of straight lines, so that the framework can be set up in perspective. The points where the curve meets the framework in the plan can be located in the perspective construction and from these the view of the circle in the perspective can be drawn.

In Fig. 113, which shows a plan view of a spectator looking at a circle, it can be seen that, to the spectator, the diameter appears shorter than a line joining the points where the spectator's visual rays meet the circumference of the circle. This line joining the extremities of the circumference of the circle as seen by the spectator must be the major axis of the ellipse which the spectator sees. This means that when a circle is viewed in perspective the major axis does not, as might be expected, coincide with the diameter of the circle. Fig. 114 shows the view of the circle seen by the spectator in Fig. 113 and demonstrates the fact that the centre of the circle cannot coincide with the intersection of the major and the minor axes of the ellipse but falls behind the major axis and in the minor axis. The foreshortening of the two halves of the circle is clearly evident in this figure, which is consistent with the basic principles of perspective projection.

The method used for setting up a perspective view of a circle using a one-point construction relies on the fact that a true circle can be enclosed in a true square. Fig. 115 shows the plan of a circle prepared for perspective drawing with a square constructed around the circle with the vertical and horizontal axes and the diagonals drawn. Once this plan of the circle has been prepared the problem is simply one of drawing a square in perspective, using one-point construction. Fig. 116 shows the method. Once the square is drawn in the perspective view, complete with the vertical and horizontal axes and the diagonals, visual rays can be drawn through the points where the circumference of the circle intersects the axes and diagonals in the plan. These points can then be

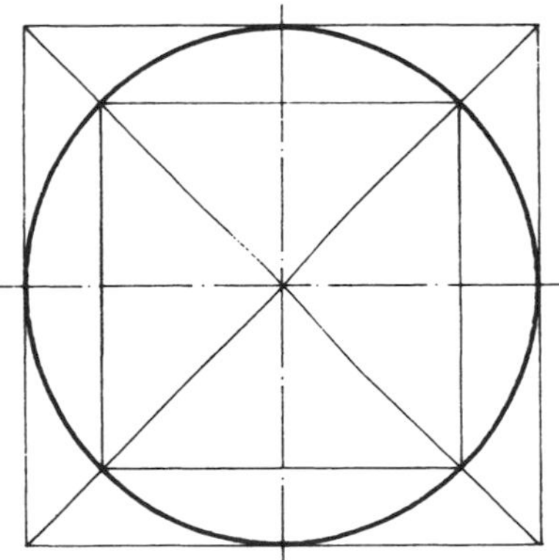

112 The geometry of the circle.

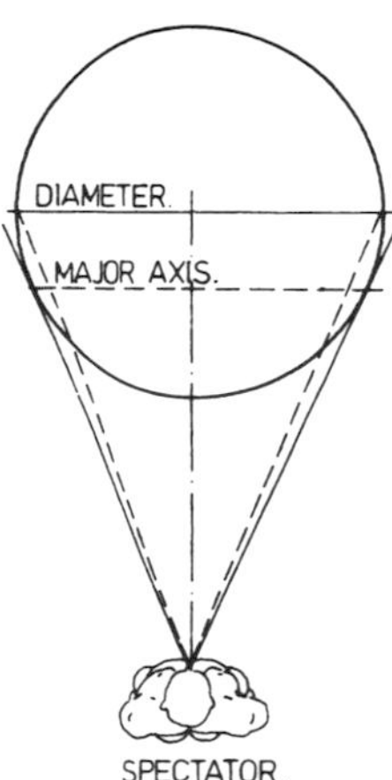

113 Looking obliquely at a circle, showing how the major axis of the resultant ellipse is arrived at.

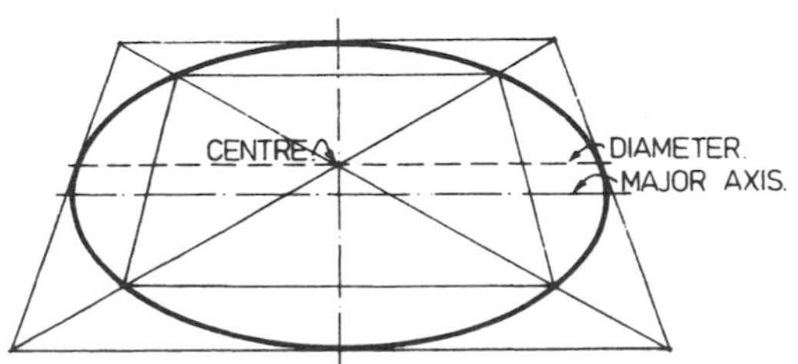

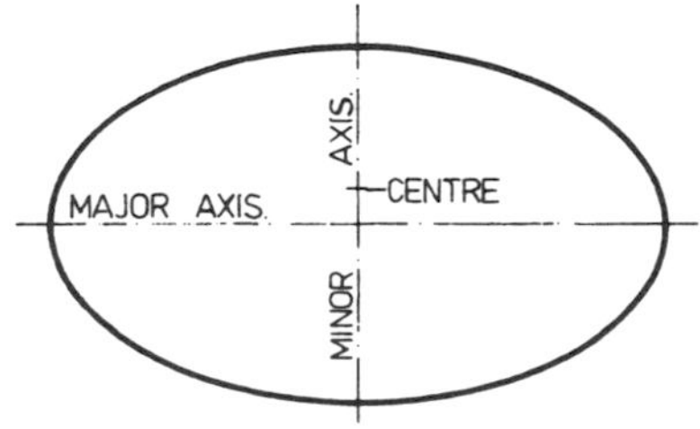

114 The spectator's view of the circle in Fig. 113.

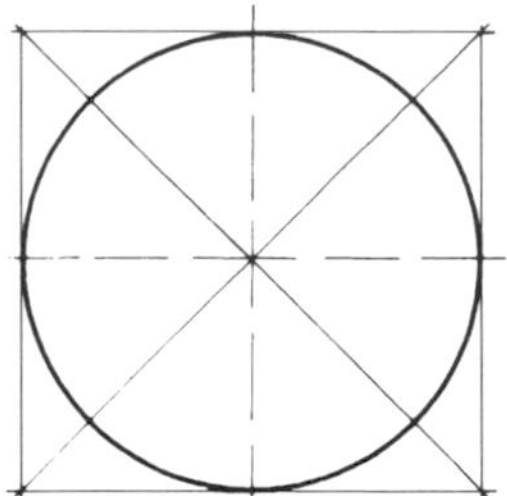

115 Circle prepared for perspective drawing.

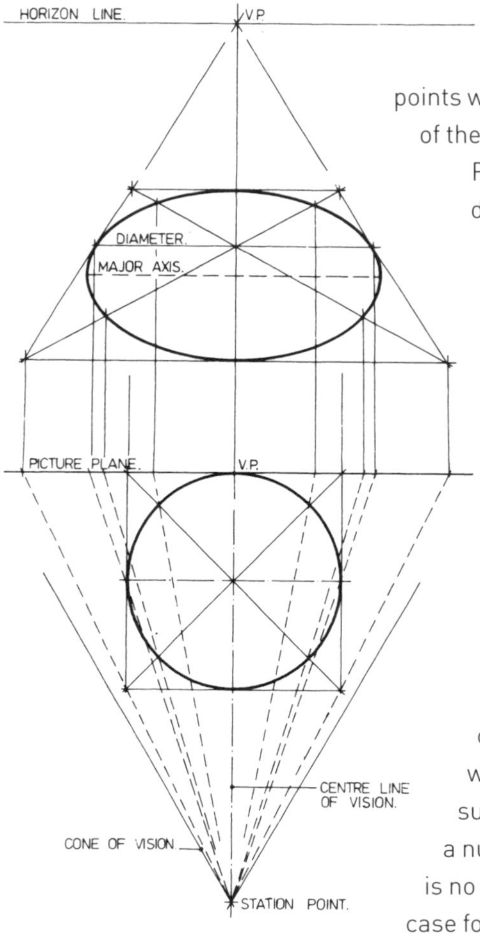

projected up and located in the perspective view. By joining these points with a freehand line the ellipse (the view of the circle in perspective) can be drawn.

Fig. 117 shows the method used for drawing the circle in perspective using a two-point construction. Once the plan is prepared as in Fig. 115 the object to be set up becomes a square which can be set up in the normal way. The points of intersection of the circumference on the axes and the diagonals are located in the perspective view in the same way as they were located in Fig. 116. The ellipse is then drawn by joining these points of intersection with a freehand line.

In Figs. 116 and 117 the centre line of vision passes through the centre of the circle, i.e. the centre line of vision coincides with the minor axis of the ellipse. If the subject of a perspective drawing consists of a number of circles as shown in Fig. 118 this is no longer the case. Rather it is no longer the case for the two outer circles although the middle one still conforms because its centre coincides with the centre line of vision.

116 Drawing a circle in one-point perspective.

It is at this point that one of the anomalies of perspective projection occurs because if the normal method of construction is used, as shown in Fig. 119, the two circles whose centres do not fall in the centre line of vision appear different from the one

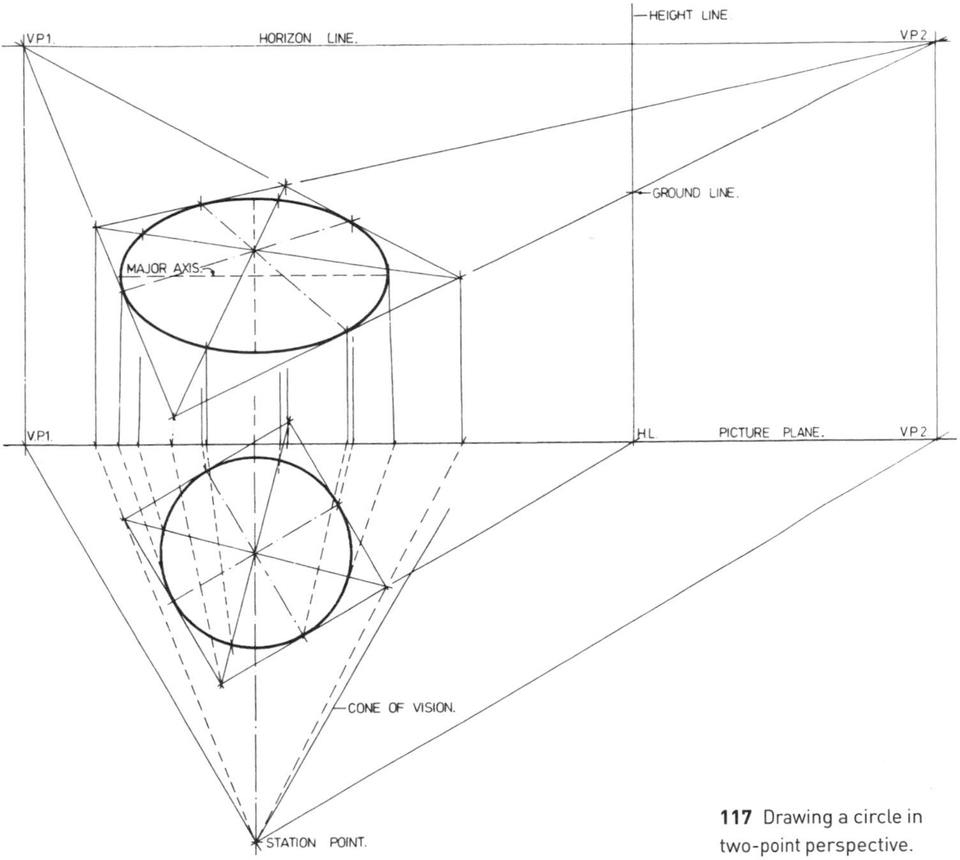

HEIGHT LINE.
V.P.1. HORIZON LINE. V.P.2.
GROUND LINE.
MAJOR AXIS.
V.P.1. H.L. PICTURE PLANE. V.P.2.
CONE OF VISION.
STATION POINT.

117 Drawing a circle in two-point perspective.

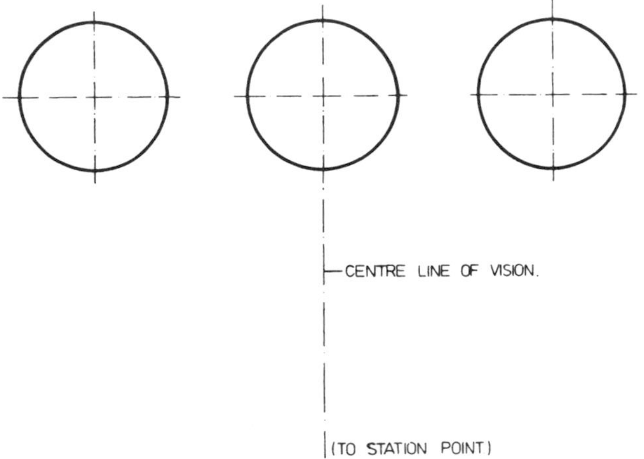

118 Three circles seen from one station point.

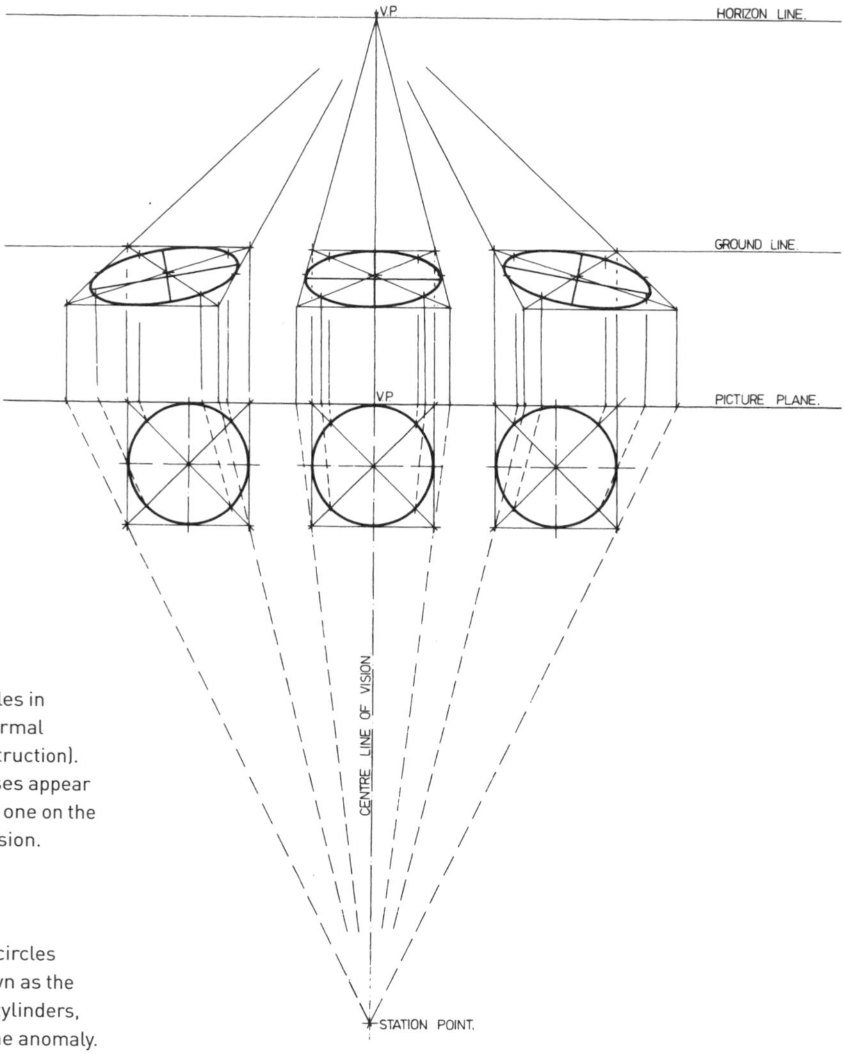

V.P
HORIZON LINE.
GROUND LINE.
V.P
PICTURE PLANE.
CENTRE LINE OF VISION
STATION POINT.

119 Three circles in perspective (normal one-point construction). The outer ellipses appear longer than the one on the centre line of vision.

120 The three circles of Fig. 119 shown as the bases of three cylinders, to emphasize the anomaly.

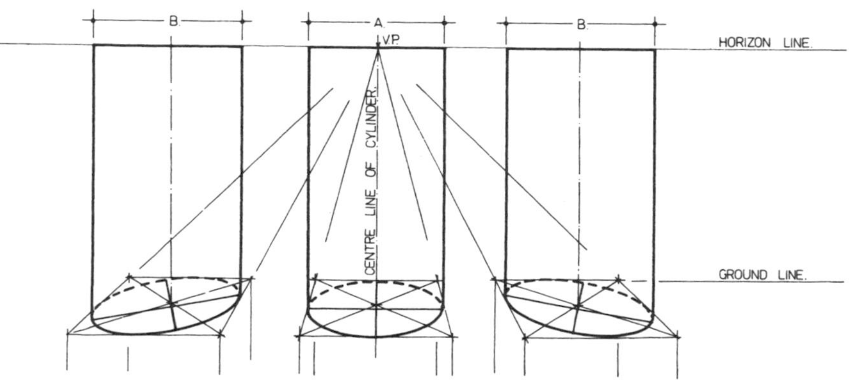

whose centre does coincide with it. When the two outer circles are examined it can be seen that their major and minor axes are no longer horizontal and vertical and in fact the ellipses representing these circles as seen by the spectator appear larger than the middle one. If these three circles are considered as the bases of three cylinders (Fig. 120) it can be seen clearly that the cylinders on either side of the middle one appear distorted. In addition they appear wider than the middle one, which means that they must be closer to the spectator than the middle one. Simple observation of the diagram shows that this cannot be so: therefore the solution shown in Fig. 120 is contrary to the laws of perspective. (Things appear to become smaller as the distance between them and the spectator increases.) Furthermore, the outer sides of the outer cylinders appear to be longer than the sides adjacent to the middle cylinder which again is a contradiction of the laws of perspective.

A
B
C
STATION. POINT.

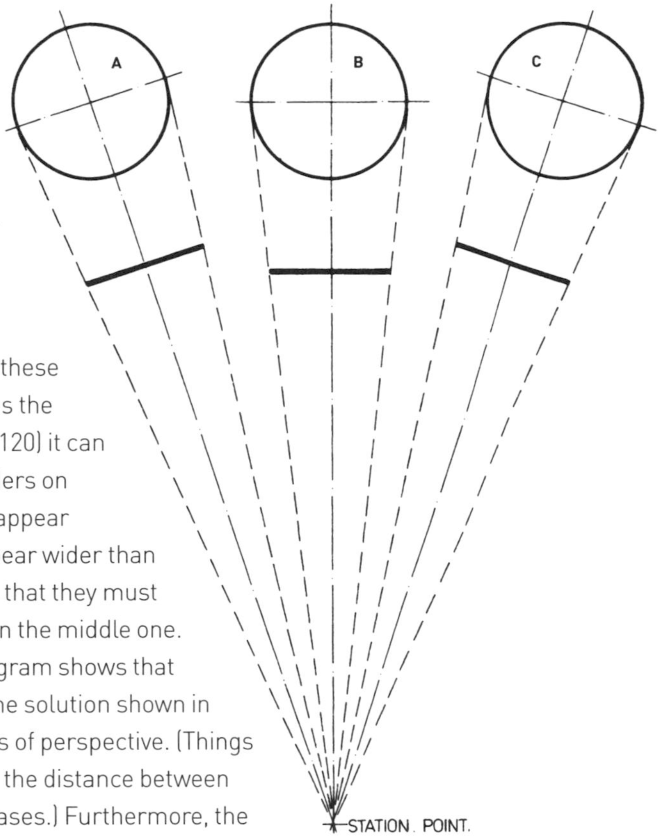

121 The three circles and their relation to the station point. The lines between the visual rays (at the same distance from the centre of the circle in each case) prove that the circles must seem very nearly identical in size to the spectator.

Fig. 121 shows that the spectator in fact sees three cylinders as being virtually the same size. The line between the visual rays in each case is located at the same distance from the centre of each circle. The difference in distances between the spectator and the cylinders is very small in this example and for all practical purposes can be disregarded. However, it could be argued that the distance between the two outer cylinders and the spectator is very slightly greater than the distance between the spectator and the middle one. This would mean that, in theory, the two outer ones should be slightly smaller than the middle one, not larger as they appear in Fig. 120.

Before proceeding further at this stage it is necessary to examine a little more closely what is seen by a spectator when he looks at a circle. It is a fact that a number of spectators

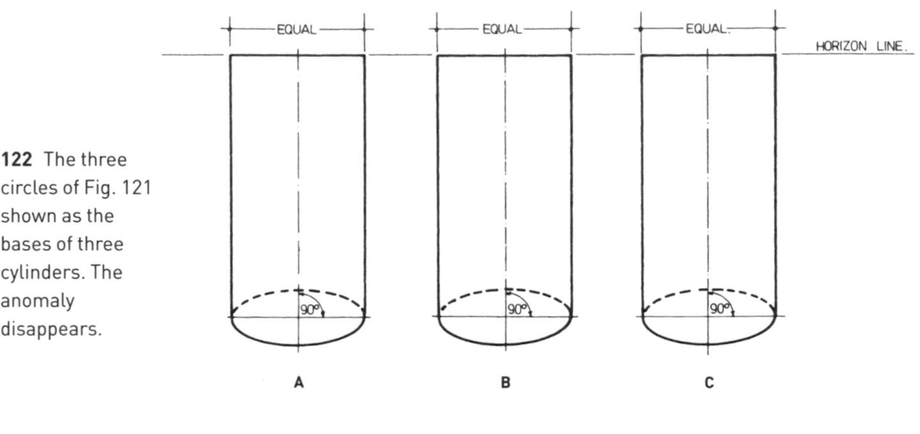

122 The three circles of Fig. 121 shown as the bases of three cylinders. The anomaly disappears.

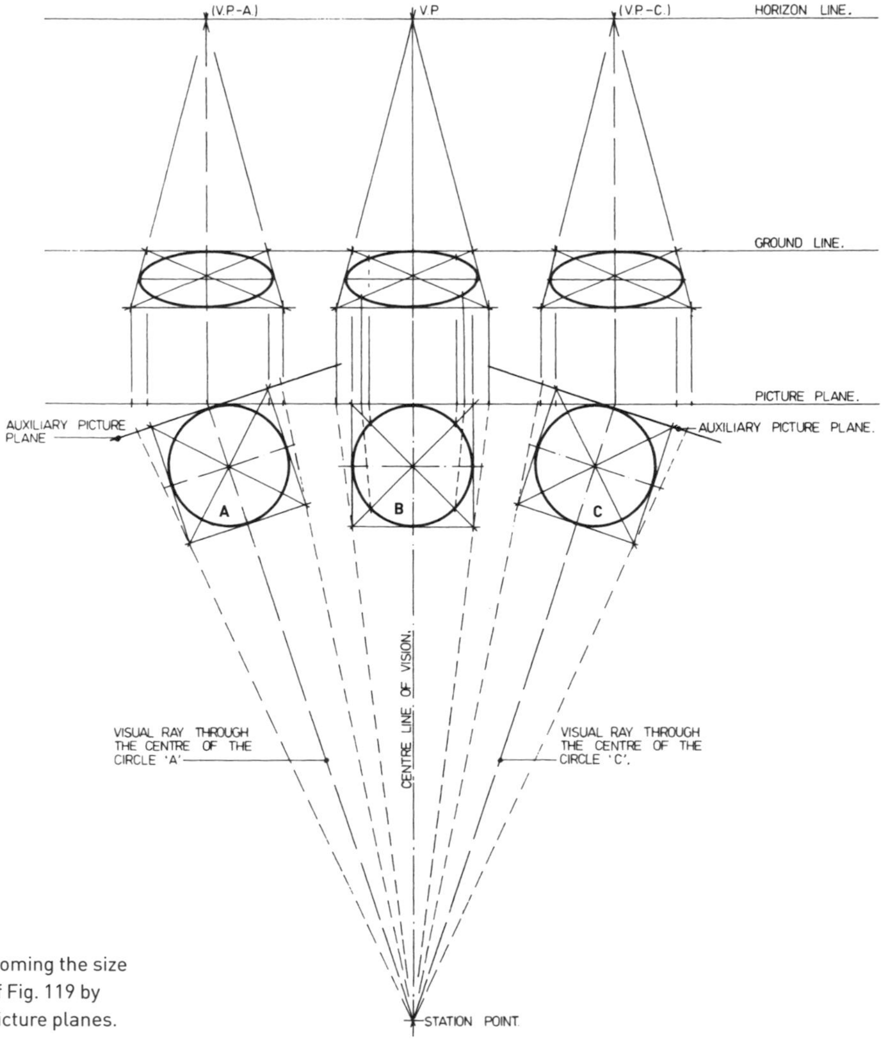

(V.P-A.)
V.P
(V.P.-C.)
HORIZON LINE.
GROUND LINE.
PICTURE PLANE.
AUXILIARY PICTURE PLANE
AUXILIARY PICTURE PLANE.
A
B
C
VISUAL RAY THROUGH THE CENTRE OF THE CIRCLE 'A'
CENTRE LINE OF VISION.
VISUAL RAY THROUGH THE CENTRE OF THE CIRCLE 'C'.
STATION POINT.

123 Overcoming the size anomaly of Fig. 119 by auxiliary picture planes.

looking at a circle from different directions, provided they are all at the same distance from the circle and have the same eye level, will see the same shape, i.e. an identical ellipse. Additionally, a spectator looking at a number of circles equidistant from him will see the same shape for each of them because, no matter where he stands to look at the circles, so long as his eye level and his distance from the circles remain constant he will see the same shape. Many authorities appear to become confused on this point and in the past few, if any, have discovered the answer to the anomaly in Fig. 119.

The statement that a circle looked at from any angle will appear as the same shape, provided the distance between the spectator and the circle and his eye level remain constant is the key to answering this question once and for all. In the light of the foregoing, Fig. 122 shows the three cylinders as they will appear to the spectator. Before leaving this explanation it is worth pointing out that further proof of the answer given in Fig. 122 can be obtained by referring to pp. 42–48 of this book, dealing with one-point perspective.

It has been shown in Figs. 119 and 120 that a correct result cannot be obtained by using the normal perspective construction: therefore it is necessary to overcome this anomaly by modifying the construction so that the correct results are obtained. There are a number of ways in which this can be done, the simplest method being the introduction of an 'auxiliary picture plane' for each of the circles whose centre does not coincide with the centre line of vision of the main perspective construction. This method is shown in Fig. 123 where, in each of the cases in which the centre of the circle does not coincide with the centre line of vision, a visual ray is drawn through the centre and, using this ray in a similar way to the centre line of vision, an auxiliary picture plane is drawn at right angles to it at the same distance from the centre of the circle as the main picture plane. Circle *B* has its centre coinciding with the centre line of vision and can be drawn in the 'normal' way. Circles *A* and *C* are drawn using auxiliary picture planes with the squares constructed around them in the directions of the visual rays through their centres and the auxiliary picture planes as shown. The points are then located

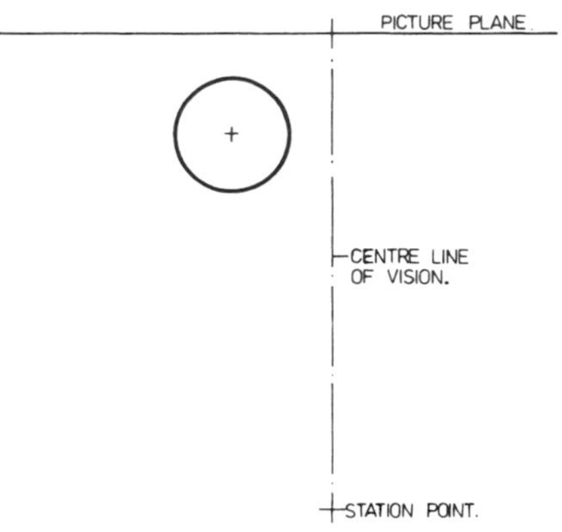

124 A circle occurring off the centre line of vision.

on the auxiliary picture plane and transferred to the main picture plane by measurement either side of the intersection of the visual ray through the centre of the circle and the main picture plane. This locates the circle accurately in the overall perspective construction and from this point forward the construction is exactly the same as for circle *B*.

From Fig. 123 it can be seen that when the centre of a circle in a perspective construction does not coincide with the centre line of vision, irrespective of whether the main construction is one-point or two-point, the circle can be drawn within the construction using a simple one-point construction and an auxiliary picture plane.

The results obtained in Fig. 123 show that the spectator will see the three circles as the same shape and because the variation in distance between the spectator and the circles is negligible they will appear to be the same size. For all practical purposes this variation in distance is so small that it can safely be ignored. In this example the spectator is looking at three identical circles from virtually the same distance and with the same eye level so the three cylinders will give the correct answer (see Fig. 122). Because this answer is at variance with most printed works on the principles of the circle in perspective projection, the method is shown in Figs. 124 and 125. Fig. 124 shows a circle occurring in any perspective construction in which the centre of the circle does not fall in the centre line of vision. Fig. 125 shows the six steps required to draw a perspective view of the circle. The steps are:

Step 1. From the station point draw a visual ray through the centre of the circle to meet the picture plane.

Step 2. Construct a square around the circle using the visual ray as the main axis (vertical axis when the centre line of vision passes through the centre of the circle). Locate the other axis at right angles to this one and then locate the diagonals.

Step 3. Locate the auxiliary picture plane at right angles to the visual ray through the centre of the circle, the same distance from the centre of the circle as the main picture plane.

Step 4. Project up from the intersection of the visual ray through the centre of the circle and the main picture plane and locate in the horizon line a vanishing point for the square around the circle (already located for the main construction). Also project the two sides of the square parallel to the central visual ray back to the auxiliary picture plane; these are then transferred by measurement to the main picture plane where they are located at the correct distance on either side of the intersection of the main picture plane and the central visual ray. These two points are then projected up to the ground line.

Step 5. Using the vanishing point for the circle, lines are drawn through the points (obtained in Step 4) which represent the sides of the square surrounding the circle in the perspective view. The square can then be completed in the perspective view by sighting the required corners, which are transferred to the main picture plane and projected up in the normal way. The diagonals can then be drawn simply by joining the opposite corners of the square in the perspective view.

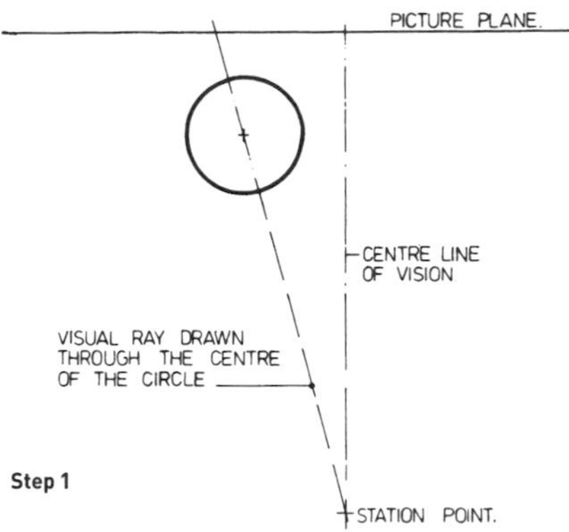

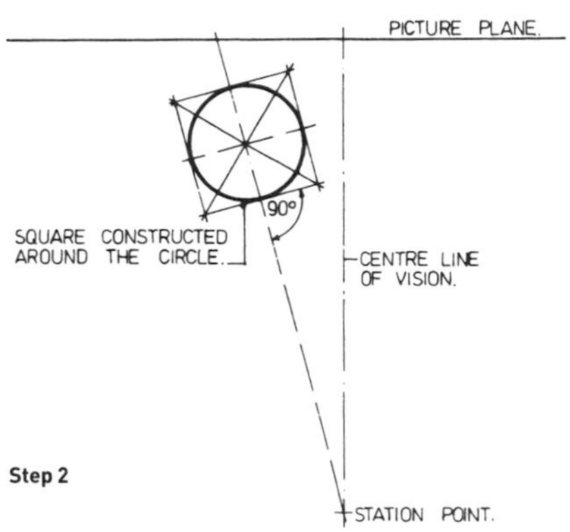

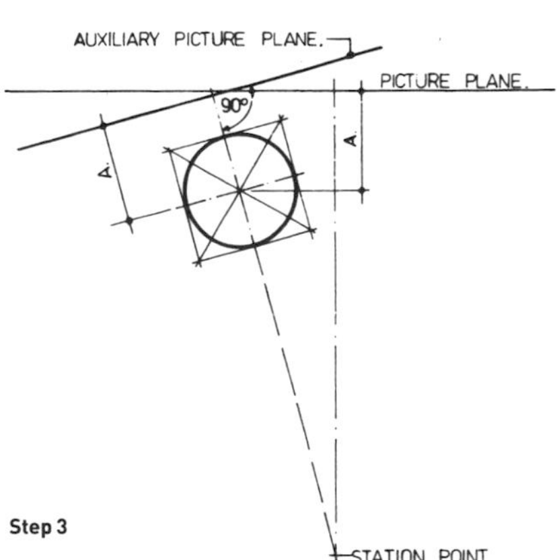

125*a* Drawing a perspective view of the circle in Fig. 124. Steps 1–3.

125*b* Drawing a perspective view of the circle in Fig. 124. Steps 4– 6.

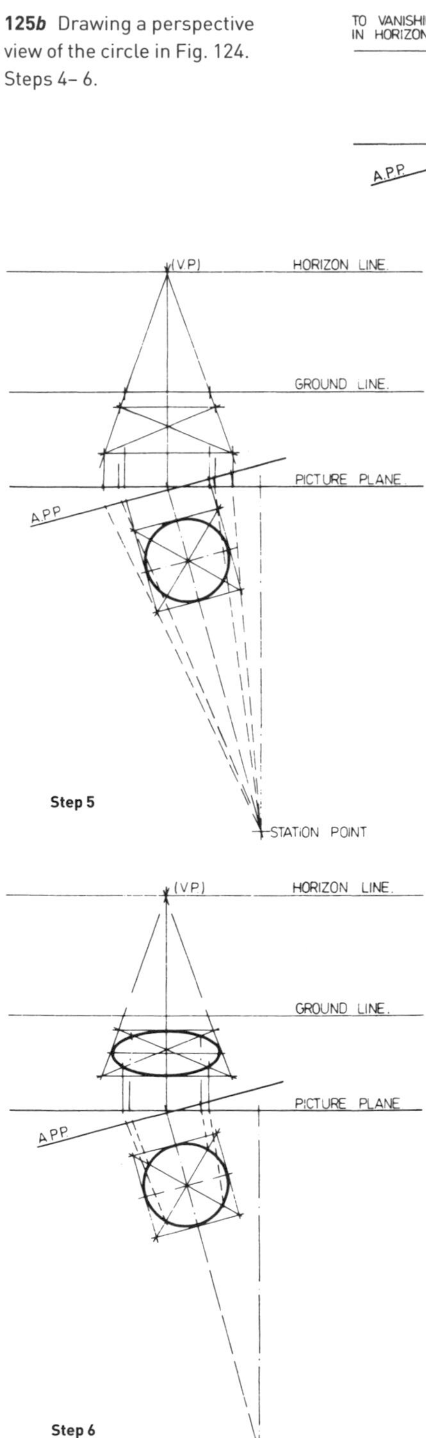

Note: sides of square parallel to visual ray projected back to A.P.P. These are then located on the P.P. by measurement.

Step 6. The intersections of the circumference of the circle and the diagonals are sighted and the points located on the auxiliary picture plane; from here they are transferred to the main picture plane, where they can be projected up to locate these intersections in the perspective view. The ellipse, i.e. the view of the circle in perspective, can then be drawn through these points.

Once the shape of the circle is drawn in perspective the auxiliary picture plane which was introduced to enable the correct shape to be obtained is of no further use. To obtain points on the circumference of the circle or within it the main picture plane is used in the normal way. Fig. 126 shows the method used for locating points *A*, *B*, and *C* on the circumference of the circle in their correct relationship to the circle as seen by the spectator located at the station point. From this it can be seen that nothing changes in the final perspective view except that if the auxiliary

126 Locating points on the circumference of a circle drawn in perspective.

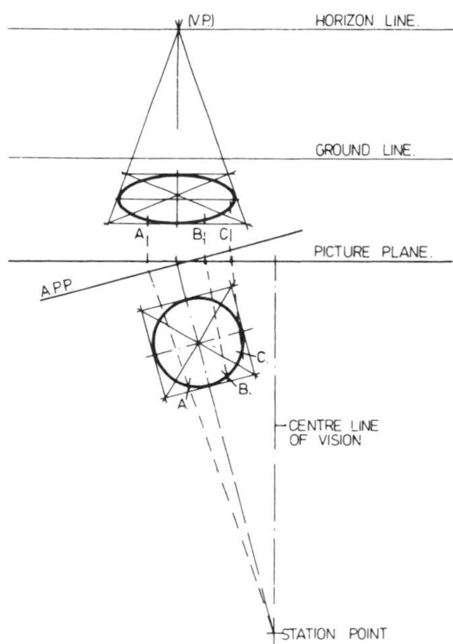

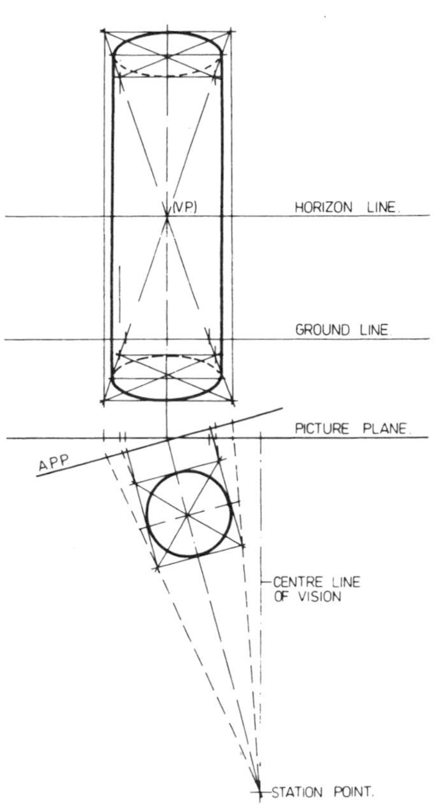

127 Perspective construction of a cylinder whose main axis lies off the centre line of vision.

picture plane is used to draw the shape of the circle as seen by the spectator it will result in a correct representation of what he will see as opposed to an incorrect representation if it is not used.

From the foregoing explanation of the method used to produce perspectives of circles it can be seen that cylinders follow the same basic rules. Fig. 127 shows the construction of a cylinder when the centre line of vision does not pass through the main axis of the cylinder. From the previous explanation it can be seen that the major axis of an ellipse, which is the result of viewing a circle in the horizontal plane, will always be horizontal, i.e. it will always be at right angles to the main axis of the cylinder of which it can be said to form an end. In this case the main axis of the cylinder will be vertical, which means that the minor axis of the ellipse will coincide with the main axis of the cylinder. It is this fact which explains the most important rule to remember when drawing

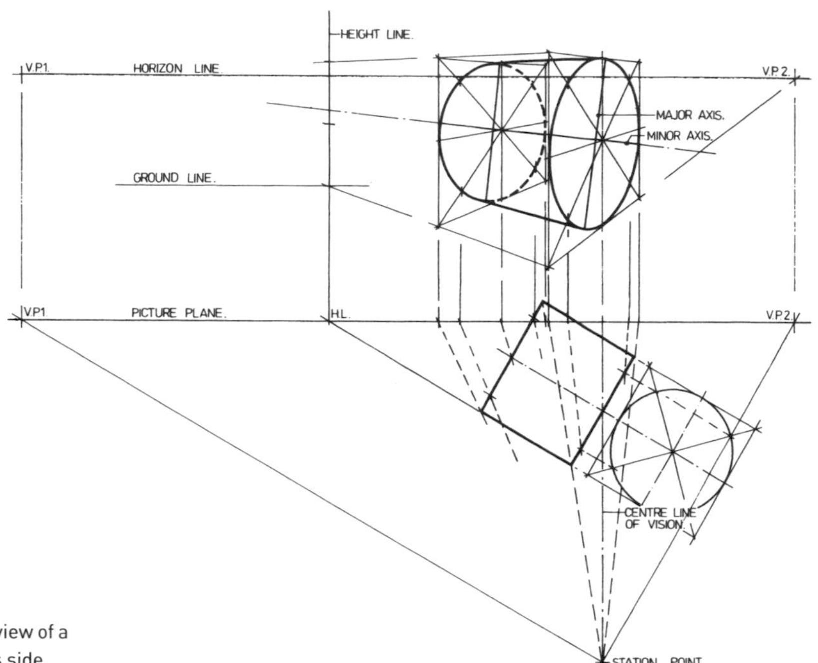

128 Perspective view of a cylinder laid on its side.

circles in perspective, regardless of whether they fall in the horizontal or vertical plane: *The major axis of the ellipse will always be at right angles to the main axis of the cylinder of which it can be said to form an end.* Therefore the minor axis will always coincide with this main axis and the centre of the circle will always fall in the minor axis behind the intersection of the major and minor axes. If this basic rule is remembered circles will cause the delineator very little trouble.

In Fig. 128 the main axis of the cylinder is horizontal, i.e. parallel to the ground, and its ends are in a vertical plane, which means that it will 'vanish' to V.P.1. Because the major axis of the ellipse is always at right angles to the main axis of the cylinder it will no longer be vertical. If the square surrounding the circle is constructed in the normal way, together with the diagonals and the vertical and horizontal axes, each end of the cylinder can be located in the perspective view by simple projection or at least the squares containing the ends of the cylinder can be located. Next it is necessary to locate the intersections of the circumference and the diagonals in the plan so that they can be located in the perspective view. But these intersections cannot be located immediately in the plan because the circular ends appear as straight lines and therefore it is necessary to set up an elevation. If this is set up in the correct relationship to the plan (as shown) it can save a good deal of extra work. The intersections of the circumference and the diagonals can be projected directly onto the plan, and from there they can be located in the perspective view. The perspective view of the ends of the cylinder can then be drawn by producing an ellipse through the points of intersection of the circumference of the circle and the diagonals and the vertical and horizontal axes of the circular ends.

Because circles and cylinders are so similar in their construction in perspective drawing it is unnecessary to study cylinders further at this stage. However, one variation to the method already shown is of use for drawing circles in perspective when they occur in a horizontal plane. The variation consists of enclosing the circle in a trapezium instead of the square used in the previous examples. Fig. 129 shows the construction when the circle is enclosed in a trapezium in which two sides coincide with the visual rays forming tangents to the circle. The other two sides of the trapezium are drawn parallel with the picture plane, or with the auxiliary picture plane when the centre of the circle does not coincide with the centre line of vision of the main construction. The diagonals in this case will not intersect in the centre of the circle but instead will locate the major axis of the resulting ellipse, i.e. the major axis will fall in a straight line between the two tangent points of the visual rays used to construct the trapezium. The perspective view of this particular trapezium in this location will be a rectangle and when its diagonals are located the major axis can be drawn parallel to the ground line. The points of intersection of the circumference of the circle and the diagonals are located in the perspective in the usual way and the ellipse is shown by drawing a line through all of the relevant points.

The method of construction is the same for both circles except that an auxiliary picture plane must be used for circle *B*. The actual centre of the circle is not located in this method unless further steps are used. In order to locate the centre of the circle in the perspective view it is necessary to construct at

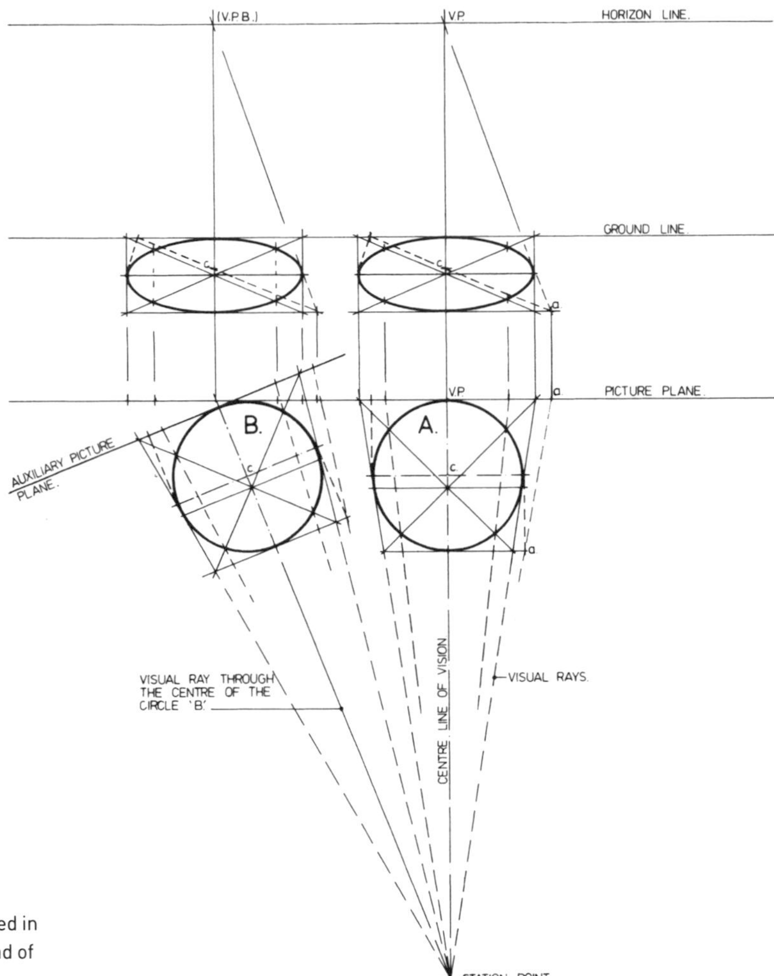

129 Circle enclosed in a trapezium instead of a square.

least two diagonally opposite corners of a square which will contain the plan of the circle. These two corners can then be located in the perspective view as shown and a diagonal line drawn. It is already known that this diagonal will intersect the minor axis of the ellipse in the perspective position of the true centre of the circle.

The development of this method is so similar to the 'square' method that it is not taken any further here but those who are attracted to this method rather than the 'square' should note that it can be used not only for circles but for those cylinders whose ends fall in a horizontal plane.

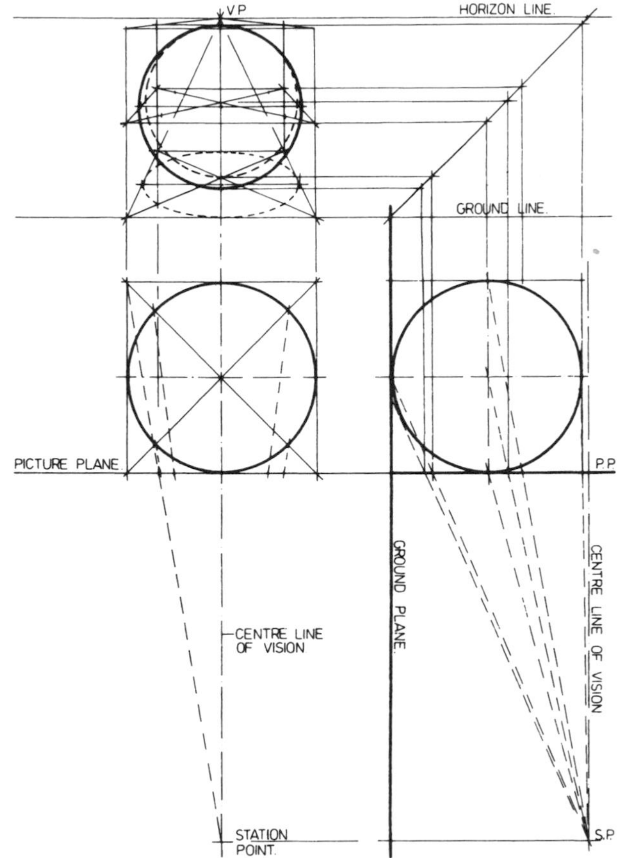

130 Drawing a sphere in perspective.

Once the circle and the cylinder in perspective projection are understood the sphere can be drawn in perspective with very little trouble. The basic theory of the sphere is very similar to that of the circle and the cylinder although it is a little more complicated to draw. The explanation of the method is shown in Fig. 130 where an elevation has been set up in a similar way to the ones used in three-point perspective constructions. From this it can be seen that the plan and the elevation have squares constructed around the sphere in each view. This has the effect of putting the sphere in a 'box', which is consistent with the methods for drawing other complex shapes. The box containing the sphere can be set up in the perspective view in the usual way. Once this is done it is possible to locate the diagonals on the base of the box and on these to locate their intersections with the circumference of the plan of the sphere. Next the plan of the sphere, which will of course be an ellipse, can be drawn in the perspective view. The major axis of this ellipse can be located (through the middle of the ellipse). Where this major axis intersects the sides of the square in the perspective view are the tangent points formed by the visual rays i.e. the furthest edges of the view of the sphere seen by the spectator. In other words, this will be the diameter of the sphere in the perspective view or, to be more accurate at this stage, it will be the width of the sphere through its centre. Because of this it is necessary to locate a horizontal plane through the centre of the sphere as shown in Fig. 130. The diagonals of this square plane through the centre of the sphere will intersect in the true centre of the sphere.

At this stage it is necessary to clarify exactly what we see when we look at a sphere. From the previous section about circles it can be said that a spectator looking at a sphere from any angle will see the same shape. It is not necessary to go into further explanation of this point because the arguments have been discussed previously. However, exactly what that shape is that the spectator sees from any angle is extremely important when drawing spheres in perspective.

It is a common assumption that the shape he sees is a perfect circle. If this were the case it would be necessary to construct the circle using the centre of the sphere located by constructing the horizontal plane through its centre. If this is attempted it will soon be learned that the circle drawn using this centre is in fact a circle representing the horizontal axis

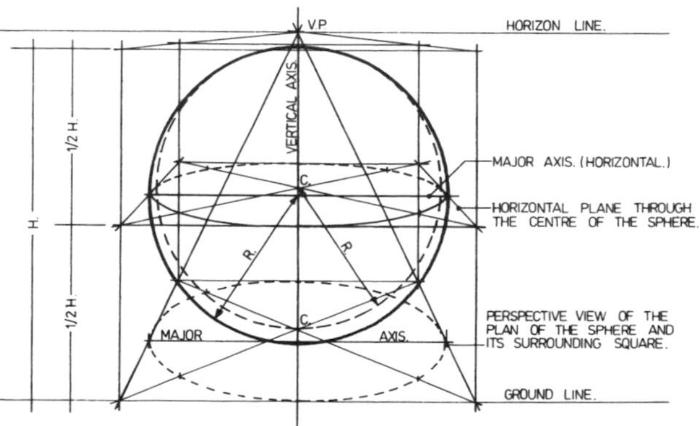

131 Enlarged detail from Fig. 130.

of the plan of the sphere. This cannot be the shape seen by the spectator because this line coincides with the diameter of the circle seen in plan and this possibility has already been eliminated (see Fig. 113, p. 135). In fact the spectator cannot see a true circle when he looks at a sphere.

The only other logical alternative is that he sees an ellipse. If this is so, then the centre of the ellipse is the intersection of the major and minor axes. Mathematics tells us that a circle is only a special kind of ellipse; therefore what the spectator sees is not a circle but a circular ellipse i.e. an ellipse in which the two foci coincide. It follows that the shape seen by the spectator can be drawn with a compass, using the intersection of the major and the minor axes and a radius equal to half the length of the major axis. This may seem at first sight like splitting hairs but if the foregoing facts are checked against the introduction to this chapter (p.129) it will be seen that an understanding of them is necessary to the satisfactory understanding of spheres in perspective projection. Fig. 131 is an enlargement of the results achieved in Fig. 130 and should be self-explanatory. An elevation of the construction was included in Fig. 130 to help in the explanation of constructing a perspective view of a sphere but it can be readily seen that this elevation is not necessary for the construction.

Of the two spheres in Fig. 132, sphere *A*, which has its centre in the centre line of vision, is drawn in perspective using the 'square' method. Once the square is set up in the perspective view the horizontal plane can be located by measurement on the picture plane and its diagonals drawn. The intersections of the circumference and the diagonals can be located, by projection from the plan, on the diagonals of both the base plane and the central plane of the box. In any perspective view of a sphere which is intended to form the basis of a rendering it is important that the plan view of the sphere be located on the base plane of the box. The reason for this will be made clear in the chapter on shadow projection; sufficient here to say that it is necessary and can be done with very little extra work at this stage. Once the major axis is located by measurement the line of the ellipse can be drawn

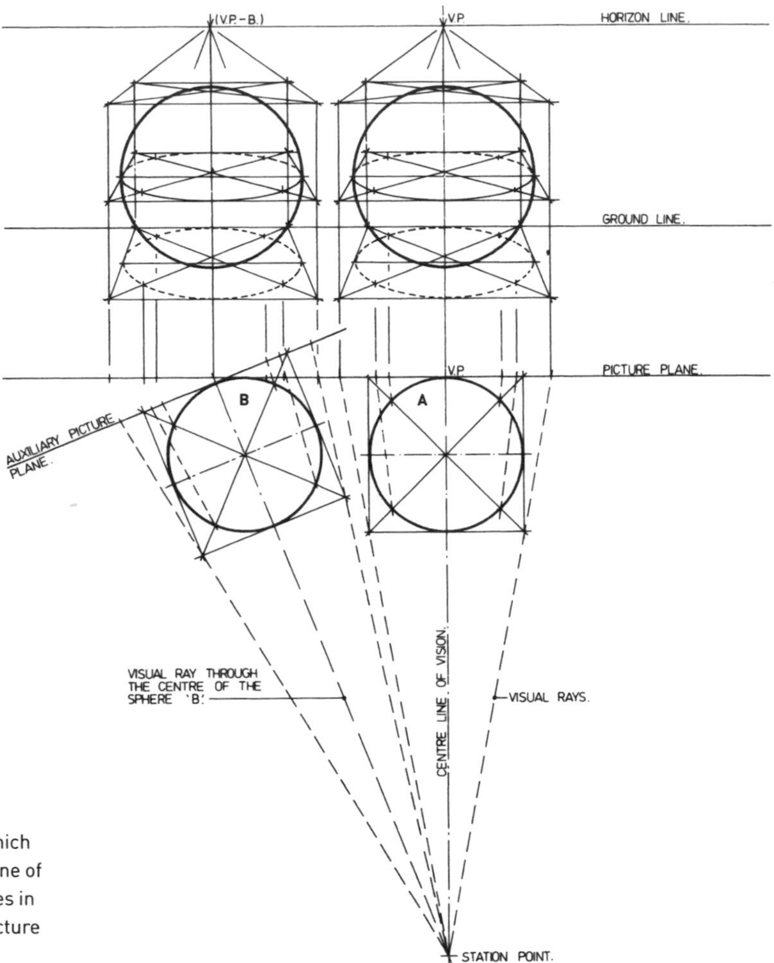

132 Two spheres, of which one lies off the centre line of vision. As with the circles in Fig. 123, an auxiliary picture plane is used.

on these two planes. Using the intersection of the major and the minor axes as the centre and a radius of half the major axis the sphere can be drawn in the perspective view.

Sphere *B* does not have its centre in the centre line of vision, therefore it will be necessary to use an auxiliary picture plane because it can be readily understood that the spectator will see each sphere as the same shape. The actual construction is similar to that for sphere *A* except that all of the points located on the auxiliary picture plane must be transferred by measurement to the main picture plane. Once the shape of the sphere has been drawn in the perspective view the auxiliary picture plane is of no further use and the

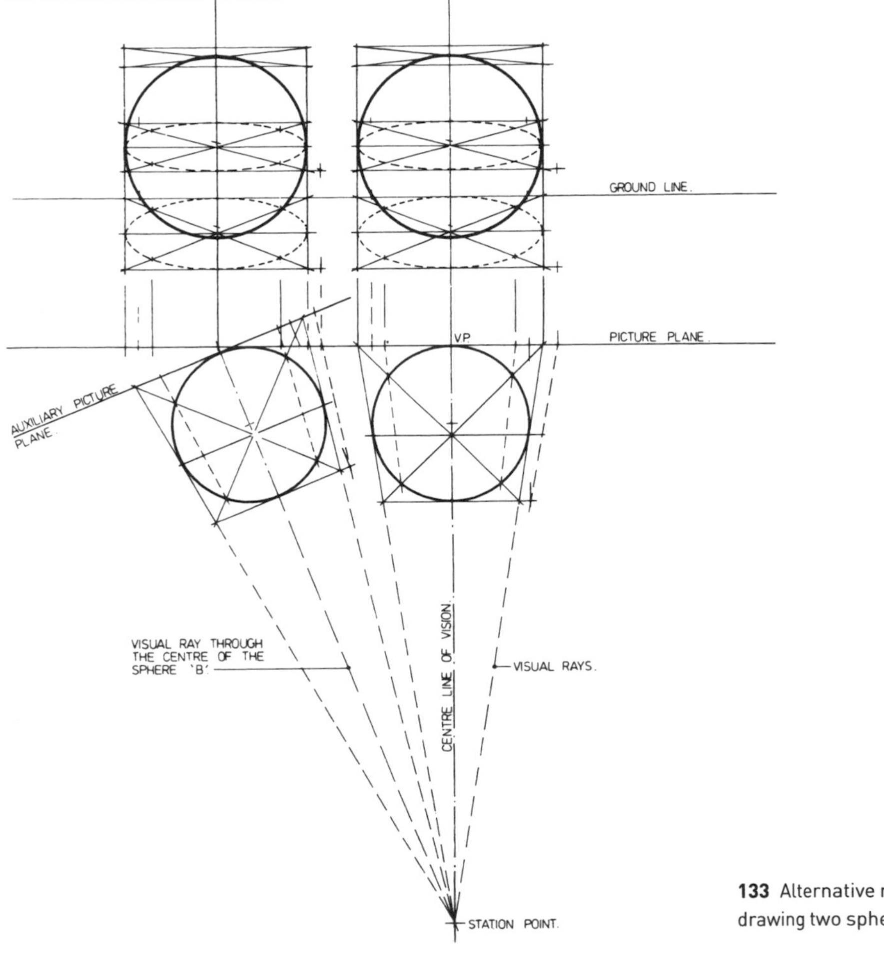

133 Alternative method for drawing two spheres.

main picture plane is used to locate points or lines on the surface of the sphere.

Fig. 133 shows an alternative method for drawing the sphere in perspective where sphere *A* has its centre falling in the centre line of vision and sphere *B* does not. This alternative method consists of the use of a trapezium to enclose the plan view of the sphere in the same way as was described in the section dealing with circles. The method will be easily understood by reference to Fig. 133, where it will be seen that it is only a combination of the constructions shown in Figs. 129 and 132.

Fig. 134 shows the method used for locating a horizontal plane through a sphere other than through the centre. The

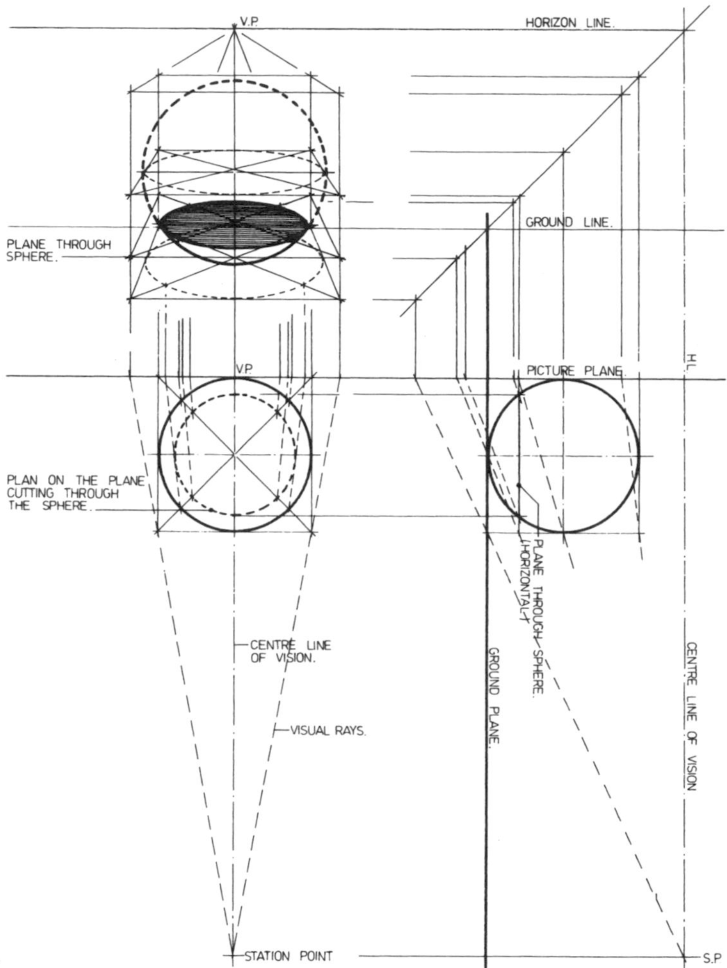

134 Locating a horizontal plane through a sphere, in cases where the plane does not pass through the centre.

sphere is drawn in the perspective view using the square method described in Fig. 132 (sphere *A*). When this is done it is necessary to set up an elevation of the construction in the usual way. The horizontal plane through the sphere is located on the elevation of the sphere and from this the plan of the sphere at this plane can be drawn on the plan (shown as a broken line on the plan). By means of projections in both the plan and the elevation, the plane at this level can be located through the perspective view of the box containing the sphere. The diagonals can be drawn in the usual way. Projections of the intersections of the circumference of the circle on the plane through the

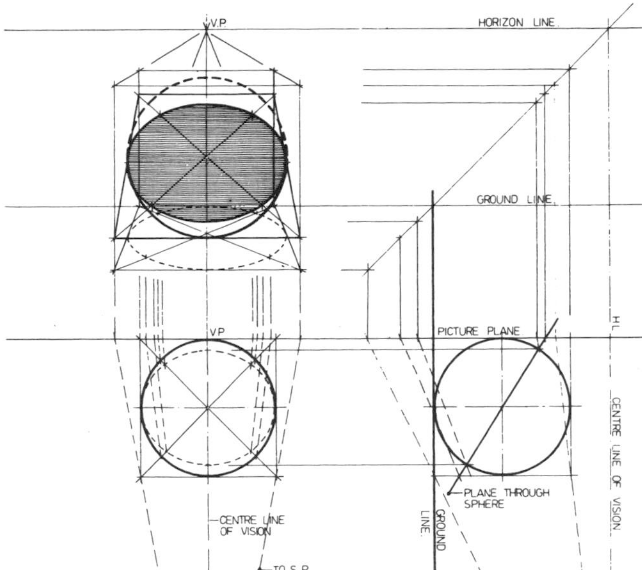

135 Drawing a sphere cut by an inclined plane.

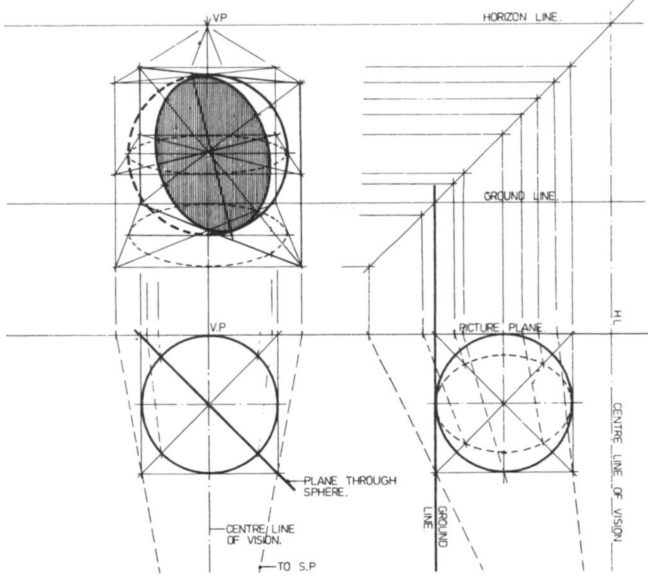

136 Drawing a sphere cut by a vertical plane.

sphere with the diagonals in the plan are used to produce the ellipse seen by the spectator when the sphere is cut at this level.

To draw a sphere cut by an inclined plane (Fig. 135), the method is similar to the one described for Fig. 134 so it need not be repeated. However, it should be pointed out that although the plane cutting the box containing the sphere will be inclined, not horizontal, it can easily be located by projections from the elevation.

Fig. 136, the last figure in this chapter, shows the method used for setting up a perspective view of a sphere which has been cut with a vertical plane. The sphere is drawn in the perspective view using the square method and again it is necessary to set up an elevation of the construction in the usual way. The vertical plane cutting the sphere is located on the plan view (in this example it coincides with one of the diagonals). This plane through the sphere is then located on the elevation together with its diagonals on which the points of intersection of the circumference of the circle formed by the cut can be located by projection from the plan to enable the ellipse formed by the cut to be drawn in the elevation. The plan and the elevation are used to locate the plane in perspective with its diagonals and the intersections of the circumference of the circle formed by the cut. Using these points of intersection, the ellipse which will be seen by the spectator in the circumstances shown here can be drawn in the usual way.

Because of the confusion, in the existing published works, on the whole subject of circles, cylinders and spheres in perspective projection, it should again be emphasized that the solutions described and illustrated here are based on one simple logical fact. When a spectator views a circle in a horizontal plane from any direction, at a constant distance from the circle and a constant eye level, he will see the circle as an identical ellipse. When viewing a cylinder, of which the axis of symmetry is vertical, from any direction at a constant distance from it and a constant eye level, he will see the cylinder as an identical shape. When a sphere is viewed from any angle, at a constant distance from it and constant eye level, it will be seen as an identical shape. Because of this it must be obvious that the basic method of perspective projection is not suitable when the circle, cylinder or sphere does not have its centre falling in the centre line of vision. This anomaly can be overcome by the use of an auxiliary picture plane so that the results obtained are consistent with the logical requirements.

.6 Reflections

Reflections occur often in rendering because many surfaces are capable of reflecting images with varying degrees of clarity. Glass in the windows of a building will often reflect images of those things near it, the surface of still water will reflect a mirror image of everything located in the correct relationship to it and even a wet road or pavement will reflect its surroundings. Therefore it is necessary to understand the basic principle of reflection: a reflected image of an object will always appear to be the same distance behind the reflecting surface as the object is in front of it. Fig. 137 shows a rectangular prism placed a short distance from a mirror. The mirror reflects not only the object but the ground or floor between the object and the mirror. It is this which makes the reflection of the object look as though it is the same distance behind the reflecting surface as the object is in front of it. When this is thoroughly understood the construction of reflections in perspective is a simple exercise.

If the reflection of an object will appear to be the same distance behind the reflecting surface as the object is in front of it, then a second or 'image' object can be drawn in the plan (Fig. 138). The object and its reflection can be located in the perspective drawing in the normal way. When the object is a simple rectangular prism, as shown in Fig. 138, this is not a long or involved process. However, if the object is more complicated this method can become unwieldy and then it is necessary to look for a simpler, quicker method of setting up reflections in a perspective drawing. The use of short cuts in perspective drawing enables many long and laborious exercises to be carried out with a minimum expenditure of time and effort. These short cuts are dealt with fully in a later chapter in this book but because one of the basic short cuts is required at this stage it is best to introduce the principle behind it here.

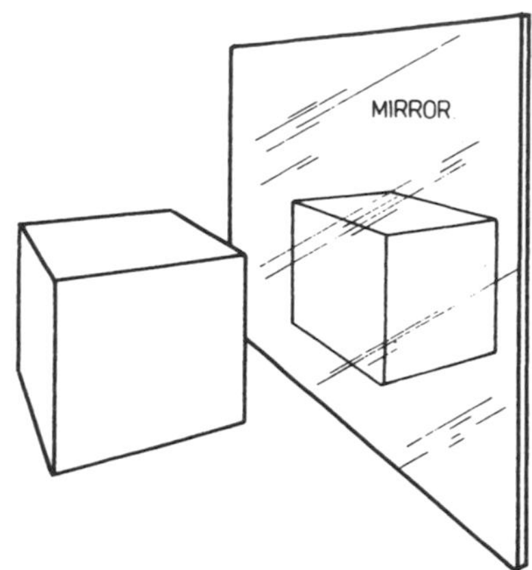

137 Reflection: a rectangular prism, and its image in a mirror.

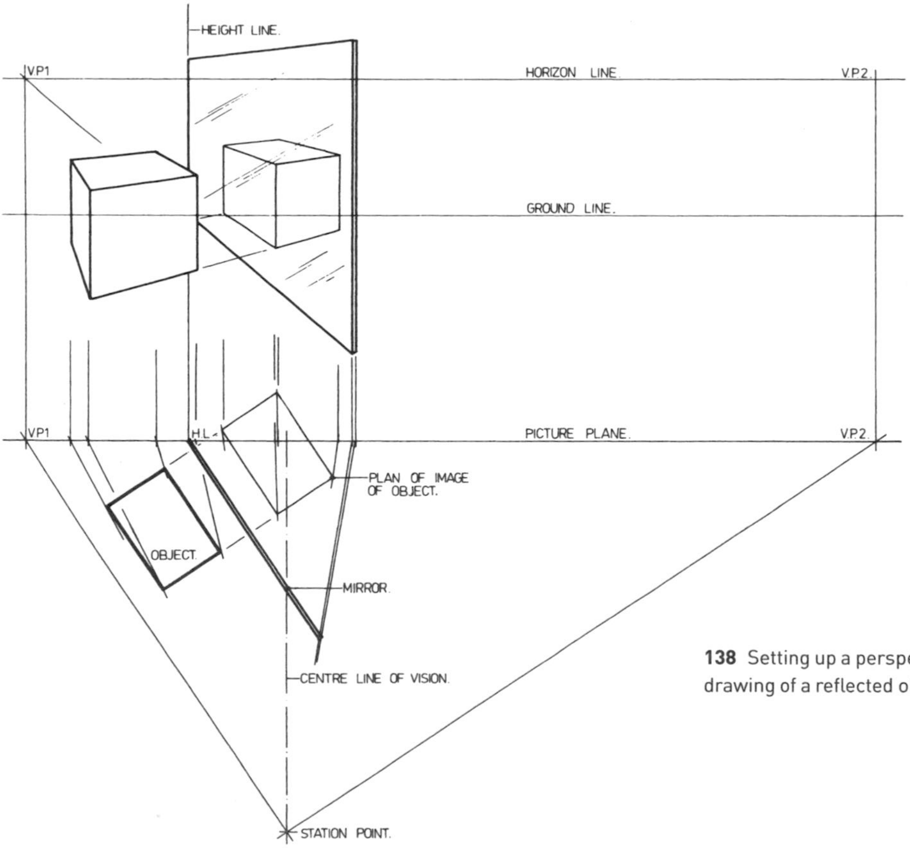

To understand one of the most useful short cuts in perspective projection it is necessary to go back to plane geometry. It is known that the diagonals of a square intersect in the centre of the square (see Fig. 112), and similarly the diagonals of a rectangle will intersect in the centre of the rectangle. If a square prism and a rectangular prism are set up and drawn in perspective, together with the diagonals on each of the visible faces, these diagonals must still intersect in the centre of each face (Fig. 139). These constructions show that the diagonals locate the centre of each face of each object in the perspective drawing. In other words, the perspective drawing shows not

138 Setting up a perspective drawing of a reflected object.

only the face of the object but also whatever is on its surface. Viewing an object from a different position does not change anything in its surface in reality; therefore, the diagonals must still intersect in the centre of the square or the rectangle.

Using this centre point of the face of the figure, each face can be divided into four equal parts in the perspective drawing, as shown in Fig. 140, which can be checked by projection back to the plan. Once this is understood, it can be

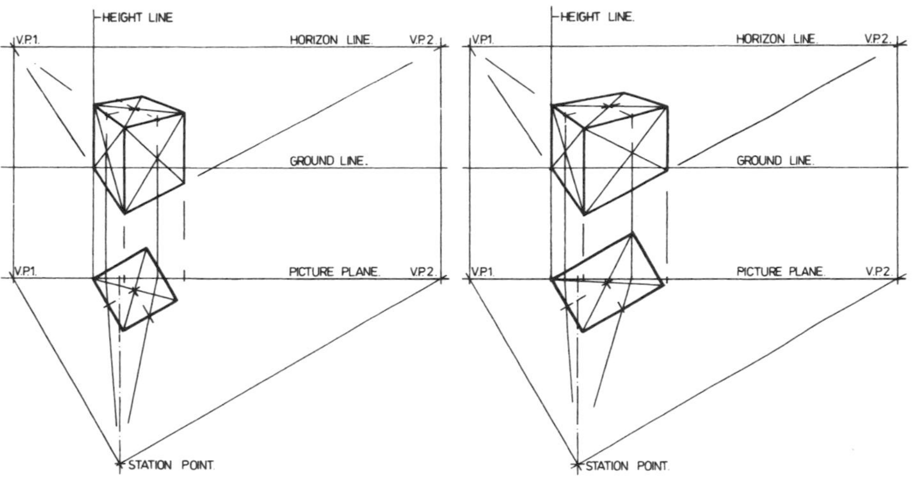

139 A square prism and a rectangular prism drawn in perspective, with the diagonals on each of the visible faces.

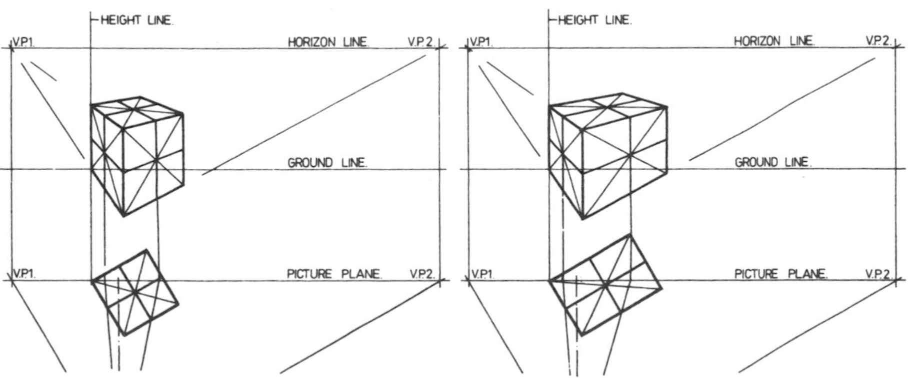

140 Division of each face of a prism into four equal parts with the help of the diagonals.

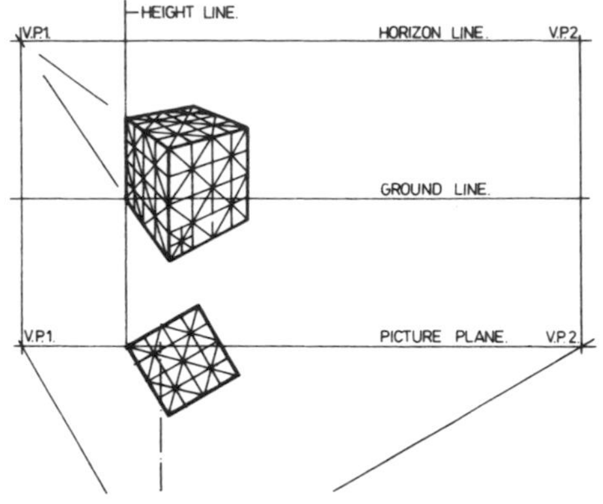

141 Dividing and subdividing the face of a cube.

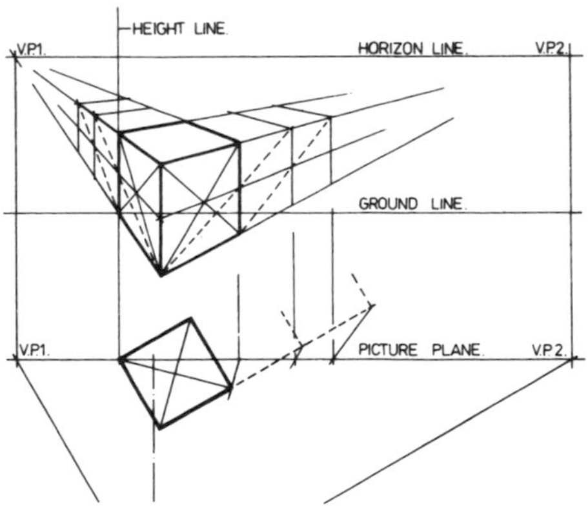

142 Multiplying a cube by the same principle of diagonals.

used to advantage in perspective drawing. The principle can be expressed simply: *The diagonals of a square or rectangle can be used to divide the figure exactly in half.* Therefore each half can again be treated as a square or rectangle and be divided in half repeatedly until the object is divided into a great many equal parts. Fig. 141 shows how this can be done using a simple cube. Obviously the rectangular prism can be dealt with in the same way.

This is not the only result which can be obtained from this principle; if it remains true for division of square and rectangular shapes it must remain true for multiplication of the same shapes. Fig. 142 shows a cube which has been set up using a simple two-point perspective construction. To this cube it is required to add more cubes of exactly the same size, which can of course be done by adding more squares to the plan and then projecting them up in the normal way. The same result can be obtained in about half the time by using an adaptation of the principle of diagonals. One face of the cube could be thought of as half of a rectangle which is made up of two identical squares, one of them being a face of the cube under consideration. The diagonals of this rectangle would pass through a point in the middle of a side of the square, as shown in Fig. 142, and if the top and bottom sides of the square were extended as necessary the rectangle equal to two squares could be drawn. This exercise could be repeated many times, resulting in a large number of squares being drawn, each equal in size to the original one. Because this can be done directly in the perspective view without further reference to the plan it is a great time-saver, and because it is based on a geometric fact, it does not suffer any loss of accuracy. This is one of the most valuable short cuts in perspective projection and has a number of other important uses which are dealt with more fully later. At this stage it is sufficient to understand the basic principle, which is used to set up reflections without unnecessary work and loss of time.

If the same cube as used in Figs. 141 and 142 is set up in front of a mirror in the same way as the rectangular prism was in Fig. 138 it can be drawn in perspective in the normal way together with the mirror. However, once the cube and the mirror are drawn in perspective as shown in Fig. 143 the reflection can be completed using diagonals without further reference to the plan. Fig. 144 shows how this is done, together with a diagram illustrating the principle involved. From the example it can be seen that this is a much quicker way than that shown in Fig. 138, but identical results will be obtained whichever method is used.

To this stage, the reflecting surface has been placed at right angles to the ground plane. Fig. 145 shows a rectangular prism placed on a horizontal reflecting surface and set up in perspective. The advantage of using diagonals to locate the reflection can be seen clearly in this example. If the object is raised above the reflecting surface as shown in Fig. 146 the diagonals can be used again to advantage and a great deal of time and effort can be saved. Fig. 147 shows one object placed on top of another with the two objects drawn in the perspective view in the normal way. By using diagonals, as shown, the reflections of both of these objects can be located and drawn. If it is remembered that the

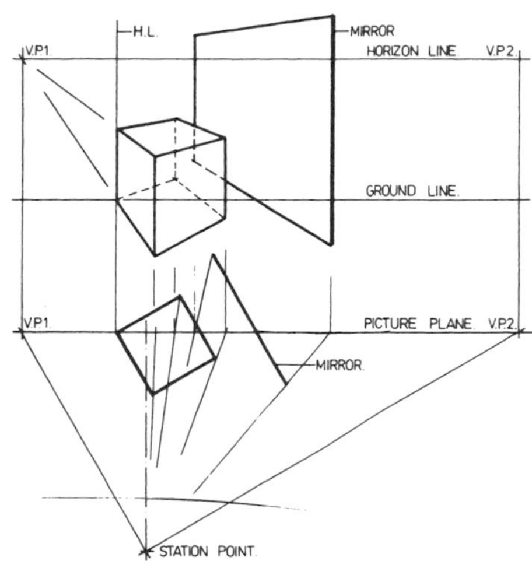

143 A cube and a mirror set up in perspective.

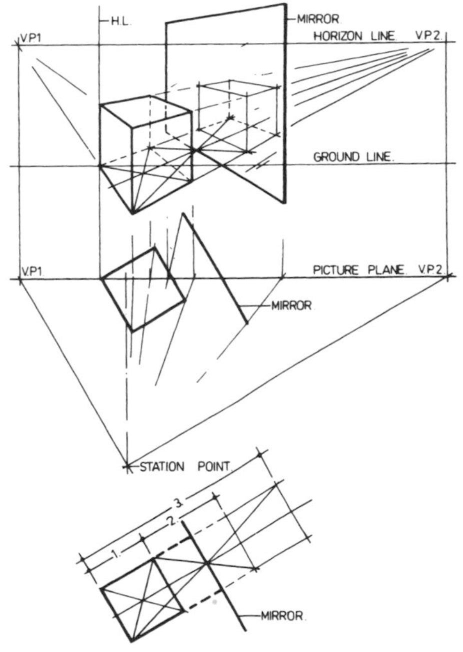

144 The reflection added to Fig. 143, showing how the diagonals are used to save time and labour.

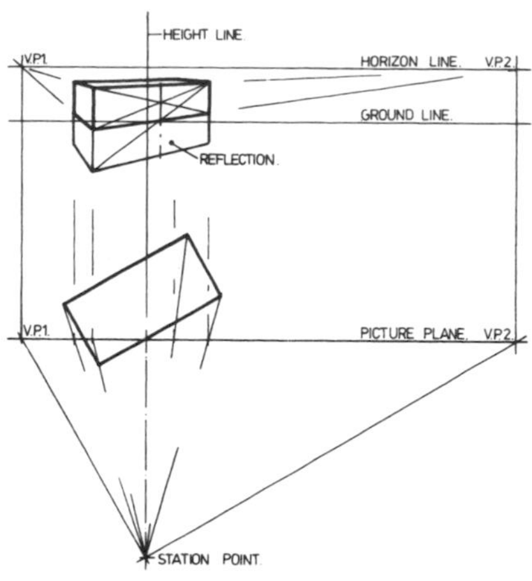

145 A rectangular prism standing on its own reflection.

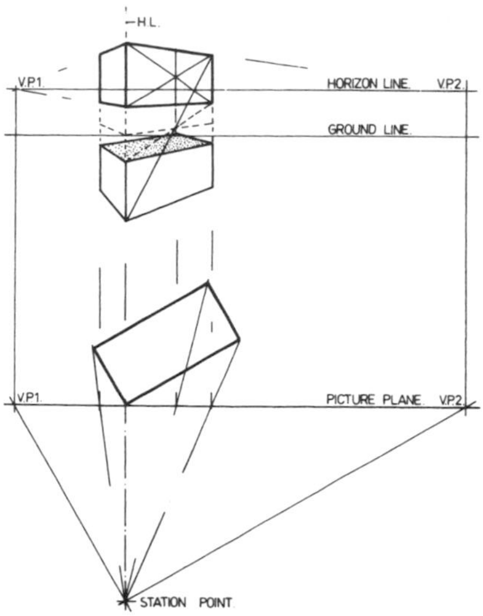

146 A rectangular prism standing above a horizontal reflecting surface.

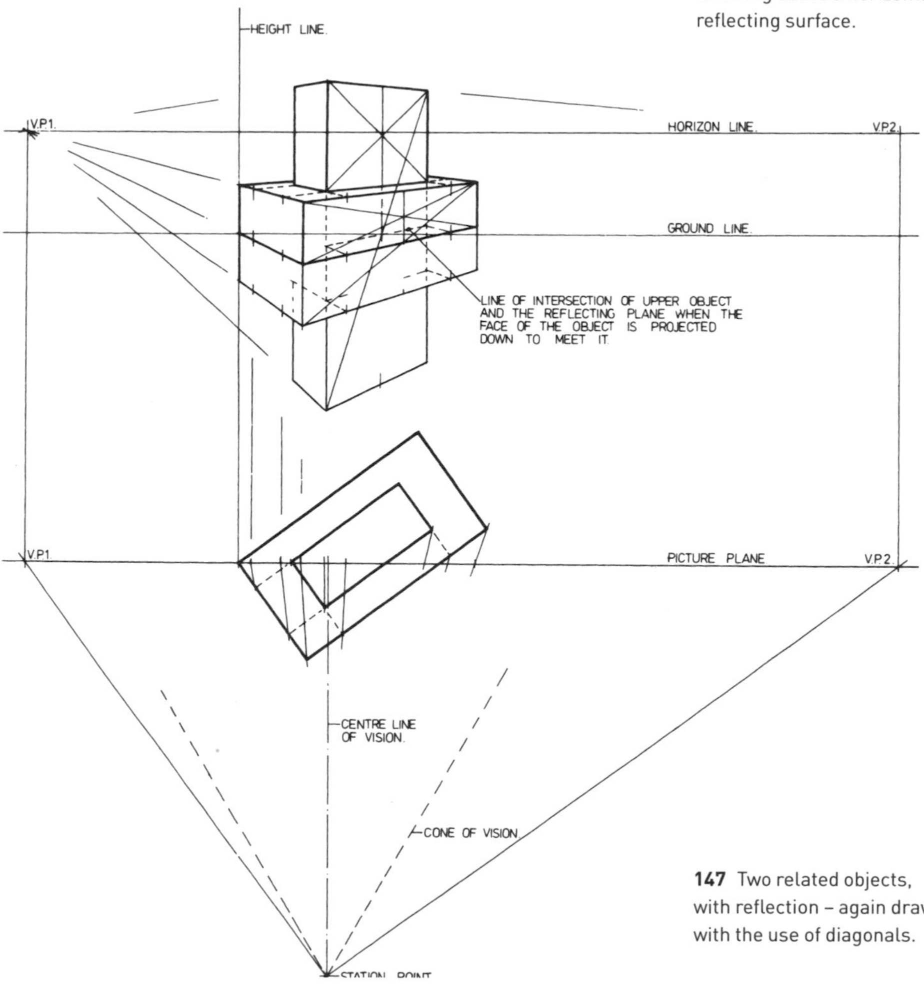

147 Two related objects, with reflection – again drawn with the use of diagonals.

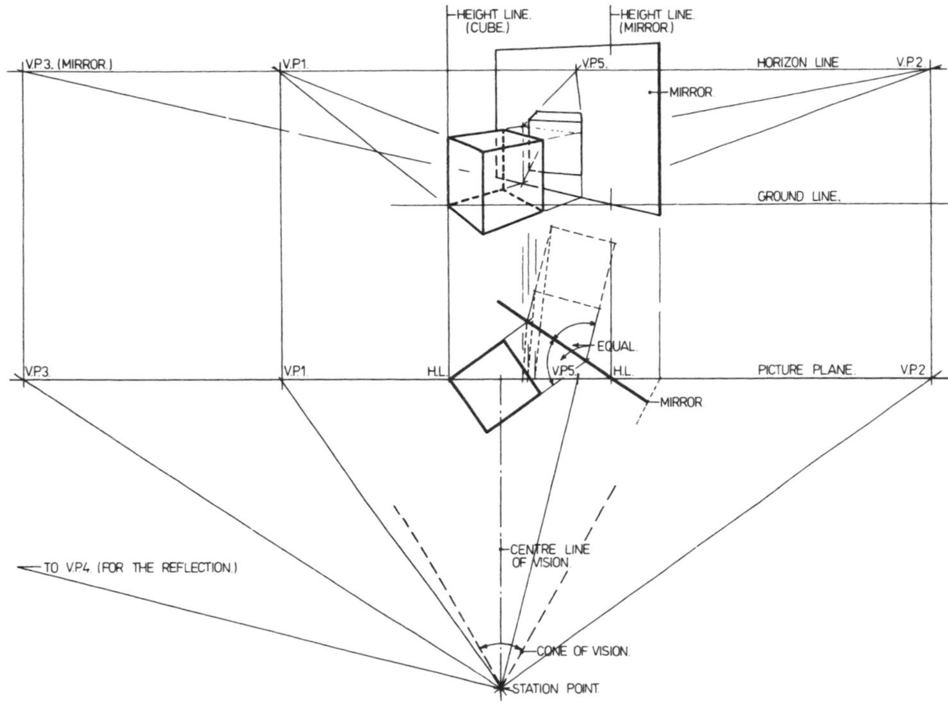

148 Object and reflecting surface not parallel.

reflection of an object will appear to be exactly the same distance behind (or below in this example) the reflecting surface as the object is in front (or above) it, this type of subject is fairly simple and straightforward.

There are two sets of conditions which have, as yet, not been discussed. These are a little more complex than the ones dealt with so far because they consist of *(a)* objects and reflecting surfaces which are no longer parallel to each other and *(b)* reflecting surfaces which are neither vertical nor horizontal. The first of these two sets of conditions is shown in Fig. 148 where the reflecting surface is not parallel to a side of the cube. In this example the cube is drawn in the perspective view in the normal way using V.P.1 and V.P.2. The mirror is then drawn, again in the normal way, using V.P.3. Because the reflection of the cube will appear to be the same distance behind the reflecting surface as the object being reflected is in front of it, the plan of the cube representing the reflection can be drawn behind the mirror using the same angles as

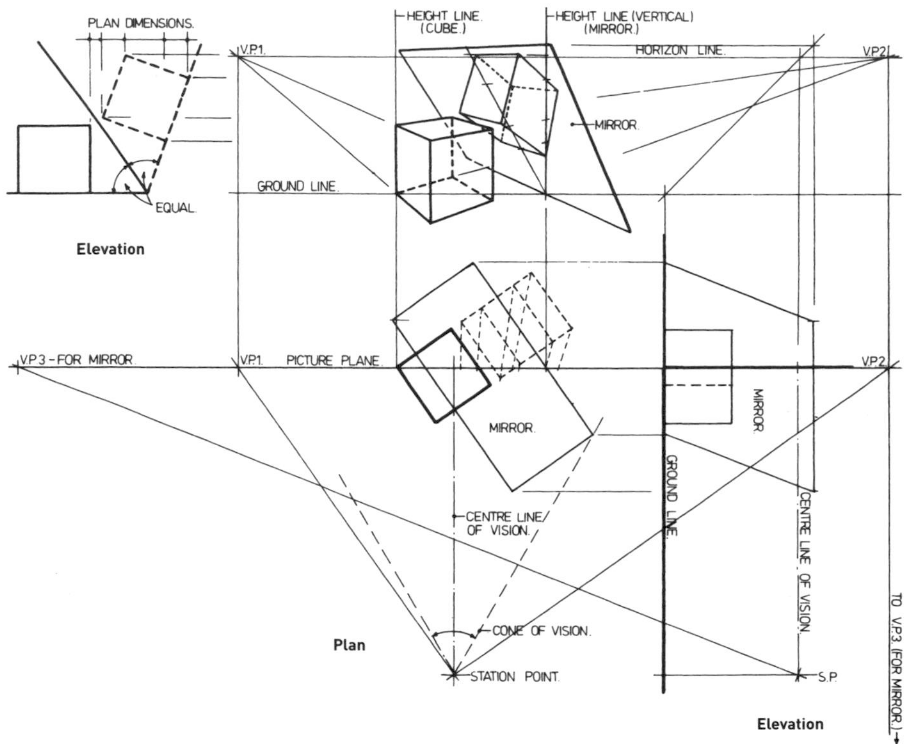

149 Reflecting surface inclined to the ground plane.

used for the cube being reflected (see Fig. 138). When this 'second' plan is located in the plan construction its vanishing points can be located in the usual way. By using these vanishing points (V.P.4 and V.P.5) for the 'second' cube in the usual way, the reflection of the cube can be drawn in the perspective view.

The second of these two sets of special conditions occurs in Fig. 149, which shows the method used for locating and drawing the reflection of a cube when the reflecting surface is inclined to the ground plane, i.e. is neither vertical nor horizontal. This example looks a little more complicated than the previous ones in this chapter because the reflecting surface, which is an inclined plane, requires an elevation of the construction to locate the vertical vanishing point (V.P.3). Once this has been found, both the cube and the mirror are set up and drawn in the perspective view in the normal way. As with the preceding example, it is necessary to locate a plan view of the 'reflection' before it can be located and drawn in the perspective view. To obtain this plan view of the 'reflection', it is necessary to set up an elevation of the cube and the mirror as shown at the left of Fig. 149. This is set up at a convenient distance from the main construction and to save time, as will be seen later, with its ground line coinciding with the ground line of the perspective. Because the object and the reflected image will appear to occupy corresponding respective positions in front of and behind the reflecting surface, an 'elevation of the reflection of the object' can be set up behind the mirror, using equal angles as shown. From this elevation, dimensions can be obtained and used to locate the 'plan of the reflection of the cube' in the plan construction as shown. Once this plan view of the 'reflection of the cube' has been located it is possible to sight its corners and project them up from the picture plane in the normal way. These corners can be located in the perspective view by projecting across horizontally from the previously prepared elevation to the vertical height line for the mirror. Using V.P.2 these 'heights' on the height line can be located by projection to a line on the inclined surface of the mirror. The reason for this last step should be obvious because the height line used for the mirror is a vertical line and the surface of the mirror is inclined, which means that 'heights' projected across from the elevation must be located on that surface where the reflection will be drawn. The corners of the reflected cube are located using the 'heights' on the inclined line on the surface of the mirror, V.P.1 and the projections up from the plan. This may sound a little complicated at first but, if the basic principles of perspective projection are fully understood, such a reflection as the one described here should not prove difficult when attempted.

To sum up, the most important single fact to remember when dealing with reflections in perspective projection is that the reflection of the object will always appear to be the same distance behind the reflecting surface as the object being reflected is in front of it. If this is learned thoroughly from the very beginning, reflections are quite a simple exercise and need not be time-consuming.

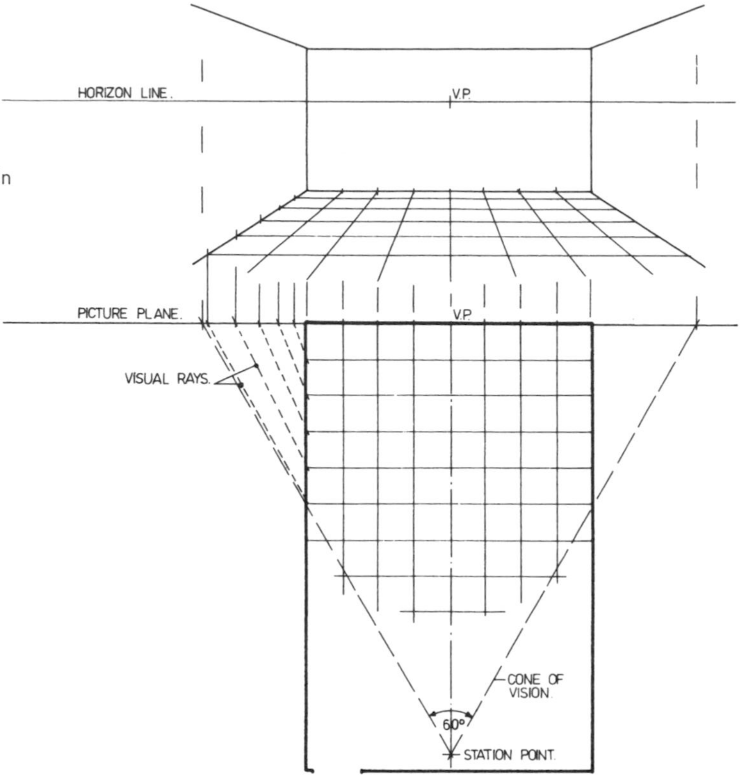

150 Interior of a room, in one-point perspective.

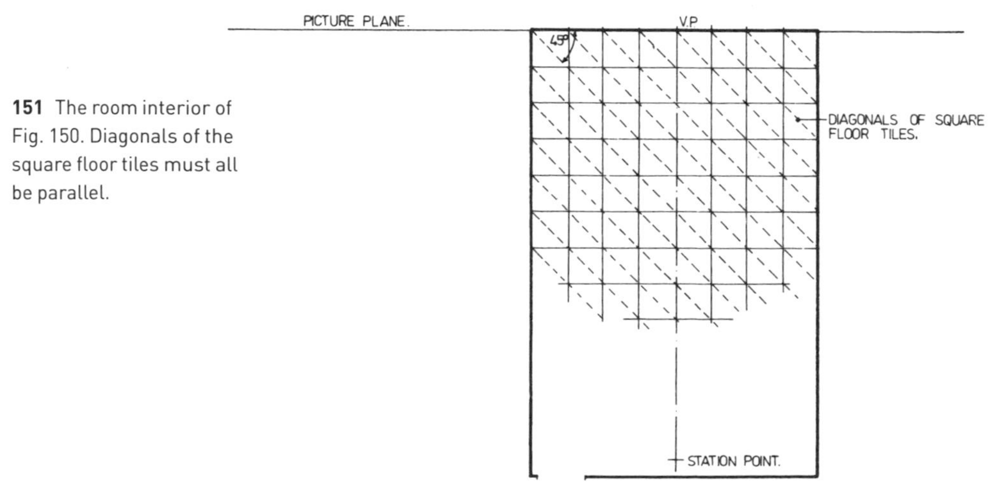

151 The room interior of Fig. 150. Diagonals of the square floor tiles must all be parallel.

.7 The Use of Measuring Points

The point known as a measuring point in perspective projection is in reality a vanishing point but, unlike the true vanishing point, which is located by using a sight line parallel to a side or line of an object, a measuring point is located by using a sight line parallel to some construction line, such as a diagonal line of a face of a figure, usually a square or a rectangle.

To explain this more fully, Fig. 150 shows a simple interior of a room set up in perspective using a one-point construction. The floor tiles have been drawn in the perspective view using the normal method of sighting them in the plan and projecting them up to the perspective view. Because these floor tiles are square, diagonals drawn on them will be at an angle of 45° to the picture plane (Fig. 151). Because all of the tiles are the same size and all are square their diagonals will be parallel as shown, therefore they will converge to a common vanishing point in a perspective projection. From Fig. 151 it can be seen that a diagonal drawn from a corner of the room crosses a tile in each 'vertical' and 'horizontal' row until it reaches the opposite wall. It is unnecessary to draw any other diagonals in this method of perspective projection.

Fig. 152 shows the method of setting up the floor tiles using a measuring point. The diagonal drawn will be parallel to all of the other diagonals of the tiles (in this direction). Therefore a vanishing point for these diagonals could be located by drawing a sight line from the station point parallel to the diagonal to meet the picture plane. These diagonals do not exist as a part of the actual view but are in fact construction lines, so this vanishing point is known as a measuring point. Because the end wall of the room in Fig. 152 coincides with the picture plane, the floor tiles can be measured along this wall in the usual way and, by using the vanishing point for the room, the 'vertical' divisions between the tiles can be drawn.

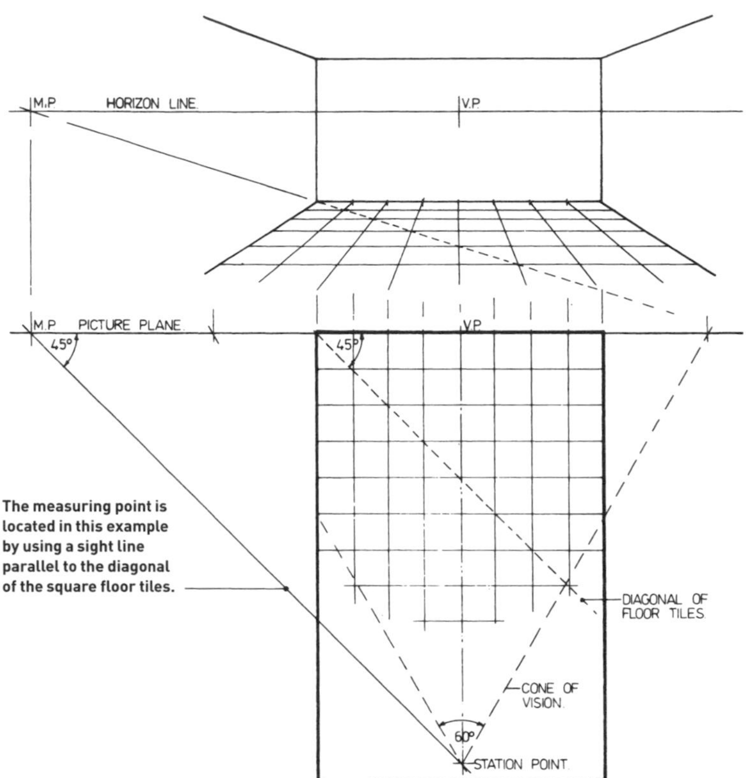

152 Method of setting up the floor tiles using a measuring point.

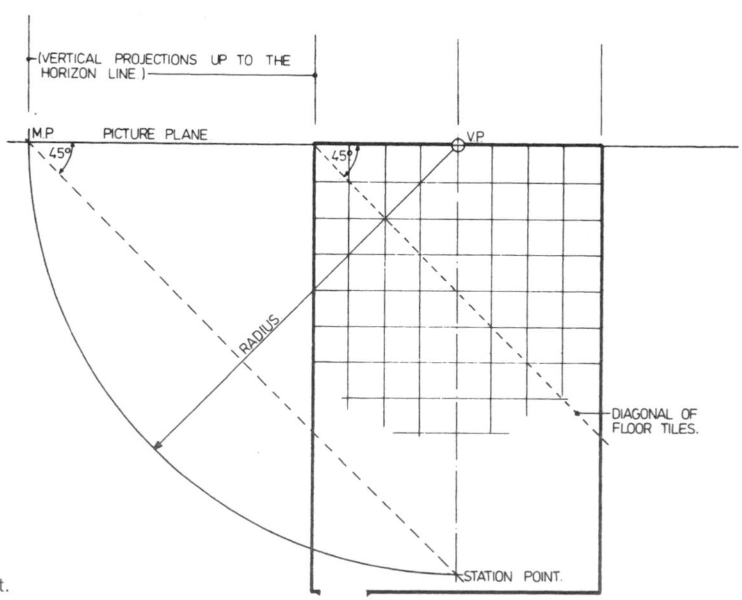

153 Two short cuts for locating a measuring point.

At this stage the knowledge that a diagonal line drawn from the corner of the room will cross a tile in each 'vertical' row and each 'horizontal' row (until it reaches the opposite wall) can be used to save a considerable amount of time and effort. If the measuring point located in the plan construction is projected up to the horizon line (the diagonals are in the horizontal plane) the diagonal line located in the plan can be located in the perspective view by drawing a line from the measuring point in the horizon line through the appropriate corner of the room until it meets the opposite wall. Where this perspective view of the diagonal line meets the 'vertical' divisions of the floor tiles, will be located the 'horizontal' divisions and therefore the floor tiles can be completed in this view by drawing these in as 'horizontal' lines (i.e. parallel to the picture plane).

Because the diagonals of a square are at 45° to a base line of that square – which, in this example, is parallel to the picture plane – there are a number of alternative short cuts for locating a measuring point. Fig. 153 shows the two most favoured ways, superimposed on the room used for the previous examples. The first of these uses the knowledge that the diagonal of a square tile in this example will be at 45° to the picture plane. Therefore it will not be necessary to do more than draw a line from the station point to meet the picture plane at an angle of 45°. This point of intersection must be the vanishing point for the diagonals of the square floor tiles. The second method for obtaining a measuring point for the diagonals of square floor tiles consists of drawing an arc using the plan position of the vanishing point as the centre and a radius equal to the distance between the vanishing point and the station point. This arc is swung to meet the picture plane and it is this intersection of the arc and the picture plane which is the plan position of the measuring point. When the measuring point is located in the plan it is then projected up to the horizon line in the normal way.

Another method of obtaining a measuring point is not shown but should be obvious from the methods shown so far. This is probably the simplest method of all as it consists simply of measuring the distance between the station point and the vanishing point in the picture plane and transferring this measurement along the horizon line using the vanishing point in the horizon line as the starting point. Regardless of which of the methods shown or described here is used, the principle remains the same and the results obtained will be identical.

The previous examples show a simple use of a measuring point to save time and effort without loss of accuracy. However, the use of a measuring point, or measuring points, is not limited to this type of example only. Measuring points can be used to produce more squares or rectangles, as shown in Fig. 154 where a square is set up in plan in the normal way and the perspective view of it is drawn. If a diagonal is drawn on the perspective view and continued until it intersects the horizon line, this intersection can be used as a measuring point, i.e. the vanishing point for the diagonal of the square and all other lines parallel to it. If any pair of parallel sides of the square are extended, the measuring point can be used to draw another diagonal so that another square of identical size can be added to the first. This can be done using any one of the four sides of the square to add another square or, if

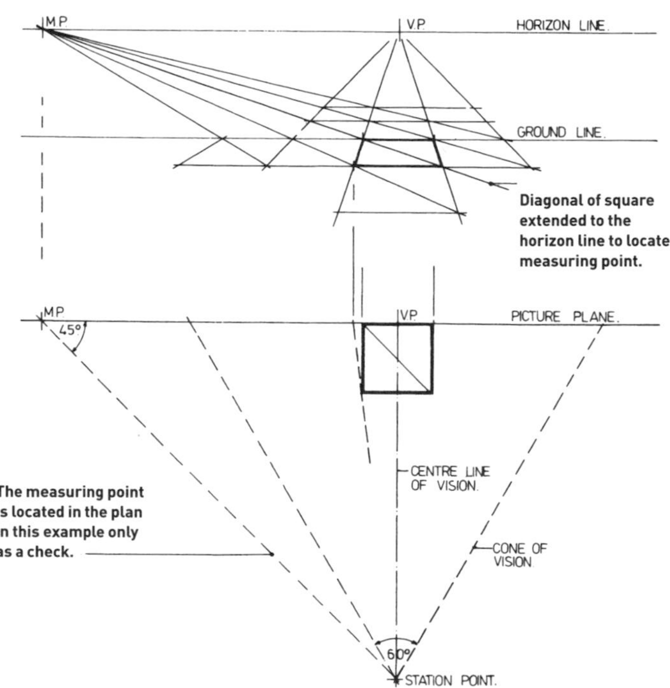

154 Use of a measuring point to draw a series of squares in perspective from one square in plan.

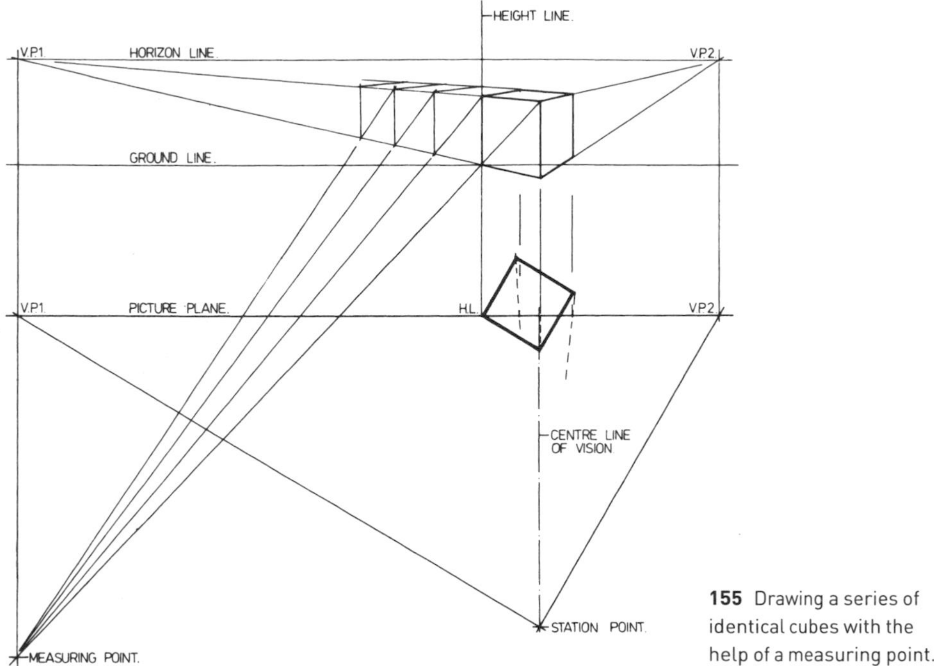

155 Drawing a series of identical cubes with the help of a measuring point.

necessary, all four sides as shown. The only limitation to the addition of an almost endless number of squares in any direction is the cone of vision. Squares constructed outside of the cone of vision will be subject to distortion in the same way as in any other method of perspective projection.

In the examples to date the measuring points have occurred in the horizon line because each of the figures used has been either in the ground plane or parallel to it, which means that the diagonals used to locate the measuring points have been parallel to the ground. The vanishing points for lines either in or parallel to the ground plane are located in the horizon line. In the example shown in Fig. 155, the side of a cube, which has been set up in perspective using a two-point construction, is used to locate a measuring point. If the diagonal of a side is drawn as shown, it can be seen that it is a line inclined to the ground plane. The diagonal drawn on the face of the cube will be in the same direction, when seen in plan, as the top and bottom edges of the cube, so that its vanishing point will be either directly above or below V.P.1.

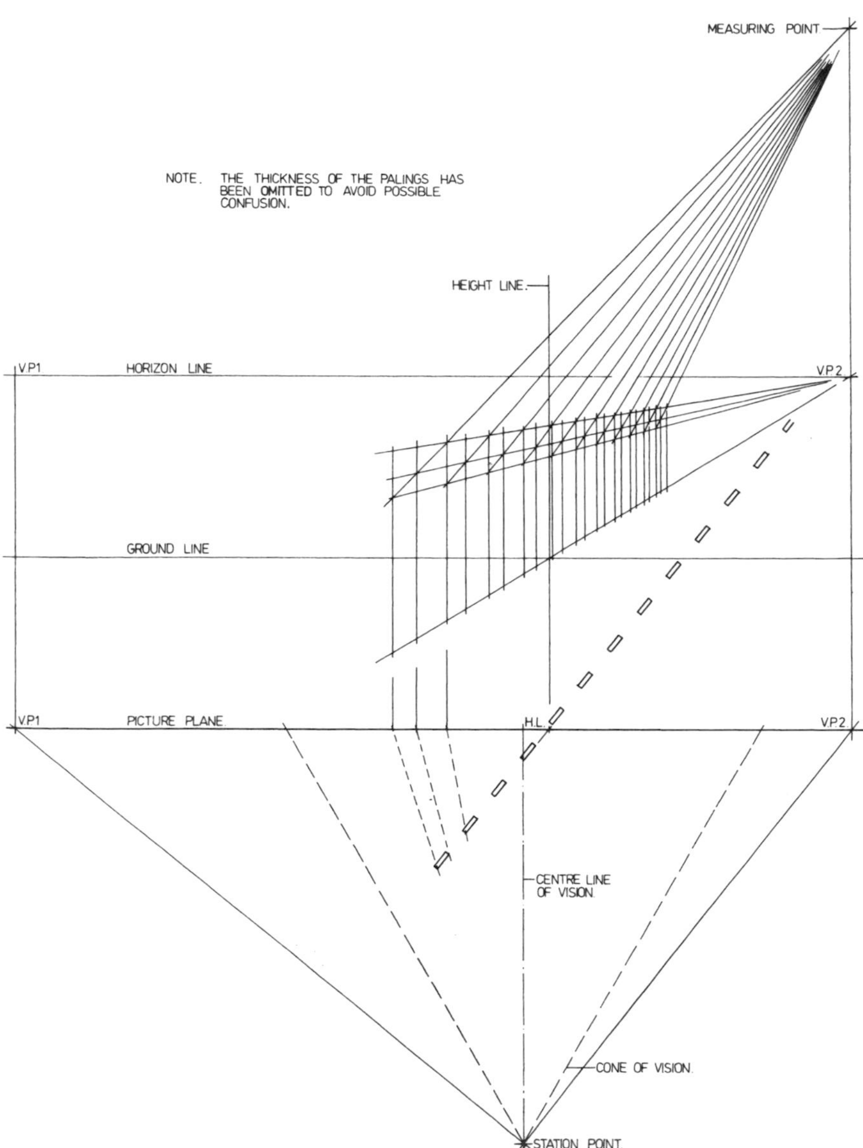

156 Use of a measuring point to subdivide a surface – in this case a line of palings.

In the example shown here a measuring point (vanishing point for the diagonal and all lines parallel to it) will be below V.P.1. By extending the top and bottom lines of the appropriate side of the cube, more identical cubes can be drawn using the measuring point to draw another diagonal as each cube is completed. This can be repeated until the required number of cubes is produced. More cubes could be added in another direction if a diagonal were drawn on the other visible vertical face of the cube and extended to meet a vertical line through V.P.2. This second measuring point could then be used in the same way as the previous one to add more cubes on this side.

Another use of the measuring point is the subdivision of a surface similar to the one shown in Fig. 156. The problem illustrated here represents a paling fence with palings of one width and spaces of another. This can be set up in perspective using the normal method of projection, but it would be a long and laborious process. If the top and bottom lines of the palings are set up using the normal method of perspective projection the first paling and the first space can be located as shown. Using a convenient angle, a line is drawn through the intersection of the top line of the fence and the top corner (next to the first space) of the second paling and continued in both directions to intersect the sides of the first paling in one direction and a vertical line drawn through V.P.2 in the other. The intersection of this line and the vertical line through V.P.2 is the measuring point, i.e. the vanishing point for this line and all others parallel to it. From the points of intersection of the line and the sides of the first paling perspective lines are drawn back to V.P.2 as shown. A line drawn from the intersection of the lower of these two perspective lines and the side of the second paling (already located) to the measuring point will locate the width of the second paling and the space between it and the third paling. This exercise can be repeated until the required length of fence has been drawn.

To sight and locate each paling by projection would require a great deal of patience together with a possible loss of accuracy as the distance between the spectator and the palings increases. Though the measuring point in this case is an arbitrary one its use is no less accurate than those which were constructed in the previous examples. The basic principle, that shapes can be repeated in perspective projection using diagonals and their vanishing points (measuring points), remains the same.

Fig. 157 shows this method used for drawing a railroad track in perspective. This is always a difficult subject because if it is not drawn accurately in the first place it can cause no end of difficulty and frustration. Because the diagonals are

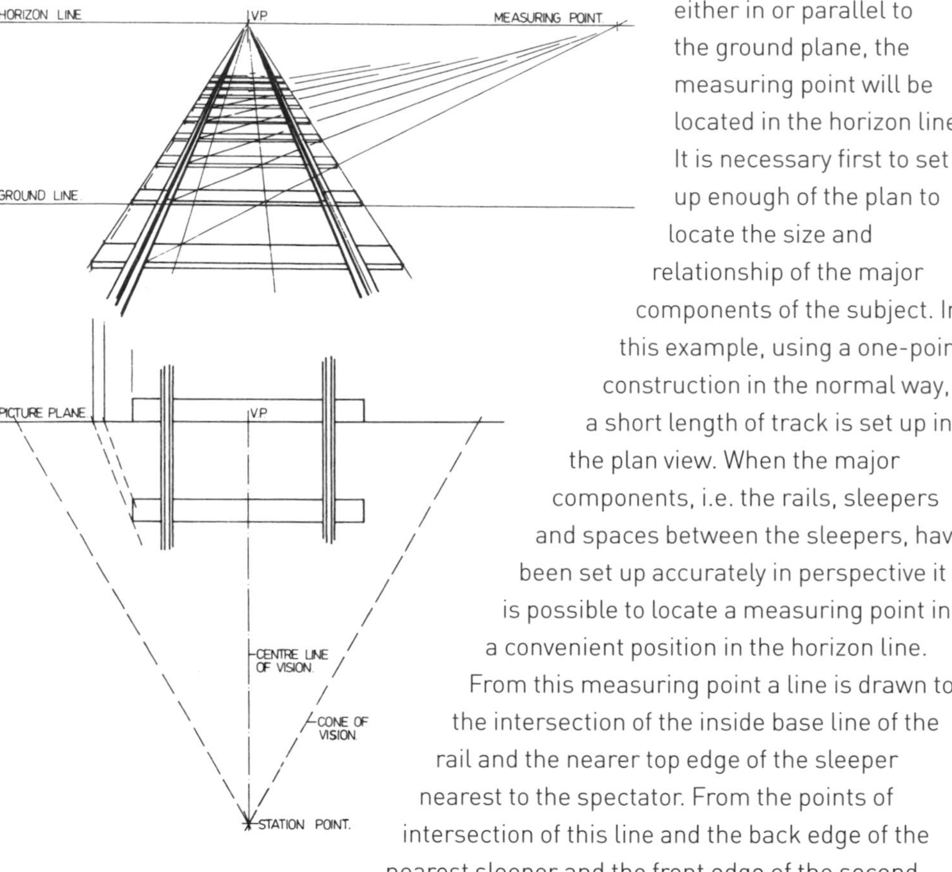

157 Another example of a measuring point used to subdivide a surface; here the measuring point is in the horizon line.

either in or parallel to the ground plane, the measuring point will be located in the horizon line. It is necessary first to set up enough of the plan to locate the size and relationship of the major components of the subject. In this example, using a one-point construction in the normal way, a short length of track is set up in the plan view. When the major components, i.e. the rails, sleepers and spaces between the sleepers, have been set up accurately in perspective it is possible to locate a measuring point in a convenient position in the horizon line. From this measuring point a line is drawn to the intersection of the inside base line of the rail and the nearer top edge of the sleeper nearest to the spectator. From the points of intersection of this line and the back edge of the nearest sleeper and the front edge of the second sleeper, perspective lines are drawn back to the vanishing point. It can be seen from Fig. 157 that the diagonals are drawn back to the measuring point and the sleepers and the spaces between them are located and drawn until the required length of track has been produced.

From the few examples shown here it can be seen that the use of the measuring point can save a great deal of time and needless effort without significant loss of accuracy. These examples are by no means all of the uses to which measuring points can be applied but once the principle is thoroughly understood it can be developed, expanded and used to solve many otherwise complex problems.

Measuring points can also be used to set up a perspective view of an object. This is known as the measuring point method for setting up a perspective and the basic principle of it is shown in Fig. 158 where, by its use, one line is located in a perspective view. In this figure the line to be drawn in perspective is located in the ground plane with, in this case, end *B* coinciding with the picture plane. The station point and the picture plane are selected in the same way as in previous constructions. To eliminate the possibility of distortion the position of the station point should be checked with the cone of vision to make sure that the spectator can in fact see all of the object from the chosen station point. This step important in any perspective drawing and is, unfortunately, often forgotten. The vanishing point for the given line is found by drawing a sight line from the station point parallel to the line to meet the picture plane. The point of intersection of this sight line and the picture plane is the plan location of the vanishing point (V.P.). The measuring point is located in the picture plane (plan) by using the vanishing point as the centre of an arc whose radius is equal to the length of the line from the station point to the vanishing point. The point where the arc intersects the picture plane is the plan location of the measuring point. The location of the horizon line is a matter of convenience; it can be located either above or below the plan construction without altering the final drawing. In Fig. 158, the horizon line is located above the plan construction and the ground line is located below the horizon line at a distance equal

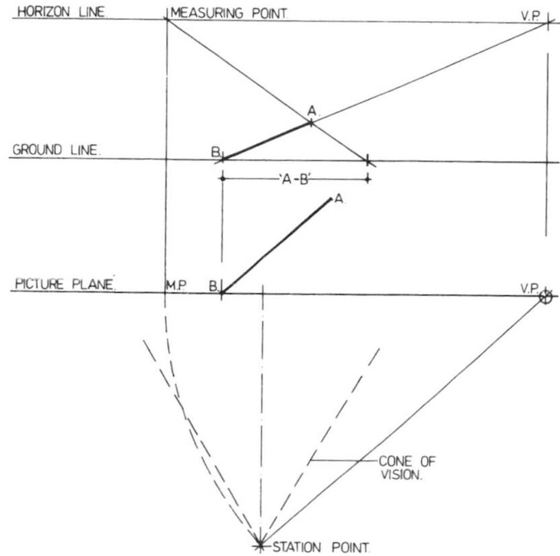

158 Locating one line in a perspective view by the measuring-point method.

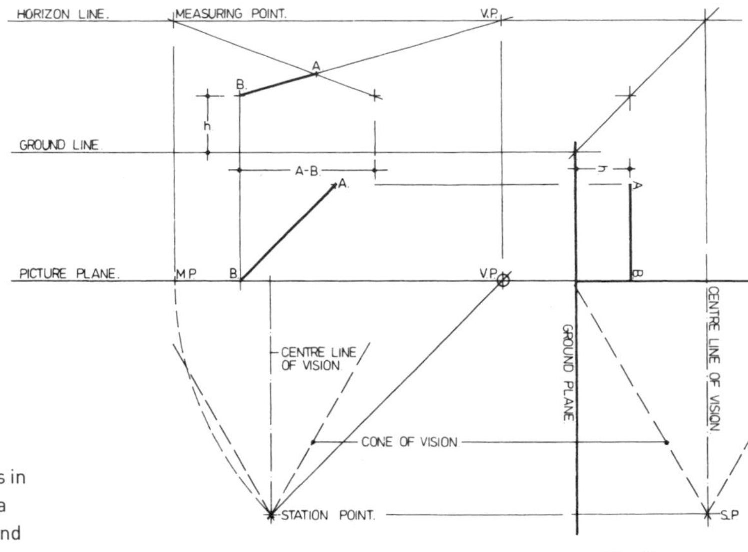

159 Locating one line, as in Fig. 158, but in this case a line which is parallel to and above the ground plane.

to the required eye level. It is this distance which determines the height of the spectator's eye above the ground and it is therefore the relationship between the horizon line and the ground line which is important, not the relationship between the horizon line and the picture plane in the plan construction, as the student sometimes mistakenly assumes.

To locate the vanishing point and the measuring point on the horizon line, where they must be located because the line which is the subject of the perspective drawing is located in the ground plane, is a simple matter of projecting up vertically to the horizon line. If the horizon line was below the plan of the picture plane, projections would be down vertically. Because point *B* coincides with the picture plane and is in the ground plane it can be located in the perspective view by simple vertical projection up to the ground line. The line *AB* will lie in a line from point *B* to the vanishing point (the vanishing point was located by drawing a sight line parallel to the plan of line *AB*). The length of the line *AB* is measured in the plan and from point *B* in the ground line this length is measured along the ground line and marked, as shown. (This line must always be marked off on the opposite side of the line from *B* to V.P. to the measuring point.) By joining the measuring point and the point in the ground line marking off the length of the line *AB*, point *A* is located in the line from *B* to V.P. The result of this exercise is a drawing of the line *AB* in perspective.

Once it is possible to locate one line in a perspective view it is possible to locate any number of lines. Because a perspective drawing is essentially a line drawing and an object can be considered as simply a collection of lines, it must be possible to draw objects in perspective using the method described here for a single line. However, before proceeding with an object such as a simple rectangular prism, it is necessary to look at a few variations to the location of the single line. The first is a line which is still parallel to the ground plane but no longer situated in it. In Fig. 159, the line *AB* is at a height *h* above the ground plane but in all other respects the circumstances are the same as those in Fig. 158. For the purpose of explanation, an elevation of the plan construction is shown and, as is usual, it is at a convenient distance from the plan construction. The relationship between the eye of the spectator and the height of the line *AB* can be seen from the elevation. The location of the station point, the picture plane, the vanishing point and the measuring point is carried out in exactly the same way as in Fig. 158. In this case point *B* is located at a height *h* above the ground plane (this is measured from the elevation), therefore point *B* in the perspective view will be at a height *h* above the ground line (point *B* coincides with the picture plane). Line *AB* will be located in the line joining point *B*, at height *h* above the ground line, to the vanishing point, i.e. in the line from *B* to V.P. Because the line *AB* is at a height *h* above and parallel to the ground plane it will be necessary to locate the length of the line *AB* at a height *h* above the ground line in the perspective view. This point defining the length of the required line can then be joined to the measuring point and point *A* located in the line from point *B* to the vanishing point. The result of this exercise is a perspective drawing of the line *AB* when it is at a height *h* above the ground plane.

The second variation to the location of a single line in perspective using the measuring point method is an inclined line, i.e. a line inclined to the ground plane. If the elevation in

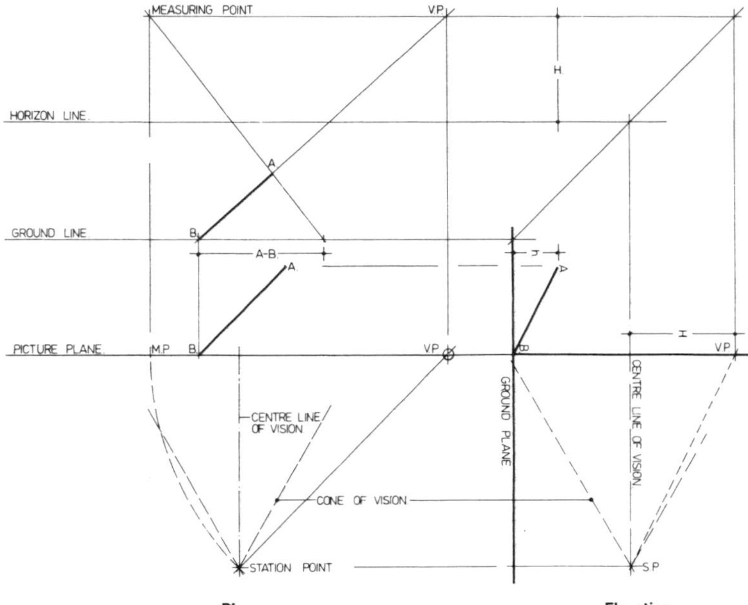

160 Locating an inclined line by the measuring point method.

Fig. 159 is examined it will be seen that if one end of the line *AB* were to be lifted higher than the other, the sight line parallel to it would intersect the picture plane no longer in the horizon line but either above or below it depending on which end of the line was raised. This means that the vanishing point (and the measuring point) for an inclined line would be either above or below the horizon line and located in a vertical line through the plan location of the vanishing point (and measuring point).

Fig. 160 shows the construction required when the line *AB* is inclined to the ground plane. In this example it is necessary to prepare an elevation of the plan construction to obtain the height of the vanishing point and the measuring point above or below the horizon line. Both the plan construction and the elevation are prepared in the normal way, as previously described. Point *A* is higher than point *B* which, in this case, is located in the ground plane. From the elevation the height of the vanishing point and the measuring point is measured from the horizon line. This height is then located, in this case above the horizon line, and a line drawn horizontally to enable the measuring point to be located at the same height above the horizon line as the vanishing point. The measuring point is located in this line by projecting up from its position in the plan view of the picture plane in the normal way. Line *AB* is drawn in the perspective view in exactly the same way as it was in the two preceding examples, the only difference being that the vanishing point and the measuring point are no longer located in the horizon line but in a horizontal line above it. From point *B* in the ground line the true length of line *AB* is measured. It should be noted that neither the plan view nor the elevation of the construction shows the true length of line *AB*, so a simple projection exercise is necessary to obtain its true length. As previously described, once the true length of the line *AB* is established, the perspective view of it can be drawn using the vanishing point and the measuring point.

In each of the previous examples of perspective drawing by the measuring point method, one end of the line to be drawn has been located in the picture plane. In the last example of single lines in perspective using this method, neither end of the line is located in the picture plane so the line must be extended to meet the picture plane at point *O*. Fig. 161 shows the construction required under these circumstances. The only difference between this and the previous construction

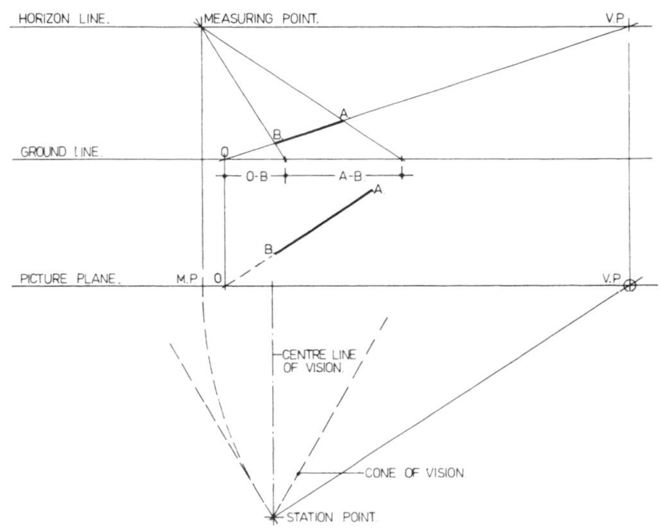

161 Locating a line of which neither end is in the picture plane.

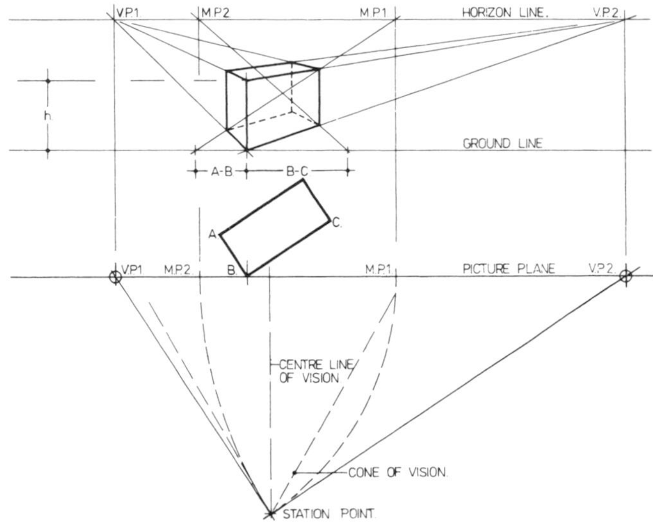

162 The measuring point method extended from a single line to a figure bounded by a number of lines.

shown in Fig. 158 is that the distances from point *O* of both ends of the line must be measured and located on the ground line. By joining both of the measured distances on the ground line to the measuring point the ends of line *AB* can be located.

When the basic method of constructing a perspective view using the measuring point method is understood it can be used to set up actual objects, i.e. objects consisting of a number of lines. Fig. 162 shows the method used for setting up a perspective view of a simple rectangular prism. Because two vanishing points are required to draw this object in perspective, it will be obvious that two measuring points will be necessary. Apart from this, the figure should be self-explanatory if the previous examples have been understood.

Fig. 163 shows the same rectangular prism as used in the preceding example but this time it has been placed at a short distance behind the picture plane. Unlike the previous example in which a corner of the prism coincided with the picture plane, in this example no corner of the prism coincides with the picture plane; this means that the appropriate sides of the prism will have to be extended to meet the picture plane in the plan construction. The vanishing points, measuring points, horizon line and ground line are located as previously explained. From the point where side *AB* is extended to meet the picture plane at point *O* in the plan construction, point *O* is located in the ground line by vertical projection. From this point *O* in the ground line the lengths *OA* and *AB* are measured and marked. The line from *O* to V.P.2 is drawn, and points *A* and *B* are located in it using the measuring point M.P.2 in the usual way. Using point *O* in the ground line as a base, the height of the rectangular prism can be established by measurement, and from this height, a line can be drawn back to V.P.2 in which the top of the side *AB* will be located. By projecting vertical lines up from points *A* and *B* in the base line of the perspective view, side *AB* can be completed. Using the extension of the side *CA* to meet the picture plane at point *X* in the plan construction, the side *CA* can be drawn in the perspective view using the same method as was used for side *AB*. Obviously it will be unnecessary to locate the height of the prism because this has already been established in the perspective view when side *AB* was drawn.

While advantages are claimed by some people for this method in comparison with others, it must be admitted that it also has a number of disadvantages, not the least of which is that it seems unnecessarily complicated. When it is remembered that for each vanishing point a measuring point is required, it will be realized that the possibility of error must

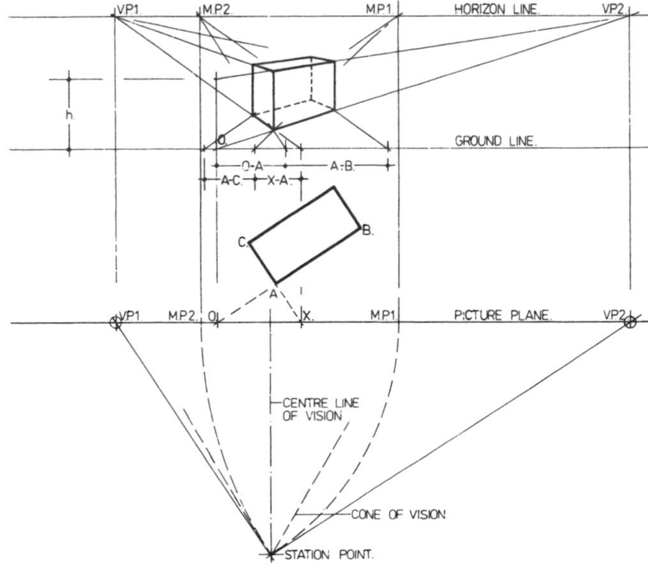

163 An adaptation of Fig. 162, where no corner of the object touches the picture plane. As in Fig. 161, two sides of the object have to be extended.

be at least twice that of the method used in this book. However, it is not intended to enter into an academic discussion of the relative merits of the various methods for the construction of a perspective view of an object. Rather, the intention here is to help the student to understand and use sound knowledge of the principles of perspective projection in developing accurate methods for setting up perspective views of objects quickly and efficiently. This criticism of the measuring-point method does not extend to the use of measuring points in cases where they can be of great value in saving time without loss of accuracy, but only to the use of measuring points as the whole basis of perspective projection.

More information regarding the use of measuring points and the measuring point method of setting up perspectives is given in Chapter 2.9, 'Short Cuts in Perspective Drawing'.

2.8 Shadow Projection in Perspective Drawing

Perspective drawing is generally only a means to an end rather than an end in itself. A perspective drawing is usually produced as a linear framework on which a rendering is based. Because light plays such an important role in what is seen, it is essential that its effect on a subject be understood so that it can be portrayed accurately when the subject is rendered. Shadow projection is seldom treated with the importance it deserves in the academic subject known as perspective, but it is nevertheless a very important part of that subject. The ability to construct accurate or, at the very least, believable shadows is one of the most important elements of rendering.

Before proceeding with the method used for constructing shadows in perspective projection it is necessary to understand a few elementary principles of light. Without light it would be impossible to see anything. An object is seen because light rays strike its surface and are reflected from that surface back to the eye of the spectator and it is only because of these reflected light rays that the spectator is able to see the object. In shadow projection it is not the reflected light ray which is of principal interest but the light ray itself. Generally speaking, there are two sources of light: the sun and the various forms of artificial light, e.g. electric light, candles, etc. Whether a light ray emanates from the sun or some form of artificial light source makes no difference to the fact that the light ray will always travel in a straight line and is incapable of changing direction unless some form of reflector is introduced. For all practical purposes light rays from the sun are considered to be parallel, unlike those from the simplest form of artificial light source which radiate from a single point. Light rays, whether from the sun or an artificial source, are incapable of penetrating solid, opaque matter. It is because of these qualities that shade and shadow exist.

To eliminate any confusion from the very beginning, it is necessary to define the difference between shade and shadow. Shade exists when a surface is turned away from the light source. Shadow exists when light rays are stopped from reaching a surface by the intervention of another object or surface. Fig. 164 shows a post seen in ordinary sunlight and from this view it is possible to see that the side facing the light source is seen in light and the side facing away from the light source is seen in shade. The line between the face seen in light and the face seen in shade is known as the line of separation. This line of separation is of considerable importance and will be dealt with more fully later in this chapter. Because the post stops the light rays from reaching the ground, the area on the ground directly behind the post will be in shadow. This shadow will start from the base of the post, i.e. where the post meets the ground, and finish with the first ray of light which is able to pass directly over the top of the post. Because, in this example, only the post is capable of stopping the light rays, the rest of the ground will be in light.

If this is related to a person standing on the ground, it will be seen (Fig. 165*a*) that his shadow will start from his feet and will finish with the topmost part of him obstructing the light rays. The only time his shadow will not start from his feet is when his feet are no longer in contact with the surface directly below him. An example of this is shown in Fig. 165*b*, where the person has jumped into the air. Because he is no longer in

164 Shade and shadow.

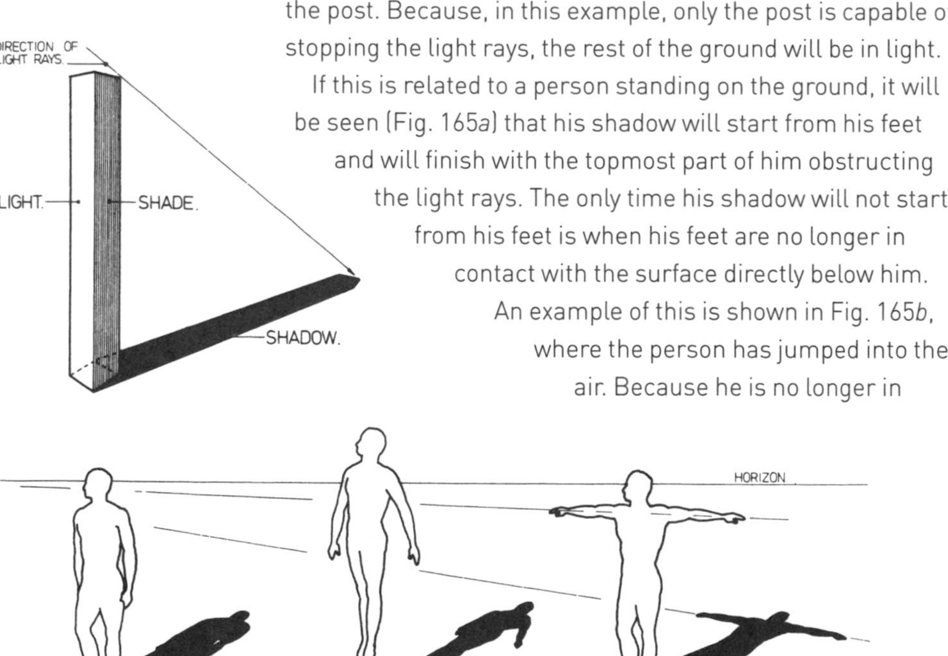

165 Shadows related to the human figure.

contact with the ground no part of him is obstructing the light rays between his feet and the ground directly below him, which means that his shadow will no longer start from his feet. Nevertheless, as soon as he lands again everything will be back to normal and once again his shadow will start from his feet. This is an important fact to remember about shadows. Another is that the shadow will always fall in the direction in which the light rays travel from the light source. The third and possibly the most important of these facts to remember in shadow projection is that parallel lines cast parallel shadows. Fig. 165*c* shows a person standing on the ground, i.e. at right angles to the ground plane, with his arms raised so that they are parallel to the ground plane. The shadow cast by his outstretched arms will be parallel to his arms, i.e. the shadow cast by his arms will appear to converge to the same vanishing point as his arms.

Knowledge of these basic facts regarding shadows can save a great deal of needless effort and wasted time in setting up shadows in perspective drawing. Though these facts are possibly the most important, they are by no means all that must be considered when setting up shadows in perspective drawing. Because many of these other factors are not common to all problems, but occur only in special circumstances, they can be dealt with as they occur in the following examples.

Of the two different sources of light the first to be considered here is sunlight. Because the rays of light from the sun are for all practical purposes considered to be parallel and because they strike the ground plane obliquely, they can be treated as any other inclined lines in perspective projection. This means that because they are parallel they will converge to a common vanishing point and, because they are inclined to the ground plane, that vanishing point will be located either above or below the horizon line in the perspective view. From basic principles it is known that the vanishing point for inclined parallel lines (the light rays) will be located either directly above or below the position of the vanishing point for those lines when they are in the horizontal plane. If the sun is located in front of the spectator the

166 Sun in front of the spectator: vanishing point for light rays is above the horizon, shadow towards the spectator.

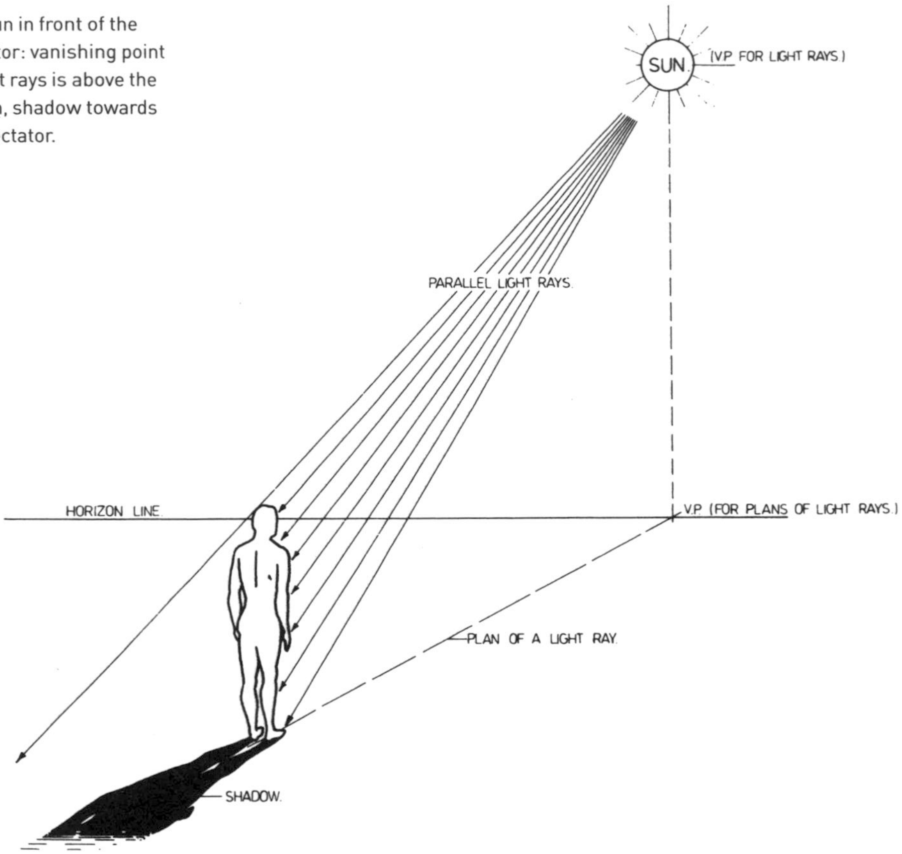

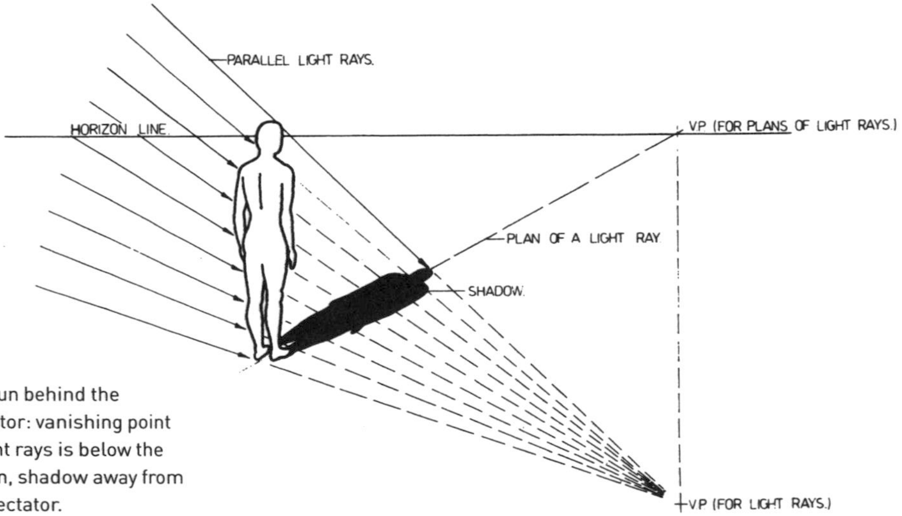

167 Sun behind the spectator: vanishing point for light rays is below the horizon, shadow away from the spectator.

vanishing point for the rays of light will be above the horizon line, as shown in Fig. 166. This means that the shadow cast by an object, in this case a person, will be towards the spectator. If, on the other hand, the sun is located behind the spectator (Fig. 167), the vanishing point for the rays of light will be below the horizon line. This means that the shadow cast by the person will be away from the spectator.

Because the shadow of an object is cast in the direction of the light rays and extends from the base of the object (if the base of the object is located in the ground plane) to the shadow point of the top of that object, it is possible to produce the shadow of a simple vertical line in a perspective view, as in Fig. 168. The line is shown at right angles to the ground plane, and the direction of the light rays appears on the ground plane in the form of a line which represents a plan view of the actual ray of light. This plan of the light ray starts from the base of the vertical line. Both ends of the vertical line will coincide when it is viewed in plan, which means that the plan of the light ray drawn is the plan of that light ray which passes through the top of the vertical line. Therefore the shadow of the top of the vertical line will be located at the intersection of the plan of the light ray and the actual light ray passing through the top of the vertical line. If this principle is applied to a line which is still vertical but does not have one end located in the ground plane,

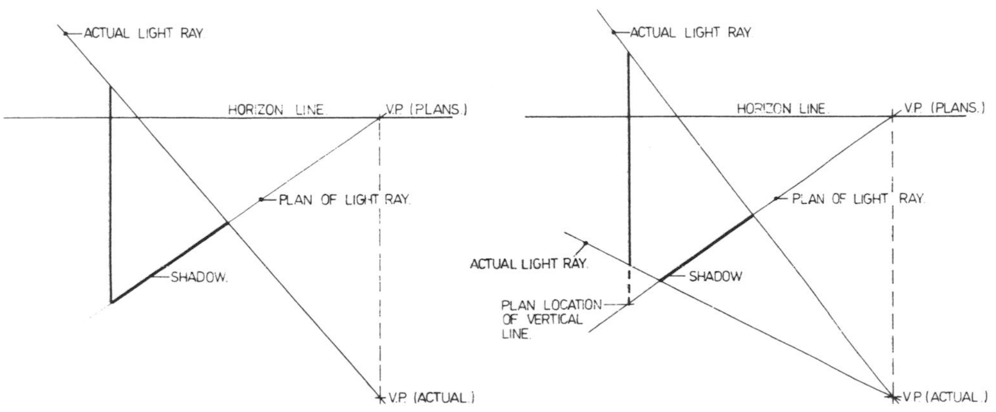

168 The shadow of a simple vertical line.

169 The shadow of a vertical line of which the lower end stands above the ground plane.

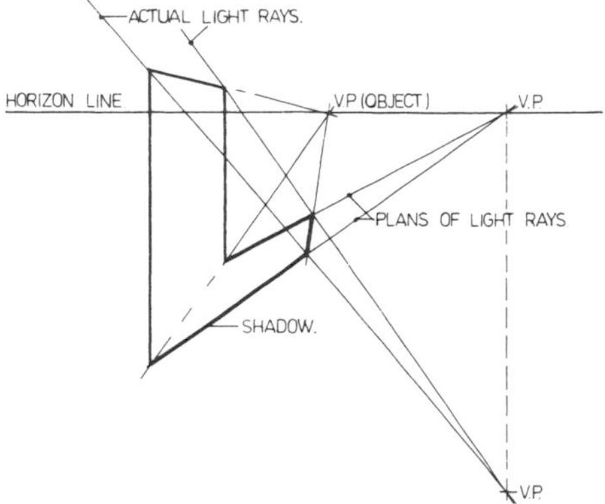

170 Shadows of two vertical lines and a cross-bar.

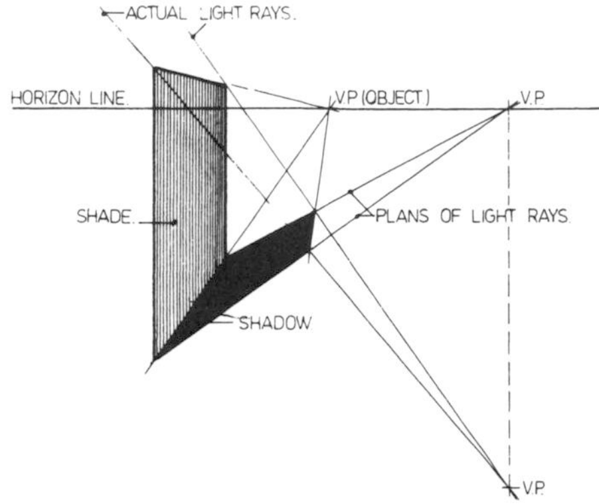

171 Fig. 170 converted into a vertical plane.

as shown in Fig. 169, it will be seen that again both ends of the line would coincide in the plan view; therefore, the plans of the light rays through the top and the bottom of the line and its plan position in the ground plane would coincide in the plan view. This means that in the view shown in Fig. 169 it is necessary to locate the plan position of the vertical line in the ground plane and the plan view of the rays of light (the ones which pass through the top and the bottom of the vertical line which will coincide in the plan view) drawn from it in the direction of the light rays. The shadow position of the top of the vertical line is located in the plan of the light ray by drawing the actual light ray through the top of the vertical line to intersect the plan line. The intersection of the actual light ray and the plan of the light ray will be the shadow point of the top of the vertical line. The shadow point of the bottom of the vertical line is located in the plan of the light ray by drawing the actual light ray through the bottom of the vertical line to intersect the plan of the light ray. The intersection of the actual light ray and its plan will be the shadow point of the bottom of the vertical line. The part of the plan of the ray of light between these two points will be the shadow cast by the vertical line.

The third of these simple explanations concerns two vertical lines set apart with a horizontal line joining their tops. Fig. 170 shows the plan of the light ray for each vertical line drawn from their intersections with the ground plane. The shadow points of the tops of each line are located on these plan lines by drawing the actual light rays through the tops of these lines to meet the plans of the light rays, as previously described. The line joining the tops of the vertical lines is horizontal, i.e. parallel to the ground plane. This means that the shadow of this line joining the tops of the vertical lines will also be parallel to the ground plane.

Fig. 171 shows a vertical opaque plane which is produced by using the same vertical lines as in Fig. 170 but in this case joined by horizontal lines at the bottom as well as the top. The shadows of the lines surrounding the vertical plane are located in exactly the same way as for the lines in Fig. 170. In this example the lines will stop the rays of light from reaching the ground but also, because the lines enclose an opaque surface, no light ray will be able to reach the ground within an area bounded by these lines. Consequently the area between the shadows of these lines will be seen in shadow. It should be remembered that the surface of the vertical plane facing away from the light source will be in shade.

From the examples shown here it can be seen by examination, particularly of Figs. 170 and 171, that the shadows of the objects can be completed by simple

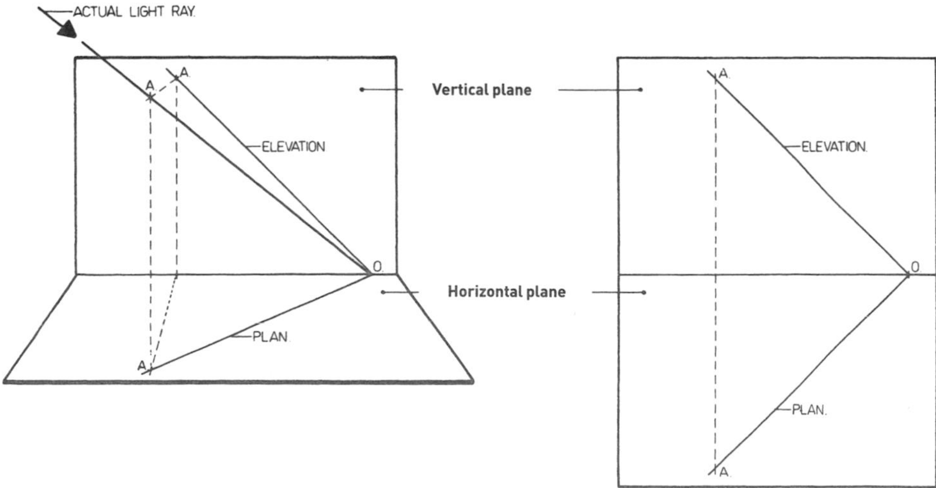

172 The relationship between an actual light ray, the ground plane and the picture plane.

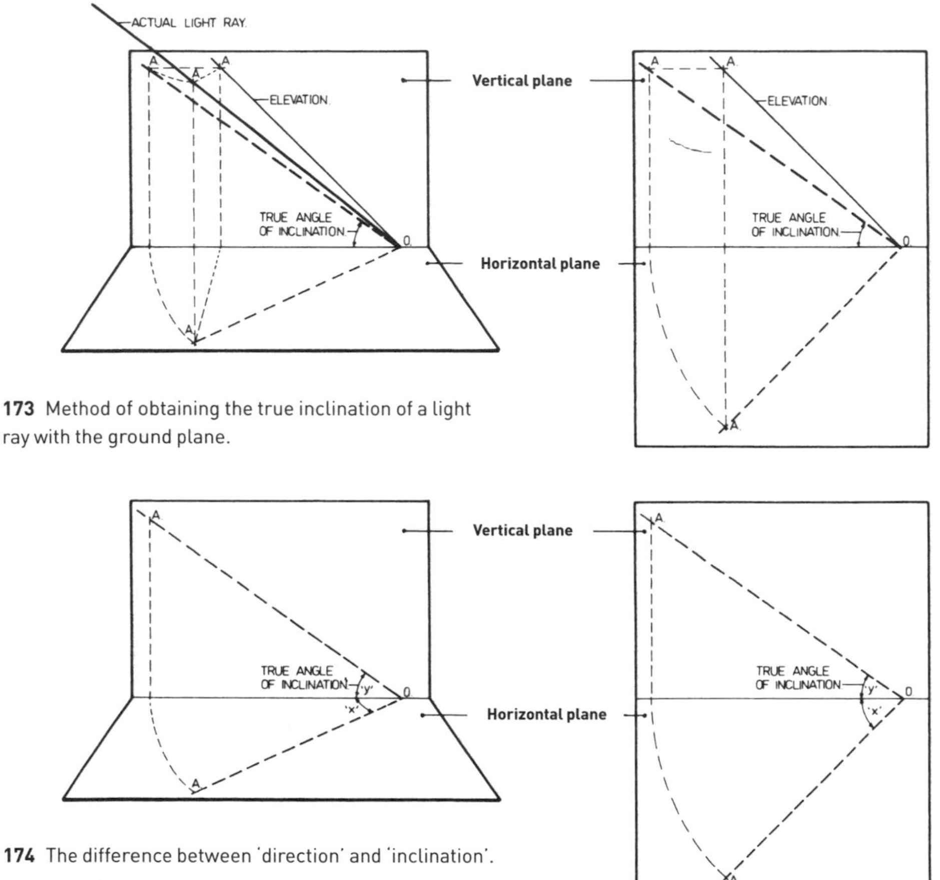

173 Method of obtaining the true inclination of a light ray with the ground plane.

174 The difference between 'direction' and 'inclination'.

observation and logic: if each object is treated as a combination of simple lines, shadows need be neither difficult nor time-consuming.

From the foregoing it should be obvious that before shadows can be constructed in a perspective projection the direction of the light rays and their angle of inclination to the ground plane must be known. Because a perspective projection is carried out in two dimensions, not three which would be necessary to take advantage of the conditions shown in Fig. 172, it is necessary to locate a plan view and an elevation of the actual light ray so that when the vertical plane is 'laid down flat', as shown, it is possible to use these views for the perspective construction. While the angle between the plan of the light ray and the picture plane is the true angle, the angle of inclination, i.e. the angle the inclined light rays make with the ground plane, shown in this view, is not. For the angle of inclination to be seen as a true angle it would have to be seen parallel to the vertical plane, therefore in this view it will appear distorted, i.e. larger than it will be in fact. In perspective projection it is necessary to produce a true elevation of the actual light ray so that the true angle the light ray makes with the ground plane can be used. The method for obtaining this true inclination of the actual light ray is shown in Fig. 173, where the angle formed by the actual light ray and the ground plane is swung through an arc which results in the true angle being located on the picture plane without distortion. When the vertical plane is 'laid down flat' it can be seen that the true angle of inclination of the light ray is much smaller than the angle shown in Fig. 172. To relate this to perspective projection the angle which the plan of the light ray makes with the picture plane is known as the *direction* of the light ray (angle *x*) and the true inclination of the light ray is known as the *inclination* (angle *y*). These angles are shown and identified in Fig. 174 to avoid any confusion.

For the purpose of explaining the method used for the construction of shadows in perspective projection a simple rectangular prism has been set up using a two-point construction (Fig. 175). When the perspective view of the object is completed, it is necessary to decide on the location of the light source, i.e. the direction (angle *x*) and the inclination (angle *y*) of the light rays. Because the light rays are parallel

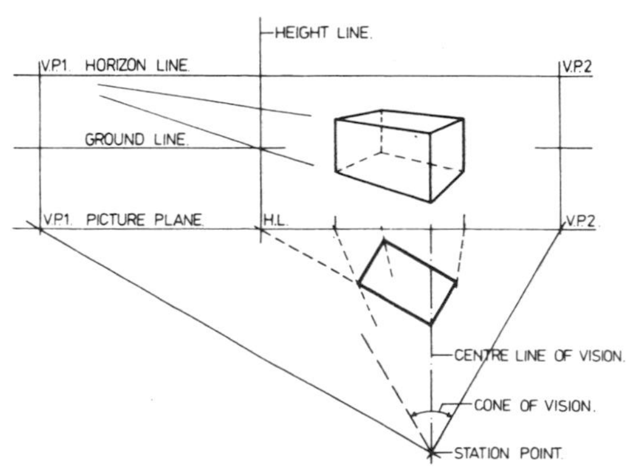

175 Rectangular prism in perspective, ready for construction of shadows.

and their plan lines are parallel it is necessary to locate vanishing points for each of them.

These vanishing points are located in three main steps (Fig. 176):

Step 1. Using the station point as the starting point, a sight line parallel to the plan view of the light ray is drawn to meet the picture plane (plan) at the angle *x*. The intersection of this sight line and the picture plane (plan) is the plan location of the vanishing points (V.1) for both the actual light rays and their plans. Because the plans of the light rays will occur in a horizontal plane (the ground plane or planes parallel to it), the vanishing point for these plan lines will be located in the horizon line. This means that V.1, which was located in the picture plane (plan), is projected up vertically in the normal way to locate it in the horizon line. It is known that the vanishing point for the actual light rays, which are simply inclined lines, will be located either directly above or below the vanishing point for their plans (V.1). This means that the vanishing point for the actual light rays will be located somewhere in the vertical line drawn through V.1.

Step 2. Before locating the vanishing point for the actual light rays it is necessary to locate the true angle *y* (the angle the light ray makes with the ground plane) on the picture plane. The sight line used to locate V.1 in Step 1 is a plan line drawn parallel to the light ray; therefore if this sight line (which is in fact a plan view of a sight line drawn parallel to the actual light ray) is swung through an arc with centre V.1 and radius V.1 to S.P. it is possible to obtain the true angle of inclination of the light ray (angle *y*) on the picture plane. Point *O* is located in the picture plane at the point where the arc intersects it. Point *O* is then located in the horizon line (because a sight line is used and the horizon line coincides with the eye level) by vertical projection in the normal way. Because point *O* in the horizon line is the equivalent of the 'eye position' and the vertical line through V.1 is the equivalent of an end elevation of the picture plane, a sight line could be drawn from the 'eye position' (point *O*) parallel to the true angle of inclination of the light ray (angle *y*) to meet the vertical line through V.1. (The equivalent of the end elevation of the picture plane.) This intersection of the sight line and the picture plane, i.e. the line drawn from point *O* at angle *y* to the horizon line to meet the vertical line through V.1, will be the vanishing point for the actual light rays.

Step 3. To locate the vanishing point for the actual light rays when the light source is located behind the spectator (which means that it will be located below the horizon line, as previously described), it is necessary to draw a line from point *O* (in the horizon line) at the angle *y* (below the horizon line) to meet the vertical line drawn through V.1. The point V.2, located at the intersection of these two lines, is the vanishing point for the actual light rays when the light source is located behind the spectator.

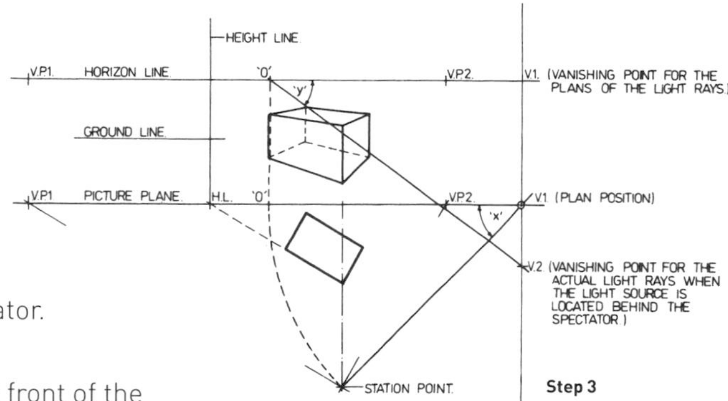

If the light source is located in front of the spectator the three steps remain basically the same except that the angle *y* in Step 3 is located above the horizon line, as shown in Fig. 177, in which V.3, above the horizon line, represents the vanishing point for the actual light rays. The sun (the light source) can be in only one place at a time, therefore either V.2 (behind the spectator) or V.3 (in front of the spectator) will be required in any perspective

176 Locating the vanishing points of the light rays, when the light is coming from behind the spectator.

177 Step 3 of Fig. 176, adapted for a light source in front of the spectator.

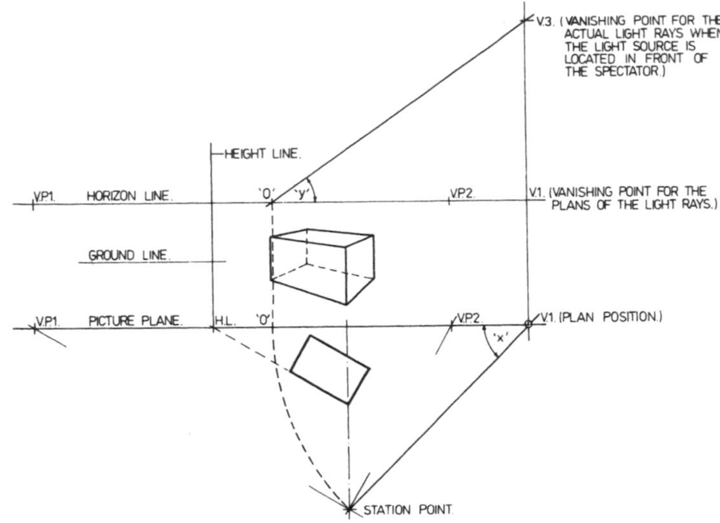

drawing but never both in the same drawing even though V.1 is common to both constructions. Needless to say, if the light source were located on the right of the spectator, instead of on his left as shown in Figs. 176 and 177, it would be necessary to locate V.1 on the other side of the construction using exactly the same method as for the examples shown.

An important factor is that the method shown here gives the student complete freedom in his choice of the direction and inclination of the light source. However, if the subject of his perspective drawing is a building or any other object which has a fixed aspect, this aspect can easily be related to the plan under projection because the angle the sun makes with both the picture plane and the ground plane can be calculated for any time of the day, for any month of the year, for any location in the world. Because this can be done, using this method, exact shadows can be cast for any set of realistic conditions anywhere in the world. To help in this and other areas relating to sun control, tables of sun angles are available for most of the major cities of the world or, at the very least, for the various latitudes of the world. However, it is not intended to pursue this aspect of shadow projection here because once the basic method is understood, whether actual angles or arbitrary ones are used, the method for carrying out the construction of shadows in perspective projection will be the same. Further information on a short-cut method of locating the vanishing points required in shadow projection is given in the next chapter (p. 229).

Once the construction required for setting up shadows in perspective has been completed, it is possible to locate and draw the shadows of the object forming the subject of the exercise. Fig. 178 shows four examples of objects and their shadows when the light source is behind the spectator (V.2 will be below the horizon line). The construction used to locate the vanishing point for the plans of the light rays (V.1) and the vanishing point for the actual light rays (V.2) is shown for the first of the four examples only (Fig. 178*a*) and would be exactly the same for the other three. Using these two vanishing points (V.1 and V.2), it is possible to construct the correct shadows of the object under these specific conditions.

In the example shown in Fig. 178*a*, it is first necessary, after setting up the vanishing points, to select a starting point for the actual construction of the shadow of the object. In this example the vertical line *AB* is chosen as the starting point. From the point of intersection of this line and the ground plane (point *B*) a line representing the plan of the light ray passing through the top of the vertical line is drawn in perspective, i.e. back to V.1. The actual light ray is then drawn through the top of the vertical line (point *A*) back to V.2. The point of intersection of these two lines is the shadow of point *A* in the perspective view. This means that the line on the ground plane between point *B* (the base of the vertical line) and point *A* (the top of the vertical line) must represent, in the

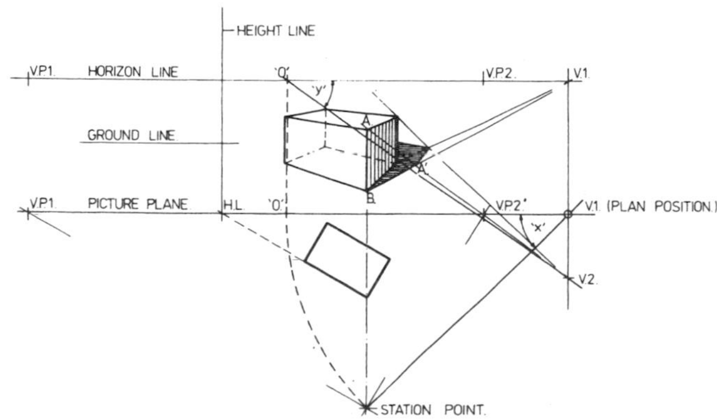

178*a–d* Four examples of objects and their shadows (light source behind the spectator).

178b

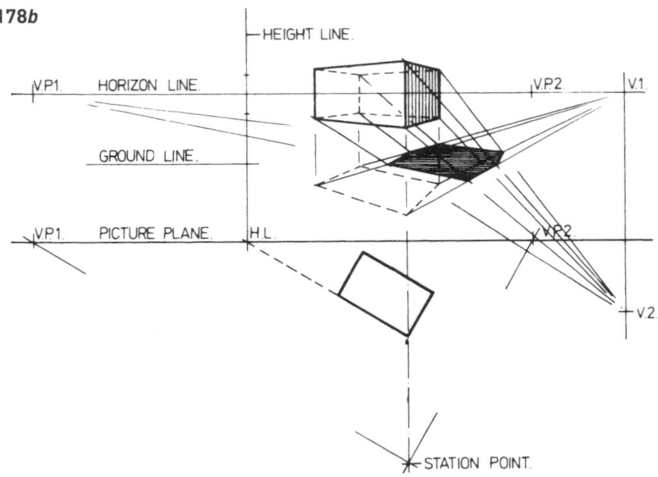

perspective view, the shadow of the vertical line *AB*. The other vertical 'edges' of the rectangular prism can have their shadows projected in the same way. If the object is examined it will be seen that these verticals form the vertical edges of solid planes which have top and bottom edges also. The top edges of these planes can be dealt with in either one of two ways. The first uses the fact that the top of the line *AB* is joined to the top of the opposite vertical edge of the plane by a straight line; therefore, the shadows of the verticals will be joined by the shadow of this straight line. In this way, the shadows of each of the planes forming the rectangular prism can be located and drawn in the perspective view.

On the other hand, it is known that parallel lines cast parallel shadows, and, because these straight lines joining the tops of the vertical lines of the object are parallel to the ground plane, the shadows cast by them will be parallel, i.e. they will be drawn using the same vanishing point as the lines themselves. It will be seen that the answer in both cases will be exactly the same; only the reasoning differs. The 'parallel line casting a parallel shadow' theory is usually preferred because it can save a great deal of time and confusion in many cases.

Once the method of actually drawing shadows in perspective projection is understood, it is a simple matter to apply it to any object, no matter how complex it might be. Basically, shadow projection is the ability to cast the shadow

178c

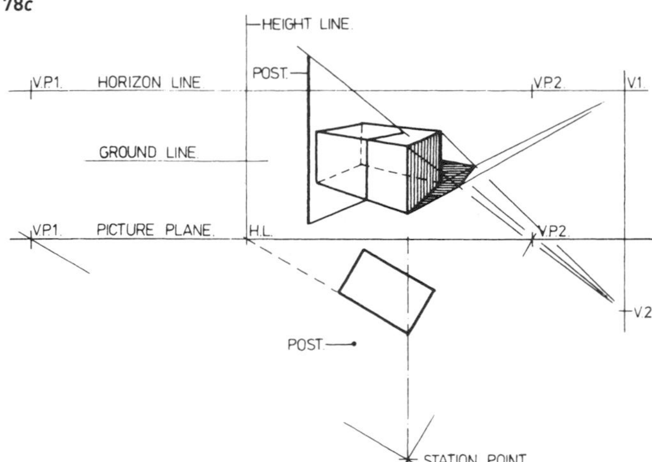

of a vertical line or 'stick' and repeat the example the required number of times, joining the tops and bottoms of these vertical lines where necessary and remembering that parallel lines cast parallel shadows.

Fig. 178*b* shows an example of an object, again a simple rectangular prism, which in this case is suspended above the ground plane. Before the shadow can be constructed in this example, it is necessary to locate the positions of the four corners of the object in the ground plane so that the plans of the light rays can be drawn. Once the plan positions of the corners of the object have been located, the shadow is constructed by locating the intersections of the plan lines (drawn back to V.1) and the actual light rays (drawn back to V.2) through the corners of the object.

Fig. 178*c* shows the same rectangular prism, in the same position as for Fig. 178*a*, with a post located so that the shadow of the post will be cast across it. The shadow of the prism is exactly the same as it was in Fig. 178*a* and is constructed in exactly the same way. The post is a little more complicated because its shadow falls not only on the ground plane but also on the surface of the rectangular prism. Therefore, it will be necessary to project the plan of the light ray on the ground plane first. This is done by using V.1 in the normal way together with the actual light ray which is drawn through the top of the post using V.2. Because the rectangular

178*d*

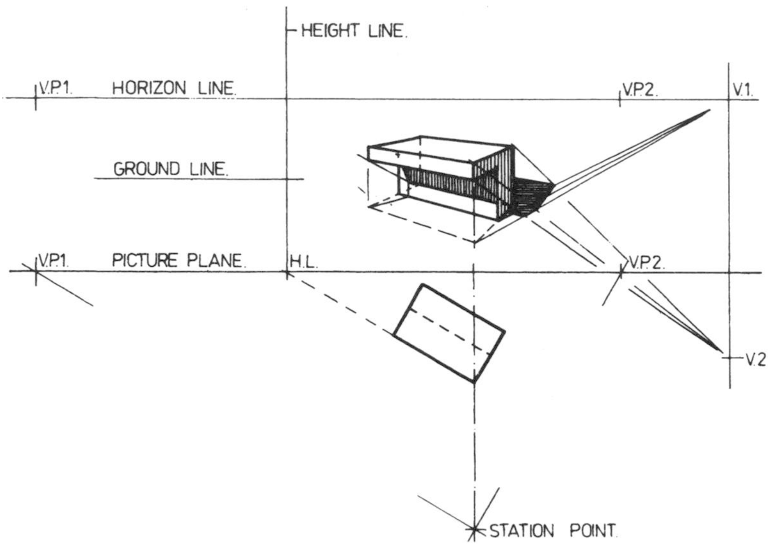

prism is opaque, the shadow of the post will not be able to penetrate the surface of the prism; therefore it must be seen on the surface of the prism. If the shadow line from the base of the post is followed, it will be seen that it will run across the ground to the base of the vertical plane forming the side of the prism facing the spectator. Because the post is parallel to that vertical side of the prism, its shadow will be parallel to the post, which means that it will run vertically up the surface of the prism. When the shadow of the post reaches the top of the vertical face of the prism, it will again encounter a horizontal plane (the top surface of the rectangular prism) which is parallel to the ground plane. This means that the shadow will continue across this horizontal plane in the same direction as it was travelling on the ground plane (using V.1), until it meets the actual light ray which will locate the shadow point of the top of the post. If the progress of a shadow is followed in a drawing in this way, the more obvious mistakes can be eliminated and, by applying a little common sense, shadows can be drawn simply and quickly and, above all, accurately.

In the final example in this figure, the rectangular prism has had a part cut out so that a shadow is cast by a part of the object on its own surface. Fig. 178*d* shows that the plan positions of the corners of the object not in contact with the ground plane must first be located in the ground plane. Once this is done, the plans of the light rays can be drawn (using V.1) on the ground plane – at least, they can be drawn as far as they go before they meet the vertical plane of the object. When they reach this vertical plane they will run up the vertical surface (vertically because parallel lines cast parallel shadows). The actual light rays are drawn through the appropriate corners of the object (using V.2) and where the actual light rays intersect the plans of the light rays (which in this case are running up the vertical face of the object) the shape of the shadow cast by the projection on the vertical surface of the object can be drawn. The shadow which the main object casts on the ground plane is constructed in the same way as already described for the other three examples in this figure.

If the four examples shown in Fig. 178 are understood, any shadows can be cast when the light source is behind the spectator whatever the complexity of the shape of the object observed. The examples shown in Fig. 178 concentrate on the construction of the shadows cast by the objects and no mention is made of the surfaces which will be seen in shade. Because shade occurs when a face of the object is turned away from the light source no construction is necessary. Instead shade is located by common sense, logical observation which is helped considerably by locating the line of separation, i.e. the line separating the faces of the object seen 'in light' and those seen 'in shade'. In the four examples in Fig. 178, the lines of separation should be obvious and most can be learned about the line of separation by observation at this stage.

Fig. 179 also consists of four examples of shadows cast by a simple object but in this case they are set up using a light source which is located in front of the spectator. This means that the vanishing point for the actual light rays will be located above the horizon line (V.3) Using the same rectangular prism and the same two-point construction as used in Fig. 178, a perspective view of the prism is set up. Fig. 179*a* shows the construction used for locating V.1 (the vanishing point for the plans of the light rays) and V.3 (the vanishing point for the actual rays when the light source is in front of the spectator). The method for carrying out this

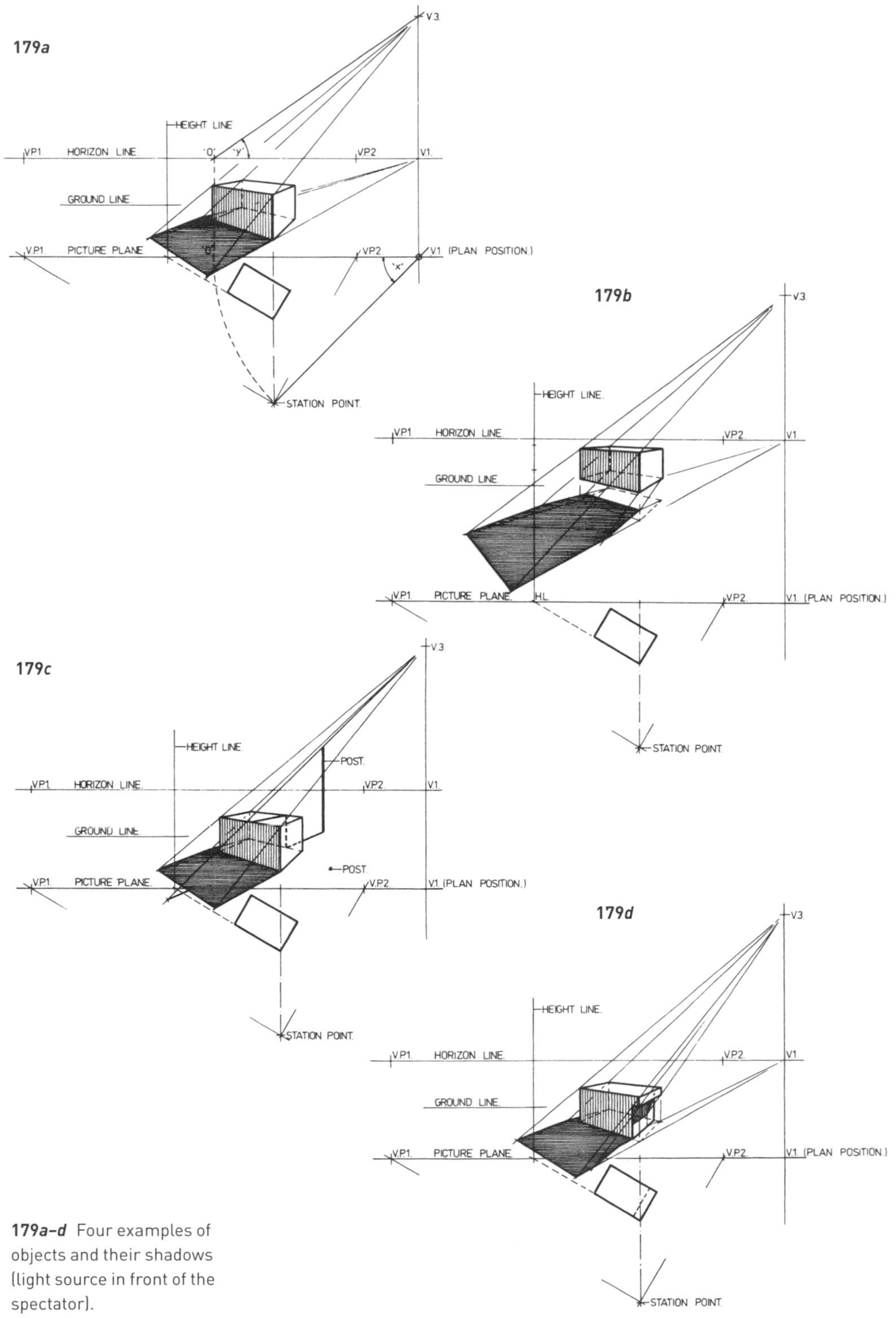

179*a–d* Four examples of objects and their shadows (light source in front of the spectator).

construction is exactly the same as the one used to locate V.2 in Fig. 178*a* except that angle *y* is set out above the horizon line instead of below it. Because the construction will be the same for all four examples in this figure it has been omitted from the other three. The shadow is constructed by drawing the plans of the light rays using V.1 and the actual light rays using V.3. The intersections of these lines are then joined up using the 'parallel lines casting parallel shadows' theory and in this way the shadow of the rectangular prism is drawn in the perspective view. In this example, the shadow of the prism will be in front of the object, which is consistent with a light source located in front of the spectator. (Note the surface of the prism which, in this case, will be in shade.)

Fig. 179*b* shows another example of a shadow cast by using a light source located in front of the spectator, in this example the rectangular prism is suspended above the ground plane. As was the case in Fig. 178*b*, it is necessary to locate the four corners of the rectangular prism in the ground plane. The plans of the light rays are then drawn using V.1 and the actual light rays are drawn using V.3. By joining up the points of intersection of these lines, the shadow of the suspended rectangular prism is drawn. Again the same face will be seen in shade as was the case in Fig. 179*a*.

Fig. 179*c* shows a post located in relation to the rectangular prism so that its shadow will fall across the prism and terminate on the ground beyond it. The shadow cast by the prism will be the same as shown in Fig. 179*a* and the same face will be in shade. The post will cast a shadow which will start from its base and proceed across the ground plane until it meets the vertical face of the rectangular prism (not seen by the spectator) where it will run up this vertical plane (vertically) until it reaches the top surface, which is horizontal (parallel to the ground plane). It will travel across this surface in the same direction as it was travelling on the ground plane, i.e. back to V.1. If the actual light ray is drawn from V.3 through the top of the post it will intersect the plan of the light ray at a point beyond the shadow of the prism; therefore the plan of the light ray will have to continue on the ground (as a continuation of the plan line established from the base of the post) until it intersects the actual light ray.

Fig. 179*d* shows a rectangular prism with a part cut out so that the part left will cast a shadow on the vertical surface of the remaining part of the prism. The plan positions of the part casting the shadow must first be located on the ground plane. Once this has been done, the plans of the light rays can be drawn (using V.1) on the ground plane, until they meet the vertical surface of the object. In this example only one of these plan lines will meet the base of the vertical face, which means that it will run up the vertical surface (vertically) until it meets the appropriate actual light ray (drawn using V.3). In this way the shadow of the projection can be drawn on the vertical surface of the object. The fact that parallel lines cast parallel shadows is used to advantage in this exercise. The shadow of the object itself is cast on the ground plane in the normal way. Finally the area seen in shade can again be determined by observation.

The foregoing examples of shadow projection have been based on two-point perspective constructions but the method of construction shown is equally suited to the other types of perspective constructions such as one-point and

180 Object in one-point perspective, light source behind the spectator.

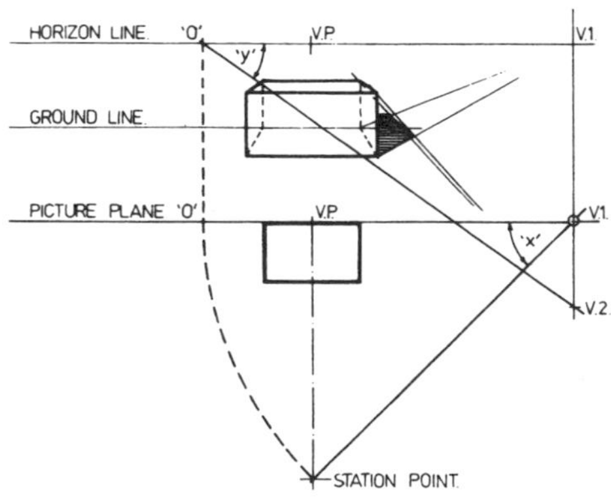

181 Object in one-point perspective, light source in front of the spectator.

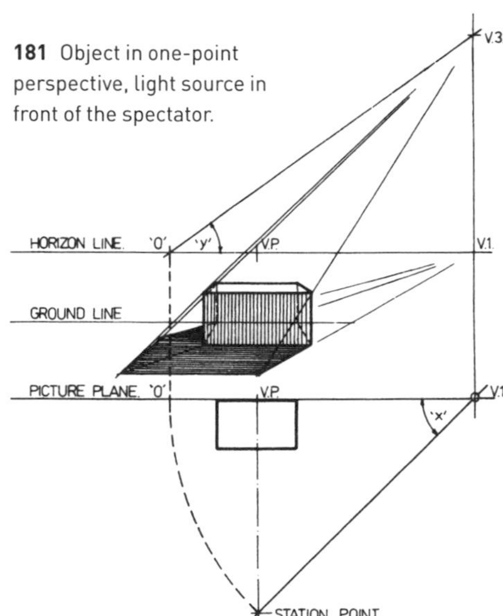

three-point. The first of these to be dealt with here is the one-point construction. For simplicity of explanation a rectangular prism is again used. The prism is set up using the normal method, described previously (Fig. 180). Assuming again that the direction of the light rays make an angle *x* with the picture plane and an angle *y* with the ground plane, the construction is identical to that described in Fig. 176. Again, if the light source is located behind the spectator the angle *y* (the angle of inclination) is set out below the horizon line as shown. If the light source is located in front of the spectator the angle *y* will be set out above the horizon line as shown in Fig. 181. From this point on, the shadow of the prism is located in exactly the same way as the ones under the same conditions in the two-point constructions, i.e. the shadow of the prism in Fig. 180 will be behind the object as seen by the spectator, and the shadow of the prism in Fig. 181 will be in front of the prism as seen by the spectator.

The third and last type of perspective construction to be dealt with here is the three-point construction. A three-point construction is required when an object is placed in relationship to a spectator so that none of its edges is either horizontal or vertical, e.g. when the object is made up of parallel sides which are at right angles to each other such as a rectangular prism. In other words, each set of parallel lines forming the shape of the object is inclined to both the picture plane and the ground plane. Fig. 182 shows a rectangular prism set up using a three-point perspective construction. The preparation of the special plan and other construction lines have been omitted from this diagram to avoid unnecessary confusion but the method used was exactly the same as previously described. From this figure it can be seen that the method used for locating the vanishing points for the plans of the light rays (V.1) and the vanishing points for the actual light rays (V.2 or V.3) is identical to the one used for both one-point and two-point constructions. Both V.2 and V.3 have been shown located but it will be realized that one or the other, never both, will be required in any one drawing.

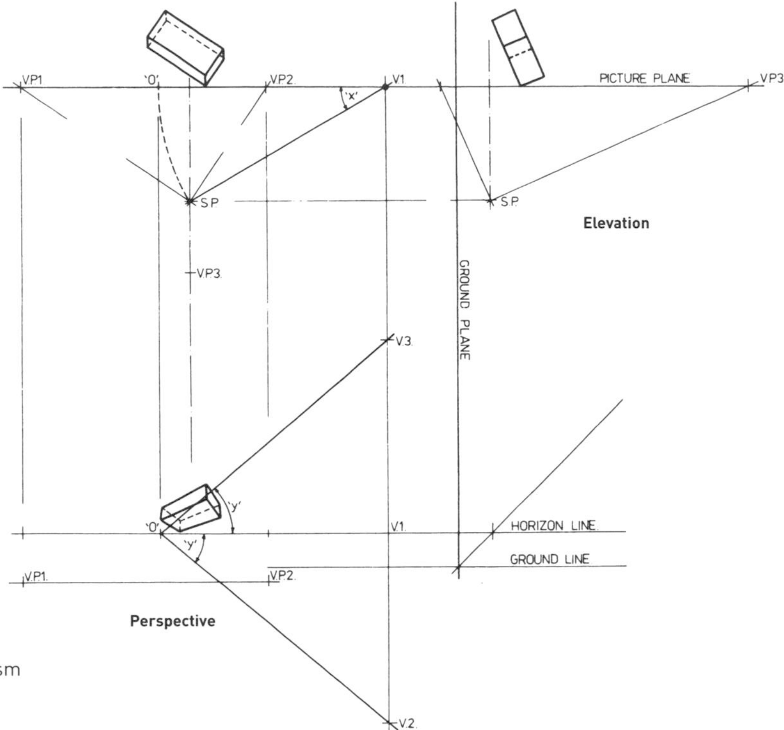

182 Rectangular prism set up in three-point perspective.

To avoid confusion at such a small scale the actual construction of the shadow has not been shown in this example but, because the prism is suspended above the ground plane, it would be necessary to locate a plan (in perspective) of the prism on the ground plane so that the plans of the light rays could be located in the normal way. The shadow cast by the suspended prism could then be completed by drawing the actual light rays using either V.2 or V.3, depending on the location of the light source, and the appropriate vanishing points. Because the method of locating the vanishing points for the plans of the light rays and for the actual light rays are identical for each of the three types of perspective construction, and the method for constructing the shadows is also identical, it is not considered necessary to show individual examples of each type of construction for the various shapes dealt with in the remainder of this section.

Fig. 183 shows a group of solid objects one of which has an inclined plane set up in perspective in which one-point and two-point constructions are included. The construction lines for the perspective constructions and the location of the vanishing points for the plans of the light rays and for the actual light rays have been omitted to avoid confusion, but it is obvious that the previously described methods have been used to produce the diagram. Apart from the fact that the shadow of the taller prism falls on the other one, little need be added to the explanations already given for constructing the shadows of these objects. As in the examples where the shadow of the post fell on the prism described previously, if the progress of the shadow is followed carefully, the problem of the shadow of one object falling on another object should not disconcert the student. (Again the areas seen in shade, together with the line of separation for each object, are worth noting.) The shadow cast on the inclined plane is simply a matter of drawing the plan of the light ray on the ground plane to meet the plan of the inclined line. From the point of intersection of these two plan lines a vertical projection is

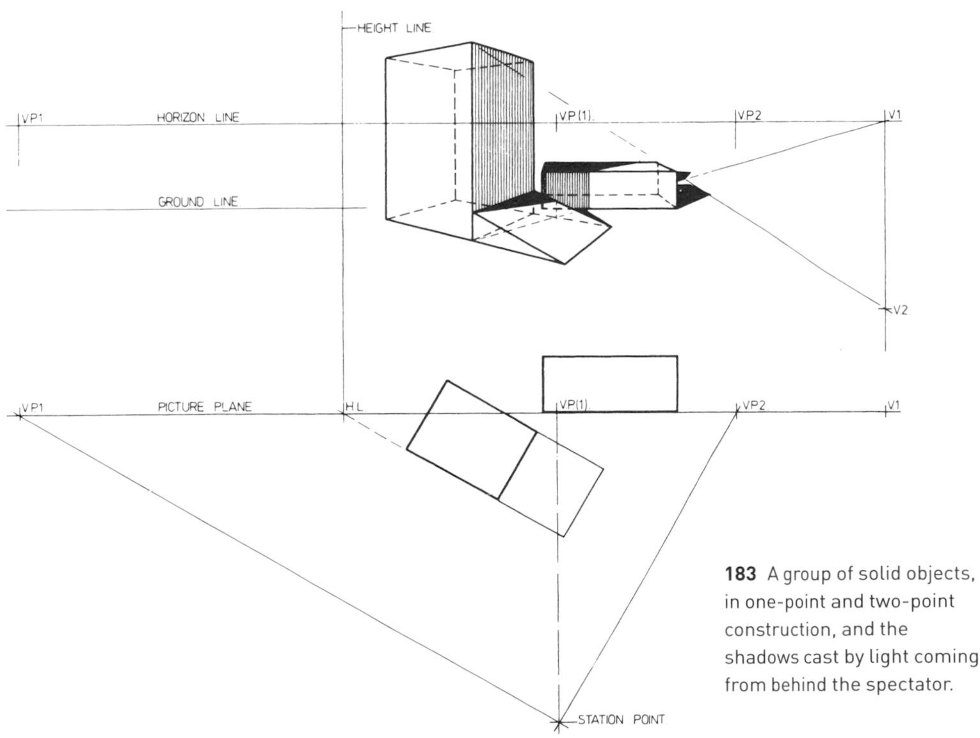

183 A group of solid objects, in one-point and two-point construction, and the shadows cast by light coming from behind the spectator.

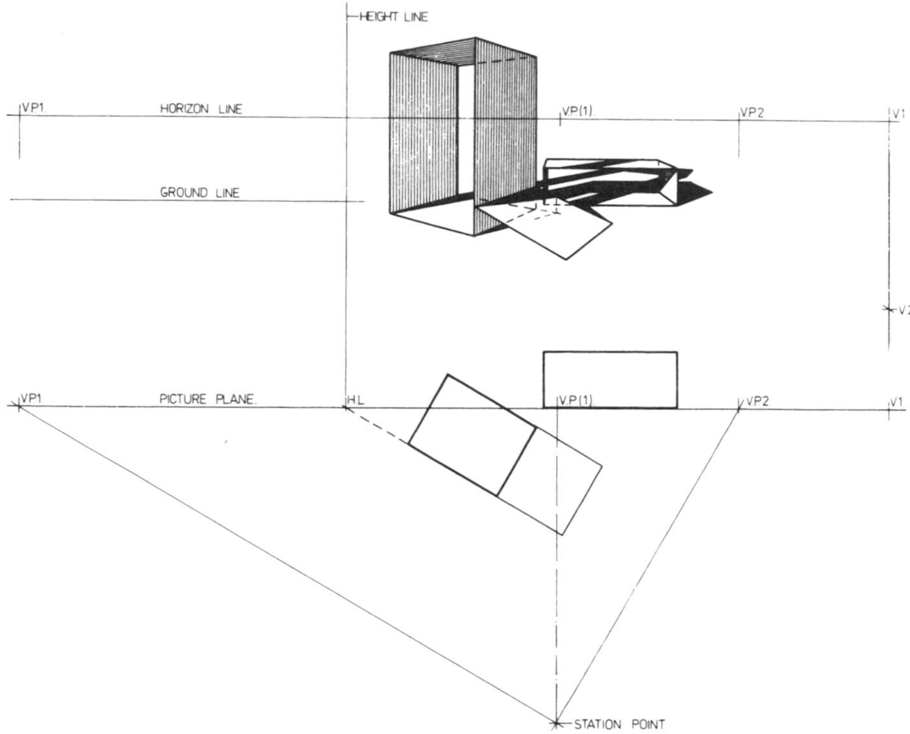

184 The same group as in Fig. 183, with the objects shown as hollow. Note the importance of the lines of separation as aids in identifying and interpreting the surfaces shown in shade.

made to meet the inclined line. From this point on the inclined line, the shadow line can be drawn back to the line of separation of the prism casting the shadow. The construction used here to locate the shadow on an inclined plane is shown and described more fully in Fig. 185.

To avoid any confusion, the shadows cast on horizontal and inclined planes are shown in solid black in Figs. 183 through to 190.

Fig. 184 is somewhat similar to the previous example but with one significant difference: the objects in this example are all hollow. This means that the number of surfaces seen by the spectator is considerably increased, with the result that not only the shadows on the ground plane, but also those which are cast on the vertical surfaces, are important. In this example the lines of separation become very important because it is from them that those surfaces which will be seen in shade can be correctly identified and shown. The actual construction of the shadows on this example can be carried out in exactly the same way as described for the previous one.

In all the previous examples where a line or plane is located above the ground plane, it is necessary to locate the plans of these lines or planes on the ground plane. This means that it is necessary, in the example shown in Fig. 185, to locate the plans of the inclined lines (the sides of the inclined plane). Once these plan lines have been located the construction is straightforward. The shadow cast by the vertical plane on the ground is located by drawing the plans of the light rays from the bases of the two vertical edges of the plane and the actual light rays through the tops of these vertical edges. The shadow cast by the inclined plane on the ground plane is located by drawing an actual light ray through the intersection of the inclined plane and the vertical plane (on the side which will cast the shadow on the ground plane). Where this light ray meets the shadow of the vertical edge of the vertical plane is the required shadow point. The shadow of the inclined plane is located by joining the shadow point of the intersection of the two edges of the planes to the intersection of the appropriate edge of the inclined plane and the ground plane. The shadow of the vertical plane cast on

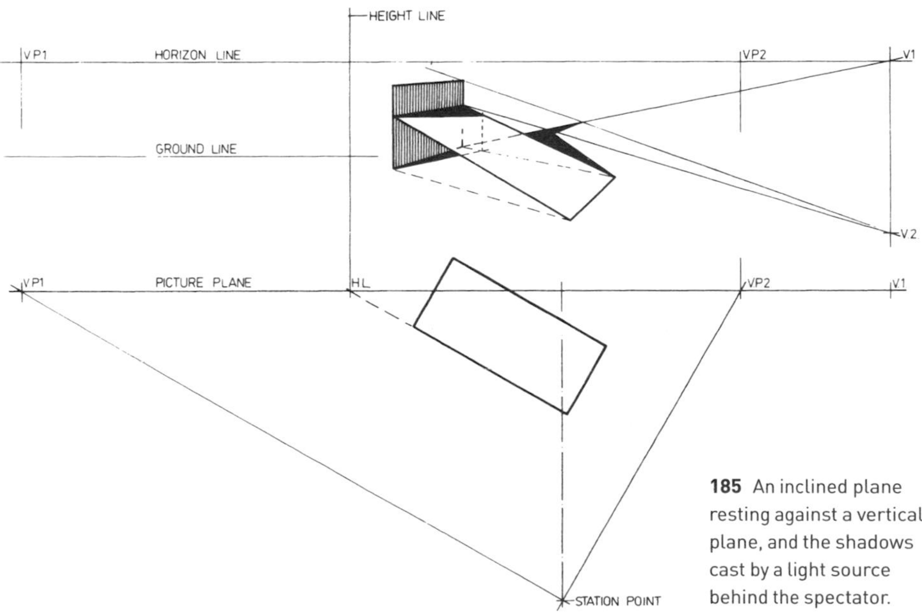

185 An inclined plane resting against a vertical plane, and the shadows cast by a light source behind the spectator.

the inclined plane is located by projecting up from the intersection of the shadow line of the edge of the vertical plane and the plan of the inclined line which represents the edge of the inclined plane. The point where this vertical projection meets the edge of the inclined plane is then joined to the point of intersection of the opposite inclined edge of the inclined plane and the vertical plane casting the shadow. Finally, as with the previous two examples, the surfaces seen in shade are identified and indicated.

Fig. 186 shows a simple recess set up in two-point perspective, with a light source located so that shadows of a side and the top will be cast on the back surface of the recess. Using V.1, the plan of the light ray is drawn from the base of the front edge of the vertical side of the recess to meet the base of the back surface of the recess where it will proceed vertically up the vertical surface (parallel lines cast parallel shadows) until it meets the actual light ray through the top of the vertical edge. Because parallel lines cast parallel shadows, the shadow cast by the top of the recess can be

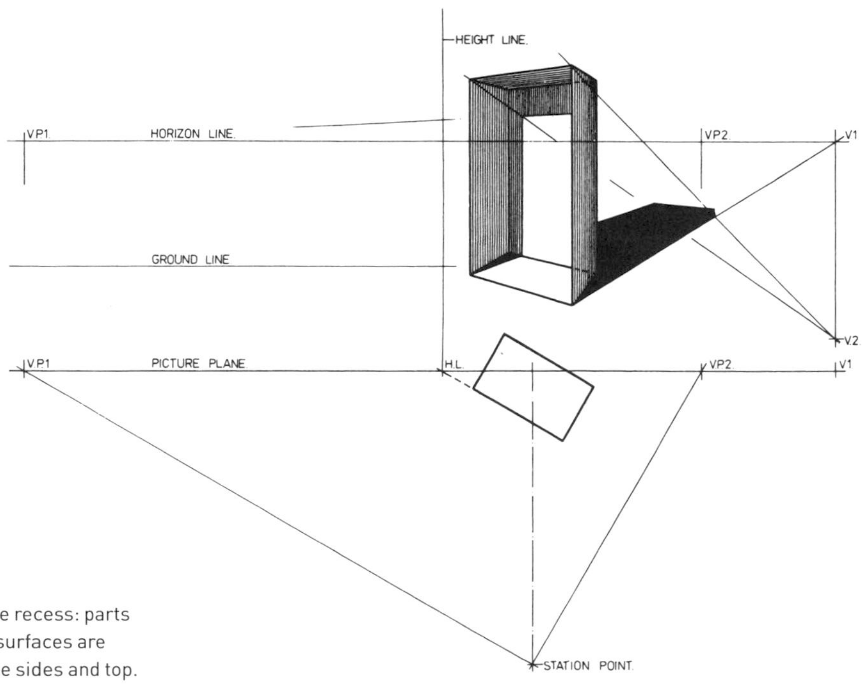

186 A simple recess: parts of the inner surfaces are shaded by the sides and top.

drawn from the shadow point of the top of the vertical side, using V.P.1. Finally, the shadow of the object is cast on the ground plane in the normal way.

Fig. 187 shows another recess: in this case the top is no longer horizontal but is made up of two inclined planes of equal length. Because the planes forming the top of this recess are inclined planes it will be necessary to locate V.P.3 and V.P.4 (vanishing points for the inclined lines) when setting up the object in perspective projection. The shadow of the vertical side is cast on the back surface in exactly the same way as for the preceding example. Because parallel lines cast parallel shadows, the shadow of the inclined lines forming the edges of the inclined planes of the top of the recess are drawn using V.P.3 and V.P.4. The shadow of the object is cast on the ground plane in the usual way.

Fig. 188 shows a hollow triangular-shaped object suspended above the ground. Once the plan of the object is located on the ground plane in the perspective view, the

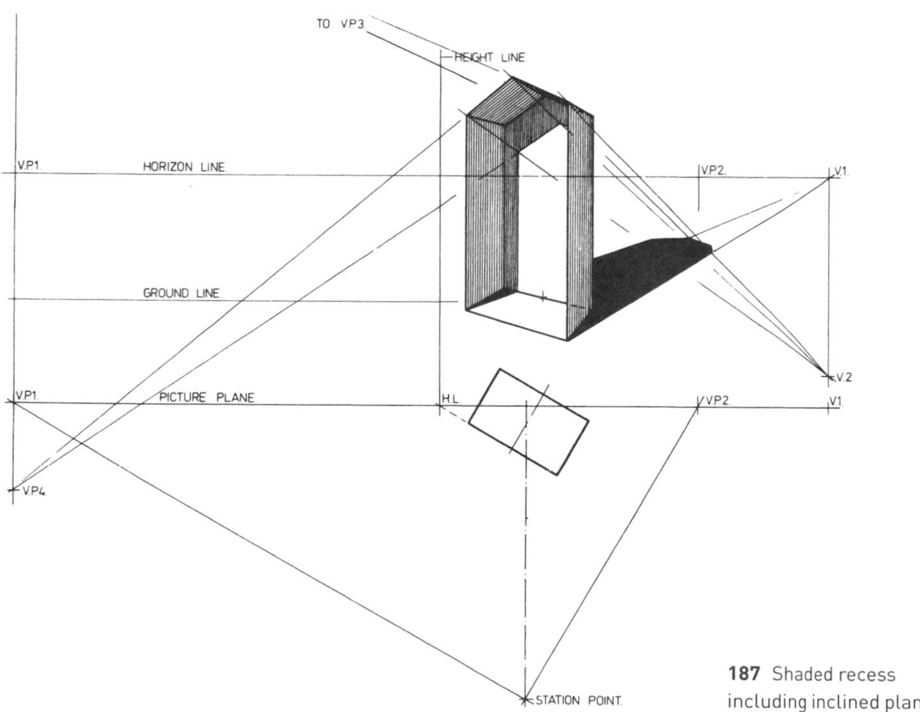

187 Shaded recess including inclined planes.

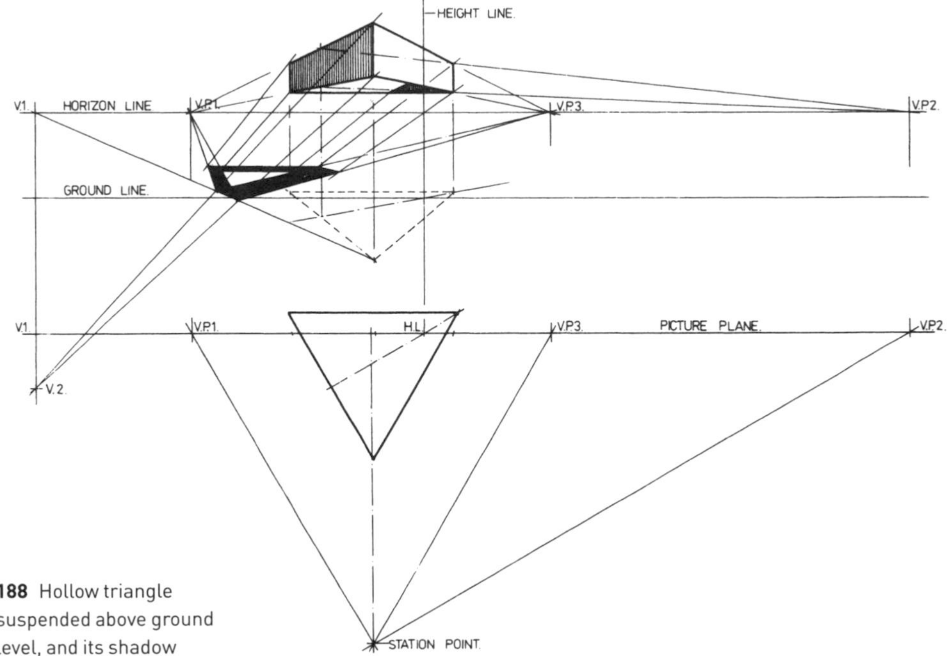

188 Hollow triangle suspended above ground level, and its shadow

shadow can be located using V.1 and V.2 in the normal way. The side seen in shade is straightforward but, because the object is hollow, it will be possible to see part of the shadow cast by one side on another. There are a number of ways in which this shadow can be located but perhaps the simplest way is to work back from the shadow cast by the object on the ground. If the shadows of the two sides under consideration are located, it will be seen that it is a fairly simple matter to locate the intersection of the shadow of the top edge of the 'front' surface and the shadow of the bottom edge of the 'back' surface. By using V.2 this point of intersection can be located on the bottom edge of the 'back' surface of the actual object. This point is then joined to the intersection of the top edges of the two surfaces under consideration. This sounds a little complicated but if the construction is followed in the example shown in Fig. 188 it will be seen that it is simply using the principles in reverse. If the principles of shadow projection in perspective have been thoroughly understood the student should have little trouble with this type of subject. Similarly circles, cylinders and spheres should be readily understood.

Fig. 189 shows a disk suspended above the ground plane, set up with a one-point perspective construction. The vanishing points for the plans of the light rays (V.1) and the actual light rays (V.2) are located as previously described. The plan of the disk is located in the ground plane in the usual way. Because it is necessary to use the perspective view of the square surrounding the circle, together with its diagonals and axes, to locate the ellipse representing the perspective view of the circle, it is also necessary to use the 'shadow' of this square to locate the shadow of the disk contained within it. It should be remembered that because parallel lines cast

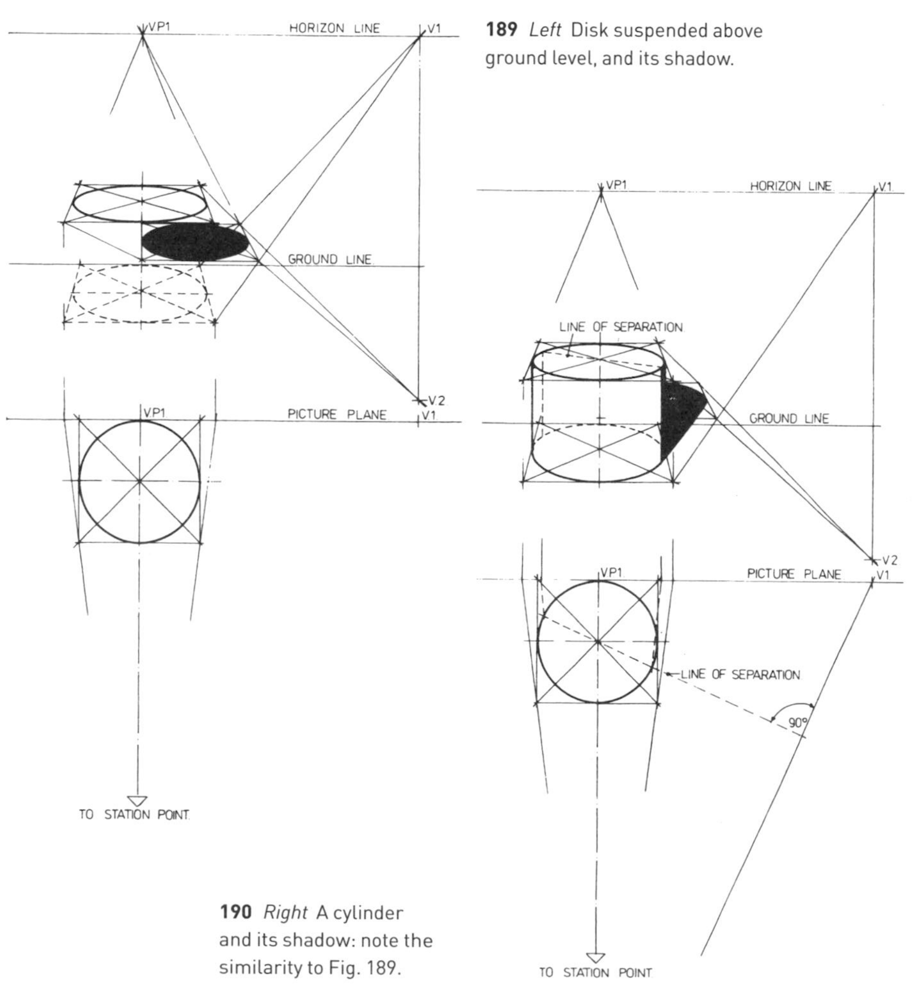

189 *Left* Disk suspended above ground level, and its shadow.

190 *Right* A cylinder and its shadow: note the similarity to Fig. 189.

parallel shadows, a disk located parallel to the ground plane will cast a circular shadow, and because the light rays from the sun are parallel, this shadow will be exactly the same size as the disk casting it. The 'shadow' of the square seen in the perspective view is located in the usual way using V.1 and V.2 together with its 'vertical' and 'horizontal' axes and diagonals. The points of intersection of the ellipse and these diagonals and axes are located in the shadow, again using V.1 and V.2. When the shadow points of the intersections of the ellipse and the diagonals and the axes are joined up they will result in the shadow shape of the disk seen in perspective.

The similarity between a disk suspended above the ground plane and a cylinder can be seen by examining Fig. 190. The shadow of the top of the cylinder is located in exactly the same way as for the disk in Fig. 189. The bottom of the cylinder coincides with the ground plane so it is unnecessary to construct a shadow for the bottom because the base and its shadow coincide. It is necessary to locate the line of separation for the cylinder so that the part of the surface of the cylinder which will be seen in shade can be located accurately and shown. This is done by drawing a line through the centre of the circle in plan at right angles to the light rays. The points where this line of separation meets the circumference of the circle representing the plan view of the cylinder are then projected up in the normal way and are located in the perspective view. Once the line of separation is located on the surface of the cylinder the points of intersection of the line of separation and the ellipses forming the ends of the cylinder can be used to locate the shadow of the side (vertical) of the cylinder.

To this stage the disks have been located parallel to the ground plane and, as can be seen from the two preceding examples, they are fairly simple to deal with when shadows are required in perspective projection. The problem is simply one of drawing the 'shadow' of a square seen in perspective. If this approach is used for a disk located at right angles to the ground plane, as shown in Fig. 191, it will be seen that the problem is again simply a matter of drawing the 'shadow' of a square together with its axes and diagonals. Using V.1 and V.2,

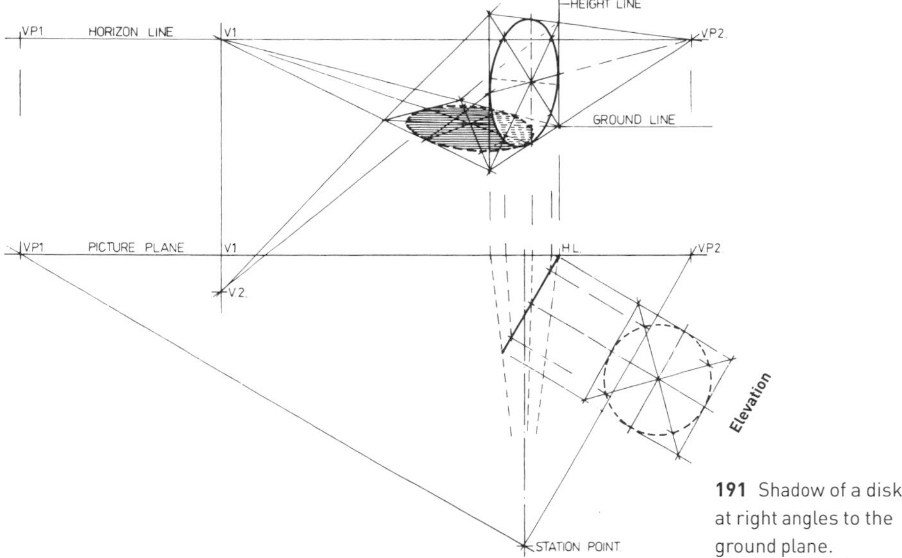

191 Shadow of a disk at right angles to the ground plane.

the shadows of the points of intersection between the ellipse and the diagonals and the axes can be located in the shadow where they can be joined up to result in the shadow of the disk on the ground plane.

Once the shadow of a disk has been mastered in both the horizontal and vertical planes, it can easily be adapted to many objects. Its adaption to the cylinder, as shown in Fig. 190, was little more than a matter of being able to draw the shadow of a disk suspended above the ground plane. The adaptation of the ability to draw the shadow of a disk to other shapes, such as the cone, should be obvious; therefore it is not intended further to pursue the matter of shadows of disks as cast by sunlight.

Fig. 192 shows a sphere set up in perspective as previously described in Figs. 130 and 131. The vanishing points for the plans of the light rays (V.1) and for the actual light rays (V.2) are located in the normal way, angle *x* representing the direction of the light rays and angle *y* their inclination. The method of locating and drawing the shadow cast by a sphere is as follows:

Step 1. The major axis of the line of separation (which will appear as an ellipse in the plan view) is located in plan view of the sphere, at right angles to the plan view of the light ray.

Step 2. At this state is is necessary to prepare an elevation of the sphere parallel to the direction of the light ray. This is done at a convenient distance from the plan, as shown. The true inclination of the light ray is drawn passing through the centre of the sphere in this elevation and then the elevation of the line of separation is drawn at right angles to the actual light ray. (For obvious reasons the line of separation on the elevation will pass through the centre of the circle representing the elevation of the sphere.)

Step 3. The plan view of the line of separation is located by simple projection from the elevation.

Step 4. Because the line of separation on the surface of the sphere will divide the sphere exactly in halves, i.e. one half will be seen in light and the other in shade, an imaginary plane can be placed through the sphere to coincide with the line of separation. The line of separation will appear as a circle on that plane, so if the imaginary plane is located, its shadow can easily be located together with its main axes and diagonals. This plane is located first in the elevation by constructing the square containing the circle representing the sphere in elevation and then continuing the elevation of the line of separation to meet its sides (top and bottom). This inclined plane is then located in the plan view by normal projection. From the plan view this inclined plane can be sighted and projected up and located in the perspective view in the usual way.

Step 5. When the inclined plane is located in the perspective view it should be remembered that this plane in its present form does not represent a square in perspective which contains the circle (line of separation) but the original plane located in the elevation. The actual square is located by projecting the intersections of the elevation of the line of separation and the circumference of the circle to the plan and then up to the perspective. Then the diagonals and axes of the square can be located and drawn. When this is done, the ellipse representing the line of separation on the surface of the sphere in

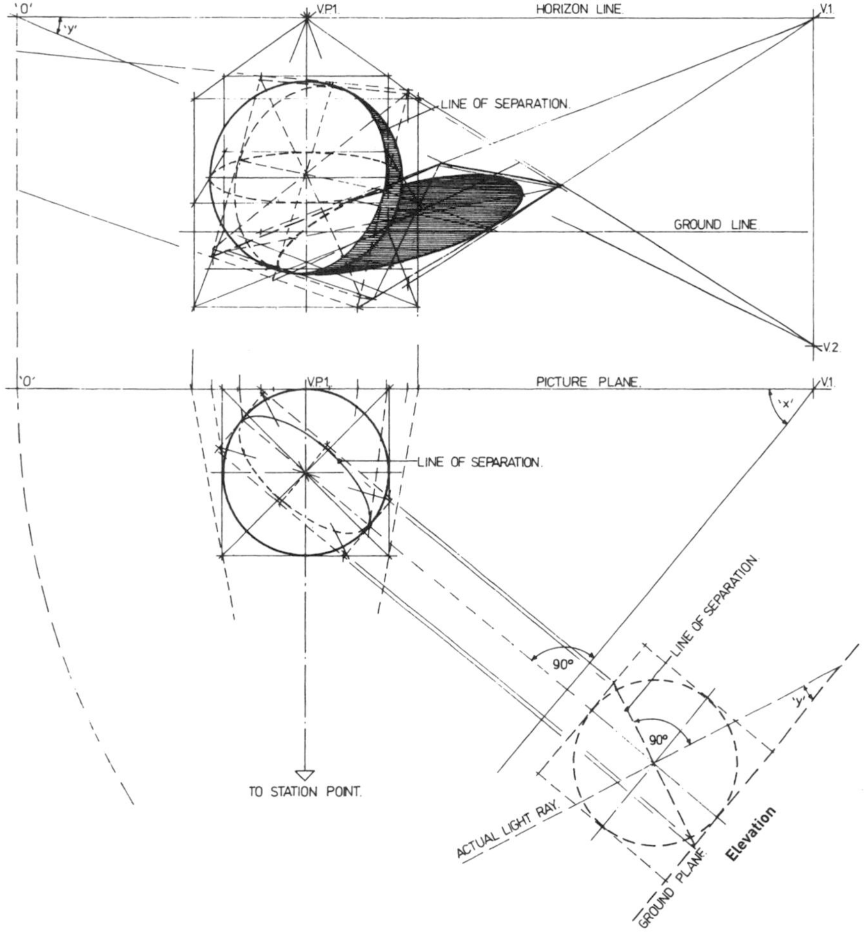

perspective can be drawn, using normal projection up from the plan.

Step 6. Using V.1 and V.2, the shadow of the inclined plane can be located and drawn on the ground plane. On this shadow of the inclined plane, the shadow of the square containing the circle (the line of separation), together with its axes and diagonals, can be located in perspective.

Step 7. Once the shadow of the square and its axes and diagonals are drawn in the perspective view, the points of intersection of the line of separation on the surface of the perspective view of the sphere and the axes and diagonals of the inclined plane can be located in the shadow by using V.1 and V.2 in the normal way.

192 The shadow cast by a sphere.

Step 8. By joining up the shadow points of the intersections of the line of separation and the axes and diagonals of the inclined plane, the shadow of the sphere is drawn as shown.

Though the diagram explaining the construction of the shadow of a sphere looks somewhat complex, if the eight steps described here are followed, the construction will prove to be simpler than it looks. In reality the shadow of a sphere can be described as the shadow of its line of separation, which is simply a circle inclined to both the ground and picture planes. Once this is understood it can be seen that most of the construction shown is needed to locate the inclined plane coinciding with the line of separation, while the construction needed for the actual shadow of the line of separation is very little different from that for any other disk seen in perspective.

Before concluding this section on shadows cast by sunlight, it is worth repeating some of the more important rules for the construction of shadows in perspective projection. The shadow of a vertical line will be cast in the direction of the light ray. If the vertical line is standing on the ground plane its shadow will start from its point of intersection with the ground plane and finish with the first light ray which can pass unobstructed over the top of it. The only time that the shadow of a vertical line does not start from its intersection with the ground plane (or any plane parallel to the ground plane) is when the line does not meet the ground plane. In this case it is necessary to locate the point where it would meet the ground plane if extended (i.e. its plan position) before the shadow of that line can be cast. Perhaps the greatest time-saver in shadow projection is the fact that parallel lines cast parallel shadows. It should be remembered that the line of separation is an extremely important line because the shadow of an object is in reality the shadow of its line of separation. Probably this could be seen most clearly in the shadow of a sphere (Fig. 192) but if all of the other examples in this section are examined it will be seen that this is always the case; therefore, if in doubt as to the correctness of the shadow cast by an object, locate its line of separation and check the result obtained.

Finally, shade and shadow in perspective projection are the result of correct construction allied to common sense and the ability of the student to understand three-dimensional representation.

The second type of light source is the artificial, which differs from sunlight in that the light rays from the sun are considered to be parallel whereas those emanating from an artificial source, in their simplest form, radiate from a single point. Fig. 193 shows a simple artificial light source with light rays radiating from it. From this diagram it can be seen that because these light rays radiate, i.e. the further away from the light source they are, the further apart they will be, the shadows cast by artificial light must differ from those cast by sunlight. However, this difference is not as great as might be expected. Light rays from an artificial light source, though not parallel, have in all other respects the same qualities as light rays from the sun. They travel in straight lines, they cannot change direction unless a reflector is introduced, they cannot pass through solid opaque matter, in other words, everything to do with individual light rays and their properties remains the same whether they originate from the sun or from an artificial source. Therefore the difference between shadows cast by sunlight and artificial light will be limited to size only. The shape will remain the same but because light rays from an artifical source are not parallel, but in fact get further apart as they travel away from their source, it should be readily understood that a shadow cast by them will be larger than that cast by parallel light rays.

The actual construction of shadows cast by artificial light is very similar to that used for the construction of shadows cast by sunlight inasmuch as they both rely on the intersection of an actual light ray and its plan to locate a shadow point. Because light rays from the sun are parallel it was necessary to locate vanishing points for the actual light rays and for their plans. Light rays from an artificial light source are not parallel; therefore vanishing points are not

193 An artificial light source is regarded as a point source, unlike the sun, whose rays are, for all practical purposes, parallel.

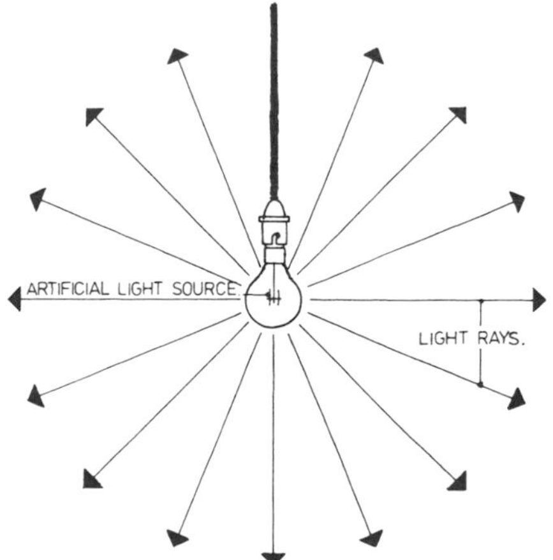

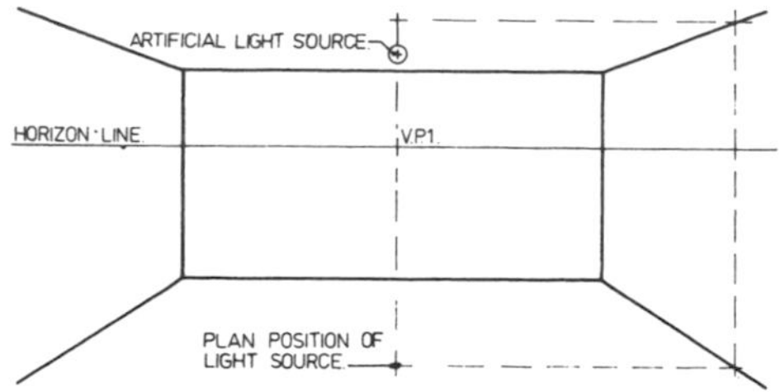

194 Locating an artificial light source.

required. The light source can be located as shown in Fig. 194 and, because plans of the light rays from this source are necessary, the plan position of that light source will have to be located. The artificial light source in Fig. 194 is shown located in a room which was set up using one-point perspective construction in the usual way (construction not shown). The plan position of the artificial light source is shown located in the floor plane by simple projection.

The four examples shown in Fig. 195 have been set up in the same way as the one shown in Fig. 194 and have the same artificial light source. Fig. 195*a* shows a single light ray, drawn at random, together with its plan. From this it should be possible to see the similarity between this type of construction and that used for constructing shadows in sunlight.

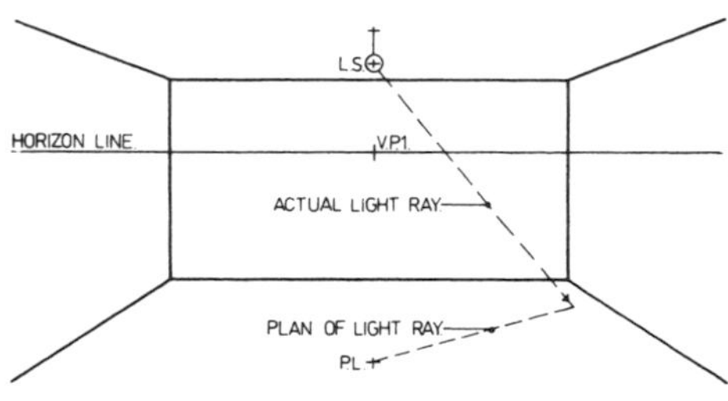

195*a* A single light ray and its plan.

Fig. 195*b* shows a single stick *ab* standing on the floor. To locate the shadow of this stick it is necessary to draw the plan of the light ray from the plan location (P.L.) of the light source, through the base of the stick *(b)*. From the artificial light source (L.S.) a light ray is drawn through the top of the stick *(a)* and continued to meet the plan line. The intersection of these two lines will be the shadow point of *a*. Therefore the shadow of the stick *ab* will be that part of the plan of the light ray between the base of the stick *(b)* and the shadow point '*a*'. The stick *cd* is placed closer to one of the walls of the room so that its shadow will not only appear on the floor but will also 'run up the wall'. The plan line is drawn from the plan location of the artificial light source (P.L.) through the base of the stick *(d)* until it meets the intersection of the horizontal floor plane and the vertical wall plane,

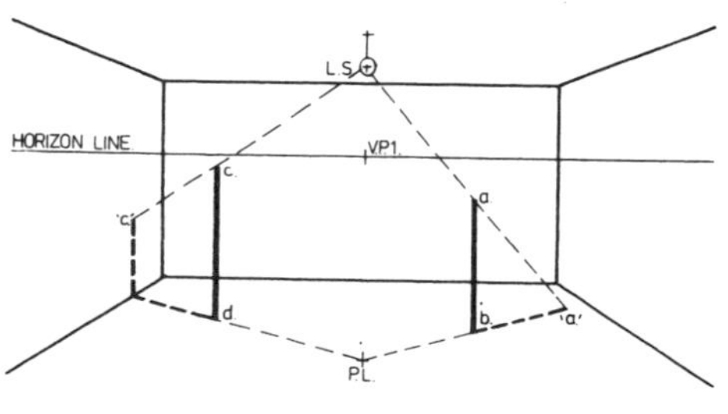

195*b* Shadows of two vertical sticks.

where it will continue up the wall vertically (parallel lines cast parallel shadows) until it meets the actual light ray drawn from the artificial light source (L.S.). In this way point '*c*', which is the shadow of the top of the stick, is located on the wall.

In Fig. 195*c* there are two sticks again but this time they are horizontal, fixed at right angles to the side walls of the room. As with shadows cast by the sun, it is necessary to locate the plan position of the object casting the shadow when that object is no longer located in the ground plane. Once the plans of these two sticks are located on the floor the shadows can be constructed in the normal way. Stick *ab* is dealt with first because its shadow is slightly simpler than the other one. First, the plan of the light ray is drawn from P.L. through the plan of end *b* of stick *ab*. The actual light ray is then drawn from L.S. through end *b* to meet the plan of the light ray which has 'run up the wall'. This point of intersection between the light ray and its plan will be the shadow of end *b*. The shadow of stick *ab* will start from the point where it joins the wall *(a)* and finish at the shadow of end *b*; therefore the shadow is drawn as a line joining these two points.

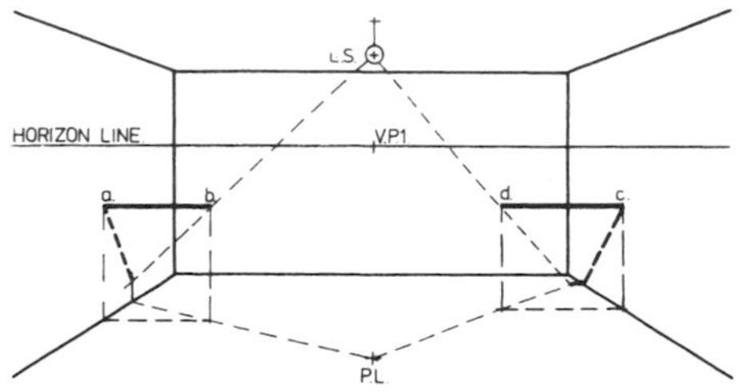

195*c* Shadows of two horizontal sticks.

Stick *cd* is placed lower down the wall, which means that a part of its shadow will fall on the floor plane. Again the plan of the light ray is drawn from P.L. through the plan position of end *d*. The actual light ray which is then drawn from L.S. through end *d* will meet the plan of the light ray on the floor plane; this means that the shadow of end *d* will fall in the floor plane while end *c* will be located in the wall plane. Again it should be remembered that parallel lines cast parallel shadows, which means that from the shadow point of end *d* the shadow of the stick, while it is cast on the floor, will be parallel to the stick. When the shadow reaches the wall it will no longer be parallel and will in fact

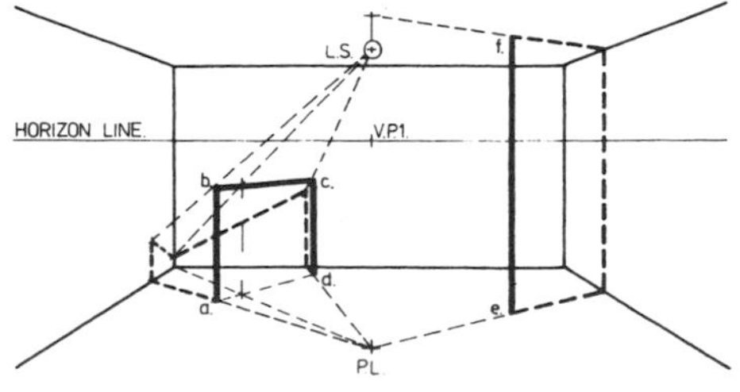

195*d* Vertical and horizontal sticks combined.

run up the wall in a straight line from its intersection with the wall to point *c*.

The fourth example in this figure (Fig. 195*d*) shows two different objects located in the room. The first is a vertical stick which touches the ceiling at point *f* and the floor at point *e*. The plan of the light ray is drawn from P.L. through end *e* in the normal way until it meets the wall of the room, where it will continue up the wall. Because the top of the stick (point *f*) is in the ceiling plane, which is above the artificial light source, a part of the shadow of stick *ef* will of course fall on the ceiling. Because the conditions will be much the same as those for the shadow falling on the floor it will be necessary to locate the 'plan' position of the light source on the ceiling. Once this is done, a line representing a plan of the light ray (on the ceiling) can be drawn from this plan position through end *f* and continued to the wall, where it will join up with the plan line from end *e* in the floor plane. This means that the shadow of stick *ef* will extend from point *f* on the ceiling across to the wall, where it will continue down the wall vertically (parallel lines...etc.) and back across the floor to point *e* in the floor plane.

The other object in Fig. 195*d* is in the form of a stool which is placed so that line *bc* is not parallel to the walls of the room. The two vertical lines of the object, *ab* and *dc*, are simple vertical lines and can be dealt with as described in Fig. 195*b*. The horizontal line *bc* is a little more difficult in this example because it no longer casts a shadow on a plane parallel to it; in fact it will cast a part of its shadow on each of the two walls. The easiest and quickest way to construct this shadow is to draw a plan of the light ray from the intersection of the two walls back to P.L. At the point where this plan of the light ray intersects the plan of line *bc* a vertical projection is made to locate this point on the line *bc*. An actual light ray drawn from L.S. through this point will locate the intersection of the two parts of the shadow of *bc* on the line of intersection of the two walls. If this point is then joined to the shadows of the tops of the two vertical sticks this will result in the shadow of horizontal stick *bc* on the two walls.

196a–d Four examples of plane surfaces, with the shadows cast by artificial light.

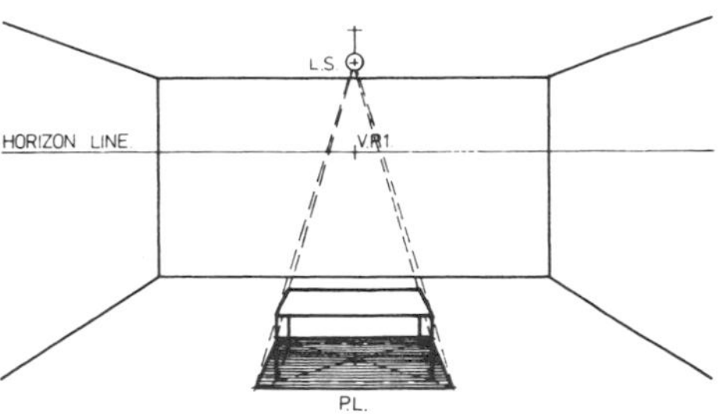

196b

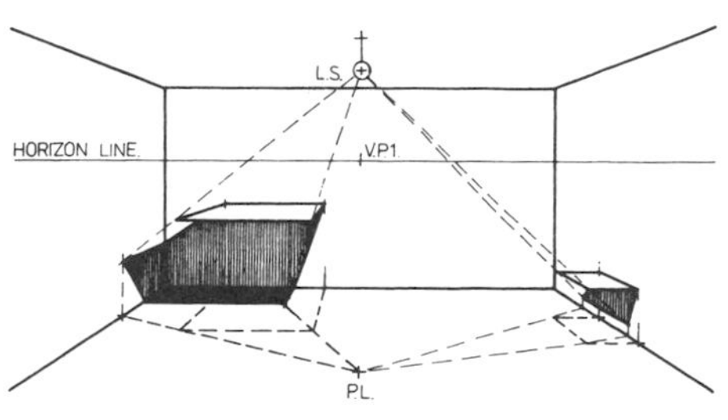

196c

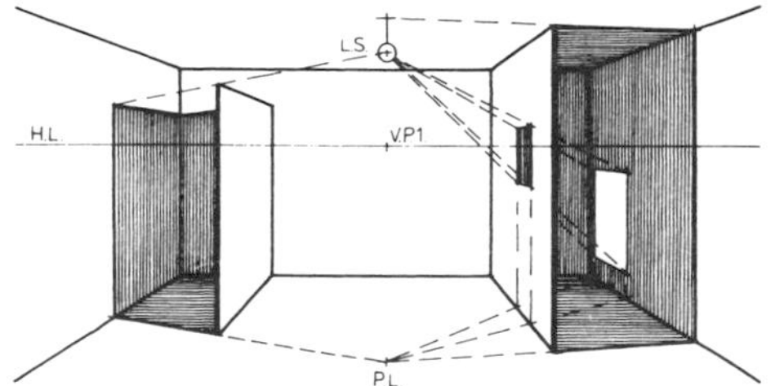

196d

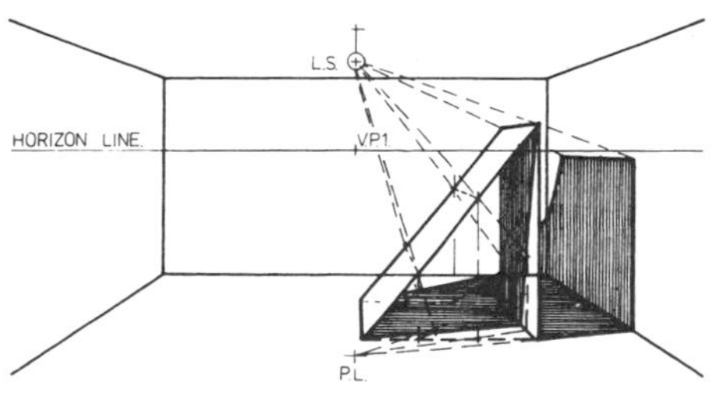

The four examples in Fig. 195 dealt with simple sticks. Fig. 196 consists of another four examples but in this case planes instead of sticks are used. Fig. 196*a* shows a horizontal plane (such as a small table) placed directly beneath the artificial light source. The plan location (P.L.) is located as previously described and is used to draw the plans of the light rays through the plan locations of the four corners of the horizontal plane. The actual light rays are drawn from L.S. through the corners of the horizontal plane to meet their plans. The shadow of the horizontal plane is drawn by joining up the four intersections of the light rays and their plans. Fig. 196*b* shows two horizontal planes cantilevered from the walls. In both cases, before the shadows can be cast it is necessary to locate plans of the planes on the floor. Once this is done their shadows can be constructed by using the L.S. and the P.L. in the normal way.

Fig. 196*c* shows two vertical planes, one of which extends from the floor to the ceiling and has a rectangular hole in it.

By reference to Fig. 195*d* the main shadow of the plane can be located. The hole is located simply by locating its plan position by vertical projection. Once this is done, plans of light rays are drawn and projected up the wall to meet the actual light rays drawn from L.S. through the four corners of the hole. The other vertical plane is dealt with initially in much the same way as a simple vertical stick. The shadow of the nearer vertical edge of the plane is located by drawing the plan of the light ray from P.L. to the wall and then up the wall until it meets the actual light ray. The shadow of the top of the plane is simply drawn parallel (in perspective) to the top of the plane until it meets the 'back' wall of the room where it changes direction and joins up to the point of intersection of the top of the plane and the wall.

Fig. 196*d* shows an inclined plane resting against a vertical plane. The shadow cast by the vertical plane is constructed in the normal way, using plans of light rays from P.L. and actual light rays from L.S. The plan of the inclined plane will be required before its shadow can be located. If the shadow of the inclined plane and the shadow of the vertical plane fell on the floor plane it would be a simple matter of joining the points of the shadow of the top of the vertical plane to the points where the inclined plane met the floor. However, in this example the shadows are cast not only on the floor but also on two walls. This means that it is necessary to locate some arbitrary points on the inclined plane so that the shadows of these points can be located. By joining up these points the correct shadow of the structure can be drawn.

The four examples shown in Fig. 195 and the four in Fig. 196 all used an artificial light source located in the same position in the room and slightly below the ceiling. Fig. 197 consists of a further four examples in which different positions are used for the light source. Fig. 197*a* shows a light source consistent with a standard lamp on a floor pedestal. This type of light source simplifies the location of the plan location of the light source (P.L.). The short stick is treated in exactly the same way as the previous ones. The horizontal stick is also self-explanatory. The taller stick *(ab)* requires a plan location of the artificial light source on the ceiling so that the shadow of

197*a–d* Four examples of shadows thrown by light sources in varying positions.

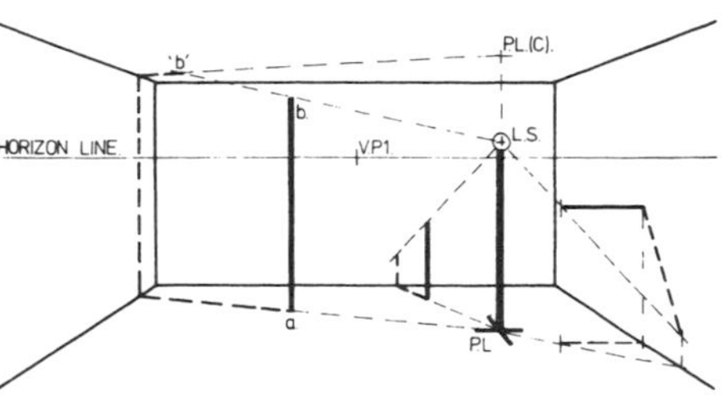

197*b*

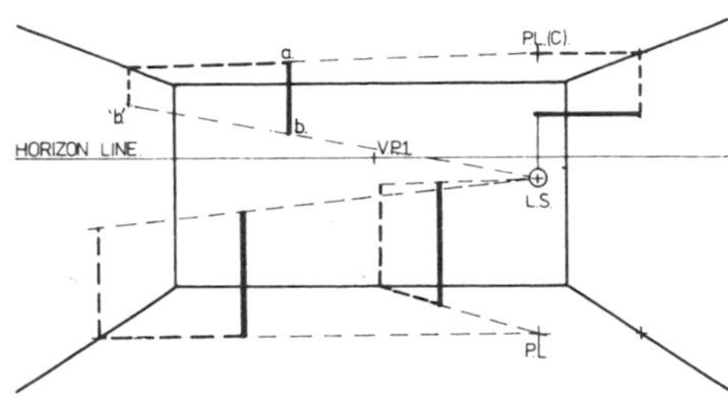

197*c*

197*d*

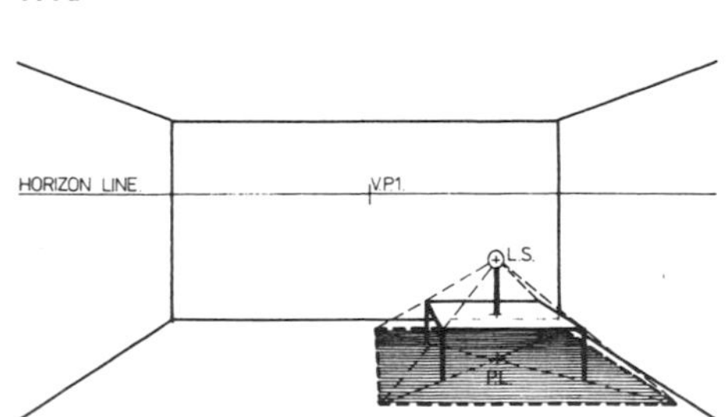

end *b* can be located on the ceiling as shown. Fig. 197*b* shows a light source suspended from a horizontal stick located on one of the walls. This means that the stick supporting the L.S. will cast a shadow on the ceiling so again the plan position of the L.S. will be required on the ceiling. Once this is done the shadow will be obvious, as should be the shadows of the vertical sticks located on the floor. The short stick located on the ceiling is a little different from the others. Its shadow is located using the plan location of the light source on the ceiling and the actual light ray.

Fig. 197*c* shows a slight variation in which two artificial light sources are used. This means that each will cast a shadow of the stick; therefore each will require its plan location on the floor plane. The two shadows are cast in the normal way. Fig. 197*d* shows a table lamp located on a low table. The plan location of the artificial light source is located on the floor in the normal way. Using this P.L. to draw the plans of the light rays through the four corners of the plan of the table, to intersect the

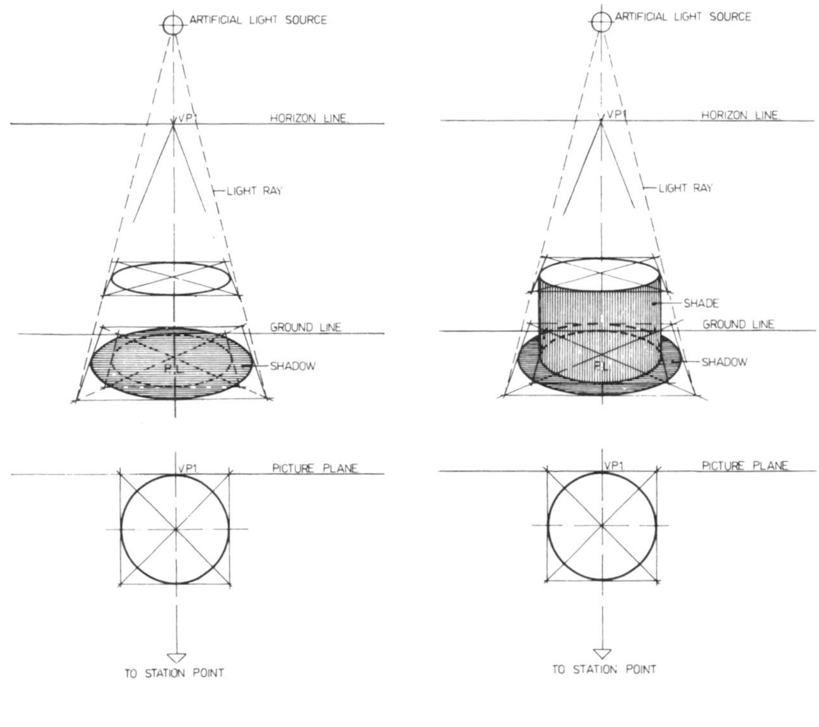

198 The shadow of a suspended disk, cast by artificial light.

199 The suspended disk of Fig. 198, converted into a cylinder.

actual light rays from the L.S. through the four corners of the table, its shadow can be drawn as shown.

The twelve examples in the preceding three figures cover most of the possibilities likely to be encountered either directly or indirectly when the subject consists of straight lines, that is to say a problem may consist of either combinations of the examples shown or simple adaptations of them.

Fig. 198 shows a disk suspended above the ground plane, set up with a one-point perspective construction as previously described. (The construction lines have been omitted, to avoid unnecessary confusion.) An artificial light source has been located directly above the centre of the circle. As with all other shadow projections, when an object is suspended above the ground plane it is necessary to locate a plan of the object on the ground plane in the perspective view. Here this is done in the normal way, using a perspective view of the square containing the circle together with its diagonals. Because the light source is located directly above the centre of the circle, the plan location of the light source will be at the intersection of the diagonals of the square surrounding the plan of the circle. As in the construction of a shadow of a disk in sunlight (Fig. 189), it is necessary to locate the shadow of the square containing the circle before the shadow of the disk can be drawn. To obtain the shadow of the square containing the shadow of the disk it is necessary to draw the plans of the light rays from P.L. through the four corners of the plan of the square containing the plan of the disk. (In this case these plans of the light rays will coincide with the diagonals.) Actual light rays are then drawn from the light source through the four corners of the square containing the disk to meet the appropriate plan lines, and these points of intersection are then joined up as shown. The shadow of the disk is then drawn by projecting actual light rays from the light source through the intersections of the ellipse representing the disk in perspective and the diagonals of the square surrounding it, to meet the diagonals of the square surrounding the shadow. The ellipse representing the shadow of the disk is then drawn by joining up these points on the diagonals. The shadow of the disk will in fact be circular because the disk is parallel to the ground plane, and therefore it will be seen as a true ellipse in the perspective view. Because the light rays emanate from a single point the shadow of the disk, for obvious reasons, will appear larger than the disk itself.

Fig. 199 shows a cylinder set up using one-point perspective construction as previously described. An artificial light source is located directly above the centre of the circular end of the cylinder. Because the construction of the shadow in this example is identical to the one described in Fig. 198, there is no need to repeat it. Sufficient to say that the sides of the cylinder will be seen in shade. This must be so because the light source is situated directly above the centre of the circular end of the cylinder, which means that the line of separation will be around the edge of the circular end.

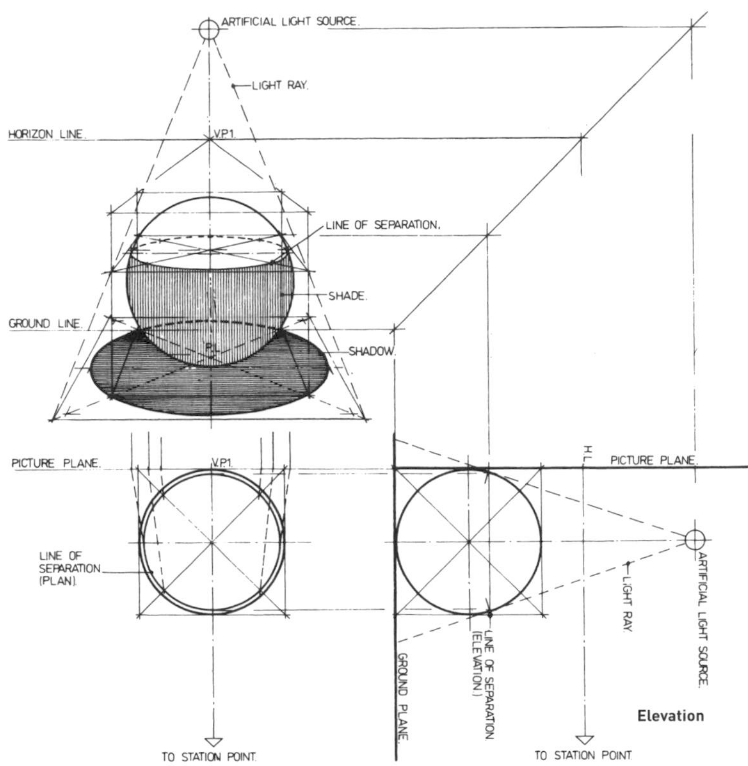

200 The shadow of a sphere, cast by artificial light

Fig. 200 shows a sphere set up using one-point perspective construction as previously described. The light source is located directly above the centre of the sphere. It is necessary to locate the line of separation on the surface of the sphere in perspective before the shadow of the sphere can be located and drawn. Before this can be done it is necessary to locate the line of separation on the plan view of the sphere which means that an elevation will be required, set up at a convenient distance from the plan. By drawing the actual light rays from the light source in the elevation, an elevation of the line of separation can be located. This line of separation is then located on the plan view of the sphere by simple projection. By locating a plane through the sphere to coincide with the line of separation in the elevation it is possible to locate this plane in the perspective view. By projecting up from the plan in the normal way, the ellipse representing the line of separation can be drawn on this plane which was located to coincide with the line of separation. This means that the ellipse is in reality on the surface of the sphere. Once the line of separation is located it is a simple matter to draw the shadow of that line of separation in exactly the same way as that described for the two preceding examples. The shadow will again be much larger than the line of separation, for the same obvious reasons.

Before concluding this section, it is worth looking at the shadow cast by a cylinder when the light source is located in a position other than directly over the centre of the circular end. Fig. 201 shows the same cylinder as was used in Fig. 199 set up as before but with an artificial light source located above and to one side of it. As with the previous examples, it is necessary to find the plan location of the light source before the shadow of the cylinder can be constructed. Once this is done the construction is much the same as the previous ones, i.e. the plans of the light rays are drawn from P.L. through the four corners of the perspective view of the square surrounding the base of the cylinder (the base corresponds to the plan). When the actual light rays are drawn through the corners of the square surrounding the top circular end of the cylinder, the square surrounding the shadow of the top of the cylinder can

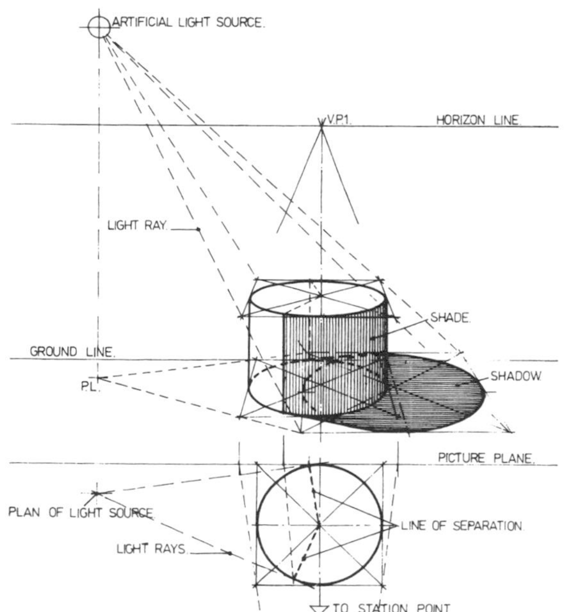

201 The cylinder of Fig. 199, with the light source moved to one side.

be drawn in perspective. The actual shadow of the top of the cylinder is drawn in the normal way by using actual light rays through the intersections of the ellipse forming the end of the cylinder and the diagonals of the square surrounding it.

The line of separation is a little more complicated in this case. The line of separation of a cylinder is always at right angles to the light rays, as previously explained. While the light rays were parallel, as for sunlight, this was a simple matter because the line of separation would have to be a diameter of the circle. In the example shown here, the light rays are no longer parallel and, because the line of separation is at right angles to the light rays, it will no longer be a diameter of the circle. Because the light rays form tangents to the circumference of the circle, the line of separation which is at right angles to the light rays will pass through the centre of the circle; this means that the line of separation will be as shown in Fig. 201. If this is compared with the line of separation of the cylinder in Fig. 190 this basic difference between the two sets of conditions should be much clearer. The other main difference is that the shadow cast by the artificial light source will become wider as it travels away from the object whereas the sides of the shadow cast by sunlight will remain parallel. There are, of course, other differences but these should be obvious to the serious student so it is not necessary to elaborate them.

In summing up, it can be fairly said that shadows are a combination of simple construction, common sense and a reasonable understanding of the two-dimensional representation of three-dimensional objects. If the basic principles are understood, shadows can be constructed on drawings of the most complex subjects without any difficulty. A reliable, accurate short-cut method for locating the vanishing points for the plans of the light rays and the actual light rays is shown in the next chapter but like most other short cuts it is of little use unless it is fully understood; therefore the student is advised to learn the basic principles before adopting this or any other short cut.

.9 Short Cuts in Perspective Drawing

Before proceeding with the final chapter of this book it is important to point out that any short cut in perspective projection which is not based on sound principles is no short cut at all but an expression of ignorance of the subject. The short cut is essential today because many of the basic methods, when applied to large, complex objects, become somewhat unwieldy and time-consuming, and thus unacceptable commercially. This is no reason to cast aside accuracy in the two-dimensional representation of three-dimensional objects, but rather a challenge to the student to acquire the knowledge and skill to produce a commodity which is acceptable in the commercial world, which he is destined to enter at the conclusion of his studies.

I propose, therefore, to introduce a number of basic short cuts and relate them back to sound principles, so that the student can use them with confidence and without loss of accuracy. The ones shown are not by any means a complete catalogue of short cuts: many of them can be adapted and/or extended to cover many problems which may be encountered, but if they are thoroughly understood this will be a comparatively simple matter.

The first of these short cuts is a two-point construction which, under certain conditions, can save a great deal of time and space. This particular short cut is divided into two parts, the first of which is the setting up of a simple cube using two-point perspective when the cube is located with its front edge (the one nearest the spectator) coinciding with the picture plane and its sides at 45° to that picture plane. Fig. 202 shows the normal method used to construct a perspective view of a cube under the conditions described here using a plan construction. If the resulting perspective view is examined certain facts are discernible, the first of which is that the two sides of the cube facing the spectator are of equal width (the sides are at 45° to

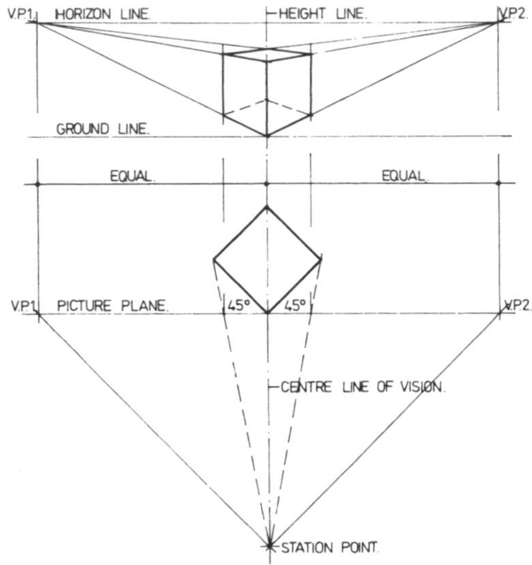

202 Two-point perspective view of a cube seen edge-on.

the picture plane), which means that the vanishing points are at equal distances from the centre line of vision (which coincides with the front edge of the cube). The second of these facts is that because the front edge of the cube coincides with the picture plane it can be used as the height line. The height of the object can be measured on this line using its true scale height which means that the front edge of the cube in the perspective view

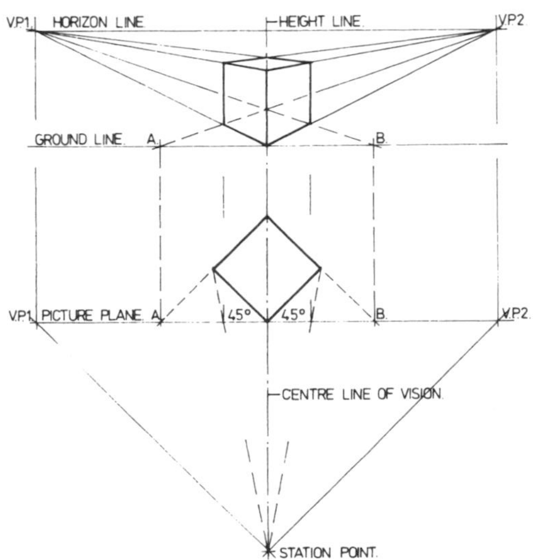

203 Two-point perspective view of a cube seen edge-on.

will be the true scale height of the cube.
The third of these discernible facts is that because the two sides seen by the spectator are of equal width the back edge of the cube will fall directly behind the front edge.

Fig. 203 shows one other useful piece of information with regard to a cube located with its front edge coinciding with the picture plane and its sides at 45° to the picture plane. The two sides forming the back of the cube as seen by the spectator can be extended forward to meet the picture plane as shown. If the points of intersection of these extended sides of the cube and the picture plane are projected up vertically to the ground line (points *A* and *B*) and these points in the ground line are joined to the appropriate vanishing points, i.e. *A* to V.P.2 and *B* to V.P.1, the bottom edges of the sides forming the back of the cube in perspective, as seen by the spectator, will fall in these lines.

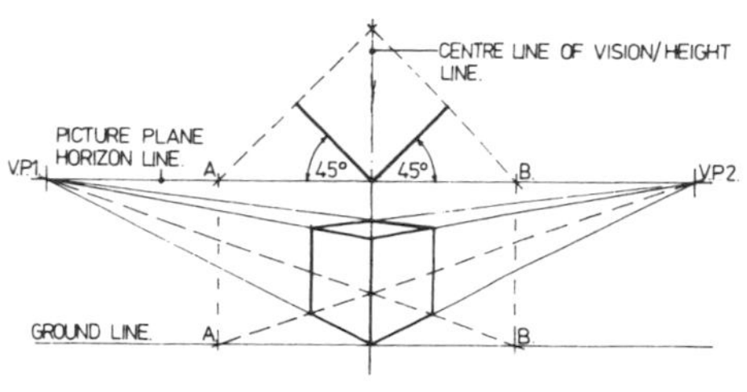

204 Perspective view of a cube seen edge-on; simplified method.

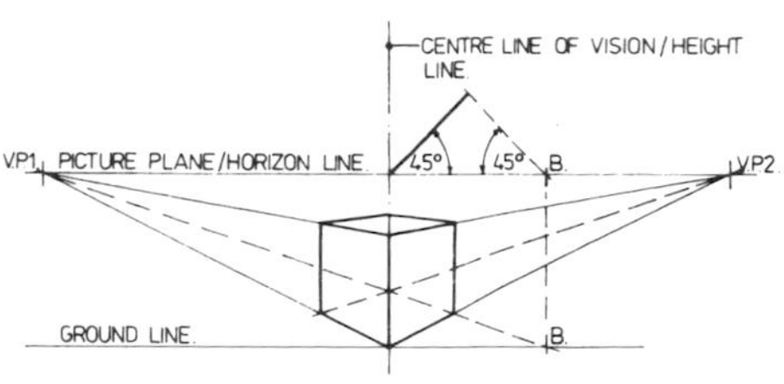

205 Perspective view of a cube: the method of Fig. 204, simplified one stage further.

If the three facts from Fig. 202 and the one from Fig. 203 are put together it is possible to use them to set up a perspective view of a cube when its front edge is located in the picture plane and its sides are at 45° to the picture plane. Fig. 204 shows how this is done when the horizon line in the perspective view is also used as a picture plane.

If this diagram is compared with those in Fig. 202 and Fig. 203 it can be seen that all of the conditions are fulfilled; therefore the result obtained is identical. This construction shown in Fig. 204 can be simplified further, as shown in Fig. 205 where the result obtained is again identical to those obtained in Figs. 202, 203 and 204. The short-cut method of setting up a perspective view of a cube with its front edge located in the picture plane and its sides at 45° to the picture plane is shown in Fig. 206 and is as follows:

Step 1. In a convenient position on the sheet of paper draw a horizontal line to represent the horizon line in the perspective view. Near each end of the horizon line locate a vanishing point (V.P.1 and V.P.2). Divide the distance between

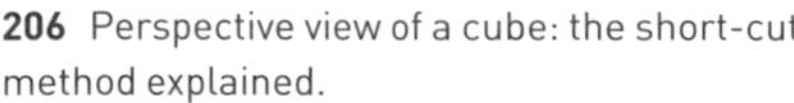

206 Perspective view of a cube: the short-cut method explained.

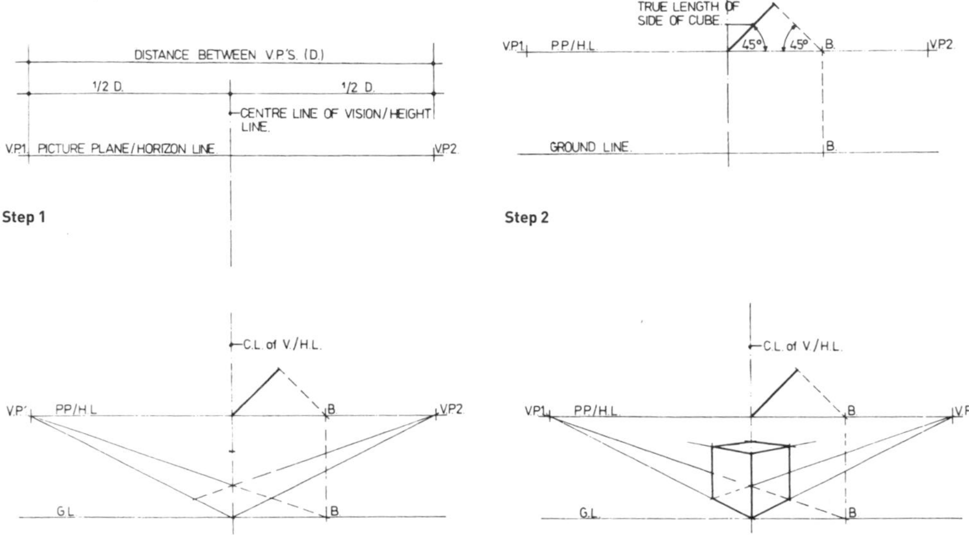

the two vanishing points exactly in half and draw a vertical line representing the centre line of vision (which coincides with the front edge of the cube, which is also the height line).

Step 2. Locate the ground line at the required distance below the horizon line. (The ground line is located with regard to the view of the cube required and the limits of the cone of vision – both subjects to be dealt with separately later.) From the intersection of the centre line of vision/height line and the picture plane/horizon line, a side of the cube is set out at 45° to the picture plane/horizon line. The extension of the side forming the back of the cube is also set out at 45° to the P.P./H.L. The intersection of the extended side and the P.P./H.L. (point *B*) is located in the ground line by vertical projection in the normal way. (The side of the cube can be set out on either side of the centre line of vision/height line.)

Step 3. From the intersection of the centre line of vision/height line and the ground line, lines are drawn back to V.P.1 and V.P.2. From point *B* in the ground line a line is drawn back to V.P.1 and from the intersection of this line and the centre line of vision/height line a line is drawn back to V.P.2, which completes the base of the cube in the perspective view. The height of the cube, measured from the ground line up, is then located on the centre line of vision/height line.

Step 4. Complete the sides and the top of the cube using the appropriate vanishing points.

Because the distance between the two vanishing points and the distance between the horizon line and the ground line are the same in this example as in the four preceding ones the result obtained will be identical. However, it should be understood that the distance between the vanishing points is arbitrary within the limits of the cone of vision i.e. if the vanishing points are too close together this will present a very close station point which could result in a distorted view of the cube. The further apart the vanishing points are placed the further the spectator is from the object viewed. Similarly, the further apart the horizon line and the ground line are placed the higher the eye level of the spectator; therefore the distance between the horizon line and the ground line is also an arbitrary dimension, within the limits of the cone of vision.

Before exploring the value of being able to set up, quickly and accurately, a cube under these conditions in perspective projection it is necessary to examine the second part of this short cut. If a cube is again located with its front edge (the one nearest to the spectator) coinciding with the picture plane and the centre line of vision, but in this case with its sides making angles of 60° and 30° with the picture plane, it is again possible to set up a perspective view of the cube using a short-cut method similar to that shown in Fig. 206. The normal method used for constructing a perspective view of a cube under these conditions is shown in Fig. 207. By examining the resulting perspective view of the cube obtained in Fig. 207 a number of facts can be discerned. The first of these is that the side adjacent to the 30° angle will appear to the spectator to be twice as wide as the side adjacent to the 60° angle. The second of these facts is that the centre line of vision/height line (which coincides with the front edge of the cube) is located at one-quarter of the distance between the vanishing points (V.P.1 and V.P.2), this one-quarter being on the side adjacent to the 60°

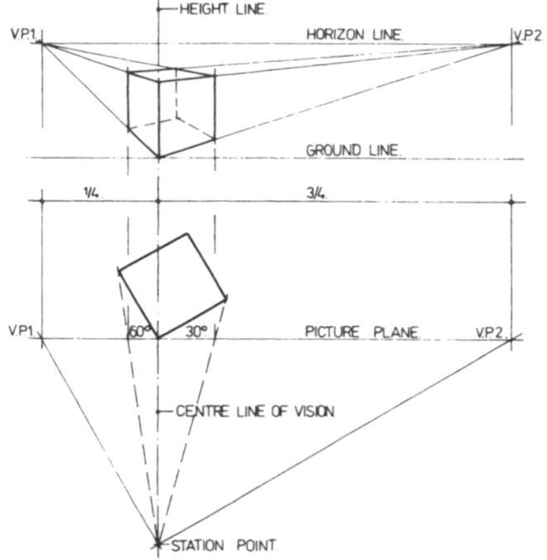

207 Cube with sides at 60° and 30° to the picture plane: normal method of two-point perspective construction.

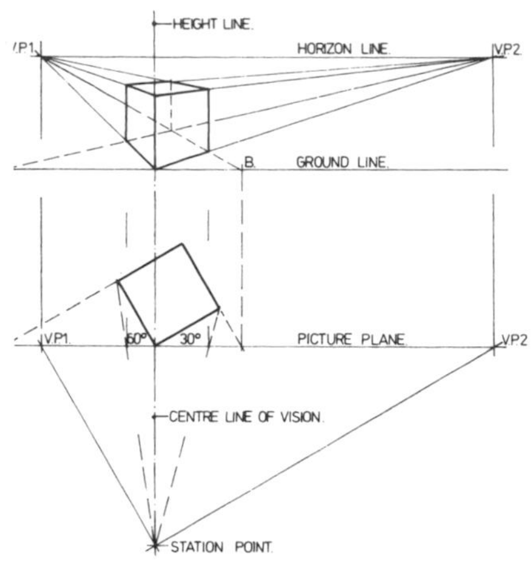

208 The cube of Fig. 207, with two sides extended to the picture plane (compare Fig. 203).

angle. Obviously the other three-quarters of the distance between the vanishing points will be on the side adjacent to the 30° angle. The third of these discernible facts is that because the front edge of the cube is located in the picture plane it can be used as the height line and because it coincides with the centre line of vision, locating the centre line of vision also locates the height line.

Fig. 208 shows in plan the two sides forming the back of the cube, as seen by the spectator, extended forward to meet the picture plane at points *A* and *B*. If the points of intersection of these extended sides are projected up vertically to the ground line and lines are drawn from them back to the appropriate

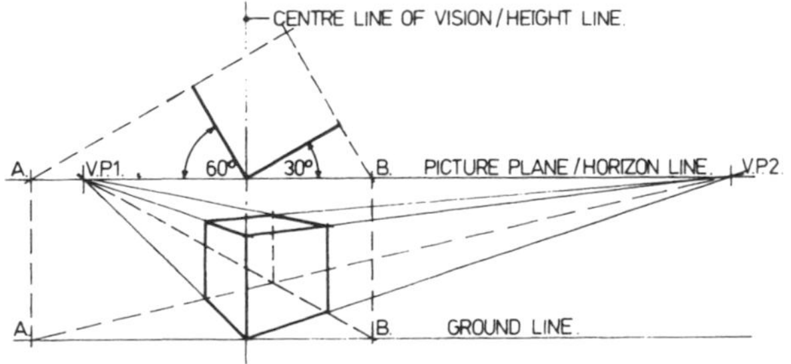

209 The cube of Fig. 207: perspective view of the short-cut method.

vanishing points (from point *A* back to V.P.2 and from point *B* back to V.P.1), the bottom edges of the sides forming the back of the cube, as seen by the spectator, will fall in these lines.

If the facts obtained from Figs. 207 and 208 are put together it is possible to use them to set up a perspective view of a cube when its front edge is located in the picture plane and coincides with the centre line of vision, one of its sides makes an angle of 60° with the picture plane and another side makes an angle of 30° with the picture plane. Fig. 209 shows how this is done without using the set-up shown in Fig. 207. This short-cut method of setting up a perspective view of the cube is shown in Fig. 210 and as follows:

Step 1. In a convenient position on the sheet of paper draw a horizontal line to represent the horizon line in the perspective view. Near each end of the horizon line locate a vanishing point (V.P.1 and V.P.2) as shown. Divide the distance between V.P.1 and V.P.2 into four equal parts and draw a vertical line through one of the quarter divisions so that the distance between the vanishing points is divided in the proportion of one-quarter to three-quarters. This line represents the centre line of vision (which coincides with the front edge of the cube and the height line).

210 The short-cut method step by step.

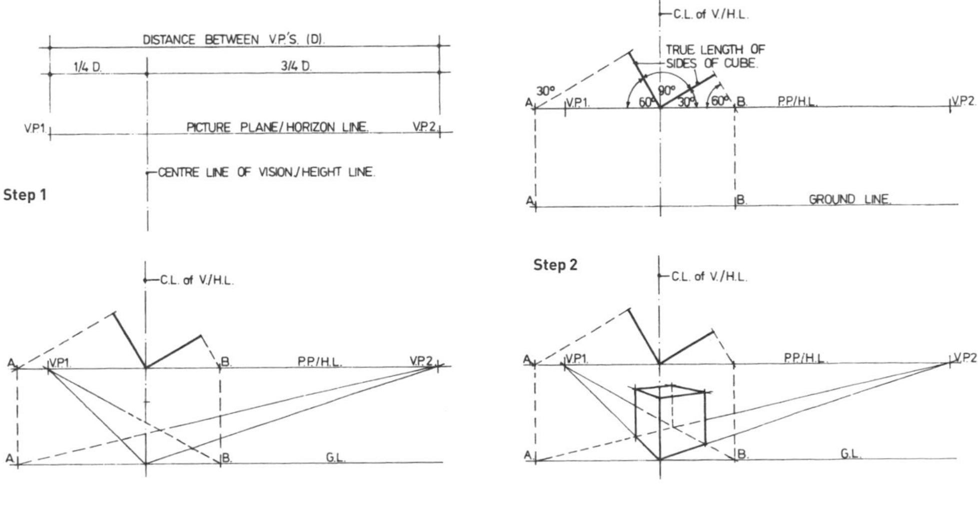

Step 2. Locate the ground line at the required distance below the horizon line. (The ground line is located with regard to the view of the cube required and the limits of the cone of vision – both subjects dealt with separately later.) From the intersection of the centre line of vision/height line and the picture plane/horizon line, a side of the cube is drawn at 60° to the picture plane/horizon line on the side with the shortest distance between the centre line of vision/height line and the vanishing point (V.P.1 in this example). A second side of the cube is set out at 30° to the picture plane/horizon line on the other side of the centre line of vision/height line. Points *A* and *B* are located on the picture plane/horizon line by extending the two sides forming the back of the cube, as seen by the spectator, forward to meet the picture plane/horizon line. Points *A* and *B* are then located in the ground line by vertical projection in the normal way.

Step 3. From the intersection of the centre line of vision/height line and the ground line, lines are drawn back to V.P.1 and V.P.2. From points *A* and *B* lines are drawn back to V.P.1 and V.P.2 to complete the base of the cube in the perspective view. The height of the cube is then located on the centre line of vision/height line (measured from the ground line up.)

Step 4. Complete the sides and the top of the cube, using the appropriate vanishing points.

Because all of the circumstances in this example are the same as those in Figs. 207, 208 and 209 the result obtained is identical. The similarity between this short cut and the one shown in Fig. 206 will be readily seen; therefore it is unnecessary to repeat the observations which follow the description of that figure. Sufficient to say that either of the two ends can be used for the one-quarter division, depending on the view of the cube required.

Because the results obtained by both of these short-cut methods are identical to the result obtained using the normal construction, they can be considered accurate and therefore acceptable. However, it should be remembered that they are accurate only for the two sets of conditions described, and are useless in their present form for any other conditions. As with

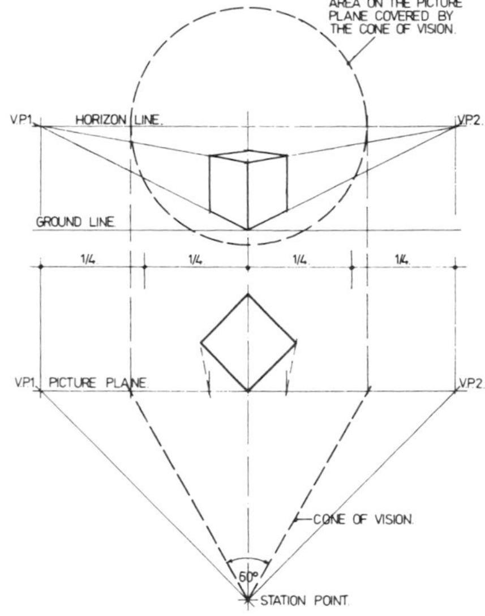

211 The cube of Fig. 202, checked for distortion in the normal way.

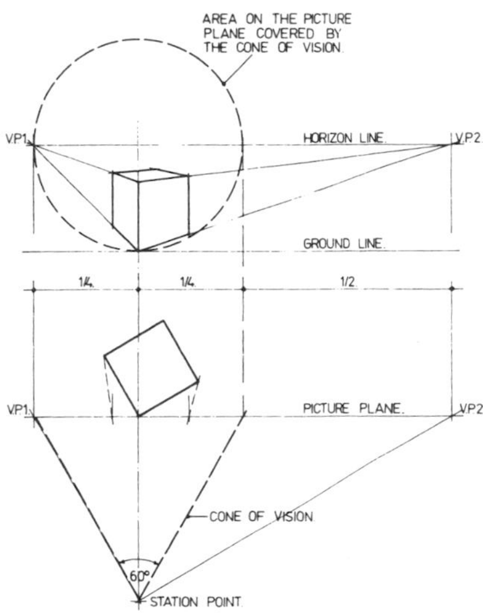

212 The cube of Fig. 207, checked for distortion in the normal way.

any other perspective construction, one of the most important steps is the use of the cone of vision to check the limits of the drawing so that distortions can be avoided. Neither of the two short-cut methods shown here has a plan construction as such, with a station point etc., which means that it is necessary to devise an alternative method for checking against distortions such as an object or a part of an object falling outside the cone of vision. To understand this alternative method or short cut it is necessary first to examine the construction shown in Fig. 211 where the same cube is set up in perspective construction under the same conditions as the one in Fig. 202. The cone of vision is shown in the plan in the normal way and the area which the cone of vision covers on the picture plane is also shown. By examination it will be found that the radius of the area covered by the cone of vision is slightly more than one-quarter of the distance between the two vanishing points; therefore if one-quarter of that distance is used it will provide a safe margin for the student. Similarly in Fig. 212, where a 60°/30° set-up is used, the cone of vision covers an area whose radius is one-quarter of the distance between the two vanishing points.

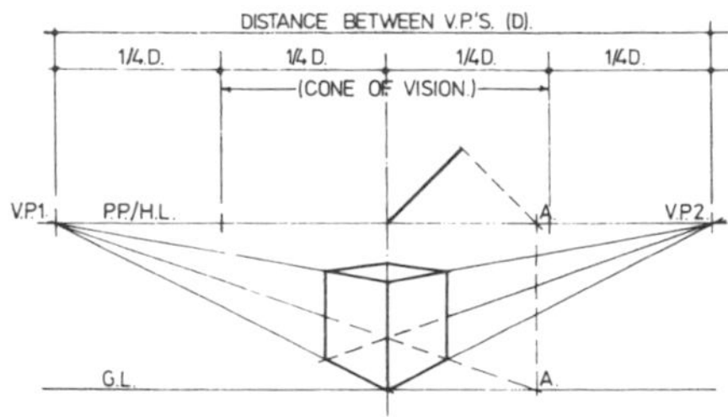

213 The cube of Fig. 206, checked for distortion by the short-cut method: the circular field of the cone of vision is reduced to a straight line (the diameter).

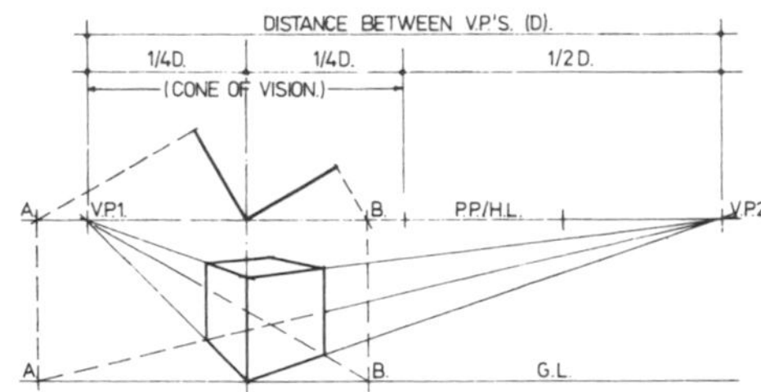

214 The cube of Fig. 210, checked for distortion by the short-cut method.

If it is known that on the picture plane the cone of vision covers a circle whose radius is equal to one-quarter of the distance between the vanishing points, this can be located in the short-cut method, as shown in Figs. 213 and 214 where the horizontal limits of the drawing can be located simply by measurement. The vertical limits are also located by simple measurement as shown in Figs. 215 and 216. In both cases the intersection between the centre line of vision/height line and the horizon line is used as the starting point for measuring both the horizontal and the vertical limits of the cone of vision.

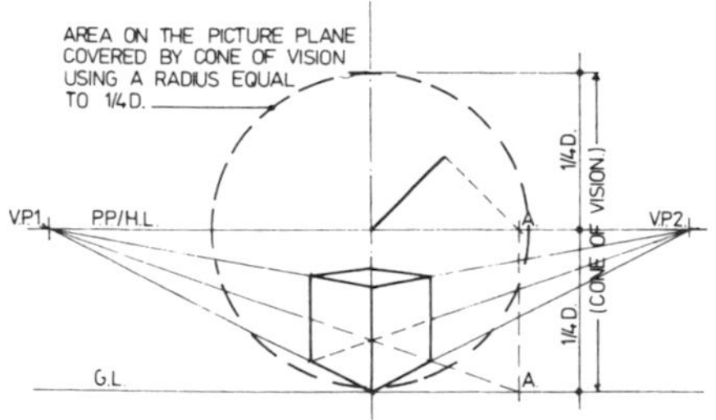

215 Locating the vertical limits by measurement.

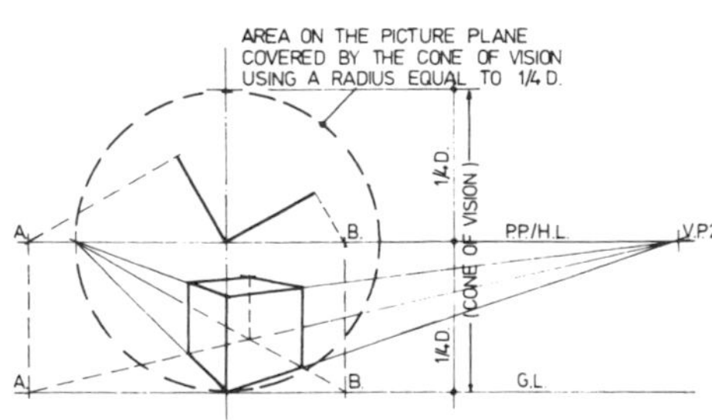

216 Locating the vertical limits by measurement.

From the examples shown in Figs. 202 through to 216, using these short-cut methods, which are quicker to carry out than to describe, it can be seen that it is possible to produce quickly a reliable, accurate view of a cube in perspective projection. It is reliable because whichever of the two sets of conditions is used the results obtained will always be identical to those obtained with the normal construction methods and those exact conditions. If this is doubted, a few simple experiments will prove convincing for even the most sceptical.

The value of being able to produce an accurate perspective view of a cube under the conditions previously described may not be fully realized until this short-cut method is related to the one explained in Chapter 2.6, 'Reflections' (see Figs. 139–142), where it was found that by the use of diagonals more identical cubes could be added horizontally, in any direction, to a single cube. To explain this more fully, a single cube is set up in perspective in Fig. 217 using the 45°/45° short-cut method. Fig. 218 shows a number of identical faces of cubes added to each of the two faces of the original cube seen by the spectator. This is done by locating the centres of the two faces of the original cube (at the intersection of its diagonals). From the centres of the two faces, perspective lines are drawn back to the appropriate vanishing points. Next, each face of the original cube is thought of as half of a rectangle, a diagonal of which will pass through the centre of that rectangle. Therefore, a diagonal drawn from the appropriate corner of the face of the original cube through the intersection of the perspective line from the centre of that face and the side opposite to the corner will intersect an extension of the top edge of the face of the original cube. This point of intersection locates the other end of the rectangle of which the face of the original cube constitutes one half. This means that the other half, which was located by using the diagonal of the rectangle, will be identical to the original half (seen in perspective). In other words, the face of a second cube, identical to the face of the original cube, has been added. By using this principle a number of faces can be added to either of the two faces of the original cube,

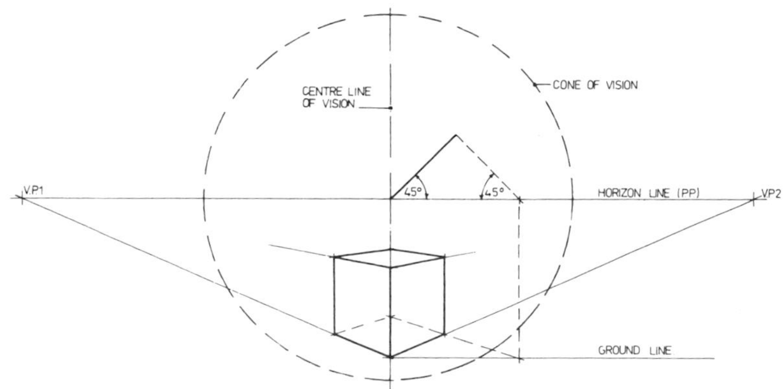

217 Multiplication of cubes by the short-cut method: first step.

218 Multiplication of cubes in two directions horizontally.

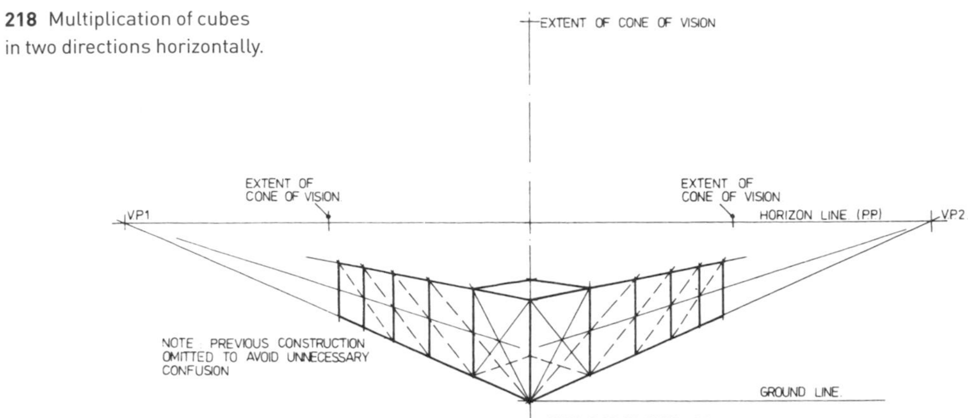

as required. The only limiting factors to adding an infinite number of faces are the vertical and horizontal limits of the cone of vision. The additional cubes can be completed by simple perspective projection, which should be obvious, therefore it is not shown in the diagrams.

Fig. 219 shows the method used for adding identical cubes vertically. Because the original cube was located with its front edge coinciding with the picture plane, this front edge could be used as the height line. Therefore, to add more cubes vertically is simply a matter of setting out the height of the cube the required number of times and completing the drawings of the additional cubes as shown. In Fig. 219 the top cube, which is shown by means of a broken line, falls partly

219 Multiplication of cubes vertically.

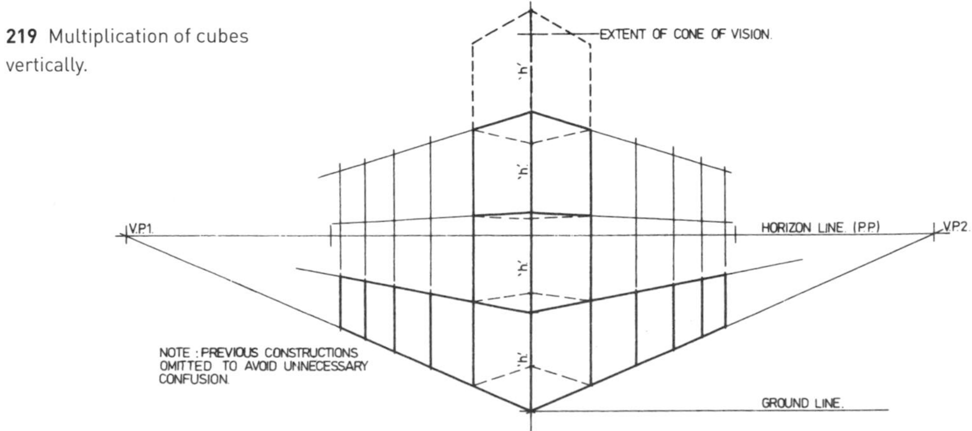

outside the cone of vision which means that normally it will be subject to distortion. However, it will be remembered that in a 45°/45° short-cut method the cone of vision used is slightly smaller than the actual cone of vision; therefore, in this case, the top cube could be drawn and, because it is so close to the limit of the cone of vision, no distortion would be expected.

Once it is possible to set up a number of identical cubes as shown in Fig. 219 it is an easy matter to set up a perspective view of any object which can be fitted into a simple cube or a series of cubes. Half-cubes and quarter-cubes can be constructed and used if necessary, which gives the student great flexibility. Little more need be said about the advantages of this short-cut method when it is related back to the 'box' method of drawing objects (Chapter 2.6).

The foregoing short-cut method of drawing a cube in perspective when it is located with its front edge coinciding with the picture plane and its sides at either 45°/45° or 60°/30° to the picture plane can be extended to rectangular prisms, which can be set up in perspective using the same basic principles.

220 Short-cut method of drawing a cube in perspective, extended to the special case of a rectangular prism which is equivalent to two or more cubes.

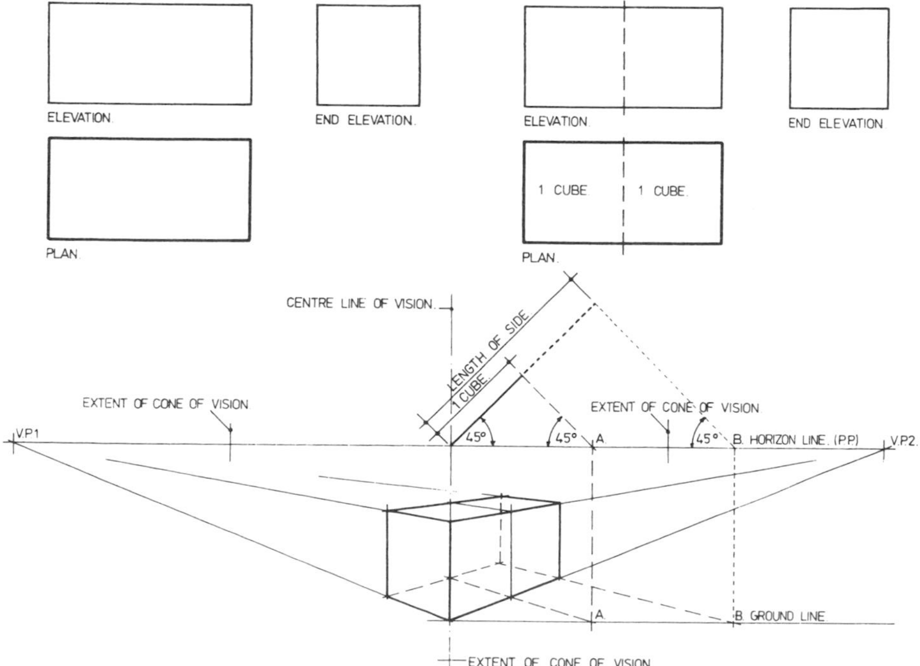

Fig. 220 shows a rectangular prism in orthographic projection (1). When this is analysed it can be seen that, in this case, the rectangular prism is made up of two identical cubes, which are also shown in orthographic projection (2). The method used for setting up the rectangular prism is as follows:

Step 1. In a convenient position on the sheet of paper draw a horizontal line to represent the horizon line/picture plane and locate a vanishing point near each end (V.P.1 and V.P.2). Divide the distance between the vanishing points in half because it is intended to view the object with its sides at 45°/45° to the picture plane in this example. Draw the vertical centre line of vision/height line through this centre measurement and locate the ground line at the required distance below the horizon line/picture plane. Locate the limits of the cone of vision in the usual way.

Step 2. From the intersection of the horizon line/picture plane and the centre line of vision/height line draw one side of a cube at 45° to the horizon line/picture plane and extend it until it equals the total length of the side of the rectangular prism. From the points indicating the measurement of a side of the cube and a side of the rectangular prism draw lines at right angles to this line to meet the horizon line/picture plane at *A* and *B* respectively. From these two points project down vertically to locate them on the ground line.

Step 3. Using points *A* and *B* in the ground line and V.P.1 and V.P.2 draw the perspective view of the rectangular prism as previously described.

Fig. 221 shows the same rectangular prism as used in Fig. 220 set up in perspective when its sides are at 60°/30° to the horizon line/picture plane. The method in this example will be the same as in the preceding one except for the obvious difference in the angles set up. Also, because it is necessary to set up two sides of the cube when using the 60°/30° method, the second side of the cube is located. From this it can be seen that this method is not limited to cubes or objects made up of a number of cubes but can be used for any object, even those which contain sloping planes.

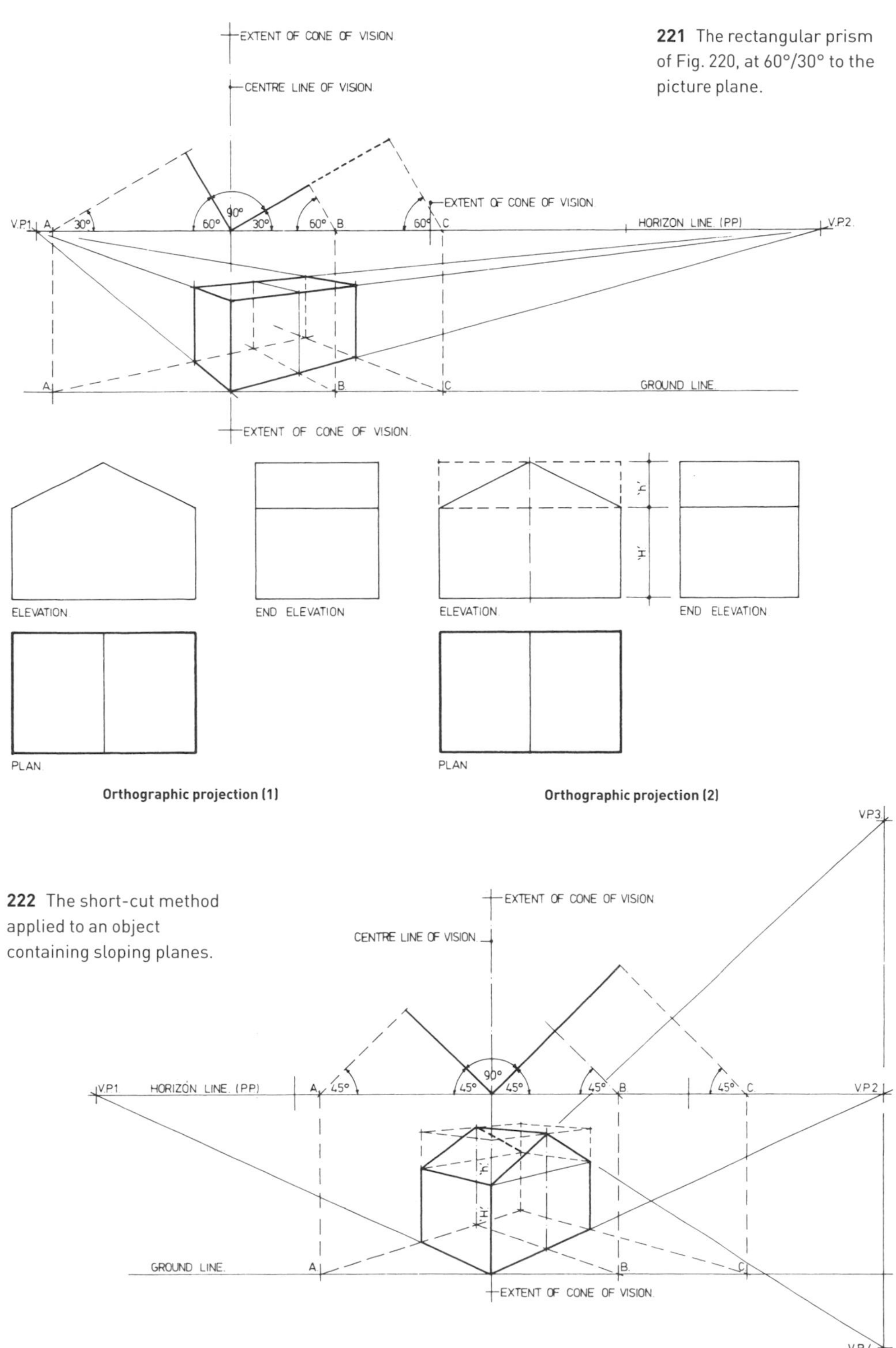

221 The rectangular prism of Fig. 220, at 60°/30° to the picture plane.

Orthographic projection (1)

Orthographic projection (2)

222 The short-cut method applied to an object containing sloping planes.

In the example shown in the orthographic projection (1) in Fig. 222, the object can no longer simply be divided into two cubes but if it is analysed, as shown in the orthographic projection (2), the whole of it, including the sloping planes, can be fitted into a simple rectangular prism. Fig. 222 shows the rectangular prism set up in the perspective view using the 45°/45° method. Because the object can no longer simply be divided into cubes it is necessary to locate two sides of the rectangular prism. Using the set-up of the rectangular prism which contains the whole of the object, the height of the lower ends of the sloping planes can be measured on the elevation (H) and located on the height line in the perspective construction. This height can then be located on each end of the rectangular prism by projection (in perspective). The centre of the rectangular prism is located from the 'plan' in the normal way and, by joining up the appropriate points in the perspective view, the inclined lines of the inclined planes can be drawn. If these inclined lines are continued to meet a vertical line through the appropriate vanishing point (V.P.2 in this case) vanishing points for these inclined lines can be located (V.P.3 and V.P.4).

Fig. 223 shows the same object as used in Fig. 222 set up using the 60°/30° method. The method should be obvious so it is not necessary to repeat the description; however, the importance of locating vanishing points for inclined lines

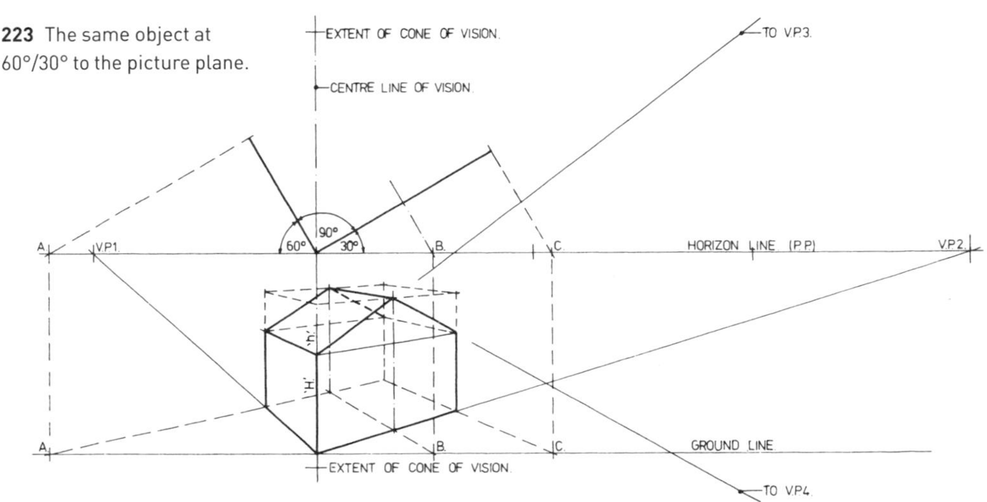

223 The same object at 60°/30° to the picture plane.

cannot be over-emphasized. They save a great deal of wasted time and effort and, in many cases, frustration if they are located and used.

Fig. 224 shows another rectangular object with, in this case, a recess in one of its faces as shown in orthographic projection (1). In this case the analysis is fairly simple: the object will not easily divide up into cubes, therefore it is necessary to set up a rectangular prism (two sides) and to locate the height, width and depth of the recess. The set-up of the rectangular prism using the 45°/45° method is as previously described. The recess is then set up on the 'plan' as shown and the same principle is applied to the recess as was applied to the rectangular prism. Fig. 225 shows the same object set up using the 60°/30° method, and is self-explanatory.

224 A rectangular prism with a recess, set up by the short-cut method.

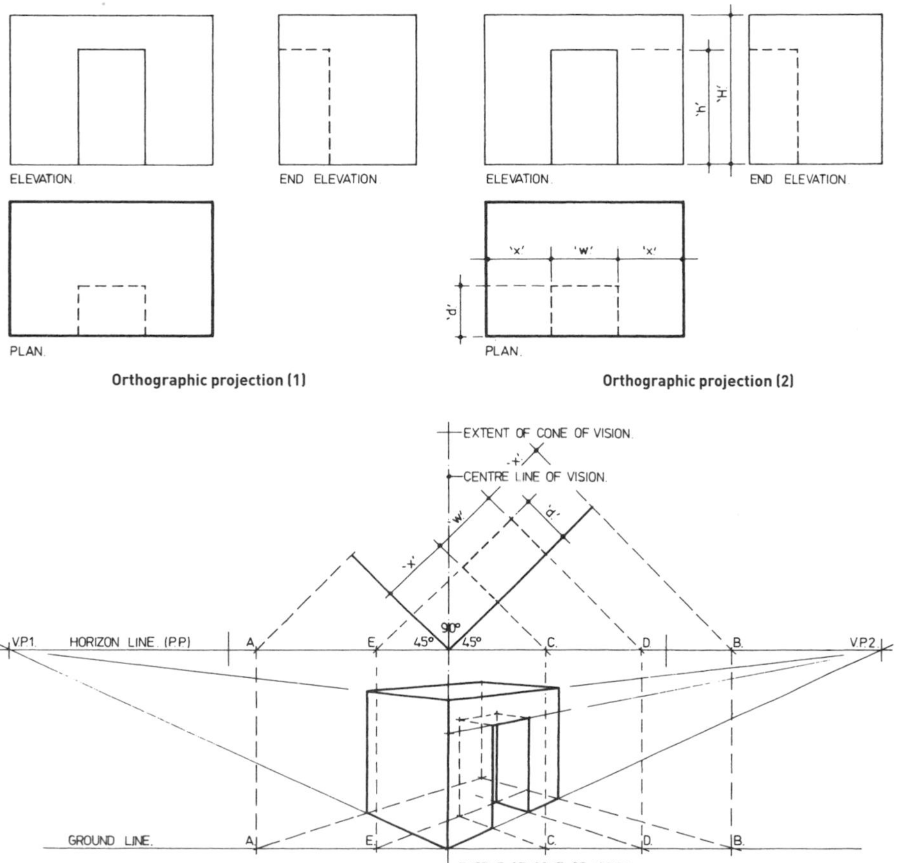

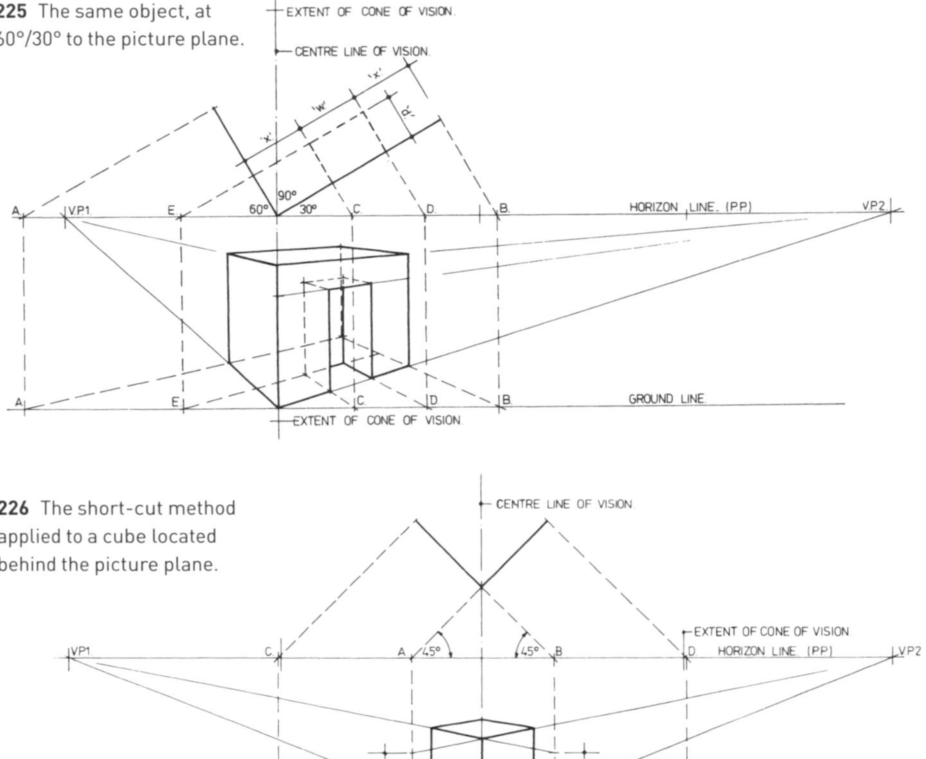

225 The same object, at 60°/30° to the picture plane.

226 The short-cut method applied to a cube located behind the picture plane.

Once the student can set up accurately a rectangular prism, inclined planes and simple recesses in perspective projection using these methods he should be able to adapt them to any object he is likely to encounter. Though the descriptions and figures have been limited to objects with their front edges coinciding with the picture plane, objects located either behind or in front of the picture plane can be set up in perspective projection using a slight variation of these methods. Fig. 226 shows a cube located behind the picture plane. This means that the front edge of the cube is no longer located in the picture plane, therefore it can no longer be used as the height line. The method used for drawing an object in perspective projection when its sides are at 45°/45° to the picture plane and located behind that picture plane is as follows:

Step 1. In a convenient position on the sheet of paper draw a horizontal line to represent the horizon line/picture plane. Locate a vanishing point near each end of the horizon line/picture plane (V.P.1 and V.P.2). Divide the distance between the two vanishing points in half. (It is intended to view the object with its sides at 45°/45° to the picture plane in this example.) Draw the vertical centre line of vision through this centre measurement and locate the ground line at the required distance below the horizon line/picture plane. Locate the limits of the cone of vision in the usual way.

Step 2. Set up two sides of the cube in the required position at 45° to the horizon line/picture plane and project each side to meet the horizon line/picture plane at *A* and *B*. Using vertical projection, these two points are then located on the ground line. From the other ends of the two sides of the cube, lines are drawn at right angles to meet the horizon line/picture plane at points *C* and *D*. Because points *A* and *B* are extensions of the two sides of the cube, lines *AA* and *BB* can be used as height lines. The height 'H' of the cube can be set out on each of them, as shown.

Step 3. Using points *A, B, C* and *D* in the ground line and the appropriate vanishing points, draw the perspective view of the cube as previously described.

The 60°/30° method is exactly the same except for the angles of the sides and the division of the horizon line/picture plane, therefore it is not considered necessary to show it. However, the 60°/30° method is used in Fig. 227 to explain the

227 The short-cut method applied to a cube located in front of, and at 60°/30° to, the picture plane.

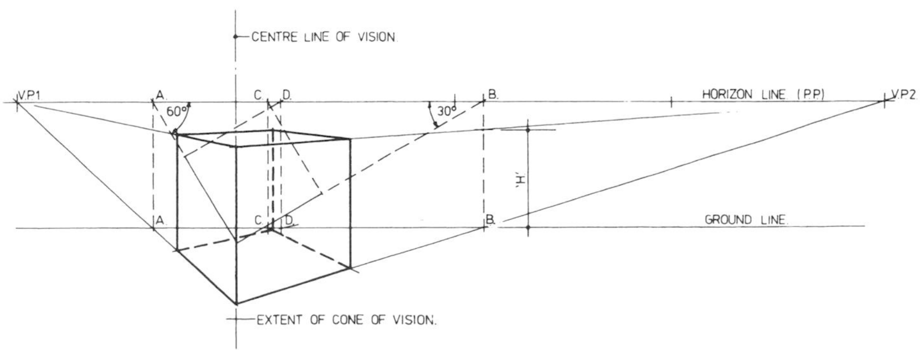

construction of a perspective view of a cube located in front of the picture plane. Again the front edge of the cube does not coincide with the picture plane, therefore it cannot be used as the height line. This means that the sides of the 'plan' of the cube will have to be projected back to meet the picture plane before height lines can be obtained. Once the height lines are located the cube can be drawn in the perspective view as shown. This example tends to look 'messy' because the perspective drawing is carried out over the 'plan'. Because of this it is less popular than the other methods, but it is not less accurate or fast than the other methods explained here.

The short-cut methods shown so far have three distinct advantages over what is known as the basic or normal method of perspective projection: (1) They are faster and as accurate; (2) they require less space; and (3) they do not require a complex and time-consuming plan set-up. However, they also have some disadvantages, one of which is that they are limited to two angles for the plan position, 45°/45° or 60°/30°. If this disadvantage is examined reasonably, it will be seen that it is not as limiting as one might think. Each method, i.e. the 45°/45° and the 60°/30° method, allows a choice of four separate views, and it would be agreed that few objects could not be provided for adequately. If a satisfactory view of an object cannot be obtained using these short-cut methods there is always the basic method to fall back on, at least for overall shapes or units.

The other main disadvantage of these short-cut methods is the difficulty of controlling from the very beginning the ultimate size of the finished drawing. Again, this is not, or need not be, a major disadvantage when the preliminary setting-up of the basic lines of the perspective view is so quick and simple. With a little common sense and practice, the required size of a perspective drawing can be quickly arrived at by trial and error.

Some of the short-cut methods can be combined satisfactorily with the basic or normal method of perspective projection, to speed up the production of a perspective drawing. The 'diagonal' is probably the most useful of all of the short-cut methods because it not only applies to the examples shown so far but has a number of other uses as well. Fig. 228 shows how

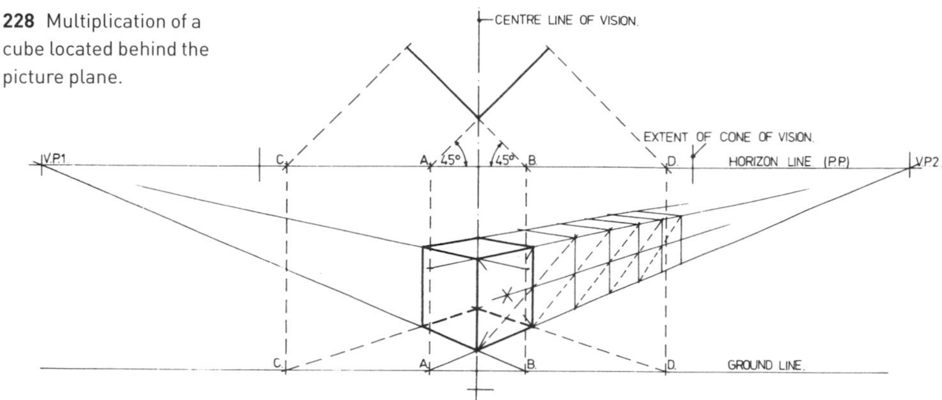

228 Multiplication of a cube located behind the picture plane.

the diagonals can be used to add more identical cubes to one located behind the picture plane. From this example and the others shown in other parts of this book (see Figs. 139–147) it should be obvious that whenever a perspective view of an object consists of square or rectangular sides, diagonals can be used either to divide up or to extend those sides.

One important use of the diagonal is the setting-up of a one-point perspective construction using a short-cut method. A basic method of setting up a one-point perspective view of the interior of a room was described in Fig. 152 (p. 168), which uses a measuring point (the vanishing point for the diagonals of the square floor tiles). Using the principles involved in the basic method, it is possible to produce exactly the same result using a short-cut method, shown in Fig. 229, as follows:

Step 1. In a convenient position on the sheet of paper draw a horizontal line to represent the horizon line in the perspective view. At a convenient point on this line locate the vanishing point (V.P.) and draw a vertical line through it to represent the centre line of vision.

Step 2. Locate the floor line (ground line) at the required distance below the horizon

229a One-point perspective of a room with tiled floor: this is Fig. 152 drawn by the short-cut method. Steps 1 to 3. (For the cone-of-vision check, see Fig. 230.)

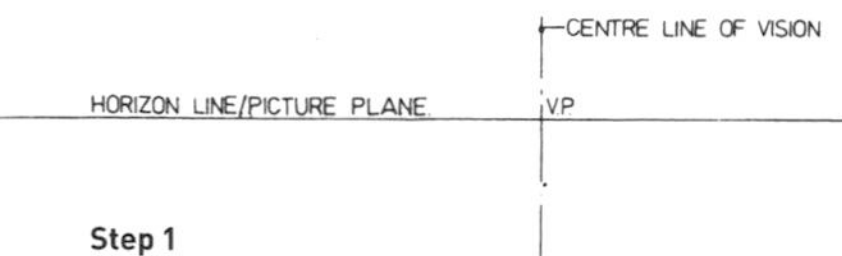

Step 1

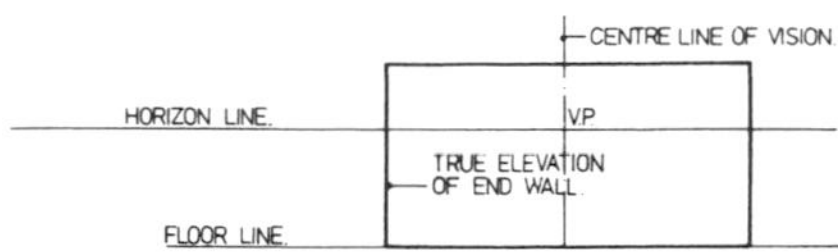

Step 2

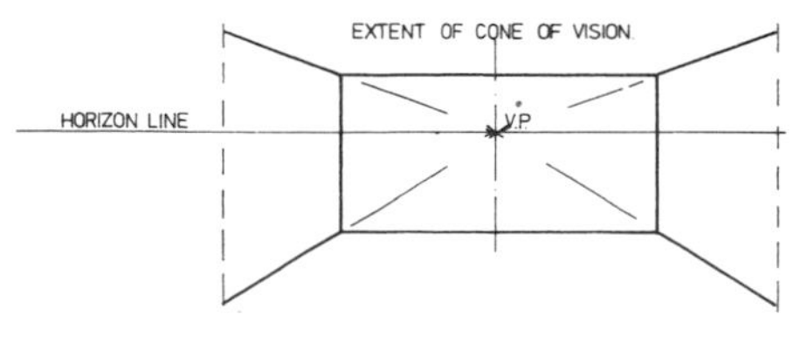

Step 3

line. When the floor line has been located it is then possible to draw a true elevation of the end wall of the room. (The end wall of the room in Fig. 152 is located in the picture plane.)

Step 3. From the V.P. a line is drawn through each of the four corners of the end wall. These lines represent the intersections of the floor and the walls and the ceiling and the walls. At this stage it is necessary to ascertain the limits of the picture, in other words to use the cone of vision.

229*b* One-point perspective of a room with tiled floor: this is Fig. 152 drawn by the short-cut method. Steps 4 to 6. (For the cone-of-vision check, see Fig. 230.)

The cone-of-vision check is shown in Fig. 230 and requires that the position of the spectator be known. This is not difficult to locate because, before a perspective drawing of a room can be carried out, there must be a room to draw. This means that its size is known and therefore the distance between the spectator and the picture plane can be established easily. When this measurement is known it is set out on an extension of the centre line of vision. From this point on the centre line of vision a line is set out at 30° to it, to represent half of the 60° cone of vision. The other half of the cone of vision can be located by measurement, as shown in Fig. 230, or by repeating the line representing half of the cone of vision on the other side of the centre line of vision. When this has been done it is possible to proceed with the construction.

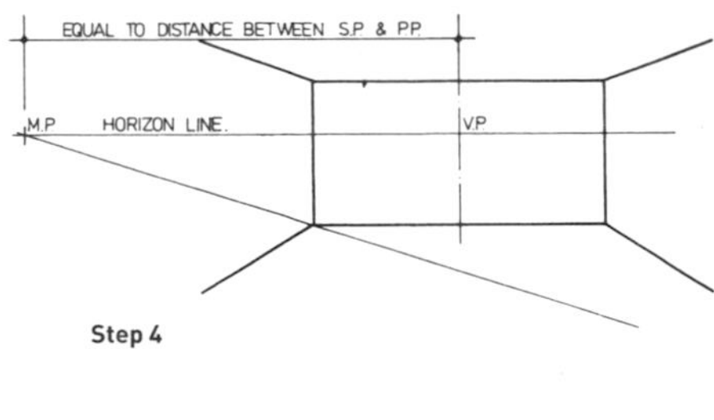

Step 4

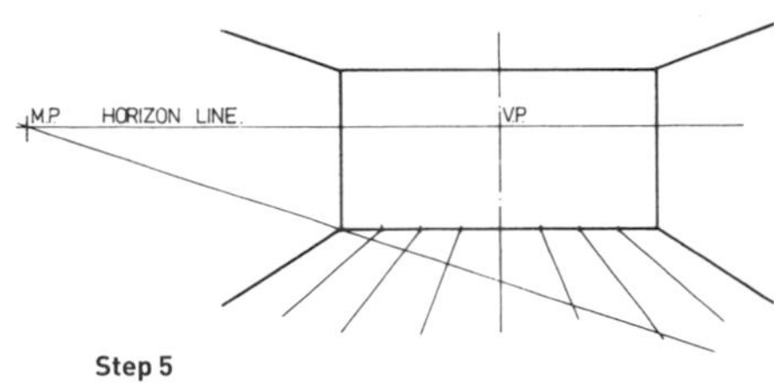

Step 5

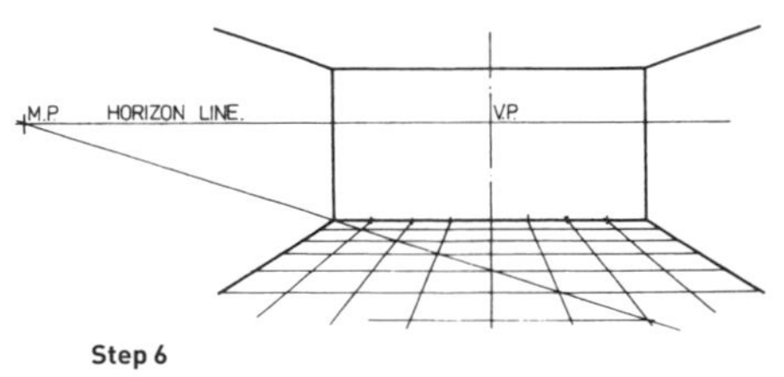

Step 6

Step 4. A measuring point for the diagonals of square floor tiles was found in Fig. 152 by drawing a sight line parallel to those diagonals and, because the diagonals of the square tiles are at an angle of 45° to the picture plane, the distances between the station point and the picture plane and between the vanishing point and the measuring point are the same. (A right

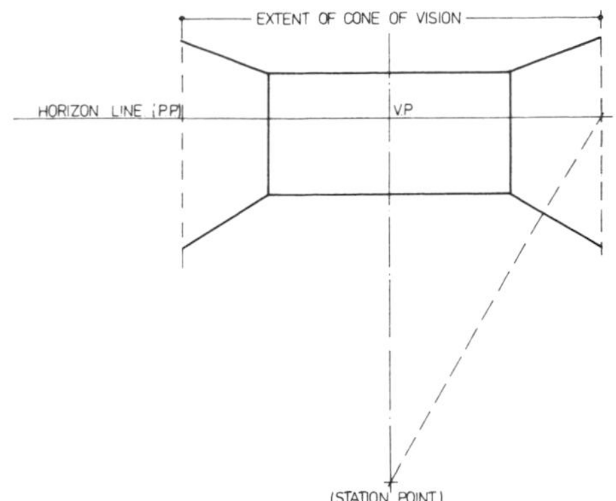

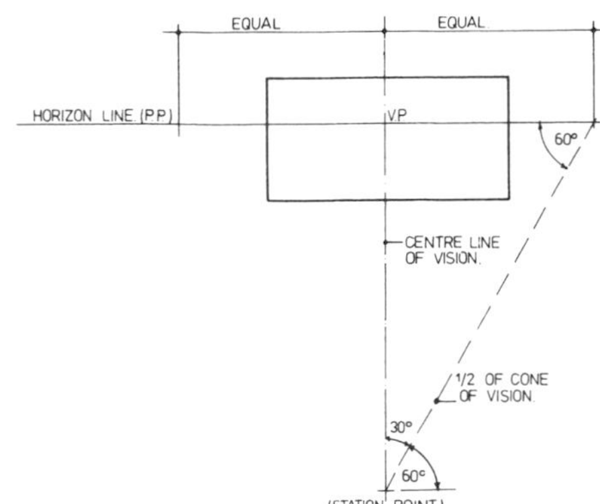

230 Cone-of-vision check for Fig. 229.

angled isosceles triangle is formed.) This means that the measuring point for the diagonals of square floor tiles will be located at the same distance from the V.P. as the spectator is located from the picture plane. This can be set out on whichever side of the centre line of vision is the more convenient. From this measuring point a line is then drawn through the nearest intersection of the end wall, the side wall and the floor. If the divisions are required on the ceiling, the intersection of the end wall, the side wall and the ceiling is used.

Step 5. Because the end wall of the room is located in the picture plane, the floor tiles can be measured and, using the vanishing point, the longitudinal divisions of the tiles can be drawn as shown.

Step 6. Using the line from the measuring point established in Step 4, the lateral divisions of the square floor tiles are located and drawn, parallel to the end wall.

Once these square floor tiles are located in the room they can be treated as units of measurement and used to locate room features such as doors and windows, furniture and fittings. One can see how easy it would be to locate a door which could be measured in units on the plan of the room, and transferred to the perspective view where it could be drawn in its correct position. Because of the simplicity of this it is not proposed to develop the idea further at this stage, but this principle is used for later examples where it is explained more fully.

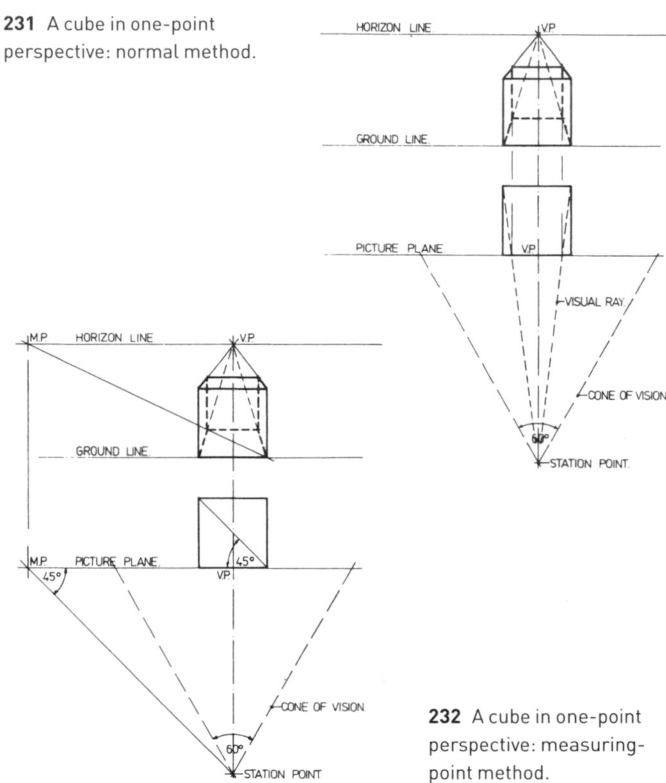

231 A cube in one-point perspective: normal method.

232 A cube in one-point perspective: measuring-point method.

Fig. 231 shows the basic or normal one-point perspective construction of a simple cube. Fig. 232 shows the measuring-point method of setting up a simple cube in perspective. If these two figures are compared it will be seen that the results obtained from identical conditions are exactly the same. From the similarity between the interior perspective constructed using the measuring-point method shown in Fig. 152 and the one-point construction of the cube shown in Fig. 232 it should be obvious that the same basic principle can be used for a short-cut method for setting up a one-point perspective view of a simple cube. The short-cut method, shown in Fig. 233, is as follows:

Step 1. In a convenient position on a sheet of paper draw a horizontal line to represent the horizon line in the perspective view. At a convenient point on this line locate

233 A cube in one-point perspective: short-cut method.

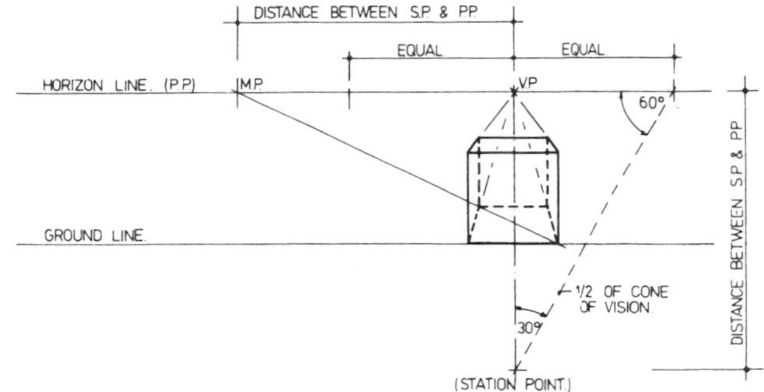

the vanishing point (V.P.) and draw a vertical line through it to represent the centre line of vision.

Step 2. Locate the ground line at the required distance below the horizon line. At this stage it is wise to check with the cone of vision and locate the limits of the picture. This is done by locating a station point, at the required distance from the horizon line (picture plane), on the extended centre line of vision. From this station point a line is drawn at 30° to the centre line of vision to represent half of the cone of vision; the other half of the cone of vision is located by measurement. By measurement along the centre line of vision, as in previous short-cut methods, the location of the ground line is checked to ensure that it is within the cone of vision.

Step 3. When the ground line has been confirmed the true elevation of the cube is drawn. (The front face of the cube coincides with the picture plane.)

Step 4. A measuring point (vanishing point for the diagonal of a square) is located on the horizon line at the same distance from the V.P. as the station point was located from the picture plane (horizon line).

Step 5. From each of the four corners of the true elevation of the cube, lines are drawn back to the vanishing point.

Step 6. From the measuring point, a line is drawn to the far base corner of the true elevation of the cube. At the point where this line intersects the line from

234 One-point perspective of a cube with its back face in the picture plane.

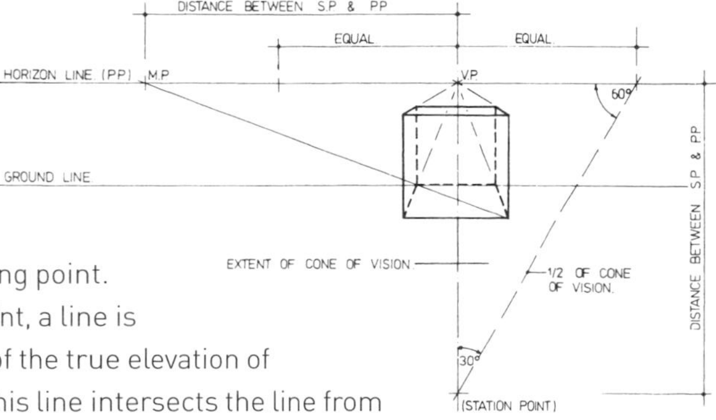

the other base corner back to the vanishing point will be located the back face of the cube. Using this, the one-point perspective view of the cube can be completed as shown.

Because the conditions used for this example are exactly the same as those used for Figs. 231 and 232 the result obtained is identical, which means that this short-cut method is reliable. It also adds another four possible views to the eight already obtainable by previous short-cut methods, i.e. 45°/45° and 60°/30°, which further reduces the possibility of not obtaining a satisfactory view of an object by using short-cut methods. Fig. 234 shows the same short-cut method as used in Fig. 233 but in this example the cube is placed so that its back face coincides with the picture plane. The only difference between this example and the one immediately preceding it is that the near base corner on the ground line is used for the line from the measuring point, and the cube is drawn in front of the ground line instead of behind it.

Fig. 235 shows one use of this principle where a grid of some required unit can be set out accurately in the perspective view so that an object can be simply constructed on it. In this example *AB* is the required unit and because the grid is to be laid out on the ground plane the unit measurement *AB* is set out on the ground line. From this stage forward the construction should be obvious; however, reference to Figs. 233 and 234 should clear up any possible confusion.

These short cuts can be of enormous help to the student once he thoroughly understands the principles behind them.

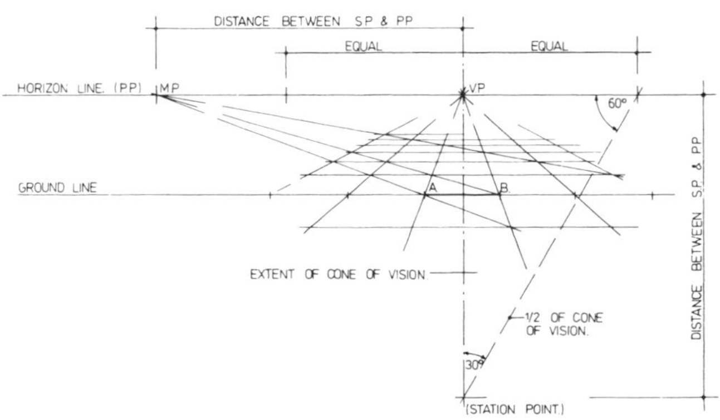

235 Construction of a unit grid in a perspective view, to help in locating objects within the view.

Their potential is limited only by lack of imagination, or unwillingness to study and understand the basic principles of perspective projection before using short cuts. The short cuts explained here are by no means all that are available but they form the basis of most, if not all, of the reliable ones and it is from these that others have been and can be evolved. However, to this stage only short-cut methods for setting up the basic shapes of objects have been considered. Others are available for setting up details, shadows etc., which can be used with equal success with either basic perspective constructions or short-cut constructions. The first of these to be considered is the short-cut method for constructing shadows on a perspective drawing.

Fig. 236 shows the normal method used for locating the vanishing points for the actual light rays and their plans. (Both V.2 and V.3 are shown but only one, never both, will be required in a drawing.) If Fig. 236 is examined (see also Figs. 175–182) it will be seen that the station point, the picture plane and the horizon line are all essential for the construction used to locate the vanishing points for the actual light rays and their plans. In the 45°/45° short-cut method and the 60°/30° short-cut method (see Figs. 206 and 210) the horizon line and the picture plane coincide, therefore both are available for use individually in the construction if necessary. The station point was not necessary in the short-cut construction so it was not

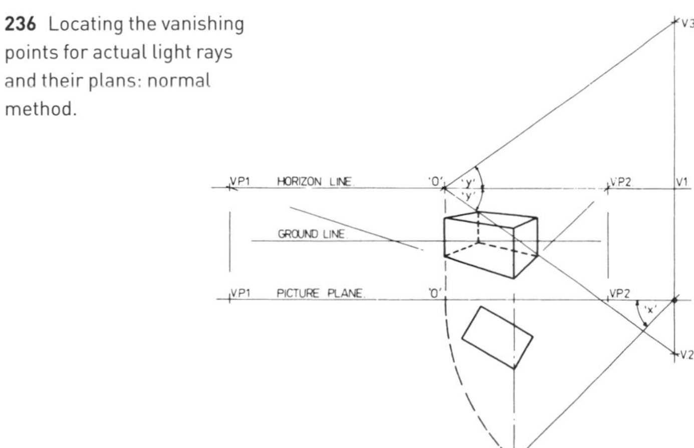

236 Locating the vanishing points for actual light rays and their plans: normal method.

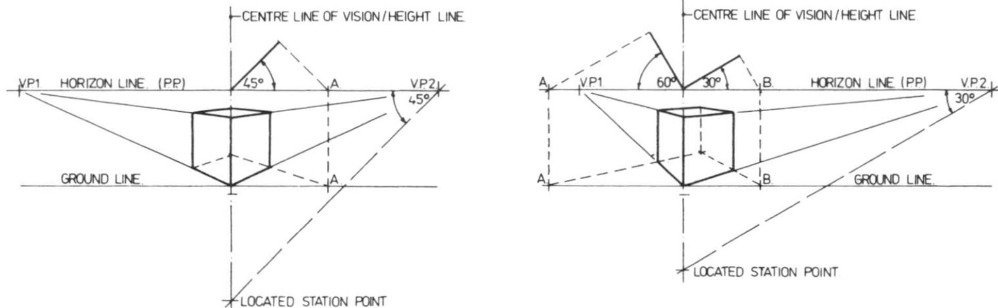

237 Cubes in the 45°/45° and 60°/30° constructions: location of the station point.

located but, because it is necessary for the construction to locate the vanishing points for the actual light rays and their plans, it will now be necessary to locate it. This simply consists of drawing a sight line parallel to a side of the object from its vanishing point back to meet the centre line of vision. The station point will be located at the intersection of this sight line and the centre line of vision. Fig. 237 shows the station points located on both the 45°/45° and the 60°/30° constructions. Once this is done all of the requirements exist on both short-cut methods for the construction to locate the vanishing points for the actual light rays and their plans.

If the light rays meet the picture plane at angle *x* and the ground plane at angle *y*, exactly the same construction as was used in Figs. 176 and 177 is used to locate the required vanishing points. Fig. 238 shows the construction superimposed on both the 45°/45° and the 60°/30° to locate the vanishing point for the plans of the light rays (V.1, which is located in the horizon line) and the vanishing point for the actual light rays when the light source is located behind the

238 Location of the vanishing points for actual light rays (V.1) and their plans (V.2). The light is coming from behind the spectator.

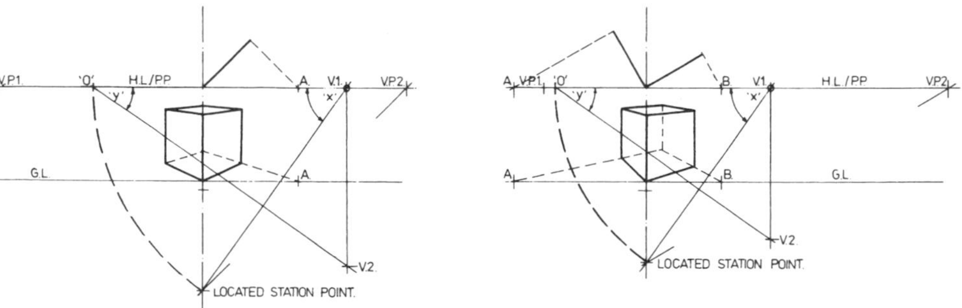

spectator (V.2, which is located below the horizon line). The steps are as follows:

Step 1. From the station point draw a line to meet the picture plane (horizon line/picture plane) at the angle *x*. The vanishing point (V.1) for the plans of the light rays is located at this intersection. A vertical line is then drawn through V.1 because the vanishing point for the actual light rays, from a light source behind the spectator, will be located directly below V.1

Step 2. Using V.1 as the centre of a circle with a radius equal to the distance between V.1 and the station point, swing an arc to meet the picture plane (horizon line/picture plane) at point *O*.

Step 3. From point *O* in the horizon line/picture plane draw a line at the angle *y* below the horizon line/picture plane to meet the vertical line through V.1. The vanishing point for the actual light rays (V.2.) will be located at this point of intersection.

Fig. 239 shows the construction for the location of the vanishing points for the actual light rays and their plans when the light source is located in front of the spectator. The difference between this example and the ones in Fig. 238 is that the angle *y* is set out above the horizon line/picture plane instead of below it. (V.3 is used when the light source is in front of the spectator.) When the vanishing

239 Location of the vanishing points for actual light rays (V.1) and their plans (V.3) with the light source in front of the spectator.

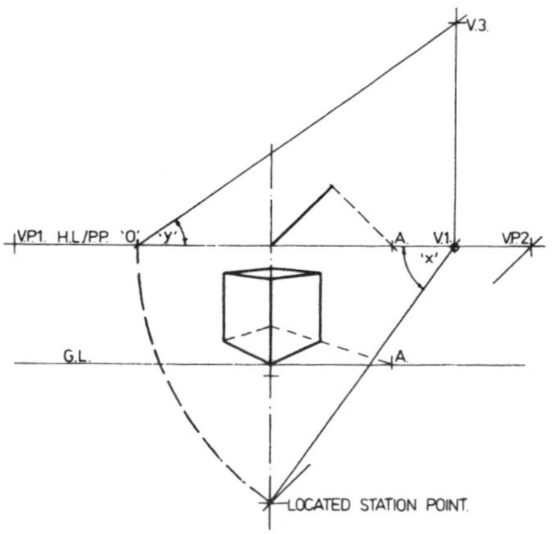

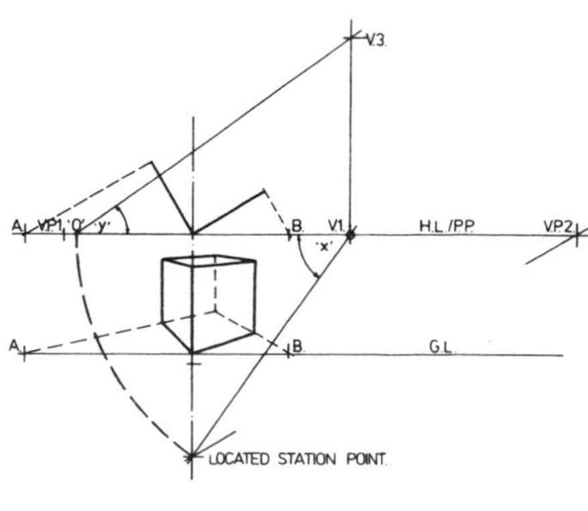

points for the actual light rays and their plans have been located the shadows are drawn in the normal way (see Figs. 178*a* and 179*a*).

Because the station point is located in the one-point short-cut method (see Fig. 233), it is a simple matter to locate the vanishing points for the actual light rays and their plans. Fig. 240 shows the construction for these vanishing points superimposed on the one-point short-cut construction with both V.2 and V.3 located on the one drawing.

This means that even if short-cut methods are employed to set up a perspective view of an object, the correct shadows can still be constructed if necessary. From these constructions used to locate the vanishing points for the actual light rays and their plans it is possible to ascertain factors which are common to all cases:

(1) The vanishing point for the plans of the light rays will always fall in the horizon line.

(2) The vanishing point for the actual light rays will always be either directly below (when the light source is located behind the spectator) or directly above (when the light source is located in front of the spectator) the vanishing point for their plans (V.1).

(3) Angle *x* (the angle which the plan of a light ray makes with the picture plane) can equal any angle between 0° and 360° unless a specific direction is given on the plan.

(4) Angle *y* (the angle which an actual light ray makes with the ground plane) can equal any angle between 0° and 90° unless a specific angle of inclination is given.

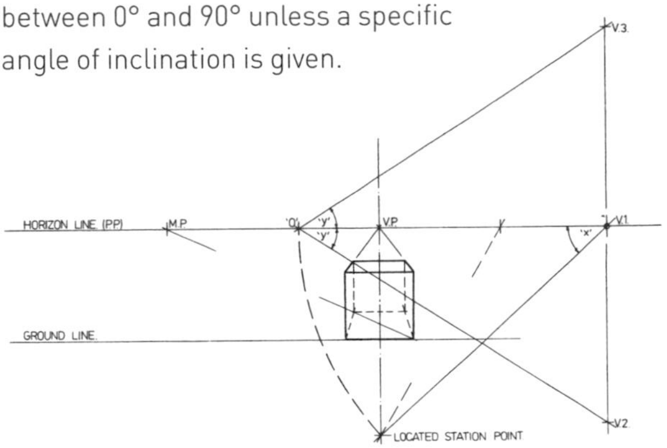

240 Location of the vanishing points for actual light rays and their plans (light source behind and in front of the spectator) superimposed on a one-point short-cut construction.

Fig. 241 shows the possible angles for the light source in relation to a plan of an object, a picture plane and a station point. Fig. 242 shows the possible angles for the light source in relation to an elevation of an object, a picture plane and a spectator point. Figs. 241 and 242 show that there is a very large number of possible combinations which can be chosen for the location of a light source. This means that if the choice of a light source is left to the student he should be able to select one which is well suited to his subject. Under these circumstances it is possible to use a short-cut method for locating the vanishing points for the actual light rays and their plans. To explain this, a simple figure is set up using the 60°/30° short-cut method (Fig. 243). (After the first diagram the perspective construction is omitted to avoid confusion.)

241 Possible angles of direction for a light source – 0° to 360°.

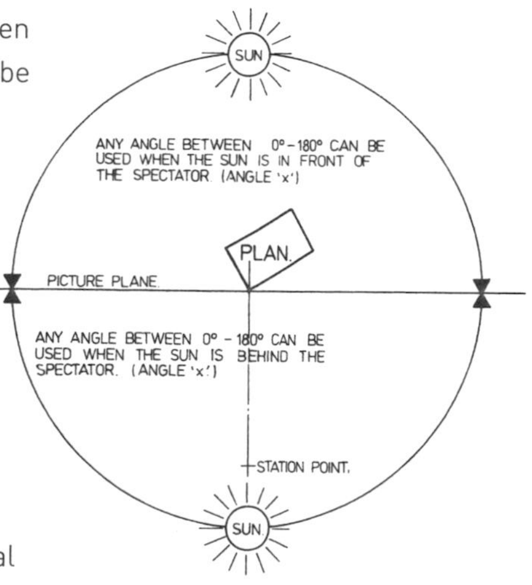

Step 1. When the direction of the light rays has been decided upon, i.e. whether the light source is to be in front of or behind the spectator and whether it is on his left or his right, one vertical of the object can be chosen as a starting point (*A–A1*). In this example a light source has been chosen behind and to the left of the spectator. From the point where the vertical meets the ground plane (*A*) a line representing a plan of a light ray is drawn in the required direction to meet the horizon line/picture plane, thus locating the vanishing point for the plans of the light rays (V.1). A vertical

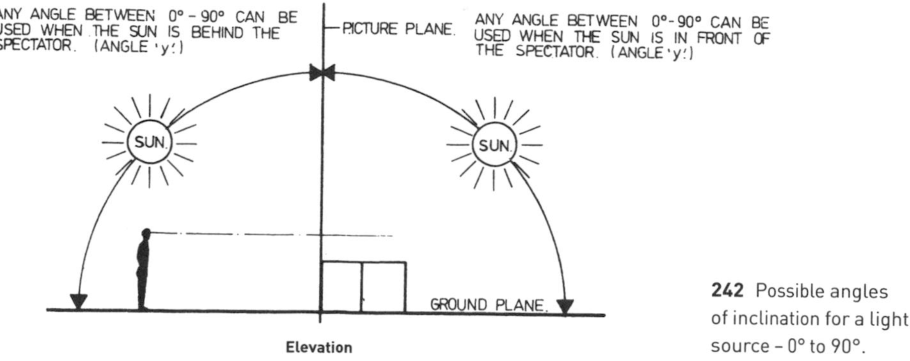

242 Possible angles of inclination for a light source – 0° to 90°.

243 60°/30° short-cut construction with light source behind the spectator.

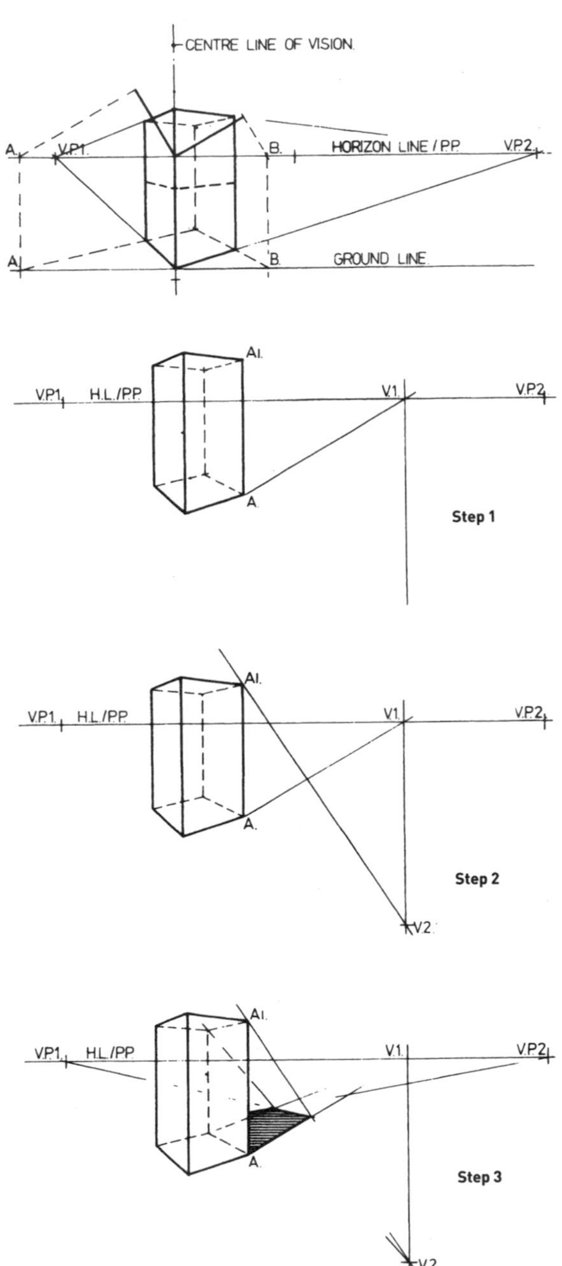

line is then drawn through V.1 (below the horizon line/picture plane in this example, because the light source is located behind the spectator).

Step 2. Through the top of the vertical line (*A1*) an actual light ray is drawn at the desired angle and continued to meet the vertical line drawn through V.1, thus locating the vanishing point (V.2) for the actual light rays.

Step 3. Once the vanishing points for the actual light rays and their plans have been located the shadow can be drawn in the usual way.

Fig. 244 shows an object set up in perspective using the 45°/45° short-cut method. In this example a light source has been chosen in front of the spectator and to his right. The vanishing point for the plans of the light rays is located in exactly the same way as it was in Fig. 243. V.3 is located above the horizon line/picture plane by drawing an actual light ray at the desired angle.

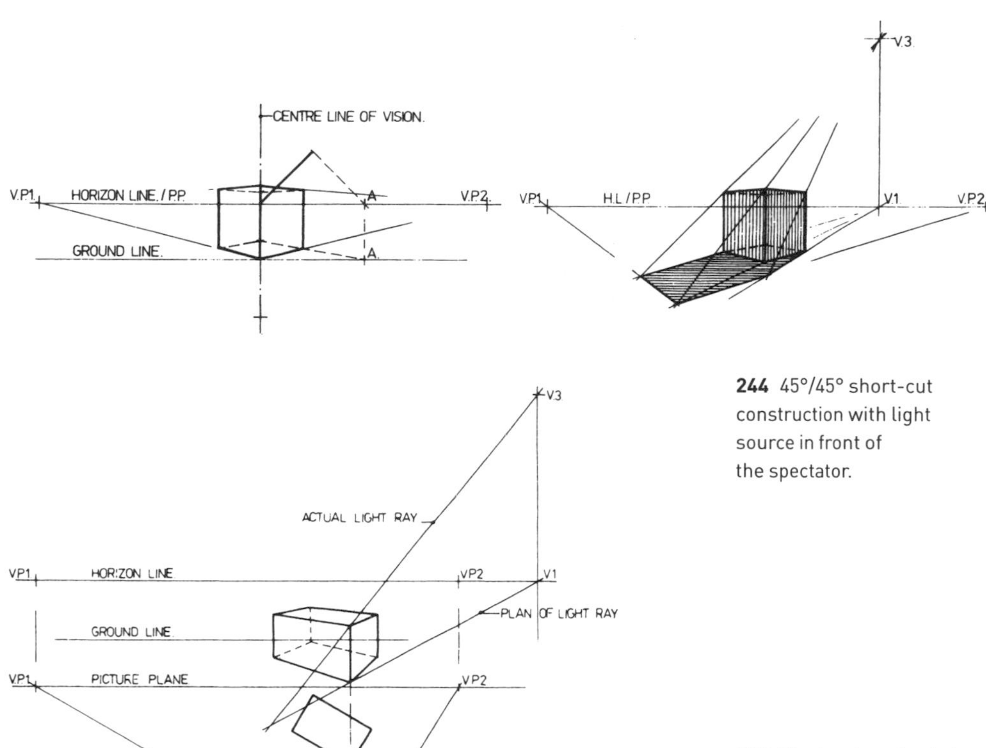

244 45°/45° short-cut construction with light source in front of the spectator.

245 Short-cut method of locating vanishing points for light rays and their plans, superimposed on a normal perspective set-up.

If the results obtained in Figs. 243 and 244 are examined it will be seen that they both contain the four common factors mentioned earlier and are therefore the correct results for the chosen sets of circumstances. In other words, even though the exact angles for *x* and *y* are not known it would be a simple matter to work backwards and find them if this were necessary. This short-cut method for locating the vanishing points for the actual light rays and their plans can be used in constructing believable shadows on a perspective set-up using the basic method. Fig. 245 shows a rectangular prism set up in perspective using the basic method. Once the direction of the light source has been decided it is a simple matter to select a vertical as a starting point and to draw from its base, i.e. its intersection with the ground plane, a line representing the plan of a light ray to meet the horizon line. Through the top of the vertical of the object an actual light ray can be drawn at the desired angle to meet a vertical line drawn through the vanishing point for the plans of the light rays (V.1). This intersection will be the vanishing point for the actual light rays (V.3 in this example, because the light source

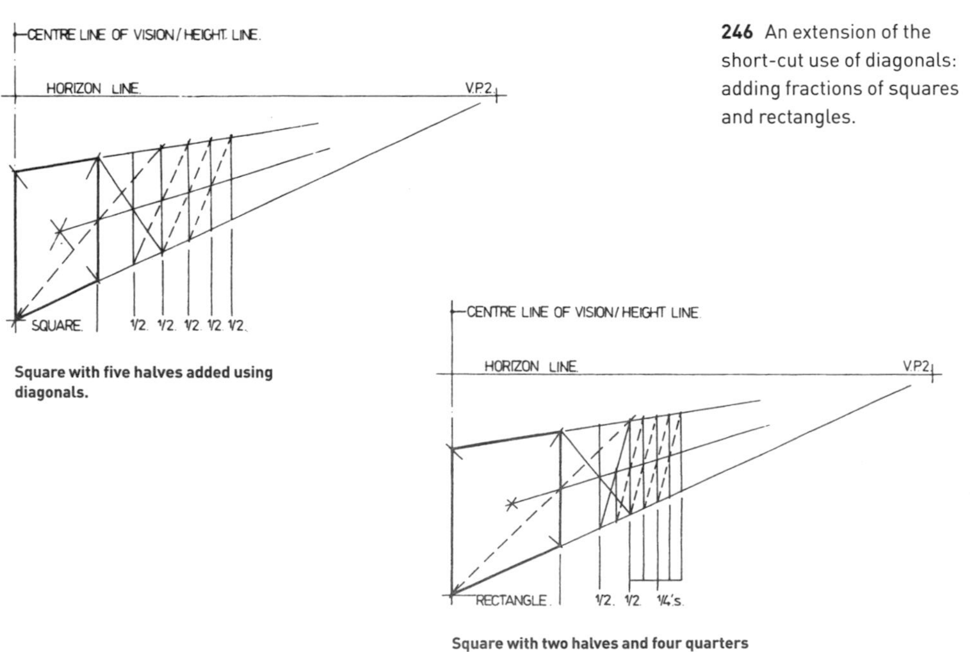

246 An extension of the short-cut use of diagonals: adding fractions of squares and rectangles.

Square with five halves added using diagonals.

Square with two halves and four quarters added using diagonals.

decided upon is in front of the spectator; if it were behind him V.2, which is located below the horizon line, would be used). When the required vanishing points have been located, the shadow can be drawn in the normal way.

Once this short-cut method is understood shadows can be located and drawn so that they are consistent, which is very important, but above all with accuracy and speed. Though, as previously stated, angles *x* and *y* are unknown, the results obtained will be accurate for the set of circumstances chosen arbitrarily. This arbitrary choice of a light source is acceptable in nearly all cases where specific directions are not known. Even if the specific directions are known this method can be used if applied intelligently, i.e. the direction of the travel of the sun would be known, which means that the light source could be placed within these limits and the elevation estimated fairly accurately for that specific position. However, it is not intended to go further into the application of the short-cut method for locating the vanishing points for the actual light rays and their plans. If the theory behind the short-cut method is fully understood the solution of any problem involving the construction of shadows on any type of perspective drawing should be simple.

To this stage, only short cuts for the construction of shadows cast by the sun have been considered. Shadows cast by artificial light sources are considered to be so simple to construct that the basic method, which is very quick and accurate, would be almost impossible to simplify further.

Another short-cut method which will be found to be of considerable use is a further extension of the diagonal theory. So far the diagonal has been used to divide squares and rectangles into equal parts or to add further squares or rectangles of equal size to the original one. The diagonal can be used in other ways as well, the obvious ones being the addition of halves or quarters of squares or rectangles, as shown in Fig. 246. These are self-explanatory and it will be realized that these additions need not be limited only to halves and quarters of squares or rectangles, but can be used for a variety of additions of various proportions as necessary. The use of the diagonal for dividing squares or rectangles in a

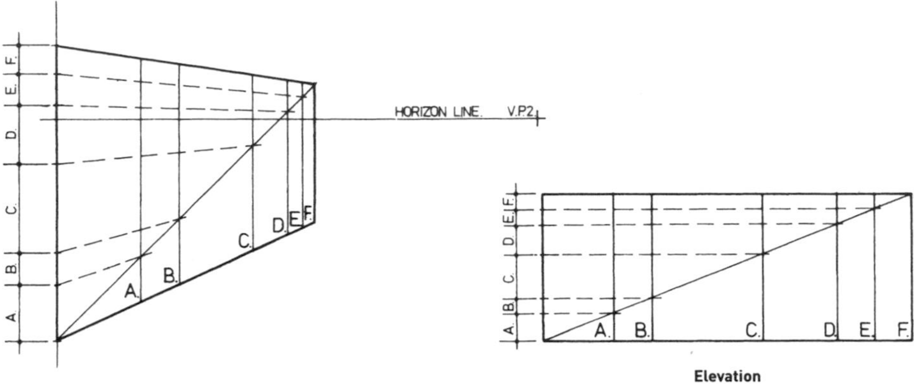

247 Dividing a rectangular surface into unequal sections by the use of diagonals.

perspective drawing into unequal parts or unequal recurring divisions can be a great time-saver.

Fig. 247 shows the method used for dividing a rectangular surface into a number of unequal parts using the diagonal. The required divisions are shown on the elevation of the rectangular surface. By drawing a diagonal on this elevation the intersections of this diagonal and the vertical divisions can be projected back to one of the ends of the rectangular surface, where they can be measured. These measurements can then be transferred to the height line in the perspective drawing and perspective lines drawn from each of these measured points to the appropriate vanishing point (V.P.2 in this example). The diagonal is then drawn on the perspective view of the rectangular surface to correspond with the one drawn on the elevation. The vertical divisions can then be drawn through the intersections of the diagonal and the perspective lines. In this example either diagonal could be used because either would produce the same result; however, it is wise to develop, from the beginning, the habit of using the diagonal which corresponds to the one used in the elevation because it can, in many cases, eliminate confusion.

The possible uses of diagonals in this way, and their variations, are almost unlimited as they can be used with all of the basic methods for setting up perspective views of objects, as well as for all of the short-cut methods. An example of the use of the diagonal in this way is illustrated in Fig. 248, which shows a rectangular face set up in the perspective view. The

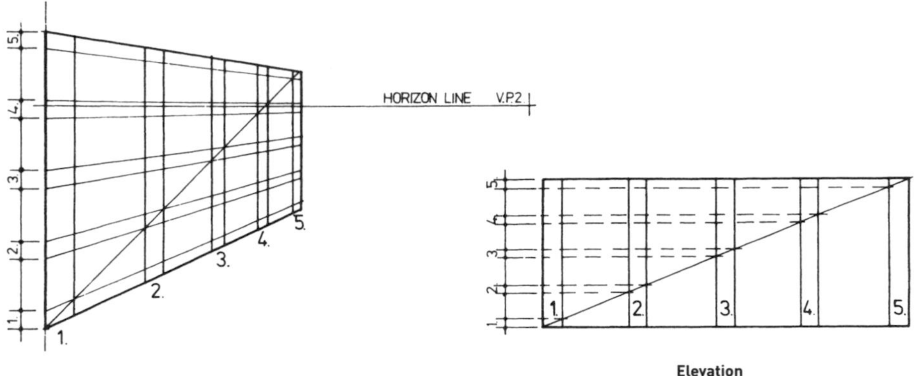

248 A rectangular surface divided into sections, drawn in perspective by the use of diagonals.

elevation in this example shows that the surface is divided into five small spaces of equal size and four large spaces of equal size. The diagonal is drawn on the elevation and the intersections of this diagonal and the vertical divisions are then projected to one of the ends of the rectangular surface where they can be measured. These measurements are then transferred to the height line of the perspective drawing, where perspective lines are drawn on the rectangular surface and the diagonal is drawn to correspond with the one on the elevation. The vertical divisions are located at the intersections of the perspective lines and the diagonal.

One application of this is the breaking-up of a surface of a building which consists of a number of columns with spaces between them. The advantages of the short-cut method in this type of drawing should be obvious. Once the columns and the spaces between them have been drawn in the perspective view it is not uncommon to have to divide the spaces between the columns into a number of further parts representing window mullions, etc.

In the example shown in Fig. 249 each space between the columns is required to be divided into four equal parts. The columns have been located using the method shown in Fig. 248 but, to avoid confusion, this construction is not shown. To divide the spaces between the columns it is necessary to measure four equal divisions on one of the verticals of the rectangular face. Any vertical may be used but normally the most convenient is chosen and any convenient divisions may be used provided they

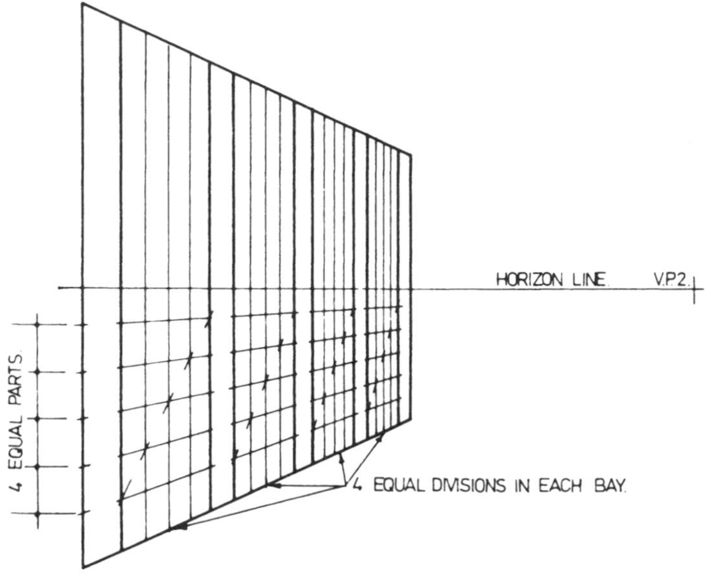

249 The short-cut method applied to the surface of a building.

are equal divisions. Perspective lines are drawn from these divisions as shown and, in this case, because it is only the spaces between the columns which are to be divided, the diagonals are drawn from the intersection of the vertical line representing a side of the column and the bottom perspective line to the intersection of the opposite vertical line representing the next column and the top perspective line. This is repeated in each space between each pair of columns. The required vertical divisions are then drawn through the intersections of the perspective lines and the diagonal. Though four spaces were required in this example, it should be obvious that any number of spaces could be produced using this method: it is simply a matter of measuring the required number of equal spaces on a vertical of the face and proceeding as described.

One variation of this method which can be used for locating the columns of a building when the ratio between the width of the columns and the width of the spaces is either known or can be ascertained is shown in Fig. 250. In this example the ratio between the columns and the spaces is 1:3. Using a convenient vertical of the rectangular face in the perspective drawing and a convenient scale, set out the required number

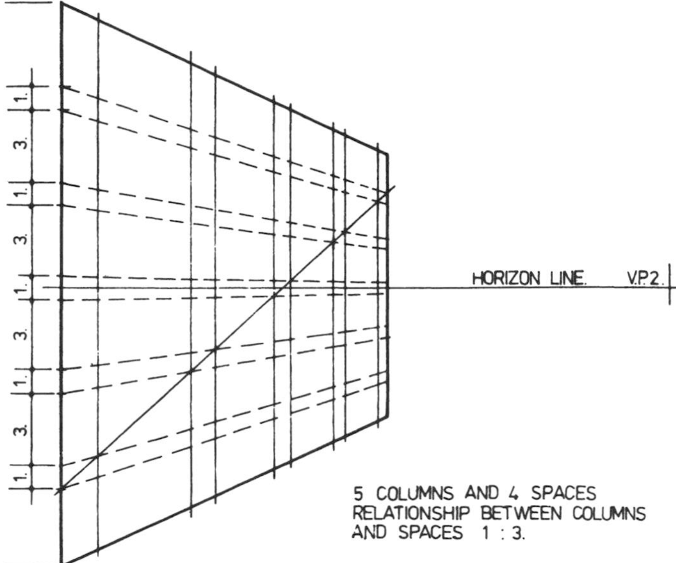

250 Spaces and columns on the side of a building.

of measurements in the proportion 1:3. These measurements can be set out anywhere on the vertical and can use either the whole of the vertical or part of it, as is the case in the example shown here.

From the preceding examples it can be seen that once the shape of the rectangular face has been located in the perspective view, irrespective of whether that face has been located using one of the basic methods of perspective projection or one of the many short-cut methods, details on that surface, whatever they may be, can be added using any one of these methods or combinations of them. Needless to say that although only vertical surfaces have been shown here the same principles apply to both horizontal and inclined planes or surfaces, therefore it is not considered necessary to show them.

Another factor which should be obvious from the preceding examples, particularly Figs. 246 and 249, is that the diagonals of equal spaces are parallel, which means that they will converge to common vanishing points (known as measuring points). Though the use of these measuring points is not essential it can be advantageous in so far as it often increases the accuracy of the resulting drawing. Fig. 251 shows in perspective a simple

251 Repetition of identical square faces by setting up a measuring point – a method which increases accuracy.

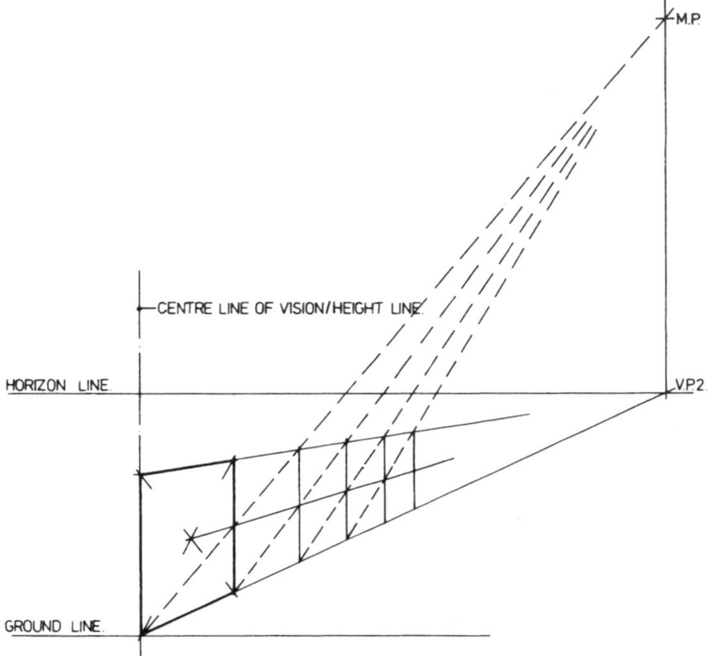

square face to which further squares are required to be added. These can be drawn as previously described. However, if the diagonal located by dividing the 'back' edge of the square in halves and drawing a line from the 'front' lower corner of the original square through the centre of the line forming the 'back' edge is continued to meet a vertical line through V.P.2, this intersection will be the vanishing point for this diagonal and all diagonals parallel to it (M.P.). The use of this M.P. will increase the accuracy of the overall drawing because the location of the vertical lines of the square faces will no longer be the result of a short line located by eye.

The short-cut methods shown here are by no means all that are available for the preparation of a perspective view of an object. They are reliable, as has been shown by relating them back to the already proven basic methods for perspective projection, which means that they can be used confidently without any loss of accuracy. It is undeniable that they are considerable time-savers when compared with the basic methods, and in most cases they also save considerable space. These two factors alone justify their use but, when accuracy is added to them, it means that these short-cut methods are indispensable to the professional renderer and therefore are of enormous value to the student. There are, in use by professional renderers and commercial artists, many variations of the short-cut methods shown here but they are nearly all based on the principles discussed here. Unfortunately there are no short-cut methods which eliminate the learning of the basic principles of perspective projection, and without a sound understanding of these basic principles, short-cut methods – both those shown here and others evolved from them – are of little use to the student; in fact they can be more of a hindrance than a help.

Because accuracy is the most important element in a perspective projection any short-cut method which cannot be proven to produce accurate results is useless and should never be used. Proving the accuracy, or otherwise, of a short cut presupposes a sound knowledge of basic perspective projection. Unfortunately, much that commonly passes for knowledge regarding perspective projection is based on some form of misinformation or half-truth which in many areas bears little resemblance to the facts. In this matter we are no doubt the victims of the prevailing atmosphere in modern-day art attitudes with their roots in Impressionism, in which perspective projection underwent a form of disintegration in favour of other elements. These present-day attitudes, whatever their validity for art, have little or no relevance to the requirements of the renderings of architects, interior designers, industrial designers and all others in the general category of technical illustrators rather than artists. The artist produces a work based on his imagination: the technical illustrator is required to produce a work of fact – which can have artistic merit, depending on the personal skill of the technical illustrator, but its first duty is technical accuracy. If the work is without accuracy its author's honesty and integrity are open to serious question. Against such a charge the only rational defence a designer possesses is his sound basic knowledge of his 'tools of trade' and his ability to use them. The ability to present a pictorial view of the true intent of his design is of paramount importance to him, both as a check for himself and as a true statement to his client and the public of his intentions.

Conclusion

There are many problems with which the student will, no doubt, come into contact which are not answered directly in this book, but if the basic principles are understood, many answers to specific questions can be found by applying these principles. There is no substitute for a sound basic knowledge of the principles of perspective, and even though there are a number of very useful short cuts, these are of limited use unless they are combined with this knowledge.

Finally, it should be remembered that a perspective drawing is a technical drawing. Like any other technical drawing, if it is not accurate, it is of little use to any one. This is too often forgotten by the very people whose designs rely on the perspective drawing to convey their intentions to a client or the public.

Index

Page numbers in italics refer to illustrations.